# Luke

# ABOUT THE AUTHORS

General Editor:

***Clinton E. Arnold*** (PhD, University of Aberdeen), professor and chairman, department of New Testament, Talbot School of Theology, Biola University, Los Angeles, California

Gospel of Luke:

***Mark L. Strauss*** (PhD, University of Aberdeen), associate professor of New Testament, Bethel Seminary, San Diego, California

*ZondervanI Illustrated Bible Backgrounds Commentary*

# Luke

**Mark L. Strauss**

**Clinton E. Arnold** ***general editor***

ZONDERVAN

*Luke*

Requests for information should be addressed to:

Zondervan, *3900 Sparks Dr. SE, Grand Rapids, Michigan 49546*

This edition: ISBN 978-0-310-52292-8

---

Library of Congress cataloged the original edition as follows:

Zondervan illustrated Bible backgrounds commentary / Clinton E. Arnold, general editor.
p.cm.
Includes bibliographical references.
ISBN 978-0-310-27829-0
1. Bible. N.T. — Commentaries. I. Arnold, Clinton E.
BS2341.52.Z66 2001
225.7 — dc21 2001046801

---

*Interior design: Sherri L. Hoffman*

# CONTENTS

# INTRODUCTION

All readers of the Bible have a tendency to view what it says through their own culture and life circumstances. This can happen almost subconsiously as we read the pages of the text.

When most people in the church read about the thief on the cross, for instance, they immediately think of a burglar that held up a store or broke into a home. They may be rather shocked to find out that the guy was actually a Jewish revolutionary figure who was part of a growing movement in Palestine eager to throw off Roman rule.

It also comes as something of a surprise to contemporary Christians that "cursing" in the New Testament era had little or nothing to do with cussing somebody out. It had far more to do with the invocation of spirits to cause someone harm.

No doubt there is a need in the church for learning more about the world of the New Testament to avoid erroneous interpretations of the text of Scripture. But relevant historical and cultural insights also provide an added dimension of perspective to the words of the Bible. This kind of information often functions in the same way as watching a movie in color rather than in black and white. Finding out, for instance, how Paul compared Christ's victory on the cross to a joyous celebration parade in honor of a Roman general after winning an extraordinary battle brings does indeed magnify the profundity and implications of Jesus' work on the cross. Discovering that the factions at Corinth ("I follow Paul . . . I follow Apollos . . .") had plenty of precedent in the local cults ("I follow Aphrodite; I follow Apollo . . .") helps us understand the "why" of a particular problem. Learning about the water supply from the springs of Hierapolis that flowed into Laodicea as "lukewarm" water enables us to appreciate the relevance of the metaphor Jesus used when he addressed the spiritual laxity of this church.

My sense is that most Christians are eager to learn more about the real life setting of the New Testament. In the preaching and teaching of the Bible in the church, congregants are always grateful when they learn something of the background and historical context of the text. It not only helps them understand the text more accurately, but often enables them to identify with the people and circumstances of the Bible. I have been asked on countless occasions by Christians, "Where can I get access to good historical background information about this passage?" Earnest Christians are hungry for information that makes their Bibles come alive.

The stimulus for this commentary came from the church and the aim is to serve the church. The contributors to this series have sought to provide illuminating and interesting historical/cultural background information. The intent was to draw upon relevant papyri, inscriptions, archaeological discoveries, and the numerous studies of Judaism, Roman culture, Hellenism, and other features of the world of the New Testament and to make the results accessible to people in the church. We recognize that some readers of the commentary will want to go further, and so the sources of the information have been carefully documented in endnotes.

The written information has been supplemented with hundreds of photographs, maps, charts, artwork, and other graphics that help the reader better understand the world of the New Testament. Each of the writers was given an opportunity to dream up a "wish list" of illustrations that he thought would help to illustrate the passages in the New Testament book for which he was writing commentary. Although we were not able to obtain everything they were looking for, we came close.

The team of commentators are writing for the benefit of the broad array of Christians who simply want to better understand their Bibles from the vantage point of the historical context. This is an installment in a new genre of "Bible background" commentaries that was kicked off by Craig Keener's fine volume. Consequently, this is not an "exegetical" commentary that provides linguistic insight and background into Greek constructions and verb tenses. Neither is this work an "expository" commentary that provides a verse-by-verse exposition of the text; for in-depth philological or theological insight, readers will need to have other more specialized or comprehensive commentaries available. Nor is this an "historical-critical" commentary, although the contributors are all scholars and have already made substantial academic contributions on the New Testament books they are writing on for this set. The team intentionally does not engage all of the issues that are discussed in the scholarly guild.

Rather, our goal is to offer a reading and interpretation of the text informed by what we regard as the most relevant historical information. For many in the church, this commentary will serve as an important entry point into the interpretation and appreciation of the text. For other more serious students of the Word, these volumes will provide an important supplement to many of the fine exegetical, expository, and critical available.

The contributors represent a group of scholars who embrace the Bible as the Word of God and believe that the message of its pages has life-changing relevance for faith and practice today. Accordingly, we offer "Reflections" on the relevance of the Scripture to life for every chapter of the New Testament.

I pray that this commentary brings you both delight and insight in digging deeper into the Word of God.

*Clinton E. Arnold*
*General Editor*

# LIST OF SIDEBARS

## Luke

# INDEX OF PHOTOS AND MAPS

# ABBREVIATIONS

## 1. Books of the Bible and Apocrypha

| | |
|---|---|
| 1 Chron. | 1 Chronicles |
| 2 Chron. | 2 Chronicles |
| 1 Cor. | 1 Corinthians |
| 2 Cor. | 2 Corinthians |
| 1 Esd. | 1 Esdras |
| 2 Esd. | 2 Esdras |
| 1 John | 1 John |
| 2 John | 2 John |
| 3 John | 3 John |
| 1 Kings | 1 Kings |
| 2 Kings | 2 Kings |
| 1 Macc. | 1 Maccabees |
| 2 Macc. | 2 Maccabees |
| 1 Peter | 1 Peter |
| 2 Peter | 2 Peter |
| 1 Sam. | 1 Samuel |
| 2 Sam. | 2 Samuel |
| 1 Thess. | 1 Thessalonians |
| 2 Thess. | 2 Thessalonians |
| 1 Tim. | 1 Timothy |
| 2 Tim. | 2 Timothy |
| Acts | Acts |
| Amos | Amos |
| Bar. | Baruch |
| Bel | Bel and the Dragon |
| Col. | Colossians |
| Dan. | Daniel |
| Deut. | Deuteronomy |
| Eccl. | Ecclesiastes |
| Ep. Jer. | Epistle of Jeremiah |
| Eph. | Ephesians |
| Est. | Esther |
| Ezek. | Ezekiel |
| Ex. | Exodus |
| Ezra | Ezra |
| Gal. | Galatians |
| Gen. | Genesis |
| Hab. | Habakkuk |
| Hag. | Haggai |
| Heb. | Hebrews |
| Hos. | Hosea |
| Isa. | Isaiah |
| James | James |
| Jer. | Jeremiah |
| Job | Job |
| Joel | Joel |
| John | John |
| Jonah | Jonah |
| Josh. | Joshua |
| Jude | Jude |
| Judg. | Judges |
| Judith | Judith |
| Lam. | Lamentations |
| Lev. | Leviticus |
| Luke | Luke |
| Mal. | Malachi |
| Mark | Mark |
| Matt. | Matthew |
| Mic. | Micah |
| Nah. | Nahum |
| Neh. | Nehemiah |
| Num. | Numbers |
| Obad. | Obadiah |
| Phil. | Philippians |
| Philem. | Philemon |
| Pr. Man. | Prayer of Manassah |
| Prov. | Proverbs |
| Ps. | Psalm |
| Rest. of Est. | The Rest of Esther |
| Rev. | Revelation |
| Rom. | Romans |
| Ruth | Ruth |
| S. of III Ch. | The Song of the Three Holy Children |
| Sir. | Sirach/Ecclesiasticus |
| Song | Song of Songs |
| Sus. | Susanna |
| Titus | Titus |
| Tobit | Tobit |
| Wisd. Sol. | The Wisdom of Solomon |
| Zech. | Zechariah |
| Zeph. | Zephaniah |

## 2. Old and New Testament Pseudepigrapha and Rabbinic Literature

Individual tractates of rabbinic literature follow the abbreviations of the *SBL Handbook of Style*, pp. 79–80. Qumran documents follow standard Dead Sea Scroll conventions.

| | |
|---|---|
| *2 Bar.* | *2 Baruch* |
| *3 Bar.* | *3 Baruch* |
| *4 Bar.* | *4 Baruch* |
| *1 En.* | *1 Enoch* |
| *2 En.* | *2 Enoch* |
| *3 En.* | *3 Enoch* |
| *4 Ezra* | *4 Ezra* |

| | |
|---|---|
| *3 Macc.* | *3 Maccabees* |
| *4 Macc.* | *4 Maccabees* |
| *5 Macc.* | *5 Maccabees* |
| *Acts Phil.* | *Acts of Philip* |
| *Acts Pet.* | *Acts of Peter and the 12 Apostles* |
| *Apoc. Elijah* | *Apocalypse of Elijah* |
| *As. Mos.* | *Assumption of Moses* |
| *b.* | *Babylonian Talmud* (+ tractate) |
| *Gos. Thom.* | *Gospel of Thomas* |
| *Jos. Asen.* | *Joseph and Aseneth* |
| *Jub.* | *Jubilees* |
| *Let. Aris.* | *Letter of Aristeas* |
| *m.* | *Mishnah* (+ tractate) |
| *Mek.* | *Mekilta* |
| *Midr.* | *Midrash I* (+ biblical book) |
| *Odes Sol.* | *Odes of Solomon* |
| *Pesiq. Rab.* | *Pesiqta Rabbati* |
| *Pirqe. R. El.* | *Pirqe Rabbi Eliezer* |
| *Pss. Sol.* | *Psalms of Solomon* |
| *Rab.* | *Rabbah* (+biblical book); (e.g., *Gen. Rab.=Genesis Rabbah)* |
| *S. ᶜOlam Rab.* | *Seder ᶜOlam Rabbah* |
| *Sem.* | *Semahot* |
| *Sib. Or.* | *Sibylline Oracles* |
| *T. Ab.* | *Testament of Abraham* |
| *T. Adam* | *Testament of Adam* |
| *T. Ash.* | *Testament of Asher* |
| *T. Benj.* | *Testament of Benjamin* |
| *T. Dan* | *Testament of Dan* |
| *T. Gad* | *Testament of Gad* |
| *T. Hez.* | *Testament of Hezekiah* |
| *T. Isaac* | *Testament of Isaac* |
| *T. Iss.* | *Testament of Issachar* |
| *T. Jac.* | *Testament of Jacob* |
| *T. Job* | *Testament of Job* |
| *T. Jos.* | *Testament of Joseph* |
| *T. Jud.* | *Testament of Judah* |
| *T. Levi* | *Testament of Levi* |
| *T. Mos.* | *Testament of Moses* |
| *T. Naph.* | *Testament of Naphtali* |
| *T. Reu.* | *Testament of Reuben* |
| *T. Sim.* | *Testament of Simeon* |
| *T. Sol.* | *Testament of Solomon* |
| *T. Zeb.* | *Testament of Zebulum* |
| *Tanh.* | *Tanhuma* |
| *Tg. Isa.* | *Targum of Isaiah* |
| *Tg. Lam.* | *Targum of Lamentations* |
| *Tg. Neof.* | *Targum Neofiti* |
| *Tg. Onq.* | *Targum Onqelos* |
| *Tg. Ps.-J* | *Targum Pseudo-Jonathan* |
| *y.* | *Jerusalem Talmud* (+ tractate) |

## 3. Classical Historians

For an extended list of classical historians and church fathers, see *SBL Handbook of Style*, pp. 84–87. For many works of classical antiquity, the abbreviations have been subjected to the author's discretion; the names of these works should be obvious upon consulting entries of the classical writers in classical dictionaries or encyclopedias.

### Eusebius

| | |
|---|---|
| *Eccl. Hist.* | *Ecclesiastical History* |

### Josephus

| | |
|---|---|
| *Ag. Ap.* | *Against Apion* |
| *Ant.* | *Jewish Antiquities* |
| *J.W.* | *Jewish War* |
| *Life* | *The Life* |

### Philo

| | |
|---|---|
| *Abraham* | On the Life of Abraham |
| *Agriculture* | On Agriculture |
| *Alleg. Interp* | *Allegorical Interpretation* |
| *Animals* | *Whether Animals Have Reason* |
| *Cherubim* | *On the Cherubim* |
| *Confusion* | *On the Confusion of Thomas* |
| *Contempl. Life* | *On the Contemplative Life* |
| *Creation* | *On the Creation of the World* |
| *Curses* | *On Curses* |
| *Decalogue* | *On the Decalogue* |
| *Dreams* | *On Dreams* |
| *Drunkenness* | *On Drunkenness* |
| *Embassy* | *On the Embassy to Gaius* |
| *Eternity* | *On the Eternity of the World* |
| *Flaccus* | *Against Flaccus* |
| *Flight* | *On Flight and Finding* |
| *Giants* | *On Giants* |
| *God* | *On God* |
| *Heir* | *Who Is the Heir?* |
| *Hypothetica* | *Hypothetica* |
| *Joseph* | *On the Life of Joseph* |
| *Migration* | *On the Migration of Abraham* |
| *Moses* | *On the Life of Moses* |
| *Names* | *On the Change of Names* |
| *Person* | *That Every Good Person Is Free* |
| *Planting* | *On Planting* |
| *Posterity* | *On the Posterity of Cain* |
| *Prelim. Studies* | *On the Preliminary Studies* |
| *Providence* | *On Providence* |
| QE | *Questions and Answers on Exodus* |
| QG | *Questions and Answers on Genesis* |
| *Rewards* | *On Rewards and Punishments* |
| *Sacrifices* | *On the Sacrifices of Cain and Abel* |
| *Sobriety* | *On Sobriety* |
| *Spec. Laws* | *On the Special Laws* |
| *Unchangeable* | *That God Is Unchangeable* |
| *Virtues* | *On the Virtues* |

| | |
|---|---|
| *Worse* | *That the Worse Attacks the Better* |

### *Apostolic Fathers*

| | |
|---|---|
| *1 Clem.* | *First Letter of Clement* |
| *Barn.* | *Epistle of Barnabas* |
| *Clem. Hom.* | *Ancient Homily of Clement* (also called *2 Clement*) |
| *Did.* | *Didache* |
| *Herm. Vis.; Sim.* | *Shepherd of Hermas, Visions; Similitudes* |
| *Ignatius* | *Epistles of Ignatius* (followed by the letter's name) |
| *Mart. Pol.* | *Martyrdom of Polycarp* |

## 4. Modern Abbreviations

| | |
|---|---|
| AASOR | Annual of the American Schools of Oriental Research |
| AB | Anchor Bible |
| *ABD* | *Anchor Bible Dictionary* |
| ABRL | Anchor Bible Reference Library |
| AGJU | Arbeiten zur Geschichte des antiken Judentums und des Urchristentums |
| *AH* | *Agricultural History* |
| ALGHJ | Arbeiten zur Literatur und Geschichte des Hellenistischen Judentums |
| AnBib | Analecta biblica |
| *ANRW* | *Aufstieg und Niedergang der römischen Welt* |
| ANTC | Abingdon New Testament Commentaries |
| BAGD | Bauer, W., W. F. Arndt, F. W. Gingrich, and F. W. Danker. *Greek-English Lexicon of the New Testament and Other Early Christina Literature* (2d. ed.) |
| *BA* | *Biblical Archaeologist* |
| BAFCS | Book of Acts in Its First Century Setting |
| *BAR* | *Biblical Archaeology Review* |
| *BASOR* | *Bulletin of the American Schools of Oriental Research* |
| *BBC* | *Bible Background Commentary* |
| *BBR* | *Bulletin for Biblical Research* |
| BDB | Brown, F., S. R. Driver, and C. A. Briggs. *A Hebrew and English Lexicon of the Old Testament* |
| BDF | Blass, F., A. Debrunner, and R. W. Funk. *A Greek Grammar of the New Testament and Other Early Christian Literature* |
| BECNT | Baker Exegetical Commentary on the New Testament |
| *BI* | *Biblical Illustrator* |
| *Bib* | *Biblica* |
| *BibSac* | *Bibliotheca Sacra* |
| BLT | Brethren Life and Thought |
| BNTC | Black's New Testament Commentary |
| *BRev* | *Bible Review* |
| BSHJ | Baltimore Studies in the History of Judaism |
| BST | The Bible Speaks Today |
| BSV | Biblical Social Values |
| *BT* | *The Bible Translator* |
| *BTB* | *Biblical Theology Bulletin* |
| *BZ* | *Biblische Zeitschrift* |
| *CBQ* | *Catholic Biblical Quarterly* |
| *CBTJ* | *Calvary Baptist Theological Journal* |
| CGTC | Cambridge Greek Testament Commentary |
| *CH* | *Church History* |
| *CIL* | *Corpus inscriptionum latinarum* |
| *CPJ* | *Corpus papyrorum judaicorum* |
| *CRINT* | *Compendia rerum iudaicarum ad Novum Testamentum* |
| *CTJ* | *Calvin Theological Journal* |
| *CTM* | *Concordia Theological Monthly* |
| CTT | Contours of Christian Theology |
| *DBI* | *Dictionary of Biblical Imagery* |
| *DCM* | *Dictionary of Classical Mythology.* |
| *DDD* | *Dictionary of Deities and Demons in the Bible* |
| *DJBP* | *Dictionary of Judaism in the Biblical Period* |
| *DJG* | *Dictionary of Jesus and the Gospels* |
| *DLNT* | *Dictionary of the Later New Testament and Its Developments* |
| *DNTB* | *Dictionary of New Testament Background* |
| *DPL* | *Dictionary of Paul and His Letters* |
| *EBC* | *Expositor's Bible Commentary* |
| *EDBT* | *Evangelical Dictionary of Biblical Theology* |
| *EDNT* | *Exegetical Dictionary of the New Testament* |
| *EJR* | *Encyclopedia of the Jewish Religion* |
| EPRO | Études préliminaires aux religions orientales dans l'empire romain |
| *EvQ* | *Evangelical Quarterly* |
| *ExpTim* | *Expository Times* |
| FRLANT | Forsuchungen zur Religion und Literatur des Alten und Neuen Testament |
| GNC | Good News Commentary |
| GNS | Good News Studies |
| *HCNT* | *Hellenistic Commentary to the New Testament* |
| *HDB* | *Hastings Dictionary of the Bible* |

| | |
|---|---|
| *HJP* | *History of the Jewish People in the Age of Jesus Christ*, by E. Schürer |
| *HTR* | *Harvard Theological Review* |
| HTS | Harvard Theological Studies |
| *HUCA* | *Hebrew Union College Annual* |
| *IBD* | *Illustrated Bible Dictionary* |
| *IBS* | *Irish Biblical Studies* |
| ICC | International Critical Commentary |
| *IDB* | *The Interpreter's Dictionary of the Bible* |
| *IEJ* | *Israel Exploration Journal* |
| *IG* | *Inscriptiones graecae* |
| *IGRR* | *Inscriptiones graecae ad res romanas pertinentes* |
| *ILS* | *Inscriptiones Latinae Selectae* |
| *Imm* | *Immanuel* |
| *ISBE* | *International Standard Bible Encyclopedia* |
| *Int* | *Interpretation* |
| *IvE* | *Inschriften von Ephesos* |
| IVPNTC | InterVarsity Press New Testament Commentary |
| *JAC* | *Jahrbuch fur Antike und Christentum* |
| *JBL* | *Journal of Biblical Literature* |
| *JETS* | *Journal of the Evangelical Theological Society* |
| *JHS* | *Journal of Hellenic Studies* |
| *JJS* | *Journal of Jewish Studies* |
| *JOAIW* | *Jahreshefte des Osterreeichischen Archaologischen Instites in Wien* |
| *JSJ* | *Journal for the Study of Judaism in the Persian, Hellenistic, and Roman Periods* |
| *JRS* | *Journal of Roman Studies* |
| *JSNT* | *Journal for the Study of the New Testament* |
| JSNTSup | Journal for the Study of the New Testament: Supplement Series |
| *JSOT* | *Journal for the Study of the Old Testament* |
| JSOTSup | Journal for the Study of the Old Testament: Supplement Series |
| *JTS* | *Journal of Theological Studies* |
| *KTR* | *Kings Theological Review* |
| LCL | Loeb Classical Library |
| LEC | Library of Early Christianity |
| LSJ | Liddell, H. G., R. Scott, H. S. Jones. *A Greek-English Lexicon* |
| MM | Moulton, J. H., and G. Milligan. *The Vocabulary of the Greek Testament* |
| MNTC | Moffatt New Testament Commentary |
| *NBD* | *New Bible Dictionary* |
| NC | Narrative Commentaries |
| NCBC | New Century Bible Commentary Eerdmans |
| *NEAE* | *New Encyclopedia of Archaeological Excavations in the Holy Land* |
| *NEASB* | *Near East Archaeological Society Bulletin* |
| *New Docs* | *New Documents Illustrating Early Christianity* |
| NIBC | New International Biblical Commentary |
| NICNT | New International Commentary on the New Testament |
| *NIDNTT* | *New International Dictionary of New Testament Theology* |
| NIGTC | New International Greek Testament Commentary |
| NIVAC | NIV Application Commentary |
| *NorTT* | *Norsk Teologisk Tidsskrift* |
| *NoT* | *Notes on Translation* |
| *NovT* | *Novum Testamentum* |
| NovTSup | Novum Testamentum Supplements |
| NTAbh | Neutestamentliche Abhandlungen |
| *NTS* | *New Testament Studies* |
| NTT | New Testament Theology |
| NTTS | New Testament Tools and Studies |
| *OAG* | *Oxford Archaeological Guides* |
| OCCC | *Oxford Companion to Classical Civilization* |
| *OCD* | *Oxford Classical Dictionary* |
| ODCC | *The Oxford Dictionary of the Christian Church* |
| *OGIS* | *Orientis graeci inscriptiones selectae* |
| *OHCW* | *The Oxford History of the Classical World* |
| *OHRW* | *Oxford History of the Roman World* |
| *OTP* | *Old Testament Pseudepigrapha*, ed. by J. H. Charlesworth |
| *PEQ* | *Palestine Exploration Quarterly* |
| *PG* | *Patrologia graeca* |
| *PGM* | *Papyri graecae magicae: Die griechischen Zauberpapyri* |
| *PL* | *Patrologia latina* |
| PNTC | Pelican New Testament Commentaries |
| *Rb* | *Revista biblica* |
| *RB* | *Revue biblique* |
| *RivB* | *Rivista biblica italiana* |
| *RTR* | *Reformed Theological Review* |
| SB | Sources bibliques |
| SBL | Society of Biblical Literature |
| SBLDS | Society of Biblical Literature Dissertation Series |

SBLMS — Society of Biblical Literature Monograph Series
*SBLSP* — *Society of Biblical Literature Seminar Papers*
SBS — Stuttgarter Bibelstudien
SBT — Studies in Biblical Theology
*SCJ* — *Stone-Campbell Journal*
*Scr* — *Scripture*
*SE* — *Studia Evangelica*
*SEG* — *Supplementum epigraphicum graecum*
SJLA — Studies in Judaism in Late Antiquity
*SJT* — *Scottish Journal of Theology*
SNTSMS — Society for New Testament Studies Monograph Series
SSC — Social Science Commentary
SSCSSG — Social-Science Commentary on the Synoptic Gospels
Str-B — Strack, H. L., and P. Billerbeck. *Kommentar zum Neuen Testament aus Talmud und Midrasch*
TC — Thornapple Commentaries
*TDNT* — *Theological Dictionary of the New Testament*
*TDOT* — *Theological Dictionary of the Old Testament*
*TLNT* — *Theological Lexicon of the New Testament*
*TLZ* — *Theologische Literaturzeitung*
TNTC — Tyndale New Testament Commentary
*TrinJ* — *Trinity Journal*
*TS* — *Theological Studies*
TSAJ — Texte und Studien zum antiken Judentum
*TWNT* — *Theologische Wörterbuch zum Neuen Testament*
*TynBul* — *Tyndale Bulletin*
WBC — Word Biblical Commentary Waco: Word, 1982
WMANT — Wissenschaftliche Monographien zum Alten und Neuen Testament
WUNT — Wissenschaftliche Untersuchungen zum Neuen Testament
YJS — Yale Judaica Series
*ZNW* — *Zeitschrift fur die neutestamentliche Wissenschaft und die Junde der alteren Kirche*
*ZPE* — *Zeischrift der Papyrolgie und Epigraphkik*
*ZPEB* — *Zondervan Pictorial Encyclopedia of the Bible*

## 5. General Abbreviations

ad. loc. — in the place cited
b. — born
c., ca. — circa
cf. — compare
d. — died
ed(s). — editors(s), edited by
e.g. — for example
ET — English translation
frg. — fragment
i.e. — that is
ibid. — in the same place
idem — the same (author)
lit. — literally
l(l) — line(s)
MSS — manuscripts
n.d. — no date
NS — New Series
par. — parallel
passim — here and there
repr. — reprint
ser. — series
s.v. — *sub verbo*, under the word
trans. — translator, translated by; transitive

# Zondervan Illustrated Bible Backgrounds Commentary

# LUKE

by Mark Strauss

## Unity and Main Themes of Luke and Acts (Luke-Acts)

It is widely recognized today that Luke and Acts are two parts of a single two-volume work (Luke-Acts). Acts picks up where the Gospel ends and claims to be a continuation of the story that began with Jesus' life, death, and resurrection (Acts 1:1–2). The two works share not only a common style and vocabulary, but also a common purpose, themes, and theology.

1. Promise-fulfillment. The central theme running throughout Luke-Acts is that the coming of Jesus the Messiah heralds the dawn of the new age—the age of salvation. What was promised by the Old Testament prophets is now being fulfilled. Through Jesus' life, death, and resurrection forgiveness of sins is now offered to all people.

2. The age of the Spirit. The new age of salvation is the age of the Spirit. In Luke's birth narrative (Luke 1–2),

EAST OF JERUSALEM TOWARD JERICHO

### Luke IMPORTANT FACTS:

- **AUTHOR:** Luke: physician, coworker, and traveling companion with the apostle Paul. Probably the only New Testament work written by a Gentile.
- **PORTRAIT OF CHRIST:** Jesus, the Savior for all people.
  Part One of a Two-Volume Work: Luke's Gospel is the first half of a single two-volume work ("Luke-Acts"), sharing purpose, themes, and theology with the book of Acts.
- **CENTRAL THEME OF LUKE-ACTS:** Luke seeks to show that *God's great plan of salvation has come to fulfillment in the life, death, resurrection, and ascension of Jesus the Messiah, and continues to unfold as the Spirit-filled church takes the message of salvation from Jerusalem to the ends of the earth.*
- **OTHER KEY THEMES:**
  1. Promise-fulfillment: The age of salvation has arrived in Jesus the Messiah.
  2. The age of the Spirit: The sign of the new age is the coming of the Spirit in the ministry of Jesus and the early church.
  3. The gospel is "good news" for all people, regardless of race, gender, or social status.
- **PURPOSE IN WRITING:** To defend and legitimize the claims of the church as the authentic people of God in the present age.
- **RECIPIENT:** Theophilus, but intended for a larger Christian audience.

the long-silent Spirit of prophecy suddenly breaks forth in praise and prophetic declaration through Zechariah, Mary, Elizabeth, and Simeon—representatives of Israel's righteous remnant. At Jesus' baptism the Spirit anoints and empowers him to accomplish the messianic task (3:22; 4:1, 14, 18). Finally, in Acts Jesus pours out his Spirit on the church, empowering its members to take the gospel to the ends of the earth. As promised by the Old Testament prophets, the coming of the Spirit means that the last days have arrived, so that "everyone who calls on the name of the Lord will be saved" (Acts 2:21, citing Joel 2:28–32).

**3. A gospel for all nations.** Closely related to the theme of promise-fulfillment is the universal application of the message of salvation. While the gospel message arises from within Israel and fulfills the promises made to her, it is a message for all people. Just as the prophets predicted, the coming of the Messiah inaugurates a new era, when all nations will be called to participate in the salvation available through Jesus the Messiah. The key for Luke is the *continuity* between the history of Israel, the person and work of Jesus, and the expansion of his church from Jerusalem to the ends of the earth. This theme is introduced in the Gospel and comes to fruition in the worldwide mission of the church in Acts.[1]

**4. A gospel for the outcasts.** The theme of God's love for all people is most evident in this Gospel with Jesus' concern for social outcasts, sinners, and the poor. The message of salvation crosses all racial and social barriers. At the inauguration of his ministry, Jesus enters the Nazareth synagogue and epitomizes his message as good news to the poor (4:16–22). He

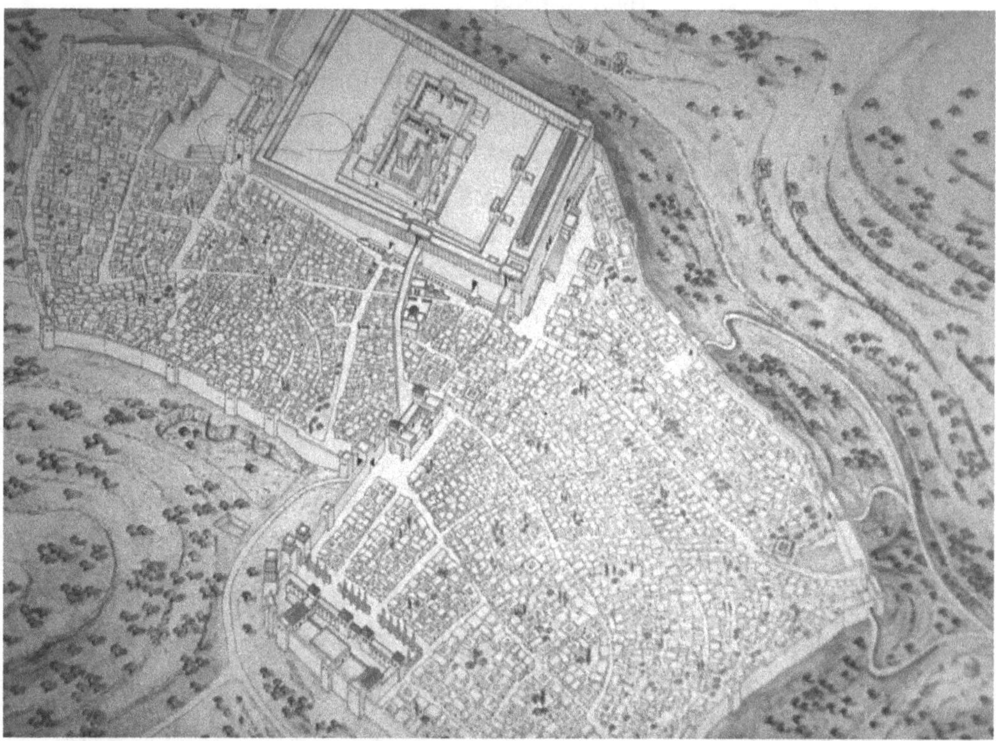

**JERUSALEM**

An artistic reconstruction of Jerusalem at the time of Christ.

associates with sinners and tax collectors, and tells parables where a hated Samaritan is the hero (10:25–37) and where a wayward son is graciously received back by his father (15:11–32). The message throughout is that God loves the lost, those who with a contrite and humble heart will return to him. Repeatedly Jesus' parables reveal the great reversal of fortunes that the kingdom of God will bring: The rich, proud, and mighty will be humbled, while the poor, humble, and oppressed will be exalted (12:13–21; 14:15–24; 16:19–31).

**5. A gospel for women.** This Gospel also crosses gender barriers, for women play a more prominent role in Luke than in the other Gospels. The birth narrative is told from the perspective of women (Mary, Elizabeth, and Anna). Women support Jesus' ministry financially (8:1–3). Mary sits at Jesus' feet, learning from him as a disciple (10:38–42). In contrast to the low status of women in Palestinian society, Jesus lifts them up to full participation in the kingdom of God. The gospel of Jesus is for all people.

## Purpose in Writing

Why then did Luke write? Luke's prologue identifies his general purpose as the confirmation of the gospel, seeking to confirm for Theophilus "the certainty of the things you have been taught" (1:1–4). More specifically, Luke appears to be writing for a Christian community—probably predominantly Gentile, but with Jewish representation—struggling to legitimize its claim as the authentic people of God, the heirs of the promises made to Israel. In defending the identity of Christ, Luke seeks to show that Jesus is the Messiah promised in the Old Testament and that his death and resurrection were part of God's purpose and plan. In defense of the increasingly Gentile church, he confirms that all along it was God's plan to bring salvation to the Gentiles, and that Israel's rejection of the gospel was predicted in Scripture and was part of her history as a stubborn and resistant people. The theme that holds these threads together is promise and fulfillment. The church made up of Jews and Gentiles is the true people of God because it is for her and through her God's promises are being fulfilled.

## The Author

The third Gospel has been traditionally ascribed to Luke, a physician, friend, and missionary companion of the apostle Paul.[2] In addition to the unanimous testimony of early church writers, there is also internal evidence consisting of several "we" sections (first-person accounts) in Acts. These reveal that the author was with Paul briefly on his second missionary journey (Acts 16:10–17), and then rejoined him at Philippi on Paul's return from his third journey (20:5–21:18). He stayed with Paul at Caesarea after Paul's arrest and accompanied him to Rome (27:1–28:16).

We know a little about Luke from Paul's letters. In two letters from prison in Rome, Paul identifies him as a physician (Col. 4:14) and fellow worker (Philem. 24). Luke also appears as Paul's faithful companion during his second Roman imprisonment (2 Tim. 4:10–11). In Colossians 4:11, 13–14, Paul associates Luke with his Gentile rather than Jewish companions. This Gentile identity helps to explain Luke's keen interest in the universal application of the gospel message. The gospel is for all peoples, Jew and Gentile alike.

Luke writes as a second-generation Christian, claiming not to have been an eyewitness of the events of Jesus' ministry, but to have thoroughly investigated the events before composing his Gospel (Luke 1:1–4). He writes as both historian and theologian, seeking to provide an accurate and trustworthy account of the events, while confirming the profound spiritual significance of these events.

## Date, Recipients, Destination

The date of the Gospel of Luke is uncertain, but it is closely tied to its companion volume Acts. Since Acts ends with Paul in prison in Rome (about A.D. 60), the book was probably written before his release, rearrest, and subsequent martyrdom. This would place its date around A.D. 60–63. The Gospel must have been completed sometime before this, perhaps in the late 50s or early 60s. It is possible, of course, that Luke wrote after Paul's death, but had a different reason for ending his two-volume work with Paul in Rome. This could be to show that the gospel had reached "the ends of the earth" (cf. Acts 1:8)—the furthest reaches of the empire. In this case, a much later date is possible, anytime from the 60s to the 80s.

Both Luke and Acts are addressed to Theophilus, who may have been: (1) the patron who sponsored the publication of Luke's work, (2) an influential unbeliever with an interest in Christianity, (3) a new Christian in need of further instruction, or even (4) the Roman official overseeing Paul's trial. This last possibility arises from the fact that Acts ends with Paul awaiting trial in Rome (Acts 28:30–31). The first of these is the most likely, perhaps in combination with the third. The writing of a book of this length was an expensive endeavor in the ancient world, both in terms of time and resources, and it was common to dedicate such a work to an influential patron. See further comments on Luke 1:3 and "The Prologues of Luke and Josephus."

Though Luke dedicates the work to Theophilus, it seems certain that he, like the other Gospel writers, writes for a wider audience. That this audience is predominantly Gentile is suggested by Luke's profound interest in the universality of the gospel message. It is good news for all peoples and for all nations.

There are few clues as to specific destination of the letter. Rome, Greece, Caesarea, and Alexandria have all been suggested.

### Historians of Luke's Time

Critics of Luke's claim to be an accurate historian have sometimes said that historical writing in the modern sense was unknown in the ancient world. Ancient "historians" played fast and loose with the facts, freely creating stories to suit their own purposes.

While it is true that some historians of antiquity were not as careful as others, it is overstating the case to deny that good history existed. The Hellenistic historian Polybius criticizes other writers for making up dramatic scenes and calls on them to "simply record what really happened and what really was said ..." (2.56.10).[A-1] Other ancient historians make similar comments. This confirms that intelligent writers and readers of the first century were concerned with distinguishing fact from fiction.

This is not so different from today, where the careful reader must discern between accurate news accounts and supermarket tabloid journalism. Luke's reliability as a historian must be judged from a careful examination of the events he records, not with sweeping generalizations about ancient history.[A-2]

## The Prologue (1:1–4)

Luke introduces his two-volume work with a formal literary prologue similar in style to the Hellenistic writers of his day (see "The Prologues of Luke and Josephus"). These four verses represent some of the finest Greek in the New Testament. The author is obviously an educated and skilled writer, a worthy candidate to compose the longest and most comprehensive account of the words and deeds of the central figure in human history.

Luke begins by setting forth the purpose of his work. What strikes the reader first is the piling up of terms of historical reliability. Not only has Luke received his information from first-generation Christians—eyewitnesses and the original ministers of God's message of salvation—but he has also gone back and carefully investigated these accounts to ensure that they are true. Yet Luke does not write from historical motivations alone. His goal is also theological. He is seeking to assure Theophilus of the truth of the gospel message.

This brings up an important point about the nature of the New Testament Gospels. None of the writers wrote from purely biographical or historical interest. All were convinced that God had acted in history to bring salvation to the world through his Son Jesus Christ. All had a burning desire to convince others of the truth of this message. The Gospel writers are called "Evangelists" (from *euangelion*, the Greek word for "Gospel") because their works are *written* versions of the *oral* proclamation of the good news about the salvation that has been achieved in Jesus Christ. The Gospels were written to be preached, and they were written to be believed.

**Many have undertaken to draw up an account (1:1).** Authors of Luke's day often cited similar works when describing their reason for writing. In some cases this was to show the inadequacy of previous writings; in others it was to justify their reason for writing or to lend credibility to their own works. In his history of the *Jewish War*, the Jewish historian Josephus claims he is writing to correct others who "misrepresented the facts" of the war to flatter the Romans or because of their hatred for the Jews.[3] The closest ancient parallel to Luke's prologue appears in the introduction to Josephus's *Against Apion* (see "The Prologues of Luke and Josephus" at 1:3).

While Luke does not say that these "many" other writings were inaccurate or inferior, he must have seen something inadequate in them for the situation he was addressing, since he felt the need to write his own. If Luke is using Mark as one of his sources, as most scholars believe, he may have wanted a more comprehensive account than Mark provided and one that addressed the universality of the gospel message more clearly.

**An account (1:1).** The term *diēgēsis* is used frequently in Greek literature of a historical narrative, especially one that set out a comprehensive and orderly account of events.[4]

**Handed down to us by . . . eyewitnesses and servants of the word (1:2).** The term "handed down" (*paradidōmi*, 1:2) often occurs as a technical term for the passing down of authoritative tradition. The rabbis of Jesus' day had a large body of oral traditions that they carefully memorized and passed on to their disciples (cf. Mark 7:13). Paul uses the same term regarding the handing down of the authoritative accounts of the Lord's Supper (1 Cor. 11:2, 23) and of the resurrection appearances (1 Cor. 15:3–8). The use of such terms indicates that the apostles, like the rabbis of their time, carefully preserved and passed on the words and deeds of their teacher. This contradicts the claim of some critics that the early church cared little about preserving accurate historical material about Jesus (see "Historians of Luke's Time").

The phrase "eyewitnesses and servants of the word" probably refers to one rather than two groups and means "the eyewitnesses who became the ministers of the message." This would refer primarily to the twelve apostles, but would also include the larger body of Jesus' disciples (see the reference to 120 believers in Acts 1:15).

**An orderly account (1:3).** Literally, "accurately in order." The phrase does not necessarily denote a strict chronological order (some events in Luke's Gospel are *not* chronological), but rather a systematic or logical account of the events.

**Most excellent Theophilus (1:3).** The word "Theophilus" means "beloved of God" or "one who loves God"; some have therefore suggested that Luke is writing generally to all believers who love God. Theophilus, however, was a common personal name in Luke's day, and it is much more likely that he refers here to an actual individual. The designation "most excellent" was used of anyone of high social status and was especially common for those of the equestrian order (the "knights") of Roman society. The term is used in Acts of the Roman governors Felix (Acts 24:3) and Festus (Acts 26:25). For more on the identity of Theophilus see the Introduction above.

## The Birth of John the Baptist Foretold (1:5–25)

Only Luke and Matthew include accounts of Jesus' miraculous conception

### The Prologues of Luke and Josephus

While there are many Greek and Roman works that have introductions similar to Luke's, the Jewish historian Josephus's two-volume work *Against Apion* is perhaps the closest. Josephus, like Luke, dedicates his work to a patron, "most excellent Epaphroditus," refers to previous works on the subject (his own in this case), and describes his purpose for writing:

> In my history of our Antiquities, most excellent Epaphroditus, I have, I think, made sufficiently clear to any who may peruse that work the extreme antiquity of our Jewish race.... Since, however, I observe that a considerable number of persons, influenced by the malicious calumnies of certain individuals, discredit the statements in my history concerning our antiquity ... I consider it my duty to devote a brief treatise to all these points; in order at once to convict our detractors of malignity and deliberate falsehood, to correct the ignorance of others, and to instruct all who desire to know the truth concerning the antiquity of our race.[A-3]

Josephus's second volume, like Acts, refers back to the first:

> In the first volume of this work, my most esteemed Epaphroditus, I demonstrated the antiquity of our race, corroborating my statements by ... citing as witnesses numerous Greek historians.... I shall now proceed to refute the rest of the authors who have attacked us.[A-4]

and birth. (Mark begins with the ministry of John the Baptist, John with a statement of Jesus' preexistence.) While the birth narratives of Matthew and Luke differ significantly from each other in terms of content, both draw strongly on the themes of messiahship and promise-fulfillment. Jesus is the promised Messiah, the descendant of David born to be king. His coming represents the fulfillment of the hopes and expectations of faithful Jews throughout the ages. Matthew's story centers on Joseph, whose dreams and actions link the narrative together. Luke's centers on Mary.

Luke's birth narrative (1:5–2:52) is not intended merely to fill in the details about Jesus' early years for the curious reader. It serves rather as an overture, setting the stage and preparing the reader for the rest of the Gospel and Acts. Many of Luke's important themes are introduced in these two chapters, including (1) the arrival of God's promised salvation and the fulfillment of his promises to Israel, (2) the place of John the Baptist as the forerunner of the Messiah, (3) the central role of the Holy Spirit in the age of salvation, (4) the gospel as good news for the poor and oppressed, (5) Jesus as the Messiah from David's line, and (6) the gospel as salvation for the Gentiles as well as the Jews.

As the reader moves from Luke's formal introduction in 1:1–4 to the story of John the Baptist, the writing style changes dramatically. From the very fine Greek literary style of the prologue, the language suddenly takes on an "Old Testament" flavor, reminiscent of the Septuagint (LXX), the Greek translation of the Old Testament. This stylistic change is used by Luke to bring the reader into another world—the world of the Old Testament and of Judaism. The characters we meet represent the righteous "remnant" of faithful Israel, Jews anxiously awaiting the coming of their Messiah. Zechariah is a priest, one of Israel's spiritual elite, and his wife Elizabeth is of priestly ancestry. Both are upright before God and faithful to his law. Zechariah is in the temple in Jerusalem, the center of Israel's religious life, offering incense before the Lord. Luke's goal here is to introduce his readers to the Old Testament people of God and to the promises that he has made to them, setting the stage for the fulfillment of those promises. The fulfillment begins with the announcement of the birth of John the Baptist, who will be "a voice of one calling in the desert" (3:4), preparing the way for the Messiah.

THE KINGDOM OF HEROD THE GREAT

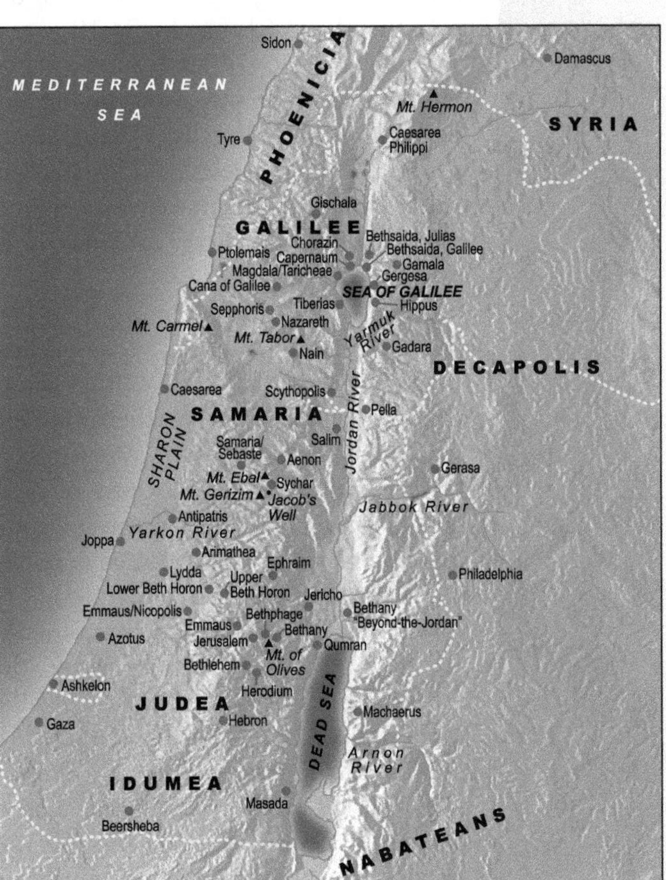

**In the time of Herod king of Judea (1:5).** In line with his historical purpose, Luke connects the birth of John the Baptist with Herod the Great, who reigned from 37–4 B.C. over a kingdom that included Judea, Galilee, Samaria, and much of Perea and Coele-Syria (see map and "Herod the Great"). When Luke calls him "king of Judea" he is probably using the term "Judea" in the broader sense of "greater Palestine," encompassing all of these regions.

**A priest named Zechariah, who belonged to the priestly division of Abijah (1:5).** The priesthood in Israel was divided into twenty-four courses, each providing temple service for one week twice a year (1 Chron. 24:1–19). Abijah is identified as the eighth division of the priesthood in 1 Chronicles 24:10.

**His wife Elizabeth was also a descendant of Aaron (1:5).** Literally, a "daughter of Aaron." Though priests could marry any godly Israelite woman, it was a sign of special piety to marry a woman of priestly ancestry.

**But they had no children, because Elizabeth was barren (1:7).** In a culture where the primary social unit was the family and where one's ancestry was of critical importance, childlessness was a cause of great concern and shame. Such shame is a common theme in the Old Testament, appearing in the stories of Sarah, the mother of Isaac (Gen. 18); Rebekah, the mother of Jacob and Esau (25:21); Rachel, the mother of Joseph (30:22–23); the unnamed mother of Samson (Judg. 13); and Hannah, the mother of Samuel (1 Sam. 1). Sarah provides the closest analogy to Elizabeth, since she was not only barren but also past child-bearing years. In all of these cases, the tragedy of childlessness provides an opportunity for God to show his grace and power. When God miraculously opens the womb, the child who is born is a special and unique gift from God and fulfills a special destiny in his plan.

**When Zechariah's division was on duty . . . chosen by lot (1:8–9).** During one of the two weeks of service for Zechariah's priestly division, he is chosen by lot to offer incense in the Holy Place. The casting of lots (something like throwing dice) was a common method of discerning God's will in the Old Testament. Proverbs 16:33 says, "The lot is cast into the lap, but its every decision is from the LORD."[5] Lots were cast by the disciples for the replacement of Judas in Acts 1:26. Regulations for the lot are given in the Mishnah.[6] In the New Testament era such a procedure is unnecessary since believers possess the permanent indwelling of the Holy Spirit for guidance (Rom. 8:14).

**To go into the temple of the Lord and burn incense (1:9).** The word "temple" here is *naos,* which Luke uses to designate the Holy Place and/or the Most Holy Place (see diagram of temple). Luke uses a different word, *hieron,* to identify the temple in general or the larger temple precincts (see comments on 2:27). The Most Holy Place, which held the ark of the covenant, was entered only once a year by the high priest on Israel's Day of Atonement, when sacrifices were offered for the whole nation (see Lev. 16:1–34; Heb. 9:6–7). Incense was offered in the Holy Place twice daily, before the morning sacrifice and after the evening sacrifice. The Holy Place held the altar of incense, the golden lampstand,

and the table of consecrated bread. The chosen priest would enter, clean the altar, and offer fresh incense. The incense was to be kept burning continually before the Lord (Ex. 30:7–8). Because of the large number of priests, this privilege may have come only once in a lifetime for a particular priest. This was a special occasion in Zechariah's life.

**An angel of the Lord appeared (1:11).** Visions or messages from God occasionally occur in the temple in the Old Testament (1 Sam. 3; Isa. 6; Zech. 3:1) and in later Judaism. Josephus describes how the Maccabean king and high priest John Hyrcanus, while offering incense in the temple, heard a heavenly voice telling him his sons had just won victory in battle.[7] Such precedents explain why in Luke 1:22 the people conclude that Zechariah has seen a vision.

In the Old Testament "the angel of the LORD" is an exalted figure who appears as God's messenger and is at times identified with the Lord himself (see Gen. 16:7, cf. v. 13). Some identify him as the preincarnate Christ. Here, however, he is identified as Gabriel (see Luke 1:19).

**Zechariah . . . was gripped with fear (1:12).** Fear is a common Old Testament response to the appearance of God or an angel. See the reactions of Gideon (Judg. 6:22–23), Manoah (13:22), and Daniel (Dan. 8:16–17; 10:10–11), and especially Isaiah's terror at his awesome vision of God (Isa. 6:5). Such fear is usually followed by a reassuring word of comfort, "Do not be afraid" (Luke 1:13; cf. 1:29–30).

**Your wife Elizabeth will bear you a son (1:13).** Predictions of the birth of a special child are common in the Old Testament and frequently follow the pattern of announcement and naming found here. See the accounts of Ishmael (Gen. 16:11), Isaac (17:16, 19; 18:1–15), Samson (Judg. 13:2–23), and "Immanuel" (Isa. 7:14). The announcement to Mary in Luke 1:30–33 will follow a similar pattern.

**You are to give him the name John (1:13).** The meaning of names, especially those bestowed by God, had greater significance in biblical times than today. They could relate to the circumstances of the child's birth or might predict his future role. "John" means "the Lord has shown favor." God is showing favor to Elizabeth by giving her a child in her old age and also to the nation Israel by providing the forerunner of the Messiah.

**He is never to take wine or other fermented drink (1:15).** The Greek word for "fermented drink" (*sikera*) can mean any alcoholic beverage not made from grapes, but usually referred to grain-based alcohol ("beer"). This abstinence from alcohol is probably to be identified with a Nazirite vow, which was for an

**THE JERUSALEM TEMPLE**

A model of the temple looking at the entrance to the holy place. This portion of the temple would have been 172′ high.

Israelite a period of special consecration to God. During the vow no alcohol was to be drunk, the hair was to remain uncut, and no dead body was to be touched (touching a body rendered an individual ceremonially unclean) (Num. 6:1–21). Though normally temporary, in the case of John the Baptist, as with Samson (Judg. 13:4–7) and Samuel (1 Sam. 1:11, 15), this vow was lifelong.

**He will be filled with the Holy Spirit even from birth (1:15).** "Even from birth" is better translated "even while still in the womb," as 1:41 makes clear. The filling of the Spirit provided an individual with God's presence and power to accomplish his sovereign purpose. While in the Old Testament period, the Spirit came upon individuals intermittently to accomplish particular tasks, John will have a permanent possession of the Spirit (cf. 1 Sam. 16:13). This previews the role of the Spirit in the church from the day of Pentecost onward.

**In the spirit and power of Elijah (1:17).** This verse alludes to Malachi, where the prophet predicts that Elijah will return before the great Day of the Lord to bring about reconciliation within families (Mal. 4:5–6) and to prepare the way for the coming of the Lord (Mal. 3:1; see Luke 1:76). The reference to Elijah's "spirit" recalls 2 Kings 2:9–10, where Elijah's successor Elisha asks for and receives a "double portion" of his spirit. The "power" of Elijah probably refers to his prophetic authority rather than to his miracles (cf. 1 Kings 17–18) since Luke does not record miracles by John. His role, rather, is to "make ready a people prepared for the Lord."

There was speculation in Judaism concerning the return of Elijah, much of it related to Elijah's role as interpreter of the law.[8] Even today Jews leave an empty chair at Passover in the hopes that the prophet Elijah will come.

**How can I be sure . . . ? (1:18).** Requests for a sign are common in the Old Testament. Abraham (Gen. 15:8), Gideon (Judg. 6:17), and Hezekiah (2 Kings 20:8) all asked for signs. Paul says in 1 Corinthians 1:22, "Jews demand miraculous signs and Greeks look for wisdom."

**I am Gabriel (1:19).** Gabriel is one of only two angels specifically named in the Old Testament, though others are named in intertestamental Jewish literature.[9] Both Gabriel and Michael appear in the New Testament (Gabriel in Luke 1:19 and 1:26, Michael in Jude 9 and Rev. 12:7). In Daniel Gabriel explains the vision of seventy weeks, a prophecy concerning the coming Messiah (Dan. 9:24–27). He will now announce the birth of that Messiah.

**The people were waiting . . . and wondering why he stayed so long in the temple (1:21).** Replacing the incense took only a short time, so the people may have been concerned that Zechariah had incurred God's judgment for some act of disrespect. A passage from the Mishnah (*c.* A.D. 200) concerning the entrance of the high priest into the Most Holy Place on the Day of Atonement provides insight into Luke's text:

> When he [the high priest] reached the Ark he put the fire pan between the two bars. He heaped up the incense on the coals and the whole place became filled with smoke. He came out by the way he went in, and in the outer space he prayed a short

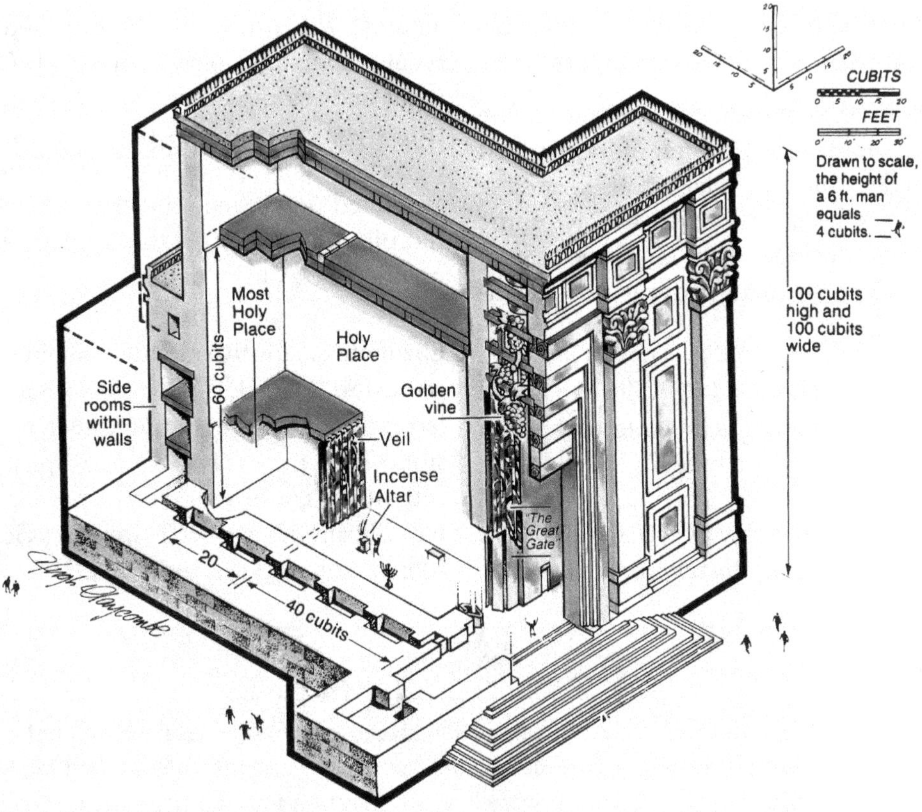

## HEROD'S TEMPLE COMPARED TO A MODERN BUILDING

CUBITS
0 5 10 15 20
FEET
0' 10' 20' 30'
Drawn to scale, the height of a 6 ft. man equals 4 cubits.

100 cubits high and 100 cubits wide

Most Holy Place

Holy Place

60 cubits

Side rooms within walls

Golden vine

Veil

Incense Altar

"The Great Gate"

20

40 cubits

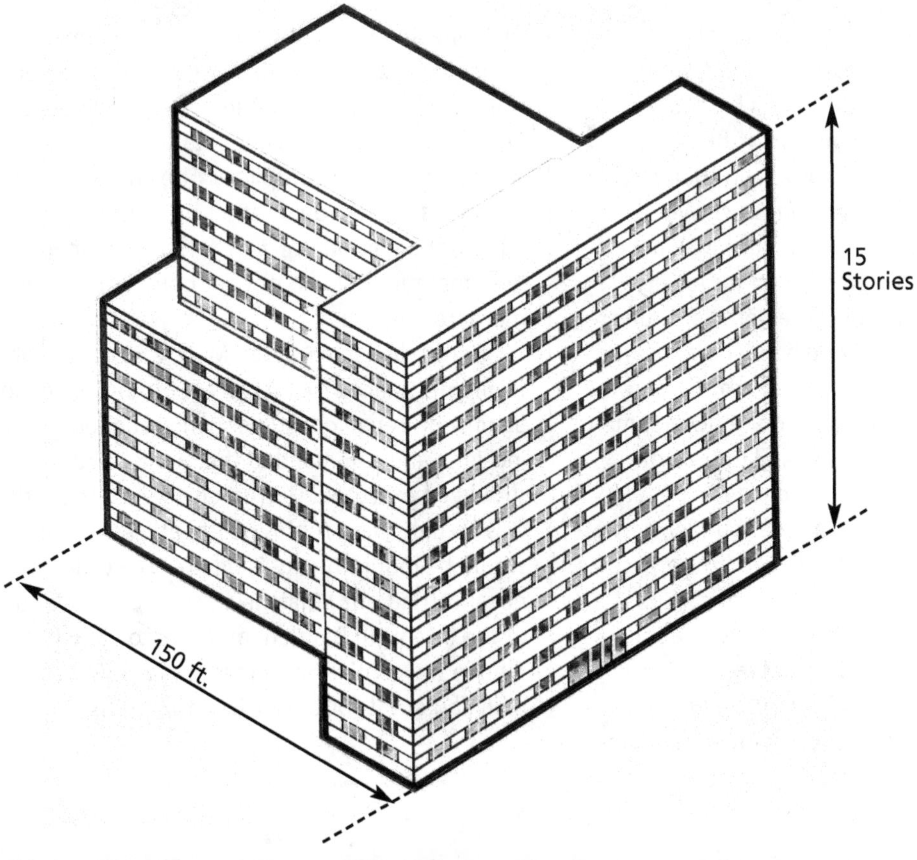

15 Stories

150 ft.

prayer. But he did not prolong his prayer lest he put Israel in terror.[10]

Though Zechariah did not enter the Most Holy Place, the altar of incense just outside in the Holy Place stood very close to the ark and hence to the awesome power and presence of God (see 2 Sam. 6:1–15 for the danger of casually touching the ark).

**He returned home (1:23).** Zechariah and Elizabeth lived outside of Jerusalem "in the hill country of Judea" (1:39). When not fulfilling his role as a priest, Zechariah probably practiced a secular trade as a small farmer or craftsman. Though the priests were supposed to receive portions of sacrifices (1 Cor. 9:13) and temple tithes (Heb. 7:5), these tithes were not always paid because of poverty or corruption, and many priests remained poor. Since they served in the temple only a few weeks a year, most practiced a secular trade.[11]

**Elizabeth . . . for five months remained in seclusion (1:24).** There is no known Israelite custom that required such seclusion. This may have been a spiritual retreat for grateful prayer, or perhaps it was Elizabeth's way of respecting God's silence imposed on Zechariah.

## Herod the Great

Herod "the Great" ruled Palestine under the Romans from 37–4 B.C. He was the son of Antipater, an advisor to the Hasmonean kings who had ruled Israel during the period of independence won by the Maccabees (see "The Maccabees"). When the Hasmonean dynasty collapsed, the Romans appointed Herod to rule as king of the Jews. A cunning politician, he had at first supported Mark Antony and Cleopatra in their struggle against Octavian (Caesar Augustus). When Octavian proved superior, Herod quickly switched sides and convinced the emperor of his loyalty.

Herod was a strange mix of an efficient ruler and a cruel tyrant. On the one hand, he appeared as the protector of Judaism and sought to gain the favor of the Jews. He encouraged the development of the synagogue communities and in time of calamity remitted taxes and supplied the people with free grain. He was also a great builder, a role that earned him the title "the Great." His greatest project was the rebuilding and beautification of the temple in Jerusalem, restoring it to the splendor of the time of Solomon (see Mark 13:2).

At the same time, Herod was distrustful, jealous, and cruel, ruthlessly crushing any potential opposition. Because he was an Edomite and not Jewish, the Jews never accepted him as their legitimate king—a rejection that infuriated him. To legitimize his claim to the throne, he divorced his first wife and married the Hasmonean princess Miriamne—later executing her when he suspected she was plotting against him. Three of his sons and another wife met the same fate when they, too, were suspected of conspiracy. The emperor Augustus once said he would rather be Herod's *hys* ("pig") than his *huios* ("son"). Herod, trying to be a legitimate Jew, would not eat pork, but he freely murdered his sons!

Herod died in 4 B.C. (cf. Matt. 2:19), probably from intestinal cancer. As an act of final vengeance against his rebellious subjects, he rounded up leading Jews and commanded that at his death they should be executed. His reasoning was that if there was no mourning *for* his death, at least there would be mourning *at* his death. (The order was never carried out.) Matthew's story of the slaughter of the infants in Bethlehem comes to life when seen in the context of Herod's extraordinary paranoia and quest for power (Matt. 2:1–18).[A-5]

**The Lord has . . . taken away my disgrace among the people (1:25).** Similar praise is expressed in the Old Testament by the barren women whom God blesses with children (Gen. 21:6–7; 1 Sam. 2:1–11). Rachel, like Elizabeth, rejoices that "God has taken away my disgrace" (Gen. 30:23).

## The Birth of Jesus Foretold (1:26–38)

Having announced the birth of John, the forerunner of the Messiah, Luke's story now turns to the Messiah himself. While Jesus and John are viewed together as co-agents in God's great plan of salvation, Jesus is superior, for he is the Messiah.

**In the sixth month (1:26).** This is the sixth month of Elizabeth's pregnancy (1:36). The reference links this story with the previous one.

**Nazareth, a town in Galilee (1:26).** Nazareth was a small and insignificant village in Galilee (see Nathanael's comment in John 1:46: "Can anything good come from [Nazareth]?"). The town is never mentioned in the Old Testament or in Jewish writings of the day. Its existence was confirmed by an inscription discovered in 1962 at Caesarea Maritima (see "Inscription Bearing the Name of 'Nazareth'").

**To a virgin pledged to be married (1:27).** The word translated "virgin" (*parthenos*) means a young, unmarried girl and normally indicates virginity. A young Jewish girl would normally be engaged between twelve and fourteen years old. This engagement was far more formal than today. A legal marriage contract would be drawn up (which could only be broken by "divorce"), the girl would be called her fiancé's "wife," and infidelity would be treated as adultery. Yet she would continue to live with her parents until the marriage ceremony a year or so later.[12]

**Joseph, a descendant of David (1:27).** Literally "of the house of David," meaning the family (= ancestry) with implications of "dynasty." Jesus is a legitimate heir to the throne of David (see 1:32–33).

**You will be with child and give birth to a son (1:31).** This verse follows a common pattern of birth announcements and especially echoes Isaiah 7:14: "The virgin will be with child and will give birth to a son, and will call him Immanuel."

**You are to give him the name Jesus (1:31).** "Jesus" is the Greek equivalent of the Hebrew *Yeshua*, or Joshua, and means "Yahweh saves." Unlike Matthew (Matt. 1:21), Luke does not specifically refer to the meaning of the name.

**Most High . . . .The Lord God (1:32).** Both of these are Greek translations of

GALILEE

Nazareth was located west of the Sea of Galilee near the Roman city of Sepphoris.

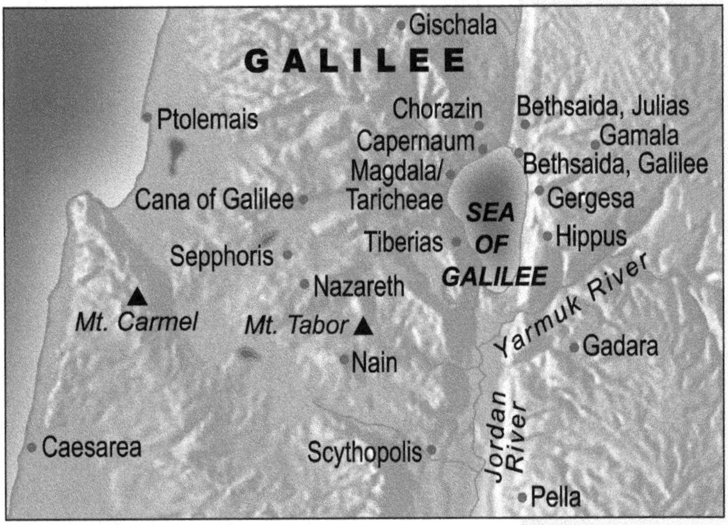

## Inscription Bearing the Name of "Nazareth"

Though the site has long been known to Christian pilgrims, until 1962 there was no literary or epigraphic evidence for ancient Nazareth. This fragmentary inscription discovered at Caesarea Maritima lists the twenty-four priestly courses (see comments on Luke 1:5), and tells in which towns they reside. The eighteenth course, Happizzez (1 Chron. 24:15), is identified with Nazareth.

Old Testament names for God. The first is from *El Elyon*, "God Most High," and the second from *Yahweh Elohim*, "Yahweh God."

**The throne of his father David . . . he will reign . . . forever (1:32–33).** The verse epitomizes the covenant made to David (2 Sam. 7; Ps. 89), where David was promised that God would raise up his "seed" after him, who would have a "father-son" relationship with God (see Luke 1:35) and who would reign forever on his throne. This promise to David was taken up by the prophets and became the foundation for Israel's hope for a coming Messiah (see "Messianic Expectation in Jesus' Day").[13] Luke repeatedly refers to this promise.[14]

**His kingdom will never end (1:33).** Though an eternal kingdom was part of the covenant made to David (2 Sam. 7:16; Isa. 9:6), the verse also recalls the eternal kingdom of Daniel 7:14.

**The Holy Spirit will come upon you . . . will overshadow you . . . (1:35).** The verb "come upon" is used similarly in Isaiah 32:15 LXX, where it refers to the Spirit's coming upon the land to make it fertile. Luke uses the same verb in Acts 1:8 of the Spirit's coming upon the believers at Pentecost. The verb "overshadow" appears in Exodus 40:35 (LXX) with reference to God's presence or Shekinah "overshadowing" the tabernacle in a cloud (cf. Num. 10:34), and a similar reference to God's overshadowing presence appears in the transfiguration account (Luke 9:34).

In the past, attempts have been made to draw parallels between this passage and pagan texts related to a god's impregnating a human woman. But there is no hint here of sexual union, and these parallels have now generally been rejected by scholars.

**The Son of God (1:35).** While the title always points to Jesus' unique relationship with the Father, it carries various nuances in the New Testament. In 1:32 the emphasis is on Jesus' messiahship, since the Old Testament promised that the Messiah would have a special father-son relationship with God.[15] This use of the title is common in the New Testa-

### REFLECTIONS

**WHEN GABRIEL ANNOUNCED TO** Mary that she would give birth to Jesus, he was proclaiming the fulfillment of a promise made nine hundred years earlier to King David. Jesus would be the promised Messiah, the king who would reign forever on David's throne. The Annunciation reminds us that God is a God who always keeps his promises. We can trust him for that today.

ment.[16] Elsewhere, as here in 1:35, the title emphasizes Jesus' essential deity.[17]

**Elizabeth your relative (1:36).** The term "relative" (*syngenis*) is not specific and could refer to a cousin, aunt, or other relation.

**Nothing is impossible with God (1:37).** The verse echoes Genesis 18:14 (LXX), "Nothing is impossible with God," a reference to God's miraculous intervention for the barren and aged Sarah. God's intervention in the case of Elizabeth (and Sarah) is proof that he can accomplish anything, even the virginal conception promised to Mary.

**I am the Lord's servant (1:38).** The term "servant" (*doulē*) is also used by Hannah (1 Sam. 1:11 LXX), whose hymn of joy has parallels to Mary's *Magnificat* in the following passage (1 Sam. 2:1–10; Luke 1:46–55).

## Mary Visits Elizabeth (1:39–45)

The stories of the births of Jesus and John now come together as Mary sets off to visit her relative Elizabeth. John's role as forerunner and witness to Christ begins already as the child leaps for joy in Elizabeth's womb at Mary's arrival. Filled with the Spirit (see comments on 1:41), Elizabeth proclaims a blessing on Mary and on her child, and Mary responds with a song of praise to God. This theme of joy and rejoicing at the arrival of God's salvation is an important one for Luke and will recur throughout his Gospel.

### Messianic Expectation in Jesus' Day

In the century leading up to Jesus' birth, when the powerful Roman empire dominated Palestine, hope for the coming Messiah to free God's people from their oppressors became particularly intense. Though these expectations were diverse in the various strands of first-century Judaism,[A-6] the dominant hope was for a messianic deliverer from King David's line. In the *Psalms of Solomon,* a pseudepigraphic work (written under an assumed name) from the first century B.C., the following hope is expressed:

> See, Lord, and raise up for them their king, the son of David,
> to rule over your servant Israel. . . .
> Undergird him with the strength to destroy the unrighteous rulers,
> to purge Jerusalem from gentiles who trample her to destruction;
> in wisdom and in righteousness to drive out the sinners from the inheritance;
> to smash the arrogance of sinners like a potter's jar;
> To shatter all their substance with an iron rod [cf. Ps. 2:9]
> to destroy unlawful nations with the word of his mouth; [cf. Isa. 11:4]
> At his warning the nations will flee from his presence;
> and he will condemn sinners by the thoughts of their hearts.
>
> (*Pss. Sol.* 17:21–25)

The Gentiles who "trample [Jerusalem] to destruction" are the Romans. It is not difficult to see why such excitement surrounded Jesus and even John the Baptist (Luke 3:15), when people suspected either might be the Messiah, the Son of David.

Similar expectations for a Davidic Messiah appear in apocalyptic Judaism[A-7] and in the Qumran (Dead Sea) scrolls.[A-8] The community at Qumran awaited two messiahs: a royal Davidic one and a priestly one from the line of Aaron.[A-9]

**A town in the hill country of Judea (1:39).** Lit. "into the hill country, to a city of Judah" (see 2 Sam. 2:1). Judah, one of the twelve tribes of Israel, occupied much of southern Canaan after the Israelites conquered the Promised Land (Josh. 15). David, a Judahite, was first made king over Judah (2 Sam. 2) and then later of all of Israel (2 Sam. 5). When the kingdom divided in civil war after the death of David's son Solomon, the southern kingdom was known as "Judah" and the northern kingdom "Israel." Luke probably uses the term to describe the whole southern region of Israel—what became the Roman province of "Judea." Luke's description of the location is imprecise, but in light of Zechariah's temple service one would expect a village in the hills near Jerusalem. Depending on the location, Mary' journey may have taken her between three and five days. If taken alone, such a journey would have been unusual and potentially dangerous for a woman of Mary's age.



HILL COUNTRY OF JUDEA

**The baby leaped in her womb (1:41).** Leaping is an expression of joy (Mal. 4:2). David "leaped" and danced before the Lord (2 Sam. 6:16). The recognition of prenatal actions as significant appears elsewhere in Jewish literature. The struggle between Esau and Jacob in the womb (Gen. 25:22) is interpreted in Jewish tradition as a conscious struggle. In another tradition, the unborn children sang a song at the Exodus.[18]

**Elizabeth was filled with the Holy Spirit (1:41).** In the Old Testament, as here, the filling of the Spirit is often associated with the prophetic gift. After four hundred years of silence, the Spirit of prophecy is appearing again in Israel (cf. 1:67; 2:25, 27).

**Mother of my Lord (1:43).** "My Lord" here is a court expression, roughly equivalent to "my king." Elizabeth recognizes

HILL COUNTRY OF JUDEA

The area just north of Hebron.

that Mary is bearing the Messiah, the future king of Israel (see 2 Sam. 24:20–21, where Araunah expresses similar unworthiness that he should be visited by King David).

## Mary's Song (1:46–56)

Mary's joyful song of praise (called the *Magnificat*, "he/she magnifies," from the first word in the Latin translation) has a strong Old Testament flavor and is the first of four similar "hymns" of praise in the birth narrative (see also 1:68–79; 2:29–32; 2:14). It has many parallels with Hannah's prayer in 1 Samuel 2:1–10, which celebrates God's blessing in overcoming her barrenness and providing her with a child. Hannah, like Mary, praised God for lifting up the poor and the humble and bringing down the mighty and the proud. This theme of the reversal of fortunes, which will accompany God's salvation (see comments on 1:52), is an important one for Luke and will appear again in his rendition of the Beatitudes (6:20–21, 24–25) and in the parable of the rich man and Lazarus (16:19–31; cf. 12:13–21; 21:1–4).

**My soul . . . my spirit (1:46–47).** Synonymous parallelism, where a second line restates the first line in some way, is characteristic of Hebrew poetry and appears throughout the Psalms. See Psalm 16:9: "Therefore my heart is glad, and my soul rejoices; my body also dwells secure" (RSV). "My soul" is a Hebrew way of saying "I" (Ps. 34:2).

**God my Savior (1:47).** God is often called "Savior" in the Old Testament, especially in the Psalms and Isaiah. Physical salvation (but always with spiritual dimensions) is usually intended.

**All generations will call me blessed (1:48).** The honor given to one's name by future generations was of great importance in the ancient Near East.

**Those who fear him (1:50).** Fear here means reverence, humility, and obedience before God's awesome person and presence. It is the appropriate attitude of all God's people.

**He has performed mighty deeds with his arm (1:51).** God's "arm" is an Old Testament anthropomorphism for God's mighty power (cf. Ps. 98:1; Isa. 40:10). It is especially used of God's strength in bringing the Israelites out of Egypt.[19]

**He has brought down rulers . . . lifted up the humble . . . filled the hungry . . . sent the rich away empty (1:52–53).** God's justice in reversing social and political fortunes is a common theme in the Old Testament. Hannah's song says, " . . . those who were hungry hunger no more. . . . The LORD sends poverty and wealth; he humbles and he exalts."[20] The theme also appears in the wisdom literature of intertestamental Judaism. Sirach 10:14 reads, "The Lord overthrows the thrones of rulers, and enthrones the lowly in their place." For the "poor" as God's righteous people, see comments on Luke 6:20.

**His servant Israel (1:54).** Israel is frequently called God's "servant" in Isaiah 41–49 (see comments on Matt. 3:22; 12:15–18).

**To Abraham and his descendants forever (1:55).** Just as Gabriel's words in 1:33–34 recalled God's covenant with David, so now Mary alludes to the Abrahamic covenant. God made an "everlasting covenant" with Abraham and with his descendants to be his God, to make his name great, to bless him, to make him the father of a great nation (Israel) and of many nations, and to give him the land of Canaan as an eternal inheritance (Gen. 12:1–3; 17:3–8). Abraham became the father of the nation Israel as well as the father of all who share his faith in God's promises (Rom. 4:16–17). Luke often refers to Abraham and his covenant.[21]

## The Birth of John the Baptist (1:57–66)

The account of John's birth centers around his circumcision and naming. Elizabeth and Zechariah demonstrate their faithfulness and obedience to God by naming the child "John" (see 1:6, 13). Their friends and neighbors are amazed at their unwillingness to name the child after Zechariah or another relative, and are astonished at the miracle that Zechariah can speak again. Word of these extraordinary events spreads throughout the countryside and all wonder what special role this child will play in God's plan. God is once again at work among his people!

**Her neighbors and relatives . . . shared her joy (1:58).** A birth, especially the birth of a son (because it meant the family name would be carried on), was a time of great celebration (as today!). For Elizabeth's family and friends, the joy was even greater since God had mercifully removed the shame of her barrenness (see comments on 1:7).

**On the eighth day they came to circumcise the child (1:59).** God commanded first Abraham and then the nation Israel to circumcise every male child on the eighth day (Gen. 17:9–14; Lev. 12:3). The procedure represented the child's incorporation into God's covenant community. Circumcision was generally viewed as essential for recognition as an authentic Jew (Phil. 3:5). At this time it was normally performed by the head of the household.

**To name him after his father (1:59).** It was common to name a son after a relative, usually either his father or (more often) his grandfather. In the Old Testament the naming normally occurred at birth (see Gen. 4:1; 25:25–26), so waiting eight days is unusual. The Greeks and Romans often named their children around the seventh or tenth day, so perhaps this practice had been adopted by some in Palestine.[22]

**He asked for a writing tablet (1:63).** This would normally be a wood board with a wax surface that could be inscribed with a sharp object.

**For the Lord's hand was with him (1:66).** Another Old Testament anthropomorphism (see 1:51). It can indicate either God's guidance and protective power, as here, or his hand of judgment, as in Acts 13:11.[23]

## Zechariah's Song (1:67–80)

Zechariah's song of praise, known as the *Benedictus* ("blessed" or "praised," after the first word of the hymn in the Latin Vulgate), is the second of four songs of praise in Luke's birth narrative.[24] Like Mary's, Zechariah's hymn has a strong nationalistic tone, focusing on Israel's physical salvation. It recalls similar psalms in the Old Testament and Judaism. Yet while Mary's was primarily a psalm of praise, Zechariah's is also prophetic, predicting the roles of Jesus and John. It is thus similar to the messianic or "royal" psalms of the Old Testament.[25] While praising God for the part his son John will play in God's plan (1:76–77), the hymn focuses especially on God's salvation through his Messiah. It is with this latter theme that the hymn begins and ends (1:68–75, 78–79).

**His father Zechariah was filled with the Holy Spirit (1:67).** See comments on 1:41.

**Praise be to the Lord, the God of Israel (1:68).** A common Old Testament phrase in hymns of praise.[26]

**Because he has come and has redeemed his people (1:68).** The idea of "visiting to redeem" recalls especially God's great act of salvation in the Exodus from Egypt (see Ex. 3:7–10, 17–20) and the "new exodus" promised by the prophets (see Isa. 40). Luke will return to this theme in 1:78 and 7:16.

**He has raised up a horn of salvation (1:69).** "Horn" indicates the horn of a powerful animal, a symbol of strength (Deut. 33:17). The lifting or exalting of a horn denotes an increase in power. The horn of David is exalted by the Lord in Psalm 89:24, a messianic context (cf. 1 Sam. 2:10). The image of "raising up" a horn is close to Psalm 132:17, another messianic passage, where it is said that a horn will "sprout" or "grow up" for David.

**In the house of his servant David (1:69).** See comments on 1:27.

**Salvation from our enemies . . . to rescue us (1:71–74).** While the language here is strongly nationalistic and political, in the Old Testament such salvation is always accompanied by spiritual and moral renewal. Notice the goal here is "to enable us to serve him . . . in holiness and righteousness" (1:74–75).

**Covenant . . . to our father Abraham (1:72–73).** See comments on 1:55.

**You will go on before the Lord to prepare the way for him (1:76).** The verse recalls God's messenger of salvation in Malachi 3:1 and the voice announcing a new exodus deliverance in Isaiah 40:3 (see comments on Luke 1:17; 3:4; 7:27).

**The knowledge of salvation through the forgiveness of their sins (1:77).** Forgiveness of sins, an important theme for Luke, was an integral part of the new covenant promised through Jeremiah.[27]

**The rising sun will come to us . . . to shine on those living in darkness (1:78–79).** The Greek word translated "rising sun" (*anatolē*; "Sunrise," NASB; "dawn," NRSV) denotes a "rising" and can refer to a rising heavenly body ("sunrise" or "east" [= where the sun rises]) or to a growing plant ("shoot" or "branch"). Both images have messianic connotations. The Messiah is called the "shoot" from David's line[28] but is also identified as a light shining on those in darkness.[29] The reference to shining here confirms that the latter sense is primary. In Isaiah 9:1–7 the light that shines on those in darkness heralds the birth of the child who will reign forever on the throne of David. Similarly, Numbers 24:17, which speaks of a star coming forth from Jacob, was widely interpreted in Judaism with reference to the Messiah.[30] Rising light imagery also appears in the Old Testament with reference to God's end-time salvation.[31]

**The child grew and became strong in spirit (1:80).** This phrase echoes the

QUMRAN

*(top)* The cliffs where the principal cave (cave 4) of the Dead Sea Scroll discoveries is located.

*(bottom left)* The remains of the scriptorium.

*(bottom right)* The entrance to cave 4.

## John the Baptist and the Community at Qumran

There has been much speculation among scholars as to whether John the Baptist may have had contact with the desert community of Essenes at Qumran, which produced the Dead Sea Scrolls. John's early years in the Judean Desert (Luke 1:80) may well have been in the vicinity of the Qumran community near the Dead Sea. If John's aged parents died before he reached adulthood, it is not impossible that he was raised by such a community. In an intriguing comment, the Jewish historian Josephus writes of the Essenes that "marriage they disdain, but they adopt other men's children, while yet pliable and docile, and regard them as their kin and mould them in accordance with their own principles."[A-10]

John's message and ministry also has some interesting points in common with the Essenes. Both share a strong expectation for the soon arrival of God's final salvation, both identify with the prophecy of Isaiah 40:3, both associate themselves with the righteous remnant called out from apostate Israel, and both practice ritual washings of some sort (baptism in John's case).

Unfortunately, there is not enough evidence either to confirm or disprove this fascinating hypothesis.

descriptions of Samson and especially Samuel.[32]

**He lived in the desert (1:80).** The reference is probably to the Jordan River Valley west of the Dead Sea. The desert in the Bible is a place of solitude and spiritual reflection, but also one of testing and preparation (see comments on 4:2 and "John the Baptist and the Community at Qumran").

## The Birth of Jesus (2:1–7)

The account of Jesus' birth in Bethlehem brings together various themes of significance for Luke. By linking Jesus' birth to the census decree of Caesar Augustus, Luke provides his narrative with a firm historical framework (cf. 1:1–4; 3:1–2) and hints at the worldwide significance of seemingly trivial events in Judea. God's sovereign control over history is evident as Caesar Augustus, emperor of the world, issues a decree that inadvertently moves God's plan forward. Joseph and Mary are required to take the arduous trip to Bethlehem and so fulfill the prophecy of the Messiah's birth (Mic. 5:2). The commonness of the birth and the lowly shepherd visitors further confirm that this child, though destined to reign in power and glory (Luke 1:32–33), will first bring good news and salvation to the humble, the poor, and the outcasts.

**Caesar Augustus (2:1).** See "Caesar Augustus, the First Roman Emperor."

**A census should be taken of the entire Roman world (2:1).** Censuses were common in the Roman empire and were used as registration for tax purposes. Although we have no written evidence of such a single worldwide census during this time, Augustus reorganized the administration of the empire and conducted numerous local censuses. Luke may be referring to an otherwise unknown census, or he may be treating a local Palestinian census as part of the emperor's administrative policy.

The Greek word *oikoumenē* (NIV: "the Roman world") literally means "the inhabited world" and is used here of the Roman empire—civilization as perceived through Roman eyes.

**The first census . . . while Quirinius was governor of Syria (2:2).** Like the census itself, the reference to Quirinius represents a historical difficulty. According to Josephus, the governorship of Quirinius over Syria began in A.D. 6–7, and a census he conducted is described for Judea around A.D. 6.[33] This particular census and the revolt that followed are also mentioned by Luke in Acts 5:37. The problem is this would be ten years too late for the present account, since the birth of Jesus occurred prior to Herod's death in 4 B.C. (Matt. 2:1–19; Luke 1:5).

Various solutions to this problem have been proposed. (1) There is some inscriptional evidence that Quirinius may have been governor of Syria twice, first in 10–7 B.C. and then again in A.D. 6–9.[34] Luke's reference would be to his first governorship and a prior census. (2) Others suggest that prior to his governorship, Quirinius held a broad administrative post over the eastern empire, and it was at this time that this first census was taken. The Greek actually says, "while Quirinius was governing [or had charge over] Syria." (3) A third possibility is that Quirinius was completing a census that a previous governor had begun. In these first three proposals Quirinius would have been overseeing a census imposed by Caesar upon Herod the Great's territory. (4) Another novel solution separates Quirinius from Luke's census by translating the Greek word *prōtē* as "before" rather than "first." Luke might be saying this census took place *prior* to Quirinius's governorship of Syria. In any case, there is not enough evidence available to draw a decisive conclusion either for or against Luke's account.

**Everyone went to his own town (2:3).** Though the Romans did not generally require citizens to return to their ancestral homes during a census, there is some Egyptian evidence that property owners had to return to the district where they owned land.[35] Perhaps Joseph owned property in Bethlehem. Another possibility is that the Romans here, as on other occasions, allowed their client states to conduct affairs according to local customs, which in the case of Judea would involve ancestral tribal divisions.

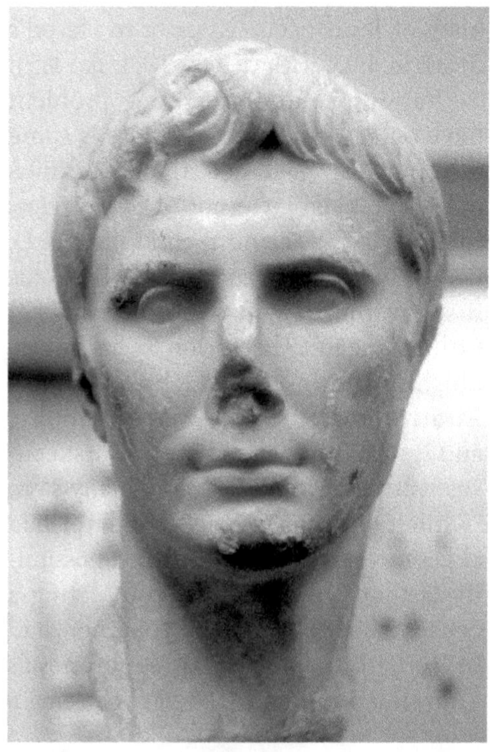

BUST OF CAESAR AUGUSTUS

COIN INSCRIBED WITH "CAESAR"

This coin depicts captives of Julius Caesar.

**So Joseph also went up . . . to Judea (2:4).** In the Old Testament one always went "up" to Judea and to Jerusalem. This is not just because of their elevation (Bethlehem is in "the hill country of Judea"; cf. 1:39), but especially because Jerusalem was the city of God.

**Bethlehem the town of David (2:4).** "Bethlehem" is from a Hebrew word meaning "house of bread." The Greek term *polis* can refer to a village, town, or city. Since Bethlehem was a small village, the NIV's "town" is accurate. Located about five miles south of Jerusalem, Bethlehem was closely associated with David in the Old Testament, being his birthplace and original home.[36] This David connection is the key to the prophecy of Micah 5:2, which predicts the Messiah's birth in Bethlehem (cf. Matt. 2:6). The Messiah was to be a new and greater "David."

**Joseph . . . line of David (2:4).** See comments on 1:27.

**Mary, who was pledged to be married to him (2:5).** See comments on 1:27.

**Her firstborn, a son (2:7).** "Firstborn" is not meant to indicate that other children would be born, but to demonstrate Jesus' consecration to God and his rights to the privileges of a firstborn son.[37]

**She wrapped him in cloths (2:7).** The traditional "swaddling clothes" were strips of cloth intended to keep the limbs straight—a sign of motherly care and affection. In Ezekiel 16:4 Jerusalem is metaphorically described as a infant for whom no one cared: "On the day you were born your cord was not cut, nor were you washed with water to make you clean, nor were you rubbed with salt or wrapped in cloths."[38]

**A manger (2:7).** A manger (*phatnē*) was a feeding trough for animals. The word could also be used of a stall or enclosure where animals would be fed, but the reference to being "placed" there suggests the former.

**Because there was no room for them in the inn (2:7).** Contrary to the traditional Christmas story, the "inn" (*katalyma*) was probably not an ancient hotel with rooms to rent and an innkeeper, but either a guest room in a private residence (see 22:11) or an informal public shelter (a "caravansary") where travelers would gather for the night.[39] In the parable of the Good Samaritan, Luke uses a different term for a public inn (*pandocheion*, 10:34). In any case, crowded conditions force Joseph and Mary from normal lodging to a place reserved for animals. This could have been (1) a lower-level room or stall for animals attached to the living quarters of a private residence, (2) a cave used as a shelter for animals (as some

## Caesar Augustus, the First Roman Emperor

Born Gaius Octavius in 63 B.C. (known to historians as "Octavian"), Caesar Augustus was emperor of the Roman world at the time of Jesus' birth. The grand-nephew of Julius Caesar, Octavian's rise to power began when Caesar was assassinated in 44 B.C. In his will, Caesar had adopted Octavian as his son. Now known as Gaius Julius Caesar Octavianus, Octavian at first shared power with a three man "triumvirate," or board of three, including himself and two of Julius Caesar's aids, Marcus Lepidus and Mark Antony. After Lepidus fell from power in 36 B.C., civil war broke out between Antony and Octavian. Antony allied himself with Cleopatra, queen of Egypt, but their combined forces were defeated by Octavian at Actium in 31 B.C. Octavian conquered Egypt in the following year and Antony and Cleopatra committed suicide. The Roman Senate recognized Octavian as supreme leader of Rome, and in 27 B.C. bestowed on him the title "Augustus" ("exalted" or "venerable" one). Augustus ruled as emperor until his death in A.D. 14, when he was replaced by Tiberius (see Luke 3:1). Demonstrating extraordinary skills as a leader and administrator, he inaugurated the *Pax Romana* ("Roman Peace"), an unprecedented period of peace and stability throughout the Mediterranean region. The freedom and relative safety of travel afforded by this peace would prove a major factor for the rapid expansion of the gospel message.

The main Roman emperors of the New Testament period following Augustus include:

*Tiberius* (A.D. 14–37). The emperor during Jesus' public ministry.

*Caligula* (A.D. 37–41). Provoked a crisis by demanding that his image be set up in the Jerusalem temple, but died before the order was carried out.

*Claudius* (A.D. 41–54). He expelled the Jews from Rome (Acts 18:2), probably because of conflicts with Christians (Seutonius, *Life of Claudius* 25:4).

*Nero* (A.D. 54–68). He persecuted the Christians after blaming them for a fire he was rumored to have set in Rome (Tacitus, *Annals* 15:44). Both Paul and Peter were probably martyred under Nero.

*Vespasian* (A.D. 69–79). He was declared emperor while in Palestine putting down the Jewish revolt. He returned to Rome, leaving his son Titus to complete the destruction of Jerusalem and the temple.

*Domitian* (A.D. 81–96). Initiated severe persecution of the church, the likely background to the book of Revelation.

ancient traditions have claimed),[40] or even (3) a feeding place under the open sky, perhaps in the town square. The present Church of the Nativity was built in the fourth century over a traditional cave site in Bethlehem. Whatever the precise location, the commonality and humility of the scene prepare the reader for the paradoxical story of the Messiah, who attains glory through suffering.

## The Shepherds and the Angels (2:8–20)

The birth of Israel's king calls for recognition and acclaim, which is provided by the story of the shepherds and the angels. The account has two parts: *a heavenly response* in the angelic announcement and praise song (2:8–14), and *an earthly response* in the praise of the shepherds and the wonder of all who hear of these events (2:15–20). The theme is central to the birth narrative and to Luke-Acts as a whole: joy, rejoicing, and praise mark the arrival of God's great day of salvation.

**Shepherds (2:8).** Later rabbinic writings describe shepherds as dishonest and untrustworthy, and some commentators have suggested that here they represent the sinners Jesus came to save.[41] Yet the biblical portrait of shepherds is almost always positive, and nothing in this context suggests otherwise. David was a shepherd; the Lord is our shepherd (Ps. 23:1); Jesus is the good shepherd (see comments on 11:23).[42] What *is* clear is that shepherds were among the lower class in Israel and so represent the poor and humble for whom the message of salvation is indeed good news (Luke 1:52; 4:18).

It has also been suggested that, considering their proximity to Jerusalem, these sheep may have been raised for

*right* ▶
**SHEPHERD**
A shepherd tends his sheep near Bethlehem.

▶
**MODERN BETHLEHEM**
Near the Shepherd's Field Church.

temple sacrifices. Though speculative, if true this could point forward to Jesus' role as the sacrificial lamb of God.

**Living out in the fields nearby, keeping watch over their flocks at night (2:8).** Shepherds normally lived outside during warmer months, perhaps March-November, though there is some rabbinic evidence for year-round grazing. The actual time of Jesus' birth is unknown. The traditional December date for Christmas seems to have arisen in the time of Constantine (306–37) to coincide with the pagan feast of Saturnalia. The NIV's "keeping watch" is literally "keeping watches"; they take turns sleeping and guarding the flock against thieves and animals.

**An angel of the Lord appeared to them (2:9).** See comments on 1:11, 19.

**The glory of the Lord (2:9).** Glory (*doxa*) is used in the LXX to translate the Hebrew *kābôd*, often referring to God's visible presence.[43] In Exodus 24:16, 17 "the glory of the LORD"—the manifestation of his glorious presence—settles on Mount Sinai and remains there.

**I bring you good news ... for all the people (2:10).** The announcement of good news (*euangelizomai*) is a common verb for Luke[44] and has its roots in Isaiah's announcement of end-time salvation (Isa. 52:7; 61:1). There is also an interesting parallel in an inscription found at Priene celebrating the birth of Augustus. The inscription calls him a "savior" and says that "the birth date of our God has signaled the beginning of good news for the world."[45] Both of these backgrounds could have had significance for Luke, who has just referred to Caesar Augustus (2:1) and for whom Isaiah's portrait of salvation plays a leading role (2:32; 3:4–6; 4:18–19). Though Augustus is acclaimed by many as the world's god and savior, Jesus is the true deliverer.

"All the people" does not here refer to all nations (though this would fit well with Luke's overall theme), but rather to all Israel. Luke always uses the singular noun *laos* in this way.

**The town of David (2:11).** See comments on 2:4.

**A Savior . . . he is Christ the Lord (2:11).** In the Old Testament, especially in the Psalms and Isaiah, God is frequently identified as the "Savior" of his people.[46] Jesus is Savior because through him God will redeem his people.[47]

"Christ" (*christos*) is a Greek translation of the Hebrew term *māšiaḥ*, meaning "anointed one" or "messiah." The title has its roots in the identification of Israel's king—especially David—as the Lord's anointed, his chosen vice-regent.[48] From this background the title "Messiah" came to be used in Judaism with reference to the coming king who would bring salvation to God's people. A manuscript fragment from the Dead Sea Scrolls says that the Messiah from David's line will "arise to save Israel"[49] (see further comments on 1:32–33; 9:20; also "Messianic Expectation in Jesus' Day).

**A great company of the heavenly host . . . praising God (2:13).** The "hosts" or "armies" (*stratia*) of heaven reveal God's sovereign power and authority (cf. 2 Kings 6:17). A common Old Testament name of God is "LORD of Hosts" (*yhwh ṣᵉbnam'oftn*; NIV, "the Sovereign LORD"). Such praise by heaven's armies appears

REFLECTIONS

**BORN TO PEASANT PARENTS, LAID** in a feeding trough, visited by lowly shepherds. The commonness of Jesus' birth reminds us how Jesus, though Lord of the universe, stooped down to our humble level to bring us salvation. As John puts it, "The Word became flesh and made his dwelling among us" (John 1:14). Jesus now calls us to represent him—to live out his incarnation—for a lost world.

in Psalm 148:2: "Praise him, all his angels, praise him, all his heavenly hosts."

**Glory to God in the highest (2:14).** "In the highest" (2:14) means "in the heavenly realms," which reflects the present praise of the heavenly hosts. It finds its counterbalance "on earth" in the next line.

**On earth peace to men on whom his favor rests (2:14).** The difference between the NIV and the traditional "on earth peace, good will toward men" (KJV) is a textual one, with the better manuscripts reading *eudokias* ("of good will") rather than *eudokia* ("good will"). The phrase "people of good will" is a Hebrew idiom referring not to the good will of humans, but to *God's* favor bestowed on his people. The phrase "a people of his good pleasure" appears in the Qumran scrolls.[50]

## Jesus Presented in the Temple (2:21–40)

The proclamation of Jesus' messianic identity continues as two prophetic heralds, Simeon and Anna, join the angels in announcing his arrival. The birth narrative theme of the righteous remnant permeates the narrative. Mary and Joseph are exemplary Jews who faithfully fulfill the Old Testament laws related to circumcision, purification, and the dedication of their firstborn to the Lord. Simeon and Anna represent faithful Israel, anxiously longing for the Messiah.

**On the eighth day, when it was time to circumcise him (2:21).** See comments on 1:59.

**He was named Jesus (2:21).** See comments on 1:31.

**Their purification according to the Law of Moses (2:22).** The Old Testament required a forty-day period of purification for the mother after the birth of a son: seven days before the circumcision and thirty-three days after (Lev. 12:1–8). During this time, "she must not touch anything sacred or go to the sanctuary until the days of her purification are over" (12:4). At the end of this time, a sacrifice was made for her purification (see Luke 2:24). The reference to "their" purification is odd, since the Old Testament set out requirements only for the mother. It is possible that Joseph was rendered unclean during the birth process or, more likely, Luke refers to the family's participation in both the purification and dedication ceremonies.

**To present him to the Lord . . . as it is written . . . (2:22–23).** The Old Testament law stipulated that every firstborn male, whether human or animal, was to be dedicated to the Lord. Firstborn animals were to be offered as a sacrifice. For humans the Lord took the Levites as his own tribe instead of the firstborn sons, but a redemption price of five shekels was to be paid.[51] Nehemiah 10:35–36 suggests that this dedication of sons was generally done in the temple. Luke

MODEL OF THE TEMPLE AND ITS COURTS

explains these requirements by alluding to Exodus 13:2, 12 in Luke 2:23: "Every firstborn male is to be consecrated to the Lord." Some scholars have suggested that since no mention is made of Jesus' redemption, he was not redeemed but wholly dedicated to the Lord, after the model of the child Samuel (1 Sam. 1–2). It is perhaps significant that there are echoes in this verse to 1 Samuel 1:24, 28 (cf. Luke 2:34, 40).

**To offer a sacrifice . . . "a pair of doves or two young pigeons" (2:24).** The quotation is from Leviticus 12:8, which concerns the sacrifice of purification for the woman, not the redemption of the firstborn. The woman was to offer a lamb and a pigeon or dove (12:6), or two doves or pigeons if she was poor (12:8). We have incidental evidence here that Joseph and Mary belonged to the lower economic classes.

**Simeon.** A common name among first-century Jews, derived from one of the sons of Jacob (Gen. 29:33; 35:23) and the tribe of Israel that came from him. It is the more Hebraic form of the name Simon. (Simon Peter is called Simeon [*symeōn*] in Acts 15:14 and 2 Peter 1:1.) Some have suggested that Simeon was a priest since he was in the temple, though the text does not say this.

**He was waiting for the consolation of Israel (2:25).** The "consolation of Israel" comes from Isaiah 40, where the prophet announces Israel's "comfort" (= salvation) after her exile.[52] The phrase represents the salvation, peace, and forgiveness Israel will receive in the messianic era. It finds a parallel in the "redemption of Jerusalem" in 2:38.

**That he would not die (2:26).** Literally "to see death," an Old Testament expression (Ps. 89:48). This suggests that Simeon was an old man, though the text does not specifically say so.

**The Lord's Christ (2:26).** This phrase is equivalent to the Old Testament expression "the LORD's Anointed" (see comments on 1:32; 2:11) and carries the sense, "Yahweh's chosen agent of redemption." Luke elsewhere uses similar expressions "Christ of God" (9:20; 23:35) and "his Christ" (Acts 3:18; 4:26).

**He went into the temple courts (2:27).** Luke uses *hieron* to refer to the general temple area (see comments on *naos* at 1:9–10). This encounter probably takes place in the Court of Women, since Mary is present and since Anna shortly appears.

**Sovereign Lord . . . now dismiss your servant (1:29).** The NIV's "Sovereign Lord" is a rare New Testament word, *despotēs* (used ten times). In parallel with *doulos* ("servant" or "slave"), it means "master," pointing to a master/servant relationship. Simeon has accomplished his task as a faithful servant and herald of his Master's salvation.

**Your salvation, which you have prepared in the sight of all people (2:30–31).** The reference to God's salvation being seen by all people captures the thought of Isaiah 52:10: "The LORD will lay bare his holy arm in the sight of all the nations, and all the ends of the earth will see the salvation of our God." The plural noun "people" (*laoi*) here means Jews and Gentiles (contrast the singular *laos* in Luke 2:10). See the following verses for more allusions to Isaiah's portrait of salvation.

HEROD'S TEMPLE FROM INSIDE THE COURT OF WOMEN

**A light for revelation to the Gentiles (2:32).** Not only will the nations see God's salvation, but Simeon now reveals that they will participate in it. He alludes to Isaiah 42:6 and 49:6, where Isaiah prophesies that the Servant-Messiah will bring salvation to the Gentiles as well as the Jews. This is the first indication in Luke's Gospel that Israel's salvation will extend to the Gentiles.

**And for glory to your people Israel (2:32).** The "light" for the Gentiles finds its parallel in "glory" for Israel. In Isaiah 46:13 Israel's glory is associated with her salvation: "I will grant salvation to Zion, my splendor to Israel." Israel's glorious salvation will serve as the attracting light that draws in the Gentiles.

**This child is destined to cause the falling and rising of many in Israel (2:34).** Though not a direct quotation, this phrase reflects a stone metaphor drawn from Isaiah 8:14–15 and 28:16. It refers to two responses to Jesus among those in Israel: To some, the Messiah will be "a stone that causes men to stumble and a rock that makes them fall" (8:14); to others, he becomes "a precious cornerstone for a sure foundation" (28:16; cf. Ps. 118:22), upon which they will rise. This dual stone metaphor was an important one for the early church, used both to explain the rejection of Israel (Rom. 9:32–33) and to express the foundation of the church (Eph. 2:20). Both images appear in 1 Peter 2:6–8, which cites all three Old Testament texts.[53] Luke uses this double stone image again in Luke 20:17–18.

**A sign that will be spoken against (2:34).** If the reference to "falling" in 2:34 is an allusion to Isaiah 8:14–15, the next phrase—that the child will be "a sign that will be spoken against"—may allude to the same context, where Isaiah and his children are said to be for "signs and symbols in Israel" (Isa. 8:18). Just as Isaiah's oracles divided Israel into a faithful remnant and an apostate majority, so the "sign" of Jesus will provoke similar opposition and division (cf. Luke 11:29–30).

**A sword will pierce your own soul (2:35).** This phrase sounds like Psalm 37:15: "But their swords will pierce their own hearts . . ." (cf. Ezek. 14:17), though that passage is in a context of judgment against the wicked. The idiom itself means to experience great pain and probably refers to the pain and sorrow Mary will experience because of Jesus' rejection and death.

**A prophetess, Anna (2:36).** Anna's prophetic office places her in a category with such Old Testament worthies as Miriam (Ex. 15:20), Deborah (Judg. 4:4), and Huldah (2 Kings 22:14). The Talmud identifies seven Old Testament women as prophetesses: Sarah, Miriam, Deborah, Hannah, Abigail, Huldah, and Esther (*b. Meg.* 14a). Prophetesses are mentioned in the New Testament in Acts 2:17–18; 21:9; 1 Corinthians 11:5. "Anna" is the Greek equivalent of the Hebrew "Hannah," Samuel's mother (1 Sam. 1–2). This is significant in light of various allusions to Samuel's dedication in the passage.

**Of the tribe of Asher (2:36).** Asher was one of the ten northern tribes of Israel, named after Jacob's eighth son Asher.[54] The reference to a northern tribe confirms that not all first-century Israelites were, strictly speaking, "Jews" (= from the tribe of Judah), and that members of other tribes had maintained their identity through the Babylonian exile. The designation Jew came to be used synonymously with "Israelite," encompassing those from other tribes as well (Paul was a Benjamite; Phil. 3:5). It is therefore not accurate to speak of the "lost (ten) tribes of Israel."

**She was very old . . . a widow until she was eighty-four (2:36–37).** In the ancient world being old was often associated with wisdom and piety. Similarly, the widow who remained single to be devoted to the Lord was a common image both in Judaism (Judith 8:4–8) and early Christianity.[55] Josephus describes Antonia, the widow of Drusus the great, as a "virtuous and chaste woman. For despite her youth she remained steadfast in her widowhood and refused to marry again. . . . She thus kept her life free from reproach."[56] Judith, the pious widow and heroine of the apocryphal work that bears her name, remained for years a widow after the death of her husband Manasseh. She "fasted all the days of her widowhood. . . . No one spoke ill of her, for she feared God with great devotion" (Judith 8:6–8). The Greek text is unclear as to whether Anna's eighty-four years refer to her present age (so NIV) or to the number of years she had been a widow after her seven-year marriage. If the latter, she would have been about 105 years old (assuming she was married at the age of fourteen: 14 + 7 + 84 = 105), the age attributed to Judith at her death.

**She never left the temple but worshiped night and day, fasting and praying (2:37).**

The statement that Anna never left the temple does not mean that she slept there (women would not normally live on temple grounds), but that she was wholly devoted to worship. This recalls Samuel's devotion to his temple service (1 Sam. 1:28; 2:11). "Night and day" follows the Jewish way of reckoning time from sunset to sunset. Fasting and prayer were common signs of deep piety in Judaism (see Judith 8:6, cited above). In the apocryphal book of 2 Esdras (*4 Ezra*) 9:44, a certain barren woman is said to have prayed for a child "every hour and every day . . . night and day" for thirty years until God answered her prayers.

**Redemption of Jerusalem (2:38).** The phrase "redemption [*lytrōsis*] of Jerusalem" is linked with the "consolation of Israel" in 2:25, both of which refer to the promised messianic salvation (cf. 1:68). The ideas of comfort and redemption appear together in Isaiah 52:9: "Burst into songs of joy together, you ruins of Jerusalem, for the LORD has comforted his people, he has redeemed Jerusalem." During the second Jewish revolt against Rome (A.D. 132–135), when messianic hopes centered on Simon Bar-Kochba, documents were sometimes dated to the years of the "Redemption of Israel."[57]

**THEATER AT SEPPHORIS**

Just a few miles from Nazareth, this city had a theater with a seating capacity of 4,500.

**And the child grew and became strong (2:40).** This verse, like the description of John in 1:80, echoes what is said about Samuel in 1 Samuel 2:21, 26. For a closer parallel, see Luke 2:52.

**He was filled with wisdom (2:40).** In Isaiah 11:2 the Messiah is said to have a special endowment of wisdom from the Spirit (see comments on Luke 2:52).

## The Boy Jesus at the Temple (2:41–52)

The Passover Jerusalem visit of the twelve-year-old Jesus is the only account from Jesus' childhood found in the canonical Gospels. Though other stories appear in the so-called "infancy Gospels," these are late, fanciful, and historically unreliable. Luke includes this story not to fill in details for the curious reader, but to reveal Jesus' real human growth, both spiritual and physical.

**Every year . . . to Jerusalem for the Feast of the Passover (2:41).** See "Passover and the Feast of Unleavened Bread."

**When he was twelve years old (2:42).** According to Jewish tradition, a Jewish boy became responsible to observe the law when he was thirteen years old—though the actual ceremony of *bar-mitzvah*, whereby a Jewish boy becomes a "son of the covenant," is of later origin.[58] Though it is not specifically stated that this is Jesus' first trip, the identification of his age as twelve probably suggests that his parents are taking steps to prepare him for his covenantal responsibility. The wisdom and spiritual awareness he demonstrates are intended to be all the more extraordinary since it takes place prior to his thirteenth year. Josephus similarly identifies

Samuel's age as twelve when he received his call from the Lord and when he began to prophesy.[59] According to 1 Kings 2:12 in the LXX, Solomon's reign began when he was twelve.

**Jesus stayed behind ... but they were unaware of it (2:43).** The journey from Nazareth to Jerusalem is about eighty miles (if they are traveling around, rather than through, Samaria); it would take approximately three days. The family is probably traveling in a caravan of relatives and friends for protection from bandits on the roads. This explains how Jesus' parents could have left without him, assuming he is elsewhere in the caravan.

**After three days (2:46).** The three days probably refers to the total time from their departure after the Feast to the discovery of Jesus (one day out, one day back, a day of searching).

**In the temple courts, sitting among the teachers (2:46).** For the temple courts (*hieros*) see comments on 2:27. Jesus is in the traditional position of a disciple, sitting at the feet of his teachers. This is the only place Luke uses the term "teacher" (*didaskalos*) for the rabbinic experts in the law. Elsewhere they are usually "lawyers" (*nomikos*) or "scribes" (*grammateus*). Luke probably seeks to retain a positive portrait here, since the other terms carry negative connotations in the Gospel.

**Listening to them and asking them questions (2:46).** Rabbis often taught in a question-and-answer format. The teachers are viewed as responding to Jesus' questions in rabbinic style with counter-questions, since it is both Jesus' "insight" (*synesis*) and his "answers" that provoke amazement among all who hear.

**Amazed at his understanding and his answers (2:47).** The motif of a hero who shows unusual intelligence as a child is common in both Greek and Jewish biography. There are similar stories told of Moses, Cyrus the Great, Alexander the Great, and Apollonius.[60] In his autobiography, Josephus describes himself in a similar manner:

*bottom left*

**ISRAEL**

The route from Galilee to Jerusaelm.

*bottom right*

**CROWDED STREET IN OLD JERUSALEM**

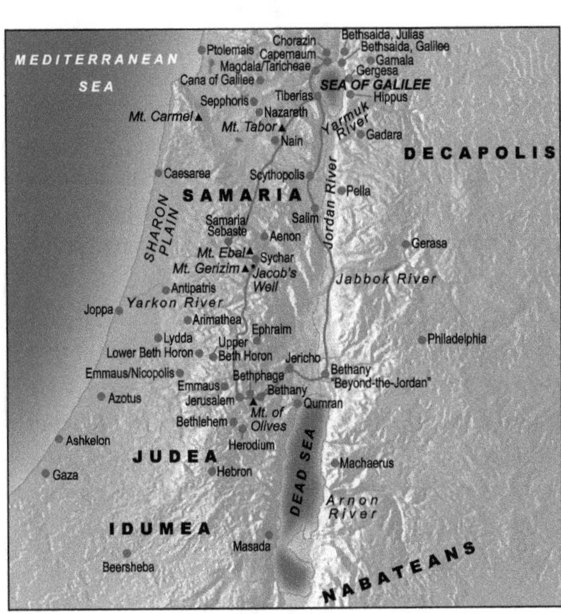

While still a mere boy, about fourteen years old, I won universal applause for my love of letters; insomuch that the chief priests and the leading men of the city used constantly to come to me for precise information on some particular in our ordinances.[61]

The most important background to this text, however, is the description of the coming Messiah in Isaiah 11:2: "The Spirit of the LORD will rest on him—the Spirit of wisdom and of understanding, the Spirit of counsel and of power, the Spirit of knowledge and of the fear of the LORD."

**I had to be in my Father's house (2:49).** Though the Greek phrase used here can be translated "about my Father's business," or even "among my Father's people," the NIV translation "in my Father's house" is probably the correct one. The idiom appears with this sense in both biblical and extrabiblical texts and fits the present context well.[62]

**He . . . was obedient to them (2:51).** Luke wants to avoid any suggestion that Jesus' priority to pursue his Father's purposes resulted in a failure to submit to his earthly parents. This statement of obedience confirms that Jesus was not the rebellious son so often condemned in Scripture.[63] The fifth commandment instructs us to honor our father and mother.[64]

**And Jesus grew in wisdom and stature, and in favor with God and men (2:52).** This verse echoes 1 Samuel 2:26: "And the boy Samuel continued to grow in stature and in favor with the LORD and with men" (cf. also Luke 1:80; 2:40). Isaiah 11:2–4 identifies the coming Messiah as one who will bear extraordinary wisdom.

## John the Baptist Prepares the Way (3:1–20)

Like the other Gospel writers, Luke begins his account of Jesus' ministry with the appearance of John the Baptist. John is the forerunner of the Messiah predicted in Isaiah 40:3–5 and Malachi 3:1; 4:5–6. For Luke he is the last and the greatest of the Old Testament prophets,

### ▸ Passover and the Feast of Unleavened Bread

Passover was the Jewish festival commemorating the deliverance of the Hebrews from slavery in Egypt. The angel of death spared the firstborn sons of the Hebrews, "passing over" those households that sacrificed a lamb and placed its blood on the doorframes (Ex. 12). It was celebrated on the 15th of Nisan (March/April), the first month in the Jewish calendar. Lambs were sacrificed in the temple on the afternoon of Nisan 14 and were roasted and eaten with unleavened bread that evening (Nisan 15 began after sunset). Family or larger units celebrated Passover together. Unleavened bread was then eaten for the next seven days—the Feast of Unleavened Bread.[A-11] The term "Passover" was sometimes used for both festivals. Extensive traditions and liturgy eventually became attached to Passover, though how much of this was practiced in Jesus' day is unknown.

Passover was one of three pilgrim feasts that Jewish males were expected to attend; the other two were Pentecost and the Feast of Tabernacles.[A-12] Because of the rigors of travel, it is a sign of the piety of Joseph's family that in 2:41 they make the journey "every year." This piety is also evident in the fact that Mary and Jesus join Joseph, since only males were required to attend (see comments on 22:1; 22:7).

a transitional figure forming a bridge between the age of promise and the age of fulfillment (Luke 7:24–28; 16:16). In light of impending judgment, John preaches a "baptism of repentance for the forgiveness of sins" (3:3), warning his hearers to produce fruit—a radical kingdom ethic—that is in accordance with their repentance.[65]

**In the fifteenth year . . . the word of God came to John (3:1–2).** The introduction to John's ministry is reminiscent of the call of Old Testament prophets, including the dating of John's career to the year of the king's reign, the establishment of his identity by his ancestry ("son of Zechariah"), and the reception of his prophetic message ("the word of God came to John"). For these elements see the opening verses of Jeremiah, Ezekiel, Hosea, Joel, Jonah, Micah, Zephaniah, Haggai, and Zechariah.

**The reign of Tiberius Caesar (3:1).** Tiberius Caesar became emperor in A.D. 14, at the death of his stepfather Augustus (cf. 2:1), and reigned until A.D. 37. A difficulty arises in establishing a firm date here, however, since Tiberius became coregent with Augustus in A.D. 11/12. Following this earlier date, some claim Jesus' ministry began in A.D. 25/26 or 26/27. Others take the later date and, depending on when the first year is reckoned to begin and end, arrive at A.D. 27/28 or 28/29.[66] A date of around A.D. 28 seems most likely. Either reckoning, A.D. 26 or 28 fits Luke's statement in 3:23 that Jesus is "about thirty" when his ministry begins.

**Pontius Pilate . . . Herod . . . Philip . . . Lysanias (3:1).** After the death of Herod the Great in 4 B.C., his kingdom was divided among his three sons. Archelaus received Judea, Samaria, and Idumea (cf. Matt. 2:21–23), Herod Antipas took over Galilee and Perea, and Philip inherited Iturea and Trachonitis, regions north and west of Galilee.[67] When Archelaus was removed from office in A.D. 6 by Augustus because of misrule (see comments on

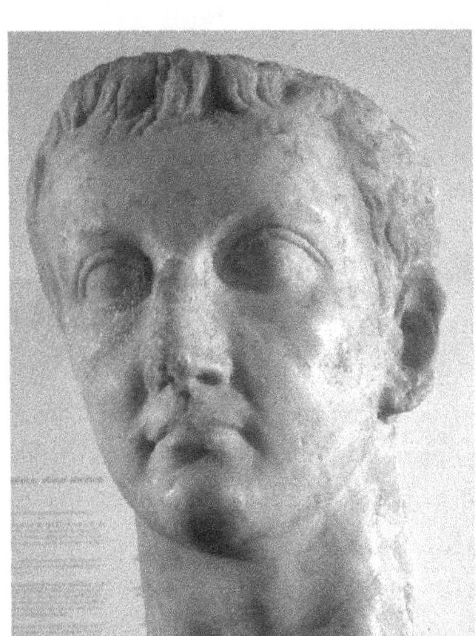

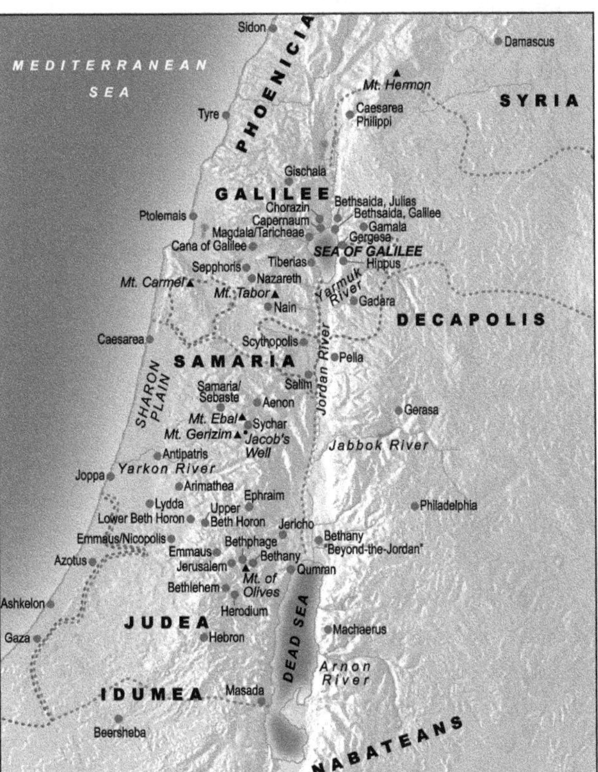


◀

THE KINGDOM OF HEROD

Showing the divisions of the kingdom among Herod's sons.

◀ *left*

MARBLE BUST OF THE EMPEROR TIBERIUS

19:14), Judea and Samaria were transferred to the control of Roman governors, known as prefects and procurators. Pontius Pilate is one such prefect, governing Judea from A.D. 26–36. In presiding over Jesus' trial, Pilate will play a key role in Luke's Gospel.[68] For more on Pilate and his harsh rule, see comments on 13:1 and the sidebar at Mark 15:1.

Herod Antipas ruled over Galilee and Perea from his father's death until he was deposed by the emperor Caligula in A.D. 39. This is the Herod who imprisoned and eventually executed John the Baptist after John spoke out against his marriage to Herodias, his brother's wife.[69] It is also Antipas who wonders about Jesus' identity (9:7–9) and whom Jesus calls "that fox" (13:31–32). Only Luke records that Jesus stood before Herod during his trial (23:7–12; cf. Acts 4:27). The title "tetrarch" originally meant ruler of a fourth part of a region, but it came to be used of any minor ruler.

Philip, the half brother of Herod Antipas, ruled as tetrarch of Iturea and Traconitis from 4 B.C. until his death in A.D. 34. Generally recognized as the best of the Herodian rulers, he died without an heir, and his territory became part of the Roman province of Syria. He is mentioned in the New Testament only here. The Philip identified in Matthew 14:3 and Mark 6:17 as the husband of Herodias and half brother of Antipas is a different son of Herod the Great. He lived in Rome and did not rule after his father's death.

The region of Abilene, over which Lysanias ruled as tetrarch, is located northwest of Galilee in Syria. The identity of Lysanias is something of a problem since Josephus mentions an individual by this name who was executed by Mark Antony in 36 B.C.[70] While some conclude that Luke is in error, Josephus elsewhere refers to another Lysanias of Abila, who ruled at a later time; there is also inscriptional evidence for such an identification.[71]

**During the high priesthood of Annas and Caiaphas (3:2).** Luke's reference to two high priests at first seems odd, since Judaism had only one high priest. Annas, who came to office in A.D. 6, was deposed in A.D. 15 by Valerius Gratus. He was eventually succeeded by his son-in-law Caiaphas, who served from A.D. 18–37.[72] Annas continued to wield enormous influence, however, and was viewed popularly as continuing as high priest.[73] In this sense there were indeed two high priests: one who held the official office and one who wielded power behind the scenes. Luke thus demonstrates an astute historical sense by identifying not only the actual office holder, but also the political intrigues behind the office.

**All the country around the Jordan (3:3).** John's ministry most likely took place in the Judean desert around the Jordan River west and north of the Dead Sea.

**A baptism of repentance for the forgiveness of sins (3:3).** The Greek term *baptizō* means to dip or immerse. In non-Christian literature the term sometimes means to plunge, sink, drench, or overwhelm.[74] Rites of washing and immersion were common in Judaism and other religious traditions. In the Old Testament bathing and sprinkling were used to remove ceremonial uncleanness.[75] The high priest bathed before and after making atonement (Lev. 16:4, 24). At the Qumran community washings were associated with participation in the end-time community of God (see quotations below).[76] Some have identified John's baptism with Jewish proselyte (new convert) baptism. John would then be calling the apostate nation to become real Jews again. While this image fits John's message and milieu, the evidence from the Talmud for such proselyte baptism is late, rendering it questionable whether such a practice goes back to the first century.[77] Since none of these parallels is exact, John's baptism may best be viewed as a unique eschatological (i.e., end times) application, drawing conceptually from the cleansing and initiatory rites of first-century Judaism.

John's baptism is described as one "of repentance for the forgiveness of sins." The Old Testament often speaks of repentance, a turning to God from sin.[78] Spiritual cleansing is frequently associated with God's forgiveness.[79] At Qumran a close connection is drawn between ceremonial washings and turning from sin. 1QS 3:8–9 reads, "By the spirit of uprightness and of humility his sin is atoned. And by the compliance of his soul with all the laws of God his flesh is cleansed by being sprinkled with cleansing waters and being made holy with the waters of repentance." It is not the act of washing, but the repentance itself that results in forgiveness, "for they have not been cleansed unless they turn away from their wickedness."[80] In John's baptism too it is not the act of immersion but the repentant heart that results in forgiveness. Josephus notes that John's baptism itself did not accomplish remission of sins, but was rather "as a consecration of the body implying that the soul was already thoroughly cleansed by right behaviour."[81]

**As is written in . . . Isaiah the prophet (3:4–6).** John's prophetic ministry is confirmed with a quote from Isaiah 40:3–5. Isaiah's prophecy, which originally referred to the return of the Babylonian exiles, had subsequently been

JORDAN RIVER

interpreted eschatologically in Judaism.[82] At Qumran the preparation of a way is identified with the community's withdrawal to their desert community to study the law.[83] Sirach too identifies Isaiah's prophecies with events of the last days: "By his [Isaiah's] dauntless spirit he saw the future, and comforted the mourners in Zion. He revealed what was to occur to the end of time, and the hidden things before they happened."[84] The prophetic announcement of deliverance from exile becomes for Luke a type or model for John's announcement of end-time restoration through the Messiah.

**A voice of one calling in the desert (3:4).** The reference to the desert presents the return from the Exile as a "new exodus," analogous to God's deliverance of his people from Egypt. In the Old Testament and in Judaism, God's final salvation is often presented as a second and greater exodus.[85]

**Prepare the way for the Lord (3:4–5).** The preparation of a way reflects Near Eastern imagery of clearing the path for a royal figure. Only a smooth, straight road is appropriate for a king. The imagery is metaphorical, referring to a people spiritually and morally prepared to welcome their Lord.

**All mankind will see God's salvation (3:6).** While Matthew and Mark cite only Isaiah 40:3, Luke continues the quotation with a confirmation of the universal application of God's message. Among the Old Testament prophets, Isaiah most stressed the universality of the gospel, that Gentiles as well as Jews will one day

## Josephus on John the Baptist

In a short passage, the Jewish historian Josephus refers to John the Baptist. When the troops of Herod Antipas were defeated by Aretas, king of Arabia, rumors spread that God was punishing Herod for his arrest and execution of John. Josephus describes this rumor and then gives a brief description of John:

> For Herod had put him to death, though he was a good man and had exhorted the Jews to lead righteous lives, to practice justice towards their fellows and piety towards God, and so doing to join in baptism. In his view this was a necessary preliminary if baptism was to be acceptable to God. They must not employ it to gain pardon for whatever sins they committed, but as a consecration of the body implying that the soul was already thoroughly cleansed by right behavior.

While the Gospel writers attribute John's arrest to his criticism of Herod's divorce and remarriage, Josephus refers more generally to the Baptist's growing influence among the people. Josephus describes the place of John's imprisonment as the castle Machaerus, which was east of the Dead Sea.

> When others too joined the crowds about him, because they were aroused to the highest degree by his sermons, Herod became alarmed. Eloquence that had so great an effect on mankind might lead to some form of sedition, for it looked as if they would be guided by John in everything that they did. Herod decided therefore that it would be much better to strike first and be rid of him before his work led to an uprising, than to wait for an upheaval, get involved in a difficult situation and see his mistake. . . . John, because of Herod's suspicions, was brought in chains to Machaerus, the stronghold that we have previously mentioned, and there put to death.[A-13]

be welcomed into God's kingdom (see Isa. 42:6; 49:6).

**You brood of vipers! (3:7).** Whereas Israelites viewed themselves as the children of Abraham (see next verse), John identifies the apostate nation as the offspring of "vipers." The image points to the destructive power of poisonous snakes, a common metaphor for evil. Israel's apostasy is similarly described in Isaiah 59:4–5: "they conceive trouble and give birth to evil. They hatch the eggs of vipers and spin a spider's web" (cf. Isa. 14:29).[86] Although "vipers" in Luke 3:7 is plural, there may be an indirect allusion to Satan as the serpent of the Garden of Eden. Similar imagery appears in the Dead Sea Scrolls and in John's Gospel, where Jesus accuses his opponents of being children of Satan (John 8:44).[87]

**We have Abraham as our father (3:8).** Descent from Abraham was a source of great pride in Judaism.[88] In the *Psalms of Solomon* it is said that while God's compassionate judgments encompass the whole world, his "love is for the descendants of Abraham."[89] According to the intertestamental *Testament of the Twelve Patriarchs*, it is this alone that had protected Israel from more severe judgment for her sins: "Unless you had received mercy through Abraham, Isaac, and Jacob, our fathers, not a single one of your descendants would be left on the earth."[90]

**Out of these stones God can raise up children for Abraham (3:8).** There may have been a pun in John's original words, since the Aramaic words for "sons" (*bebnayyam*) and "stones" (*abnayyam*) are similar.

**The ax is already at the root of the trees (3:9).** Jeremiah 46:22–23, part of an oracle of judgment against Egypt, provides an interesting parallel to Luke 3:7–9 since it contains both images of fleeing serpents and an ax cutting down trees (cf. Isa. 10:33–34).

**Every tree that does not produce good fruit (3:9).** The image of Israel as a rebellious vine that God will judge appears in the Old Testament (Jer. 2:21–22; Hos. 10:1–2) and will be taken up by Jesus later in Luke 13:7–9. There are also clear conceptual parallels to Isaiah's Song of the Vineyard, where Israel's unfruitfulness results in her judgment (Isa. 5:1–7). This song will be adapted by Jesus and applied to his ministry in the parable of the tenant farmers (Luke 20:9–19).

**Two tunics (3:11).** The tunic (*chitōn*) was a garment worn against the skin, normally under a cloak (*himation*, cf. 6:29). One might wear two tunics for warmth or could simply own a spare. In either case the exhortation is to share even the smallest surplus with those in need.

**Tax collectors (3:12).** The Roman government together with local authorities imposed a range of taxes on its citizens, from direct poll and land taxes to indirect tolls or customs on goods in transit (cf. 5:27).[91] The Romans leased out the right to collect taxes to individuals, who then took a surcharge for their own expenses. Since this charge was seldom controlled, the system was open to great abuse and corruption.[92]

Tax collectors were despised in Israel, not only because of their reputation for extortion, but also for their complicity with the hated Romans. Jesus' association with them is an important part of his identification with the poor, the lowly, and the outcasts of Israel (for more on tax collectors see comments on 18:10; 19:2).

**Soldiers (3:14).** These are probably not Roman soldiers, but Jewish troops employed by Herod Antipas (cf. 23:11). Josephus refers to such troops.[93] Their mention beside the tax collectors may indicate they were assigned to assist and protect them in their duties. John tells them not to use violent intimidation or to falsely accuse others for monetary gain, but to be content with their wages (*opsōnion*, a military term for rations or provisions). Just as tax collectors were tempted to grow rich through excessive charges, soldiers were tempted to use their position of power to intimidate and control others for financial advantage.

**If John might possibly be the Christ (3:15).** For Jewish expectation for the "Christ" see comments on 1:33–34; 2:11.

**One more powerful than I (3:16).** See 11:21–22.

**The thongs of whose sandals I am not worthy to untie (3:16).** The untying of a sandal was the duty of a slave for his master. Although Jewish disciples were expected to perform a range of menial tasks for their masters—anything a slave would do—the rabbis specifically exempted them from this as too degrading. Even Hebrew slaves were exempted from this task.[94] Yet John says he is unworthy even to carry out this lowly duty.

**Baptize you with the Holy Spirit and with fire (3:16).** The Old Testament predicted that in the end times God would pour out his Spirit on his people.[95] This prophecy was at least partially fulfilled on the Day of Pentecost (Acts 2:1–4), when a rushing wind and "tongues of fire" accompanied the coming of the Spirit. In the Old Testament and intertestamental Judaism fire is a common symbol for God's judgment,[96] and this idea is present in the context.[97] While some view these Spirit and fire baptisms as distinct, the former for the righteous and the latter for the wicked, it seems more likely that we have here one Spirit-and-fire baptism, which purifies the righteous and judges the wicked (cf. 1 Cor. 3:10–15). Isaiah 4:4 speaks in an eschatological context of a "spirit of judgment and a spirit of fire" that will "cleanse the bloodstains from Jerusalem" (cf. Mal 3:2). Such imagery was common in apocalyptic Judaism of the first century.[98]

**Winnowing fork (3:17).** After being harvested, wheat was tossed into the air with a fork-like shovel or winnowing fork. The heavier grain fell back to the ground while the lighter chaff blew away. For the

right ▶

WINNOWING FORK

A wooden pitchfork and a grain sifting net.

idea of winnowing out the wicked see Proverbs 20:26; Jeremiah 15:7.

**Unquenchable fire (3:17).** Judgment as unquenchable fire appears in Isaiah 34:10; 66:24 (cf. Mark 9:43–44, 48, where Isa. 66:24 is quoted).

**Herod the tetrarch ... Herodias (3:19).** This is Herod Antipas, the son of Herod the Great (see comments on 3:1). Antipas had divorced his first wife, the daughter of the Arabian king Aretas, and had married Herodias, his niece and the former wife of his brother Phillip (see Mark 6:17). John, in typical prophetic fashion, rebukes Herod for taking his brother's wife (see Lev. 18:16) and for other "evil things." Herod responds by imprisoning and eventually executing John (Luke 9:9). For a fuller account of these events see Mark 6:14–29 and "Josephus on John the Baptist."

John here fulfills a common role of the prophets in the Old Testament, who suffered for boldly calling Israel's king to account for breaking God's law.[99] Jeremiah was similarly treated.[100] The rejection and persecution of the prophets is a common theme in Luke.[101]

## The Baptism of Jesus (3:21–22)

Jesus' baptism marks the beginning of his public ministry. For Luke the descent of the Spirit on Jesus signifies his "anointing" as Messiah and his empowerment to accomplish the task God has set out for him (see 4:1, 14, 18). The voice from heaven provides divine confirmation that Jesus is the Messiah and Son of God (cf. Matt. 3:13–17; Mark 1:9–11).

**As he was praying (3:21).** Jesus' prayer life is an important theme in Luke's Gospel. Luke portrays Jesus praying at key points in his ministry: at his baptism (3:21), after cleansing a leper (5:16), before calling the Twelve (6:12), before Peter's confession (9:18), at the Transfiguration (9:28), before teaching the disciples to pray (11:1), for Peter that he would be restored (22:32), in the Garden of Gethsemane (22:41, 44), for his murderers from the cross (23:34), and with his last breath (23:46).

**Heaven was opened (3:21).** The opening of heaven is a common image in apocalyptic literature, often associated with the giving of revelation.[102]

**The Holy Spirit descended ... like a dove (3:22).** The symbolism associated with the dove has been much debated. Some see an allusion to Genesis 1:2, where the Spirit "hovers" over the waters at creation. Later rabbinic works interpret this "hovering" as that of a bird, and even specifically as a dove.[103] In this case Jesus can here be identified with the new creation. Others suggest an allusion to Genesis 8:8–12, where Noah's dove represents God's gracious deliverance after judgment. Neither of these have strong verbal or conceptual parallels, however, and the image may be merely a visual description of the Spirit's descent.

**You are my Son, whom I love; with you I am well pleased (3:22).** The voice from heaven alludes to at least two, and perhaps three, Old Testament passages: Psalm 2:7; Isaiah 42:1; and perhaps Genesis 22:2, 12, 16. (1) In Psalm 2:7 the messianic king's divine sonship and legitimate rule from Mount Zion are announced by God: "You are my Son; today I have become your Father." (2) "With you I am well pleased" alludes to Isaiah 42:1, where the faithful Servant of the Lord is identified as God's chosen one, "in whom I delight." (3) The clause "whom I love," may also allude to Genesis 22:2, where Isaac is described as Abraham's only son, "whom you love." This suggests an Isaac-Jesus typology, with Abraham's willingness to offer his beloved son as analogous to God's offering of his Son. If all three allusions are present, this single announcement makes an extraordinary statement about Jesus' identity: He is the promised Messiah, who will fulfill the role of the Lord's suffering Servant through his sacrificial death.

## The Genealogy of Jesus (3:23–38)

The genealogy that follows the baptism provides further confirmation that Jesus is the Christ. As in Matthew's genealogy, Jesus' ancestry is traced back through David and Abraham, confirming that he is the fulfillment of the Abrahamic and Davidic covenants. Jesus is the "seed" (NIV: "offspring") of Abraham, through whom "all nations on earth will be blessed," and the seed of David, who will reign forever on Israel's throne.[104] Yet while Matthew's genealogy begins with Abraham (in line with his Jewish emphasis), Luke's goes all the way back to Adam. This fits well his emphasis on the universal application of the gospel. Jesus is not just Israel's Messiah, he is the Savior of all humanity. For the importance of genealogies in Judaism, see comments on Matthew 1:2–16.

**Jesus himself was about thirty years old (3:23).** Thirty was viewed in both Jewish and Greco-Roman society as an appropriate age to enter public service. At thirty priests began their duties (Num. 4:3), Joseph entered Pharaoh's service (Gen. 41:46), and Ezekiel was called to his prophetic ministry (Ezek. 1:1). Most significantly, David's reign as king began at the age of thirty (2 Sam. 5:4). Jesus, the Davidic Messiah, follows in the steps of his father David. Since Luke does not give us an exact age, this reference cannot be used precisely to identify the year of Jesus' birth.

**Zerubbabel (3:27).** Zerubbabel was appointed governor of Judea by the Persian authorities when the Jews returned from Babylonian exile. He supervised the rebuilding of the temple (Ezra 3:2, 8) and was exhorted by the prophets Haggai and Zechariah to finish the task (Hag. 1:1–15; Zech. 4:6–10).

**Nathan, the son of David (3:31).** This was the third son of David, born to him in Jerusalem (2 Sam. 5:14). He should not be confused with Nathan the prophet.

**The son of Adam, the son of God (3:38).** That Adam is "the son of God" means that he came through direct creation of God rather than through human procreation. The designation "son of God" also provides an implicit comparison between Adam and Jesus. Whereas Adam, the first son of God, failed in his obedience to God, Jesus, the true Son of God, succeeds when tested (see Luke's temptation account in 4:1–13).

Philo, the first-century Jewish philosopher from Alexandria, writes similarly of Adam that his father "was no mortal, but the eternal God."[105] For Philo, however, this carried a sense of semidivinity not found in Luke. For Philo Adam lost this status at the Fall when he chose evil over good and was "condemned to change an immortal for a mortal existence . . . so as to descend into a laborious and miserable life."[106] For Luke, by contrast, all human beings, though fallen, remain God's offspring because he created them (Acts 17:28–29). Jesus shares in this sonship by virtue of his true humanity, but is also the unique Son of God by virtue of his unique relationship with the Father, his divine origin (Luke 1:35), and his unprecedented obedience to his Father (4:1–13).

## The Temptation of Jesus (4:1–13)

The temptation narrative provides the last stage in Jesus' preparation for ministry. The theme of the temptation is the steadfast obedience of the Son to the will of the Father. Two typologies appear to be present, comparing and contrasting Jesus with Adam on the one hand and with the nation Israel on the other. (1) While Adam, the first son of God, failed in his test of obedience, Jesus, the true Son of God, resists temptation and so succeeds (see comments on 3:38). (2) Even more prominent, while God's son Israel (Ex. 4:22–23) failed when tested in the desert, Jesus, the true Son of God, succeeds. Jesus' forty days in the desert are analogous to Israel's forty years, and the three Old Testament passages Jesus cites all relate to Israel's failure.[107]

Israel was tested with hunger so that she would learn dependence on God, but failed to do so. Jesus depends wholly on God for his sustenance, quoting Deuteronomy 8:3: "Man does not live on bread alone" (Luke 4:4). Israel was commanded to worship God alone (Deut. 6:13–15), but turned to idolatry (Deut. 9:12; Judg. 3:5–7). Jesus rejects the devil's offer of the kingdoms of the world in exchange for his worship, quoting Deuteronomy 6:13: "Fear the LORD your God and serve him only" (Luke 4:8). Israel doubted God's power and put him to the test at Massah/Meribah (Ex. 17:1–7; Deut. 6:16). Jesus refuses to throw himself from the temple and so test the Lord God, citing Deuteronomy 6:16: "Do not put the Lord your God to the test" (Luke 4:12). As the messianic King and Son of God, Jesus represents the nation and fulfills the task of eschatological Israel in the desert (cf. Matt. 4:1–11).

**By the devil (4:2).** In the New Testament the tempter is sometimes called the "devil" and sometimes "Satan."[108] Satan, whose name in Hebrew means "adversary" or "accuser," appears in the Old Testament as the tester or accuser of God's people.[109] The LXX translates these passages with the Greek word *diabolos*, which means "accuser" or "slanderer." In the New Testament Satan appears as a

**THE JUDEAN WILDERNESS**

Between Jericho and Jebel Quruntul (the traditional "Mount of Temptation"). ▼

ROUND LOAVES

Woman making bread in the Middle East.

personal adversary, opposing God's purpose and his people.[110]

**He ate nothing during those days (4:2).** Moses spent forty days and nights without bread or water on Mount Sinai when writing the Ten Commandments (Ex. 34:28), and Elijah was sustained for a similar period during his journey to Mount Horeb (= Sinai; 1 Kings 19:8). In light of the Israel/Jesus typology developed in this passage, the most important allusion is Israel's forty-year sojourn in the desert.

**Kingdoms of the world (4:5).** While Matthew uses the more general word *kosmos* ("world"), Luke uses *oikoumenē* ("inhabited world"; cf. 2:1). This word, often used of the Roman empire, gives this temptation a stronger political flavor and so stresses Satan's offer of messianic rule over the nations (cf. Ps. 2:8).

**For it has been given to me (4:6).** The devil's power and authority in the world is a common theme in the New Testament. In the Johannine writings he is identified as the "prince of this world" (John 12:31; 14:30; 16:11), and the whole world is under his control (1 John 5:19). Paul calls him the "god of this age" (2 Cor. 4:4) and the "ruler of the kingdom of the air" (Eph. 2:2). Yet Satan's authority is mediated by God, who is sovereign over all things (Dan. 4:32). "It has been given" is a divine passive. As in the case of Job (Job 1:12), God allows Satan a measure of freedom to test believers in the present age.

**I can give it to anyone I want (4:6).** In light of the previous note, this must be seen as a half-truth, or perhaps Satan's own self-deception. Similar arrogant boasts were made by the Caesars. The emperor Nero once said, "I have the power to take away kingdoms and to bestow them."[111]

**Highest point of the temple (4:9).** The location of this "pinnacle" (lit., "winglet") is uncertain, but has been traditionally identified with the Royal Portico on the southeast corner of the temple, overlooking the Kidron Valley. Josephus speaks of the dizzying height of this location.[112] A later rabbinic tradition (which may or may not go back to the first century) says that "when the King, the Messiah, reveals himself, he will come and stand on the roof of the Temple."[113]

right

HIGHEST POINT

The modern east wall of the old city of Jerusalem looking up at the southeast pinnacle.

**He will command his angels (4:10).** The devil responds to Jesus' Scripture quotations by quoting one himself (Ps. 91:11–12). The psalm promises divine protection for those who are faithful to God. Jesus refuses to misuse this passage by putting God to the test.

## Jesus Rejected at Nazareth (4:14–30)

The great Galilean ministry, often identified as the "period of popularity," is covered in 4:14–9:50. Throughout this period Jesus proclaims the message of the kingdom of God, calls disciples, and performs miracles demonstrating his kingdom authority. The Galilean ministry will climax in 9:20, where Peter as representative of the disciples confesses that Jesus is the Christ. From Peter's confession onward Jesus begins to clarify the nature of his messiahship by teaching his disciples that he must go to Jerusalem to suffer and die.

Jesus' public ministry begins for Luke with the sermon in Nazareth, the town where Jesus grew up (2:4, 39, 51; 4:16). Jesus enters the Nazareth synagogue and announces through a reading of Isaiah 61:1–2 that he is God's messianic herald of salvation. At first the townspeople welcome this "hometown boy made good" for his eloquent speech and his message of hope. They turn against him, however, when he points out that in the past God has sometimes chosen to favor Gentiles over his people Israel. Enraged at such heresy, the townspeople drive Jesus out of town and attempt to throw him off a cliff. Jesus walks through the crowd and escapes.

It seems likely that Luke has taken this episode from a later point in Mark's Gospel (Mark 6:1–6) and placed it first in order to introduce key themes in Jesus' ministry. Rejection by Jesus' own people in Nazareth foreshadows his coming rejection by his own nation, Israel. Jesus' announcement that "no prophet is accepted in his hometown" (Luke 4:24) becomes in turn a prediction of his own suffering fate. God's favor to Gentiles in the past—the widow of Zarephath and Naaman the Syrian—foreshadows the mission to the Gentiles in Acts.

Luke's description here and in Acts 13:14–48 represent the oldest written accounts of Jewish synagogue services. Agreements with later rabbinic sources suggest a relatively fixed order of service. This would include the recitation of the *Shema* (Deut. 6:4–9), various prayers (especially the *Shemoneh Esreh*, "Eighteen Benedictions," also known as the *Tephillah*, "the Prayer"), readings from the Law and (generally) the Prophets, an oral targum (an Aramaic paraphrase for those who could not understand Hebrew), a homily or sermon on the text or texts for the day, and a closing benediction. Psalms may also have been sung (cf. Mark 14:26). Any qualified male might be invited to read the Scripture and give instruction. Tasks were assigned and the service overseen by the synagogue ruler (*archisynagōgos*, Luke 8:49; 13:14; Acts 13:15; 18:8, 17), who would be assisted by an attendant (*hypēretēs;* see 4:20).[114]

**Jesus returned to Galilee (4:14).** Jesus' final preparation for his ministry—his baptism and temptation—took place in the Judean desert near the Jordan River (see 3:3). Jesus now returns north to his home region of Galilee to begin his preaching and healing ministry.

**He taught in their synagogues (4:15).** Visiting rabbis were normally invited to teach (cf. Acts 13:15). Jesus was earning a reputation as a respected rabbi and teacher.

**Nazareth (4:16).** See comments on 1:26 and "Inscription Bearing the Name of 'Nazareth.'"

**The scroll of the prophet Isaiah was handed to him (4:17).** Did Jesus choose this text from Isaiah or was it assigned to him? Later Judaism had a fixed three-year reading schedule from the Law, but it is uncertain whether this was established by this time and whether it would have included the Prophets. In any case, divine providence is clearly at work in the chosen text.

**"The Spirit of the Lord is on me" (4:18).** Jesus reads from Isaiah 61:1–2 with a line inserted from 58:6. The prophet Isaiah here uses language reminiscent of Israel's Year of Jubilee (see comments on Luke 4:19) to announce deliverance and release to those in Babylonian exile. Jesus takes this same announcement of release and applies it to his ministry of deliverance from sin and Satan. Jesus does not cite the last part of Isaiah 61:2, "the day of vengeance of our God," in order to highlight the positive message of salvation. Judgment will be announced only when Israel rejects her Messiah (see Luke 13:34–35).

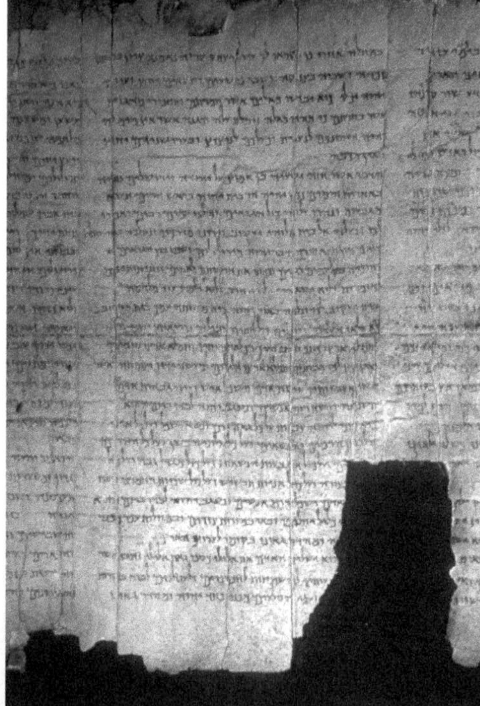

**ISAIAH SCROLL**

A portion of the famous Isaiah Scroll, the longest and oldest (c. 100 B.C.) of the "Dead Sea Scrolls" found at Qumran.

**"Anointed . . . to preach good news" (4:18).** Jesus is the Spirit-anointed prophet and Messiah, "proclaiming good news" (*euangelizomai*) to the poor (4:18). These images bring together Isaiah's related portraits of the messianic King (Isa. 11:1–2), the Servant of the Lord (42:1), and the prophetic herald of salvation (61:1–2). For the Old Testament background to *euangelizomai* see comments on Luke 2:10.

**"The year of the Lord's favor" (4:19).** Isaiah's language echoes the description of the Year of Jubilee in Leviticus 25, where every fiftieth year (after seven Sabbath years) property in Israel was to be returned to its original inheritors, debts were to be canceled, and slaves set free. In the Dead Sea Scrolls (DSS) and in later rabbinic literature, Isaiah 61 with its Jubilee imagery was interpreted with reference to God's end-time salvation. The DSS document 11QMelchizedek interprets Isaiah 61 with reference to Melchizedek, who appears as a heavenly redeemer.[115]

**Gave it back to the attendant (4:20).** The "attendant" here (Greek: *hypēretēs*) is probably equivalent to the Hebrew *ḥazzan*, an assistant to the synagogue ruler who took care of the scrolls and synagogue furnishings.

**Sat down (4:20).** While standing to read signified respect for the sacred Scripture, sitting was the traditional (though not the only) posture for teaching (see Matt. 5:1–2; 26:55; Luke 5:3). Standing is found in Acts 13:16.

**This proverb . . . "Physician, heal yourself!" (4:23).** This proverb was a common one, appearing in both Jewish and Greek writers.[116] Here it may mean, "Prove your worth as a physician." Or, the emphasis may be on "yourself," with the idea, "Heal your own people rather than outsiders from Capernaum." Both ideas may be present.

**I tell you the truth (4:24).** The Greek *amēn*, "in truth" or "truly," is from a Hebrew word traditionally used at the end of a saying to confirm its validity (much as we use "Amen"; see Deut. 27:15; Ps. 41:13; etc.). Jesus uses it in a unique sense at the *beginning* of his sayings (both singularly and doubly) to demonstrate the authority with which he spoke (lit., "Truly, truly, I say to you . . ."). Sometimes Luke leaves the term in this Hebrew form; sometimes he uses the Greek equivalent *alēthōs*.

**No prophet is accepted in his hometown (4:24).** "Acceptable" (*dektos*) is the same Greek word translated "favor" in 4:19 (the Jubilee "year of the Lord's favor"). Ironically, God's people refuse to show favor to the messenger announcing God's favor to them. For the theme of prophetic suffering see comments on 3:19–20. The following illustrations of Elijah and Elisha, two of Israel's greatest prophets, reinforce Jesus' prophetic identity.

**In Elijah's time . . . the sky was shut . . . a widow in Zarephath (4:25–26).** See 1 Kings 17–18. Elijah was God's prophet sent to announce to King Ahab judgment against Israel because of the people's unfaithfulness and worship of Baal. After hiding from Ahab and his wicked Queen Jezebel at the brook at Kerith Ravine,

MODERN NAZARETH

God sent him to a widow in Zarephath on the Phoenician coast north of Israel, between Tyre and Sidon. God's blessings came to the widow (a Gentile) in the form of the miraculous supply of flour and oil and subsequently in the raising of her son from the dead.

**In the time of Elisha . . . Naaman the Syrian (4:27).** See 2 Kings 5. Naaman was a commander in the Syrian army who came to Elisha to be cured of his leprosy. Elisha ordered Naaman to wash himself seven times in the Jordan River. Naaman reluctantly agreed and was healed. The key to both illustrations is that God has at times shown favor to Gentiles even over his people Israel. Such a statement is too much for the people of Nazareth, and they attempt to murder Jesus.

**The brow of the hill on which the town was built (4:29).** Though there is no obvious cliff just outside the city, Nazareth is in a hilly area and various plausible locations have been identified.

**In order to throw him down the cliff (4:29).** The crowd appears to be following the normal procedure for stoning, which was to cast the victim off an elevated spot so that large rocks could be thrown down on him.[117]

REFLECTIONS

IN HIS INAUGURAL SERMON IN Nazareth, Jesus announces that the message of salvation is "good news" to the outcasts of society: the poor, the oppressed, and those on the margins. If we are going to reflect the heart of Jesus to a lost world, we must demonstrate this same love for those most marginalized in our society. *To whom would God have you reach out today?*

## Jesus Drives Out an Evil Spirit (4:31–37)

In the Nazareth sermon Luke presented Jesus' announcement of the nature of his ministry: good news to the poor and release to prisoners. Now he provides examples of this ministry (4:31–44) as Jesus casts out demons and heals the sick, demonstrating his authority over satanic forces and physical infirmity. The primary focus remains on Jesus' teaching and preaching of the good news of the kingdom of God (4:31–32, 43–44). The miracles are meant to confirm the message that in Jesus the power of God's kingdom is breaking into human history (cf. Mark 1:21–28).

**He went down to Capernaum (4:31).** Capernaum was a fishing village of some prominence on the northwestern shore of the Sea of Galilee. The name means "village of Nahum," though the identity of this Nahum is not known (most scholars identify Capernaum with a site known as Tell Hum). Jesus moves from Nazareth and establishes his base of operations here during his Galilean ministry (see Mark 2:1). The statement "he went down" reflects the geography of the city, since the Sea of Galilee lies almost seven hundred feet below sea level.

**They were amazed at his teaching, because his message had authority (4:32).** Mark adds "not as the teachers of the law" (Mark 1:22). The Jewish teachers of Jesus' day taught with constant appeal to rabbis and traditions of the past. Jesus teaches with a sense of origi-

**CAPERNAUM**

Remains at Capernaum with the Sea of Galilee in the foreground.

nality and personal authority that astonishes the people. For Luke this authority comes especially from the Spirit endowment that Jesus received at his baptism (Luke 3:22; 4:1, 14, 18).

**In the synagogue (4:33).** An impressive synagogue has been excavated in Capernaum (see photo). It dates from the second century and probably lies on top of the one in which Jesus taught.

**A man possessed by a demon, an evil spirit (4:33).** Literally, "having a spirit of an unclean demon." This is probably a genitive of apposition, meaning "a spirit, that is, an unclean demon." The word *daimonion* ("demon") was used in the Hellenistic world of various spirit beings, good or evil, so Luke clarifies for his readers that these are wicked forces standing in opposition to God. He refers to them elsewhere as "unclean spirits," "spirits," and "demons," and identifies them as Satan's allies in 11:17–18. For more on demonic possession and exorcism, see comments on 8:26–39.

**Ha! . . . Have you come to destroy us? (4:34).** The demon speaks in the plural ("us"), representing the demonic hordes who are aware of Jesus' coming and quake in fear at his authority to destroy them. The word "Ha!" (Gk. *ea*) may

**AERIAL VIEW OF THE SYNAGOGUE RUINS AT CAPERNAUM**

either be an interjection of surprise and displeasure (found in Classical Greek), or may be the imperative form of the verb *eaō*, meaning "let us alone!"[118]

**I know who you are (4:34).** Knowledge of the name of a spirit being was thought to be a way of gaining power over it. This may have been the demon's futile attempt to gain power over Jesus. In the pseudepigraphic Jewish-Christian work *Testament of Solomon*, Solomon uses a magic seal ring given to him by the archangel Michael to learn the names of various demons, and then to coerce their help in building the temple.[119]

**The Holy One of God! (4:34).** "Holy One of God" is not a traditional title for the Messiah. Its sense, however, is clear: Jesus is the Righteous and Holy One set apart to accomplish God's purpose and plan. While the demon is "unclean," Jesus is "holy." In the Old Testament, nothing unclean could come in contact with God's holy presence, so conflict is inevitable. The demon shudders at the awareness that his destruction is imminent.

**"Be quiet!" Jesus said sternly (4:35).** The word "rebuked" (NIV, "said sternly"; *epitimaō*) was used in Judaism as a technical term for a command that brought evil powers into submission.[120] Jesus' ability to silence demons (cf. 4:41) demonstrates his absolute authority over them.

**All the people were amazed (4:36).** Exorcists in the ancient world often used elaborate rituals or incantations to control demons.[121] Jesus' ability to cast out demons by merely commanding them brings amazement from the people. The demon's immediate response without injuring the man further demonstrates Jesus' extraordinary authority.

## Jesus Heals Many (4:38–44)

The casting out of the demon in the synagogue is followed by further examples of Jesus' healing and exorcising ministry. Jesus heals Peter's mother-in-law and then ministers to the people in general, healing the sick and casting out demons. Once again demons recognize Jesus as the mighty Messiah and Son of God and cry out in fear. Jesus silences them with a word, demonstrating his supreme authority over them.

**The home of Simon (4:38).** Simon Peter evidently owned a home in Capernaum. John identifies Bethsaida as the town of Andrew and Peter (John 1:44), but this probably means their birthplace or the town where they grew up. Peter's present home and fishing business are in Capernaum.

**Simon's mother-in-law (4:38).** Simon's marriage is also attested by Paul in 1 Corinthians 9:5.

**A high fever (4:38).** Ancient medical writers distinguished between a "small" (*mikros*) and a "great" (*megalos*) fever. Luke clarifies that Peter's mother-in-law has the latter, thus emphasizing Jesus' healing power. Though such a clarification cannot *prove* that a physician wrote this Gospel (other educated writers might make such a distinction),[122] it provides one more piece of evidence for Luke's authorship of this Gospel.

**Rebuked the fever (4:39).** Just as Jesus "rebuked" the demon (see 4:35; cf. also 4:41), so now he "rebukes" (*epitimaō*) the fever. This does not mean that the fever is a demonic presence. Though illness was often associated with spiritual oppression in the ancient world and is sometimes so linked in Luke's Gospel (8:29; 9:39; 11:14; 13:11), elsewhere in Luke Jesus' healings are distinguished from his exorcisms (see 4:40–41; 7:21; 13:32). Jesus' "rebuke" is meant rather to demonstrate his authoritative power over all illness. Disease, like demonic oppression, is part of the evil fallen world that Jesus came to save.

**She began to wait on them (4:39).** Hospitality had great significance in this culture and the senior woman of the house would have been most responsible for it. That Peter's mother-in-law can fulfill this role demonstrates that she has been immediately and completely cured—again confirming Jesus' authority.

**When the sun was setting (4:40).** This marks the end of the Sabbath, when people could carry their sick without violating the Sabbath commandment.

**Demons came out of many people, shouting, "You are the Son of God!" (4:41).** "Son of God" is used coreferentially with the "Holy One of God" (4:34) as a title for the Messiah. This is clear from Luke's clarification that "they knew he was the Christ." For the Messiah as God's Son see 2 Samuel 7:14; Psalm 2:7; 89:26; 4QFlor (4Q174). Luke links the titles "Christ" and "Son of God" elsewhere.[123]

**But he rebuked them (4:41).** See comments on 4:35.

**The good news of the kingdom of God (4:43).** This is Luke's first explicit reference to the kingdom of God (but see 1:33). In Jewish thought God's kingdom could refer both to his sovereign reign over the whole universe and to the consummation of that reign through the establishment of a righteous kingdom on earth. To state that "God's kingdom" is near (cf. 10:9, 11) to most first-century Jews meant that God is about to intervene in human affairs to deliver the righteous, judge the wicked, and bring in an era of peace, justice, and righteousness. In some apocalyptic writings, God establishes his kingdom through a messianic agent. In others, the emphasis is on deliverance by God himself. The length of the kingdom is also debated: In some Jewish writings the kingdom is said to last for eternity[124]; in others it is an interim age or "messianic kingdom" prior to the eternal state. The rabbis speculated on the length of this interim kingdom, identifying it sometimes as four hundred years, and other times as a thousand years.[125] For more on the messianic reign see 17:20.

## The Calling of the First Disciples (5:1–11)

The Galilean ministry is marked not only by Jesus' teaching and healing ministry, but also by his calling and training of disciples. After using Simon's boat as a teaching platform to keep back the overwhelming crowds, Jesus asks the fishermen to put out into deeper water and drop their nets. Simon, discouraged from a long night of unsuccessful fishing, only reluctantly agrees. His obedience pays off, however, when the net emerges overflowing with fish. Astonished, Simon recognizes God's awesome power in Jesus' actions and falls down in unworthiness before him. In an act of grace, Jesus lifts him up and calls him to a new life of "catching" people. Simon and his companions leave everything and follow Jesus. The continuing theme of the authority and power of Jesus merges here with that of authentic discipleship.

**Lake of Gennesaret (5:1).** The "lake" (*limnē*) of Gennesaret is another name for the "sea" (*thalassa*) of Galilee. Luke prefers *limnē* to Matthew and Mark's *thalassa*, perhaps because of his more precise historical sense. The Jewish historian Josephus also prefers "lake" to "sea" when referring to Gennesaret.[126]

**Taught the people from the boat (5:3).** This becomes Jesus' preferred method of crowd control in Galilee (see Mark 3:9; 4:1). The people can sit comfortably on the beach without pressing against Jesus, and the rising shoreline serves as an amphitheater with good acoustics. A magnificent example of a first-century Galilean fishing boat was recently discovered and excavated near Kibbutz Ginosar on the Sea of Galilee (see photo).

**We've worked hard all night. . . . I will let down the nets (5:5).** The "nets" (*diktyon*) here are probably long nets supported on floats used for night fishing in deep water. They are different from the round casting nets used for shallow water day fishing (Matt. 4:18, *amphiblēstron;* Mark 1:16, *amphiballō*). A third kind of net, a dragnet (*sagēnē;* Matt. 13:47), was dragged along between two boats.[127]

**They caught such a large number of fish (5:6).** The miraculous catch recalls Old Testament miracles of multiplying food related to Elijah (1 Kings 17:10–16) and Elisha (2 Kings 4:1–10, 42–44), as well as the provision of manna and quail for the Israelites in the desert (Ex. 16).

**Their partners in the other boat (5:7).** The term "partners" (*metochos*) is often used of partners in business and refers here to James and John, the sons of Zebedee (see 5:10). Fishermen often came together in cooperatives for more efficiency. Zebedee must have been a relatively successful businessman since Mark 1:20 refers to hired servants as well as his two sons.

**Go away from me, Lord; I am a sinful man! (5:8).** Peter's awe at the overwhelming presence of God recalls Isaiah's fear when he saw the awesome glory of the Lord at his prophetic call

GALILEAN FISHING BOAT

Remains of the first-century boat recently discovered near Gennesaret.

REFLECTIONS

**WHEN JESUS CALLS ON PETER TO** trust him for a seemingly foolish request, Peter reluctantly agrees. Peter's own faith is hardly magnificent, yet the awesome object of that faith—Jesus himself—produces a transforming miracle in Peter's life. A little faith in a big God can accomplish extraordinary things.

(Isa. 6:5). Whereas Peter had earlier referred to Jesus as *epistata* ("Master"), he now calls him *kyrios* ("Lord").

**You will catch men (5:10).** The participle *zōgrōn* means "catching alive." Some have suggested that this statement alludes to Jeremiah 16:16, a passage related to judgment, but this is unlikely. All the emphasis here is on salvation.

## The Man With Leprosy (5:12–16)

Luke provides another example of Jesus' authority over illness with the healing of a man with leprosy. Lepers were social outcasts in first-century Palestine, living on the margins of society. Jesus thus continues his mission to the outcast and the oppressed that he announced in the Nazareth sermon (4:18–27). In 7:22 Jesus will identify the healing of leprosy together with other healings as evidence that the time of salvation has arrived and that he is "the one who was to come"—the Messiah.

The healing results in even greater popularity for Jesus and more and more people crowd to him for healing. Jesus, however, withdraws to a deserted place to pray. Prayerful communion with the Father is Jesus' source of strength and vitality. On the importance of this theme in Luke see comments on 3:21 (cf. Matt. 8:1–4; Mark 1:40–44).

**Covered with leprosy (5:12).** The biblical words traditionally translated "leprosy" (Heb. *ṣāraʿat;* Gk. *lepra*) do not refer to the same disease as modern day leprosy (i.e., Hansen's disease). The descriptions given in Leviticus 13–14 suggest rather a variety of skin disorders, including psoriasis, lupus, ringworm, and others. Because of the uncertainties of diagnosis and the difficulties in distinguishing highly contagious diseases from relatively harmless ones, the Old Testament set out strict guidelines for the examination and isolation of these skin disorders. If found to be "leprous" after examination by the priest, the diseased individual would be isolated from the rest of the congregation and was required to wear torn clothes, cover the lower part of his face, and cry out "Unclean! Unclean!" whenever he was approached.[128]

**Jesus reached out his hand and touched the man (5:13).** Because of fear of contagion, lepers were ostracized from society and repulsive to the common people. That Jesus is willing to touch this man shows not only his authority over the disease, but also his great compassion. There are no "untouchables" in Jesus' ministry.

**Be clean (5:13).** Leprosy results not only in social ostracism, but isolation from Israel's religious life. Jesus' words indicate spiritual as well as physical restoration.

**Show yourself to the priest and offer the sacrifices (5:14).** The Old Testament prescribed that lepers who were healed

### Scribes

The scribes were experts in the interpretation and exposition of the law of Moses.[A-14] The scribes traced their origin back to the priest Ezra, who established postexilic Judaism based on the law (Ezra 7:6, 10). As the teaching of Torah gained a more central place in the life of Judaism, the scribal office took on greater importance and influence. Later known as rabbis, scribes would be found in every village in Israel, providing exposition of the Mosaic law for everyday life and education for children in rabbinic schools.

Most scribes were probably Pharisees (Mark 2:16), though there were likely also Sadducees among them (cf. Matt. 16:1–2; 21:15). Most New Testament references to scribes are negative, and they are condemned together with the Pharisees for their legalism and hypocrisy. Jesus speaks of the validity of the office however, in Matthew 13:52: "Every teacher of the law who has been instructed about the kingdom of heaven is like the owner of a house who brings out of his storeroom new treasures as well as old."

had to be reexamined by the priest and declared "clean," and that a sacrifice was to be offered on their behalf (Lev. 14:1–32). By ordering the leper to follow this procedure, Jesus demonstrates faithfulness to the requirements of the law.

## Jesus Heals a Paralytic (5:17–26)

The account of the healing of a paralyzed man continues Luke's theme that Jesus' claims are confirmed through the power of God at work in him. Jesus' authority over disease is again evident as Luke notes that "the power of the Lord was present for him to heal the sick." Luke does not mean to suggest that such power was absent on other occasions, but that Jesus' God-given authority to heal *was obvious to all* on this occasion. No one should have missed it. This is important because this passage also presents the beginning of opposition to Jesus. The Pharisees and teachers of the law appear for the first time in Luke's Gospel, having come to observe Jesus "from every village of Galilee and from Judea and Jerusalem" (5:17). They see God's power at work but still reject Jesus' authority. When Jesus makes the extraordinary claim to forgive sins, these Jewish leaders accuse him of blasphemy by claiming it as a prerogative of God alone.

This passage is also a lesson in faith and the various human responses to Jesus' power and identity. On the negative side the religious leaders see God's power but reject the messenger. On the positive side the paralytic and his friends demonstrate extraordinary faith by tearing the roof apart to reach Jesus. The paralytic is rewarded with both spiritual and physical healing: forgiveness of sins and the ability to walk. The miracle has its intended result. The people stand in awe and give praise to God (cf. Matt. 9:1–8; Mark 2:1–12).

**Pharisees (5:17).** See "The Pharisees." This is Luke's first mention of the Pharisees.

**Teachers of the law (5:17).** The "teachers of the law" (*nomodidaskaloi*) were also called "scribes" (*grammateis;* 5:21; NIV, "teachers of the law") and "lawyers" (*nomikoi;* 7:30; NIV, "experts in the law"). See "Scribes."

**Through the tiles (5:19).** A Palestinian roof was normally flat, made of beams covered with reeds and a layer of clay. External stairs or a ladder could be used to reach the roof or upper floor. Mark speaks of the men (lit.) "digging through" the roof (Mark 2:4) while Luke refers to lowering the man down "through the tiles." Luke may be interpreting the passage for his Hellenistic readers, who were more familiar with tile roofs. The two accounts can be harmonized, however, since Mark does not specifically state the composition of the roof and tile roofs were in use in Palestine by this period.[129]

**Your sins are forgiven (5:20).** A connection between disease and forgiveness of sins is found in Psalm 103:3, where it is said that the Lord "forgives all your sins and heals all your diseases." Some Jews believed that all disease was the result of an individual's personal sin, a perspective that Jesus refutes in John 9:2–3. It is not clear in the present case, however, whether Jesus is suggesting that this man's paralysis is a result of specific sins, or whether his words merely stress the priority of the man's spiritual needs over his physical needs. The latter is more likely. Jesus' healing power is meant to confirm his authority to announce the kingdom of God and the eschatological forgiveness of sins.

**Who is this fellow who speaks blasphemy? (5:21).** In the Old Testament and Judaism "blasphemy" is sometimes defined narrowly as the misuse of the divine name "Yahweh," such as in using it in a curse (see Lev. 24:10–23). The penalty for such abuse was death. The Mishnah (c. A.D. 200) states that "the blasphemer is not culpable unless he pronounces 'the Name' [YHWH] itself."[130] Elsewhere blasphemy is identified more generally with anything that challenges or brings dishonor to God's name or authority.[131] Here the accusation is that Jesus is arrogantly usurping the authority of God.

**Who can forgive sins but God alone? (5:21).** While only God can forgive sins, he sometimes offers forgiveness through a human agent (2 Sam. 12:13). The teachers of the law and the Pharisees reject Jesus' claim to be acting with God's authority and so consider his statement to be blasphemous.

**The Son of Man (5:24).** This is the first use of Jesus' favorite self-designation in Luke's Gospel. The Greek phrase *ho huios tou anthrōpou* is a literal translation of the Hebrew *ben ʾādām* ("son of man"; Aramaic: *bar ʾenāš*), which means "a human being." It is often used in the Old Testament (especially in Ezekiel) to contrast the lowliness of humanity with the transcendence of God. A special use of

TILED ROOFS

Homes in the village of Dar Samet near Hebron.

the designation appears in Daniel 7:13, where an exalted messianic figure—one "like a son of man" (i.e., "having human form")—comes with the clouds of heaven and is given great glory and power. Jesus probably adopts the title because: (1) It stresses his true humanity; (2) it points to Daniel 7:13 and so reveals his messianic identity and the glory he will receive (see Luke 22:69); but (3) it does not carry as much political "baggage" as other titles, like "Messiah" or "Son of David." Jesus can define his messiahship on his own terms rather than on the basis of popular expectation. See also comments on 9:26.

## The Calling of Levi (5:27–32)

The call of Levi plays out in miniature a central theme in Luke's Gospel: Jesus' ministry to sinners who will repent and follow him. The great physician has not come to heal the "righteous"—that is, the *self*-righteous—but sinners who recognize their desperate need of repentance and spiritual healing. This passage is parallel to the Zacchaeus episode at the end of Jesus' ministry, where Jesus declares, "The Son of Man came to seek and to save what was lost" (19:10).[132]

**A tax collector . . . sitting at his tax booth (5:27).** For more on tax collectors see comments on 3:12. This may have been not a tax office per se, but a toll booth, where customs would be collected on goods in transit. As a tax collector (*telōnēs*), Levi is probably an agent of a "chief tax collector" (*architelōnēs*), such as Zacchaeus (19:2).

**Levi (5:27).** Since in Matthew's Gospel this individual is named "Matthew"

### ▸ The Pharisees

The Pharisees, one of several religious parties within Judaism, probably arose from the *Hasidim*, the pious Jews who had fought with the Maccabees against the oppression of Antiochus Epiphanes (175–163 B.C.). The word "Pharisee" is probably derived from a Hebrew term meaning "separatists" and was applied to this group because they separated themselves from those who did not follow their rigid standards of righteousness.[A-15]

While the Sadducees were primarily upper-class aristocrats who dominated the Sanhedrin (the Jewish high court; see 22:66) and the temple worship, the Pharisees appear to have been primarily middle-class businessmen and merchants more involved in the synagogue communities. Josephus claims that the Pharisees numbered about six thousand.[A-16] The most distinctive characteristic of the Pharisees was their strict adherence to the Torah—not only the written law of the Old Testament, but also the "oral law," a body of traditions that expanded and elaborated on the Old Testament law. Their goal was to "build a hedge" around the Torah so as to guard against any possible infringement. Their expansions of the law were also intended to apply its mandates to the changing circumstances in life. The common people had much admiration for the pious Pharisees.

Despite sharing many common beliefs, Jesus comes into frequent conflict with the Pharisees. He condemns them for raising their traditions to the level of Scripture and for focusing on the outward requirements of the law, while ignoring matters of the heart (Luke 11:39–43). For their part, the separatist Pharisees attack Jesus' association with tax collectors and sinners (7:36–50; 15:1–2, etc.) and the way he places himself above Sabbath regulations (6:1–5). Most importantly perhaps, Jesus is seen as a threat to their leadership and influence over the people.

(Matt. 9:9), we may assume he is to be identified with the disciple by that name in Luke 6:15. Some have suggested that this is Matthew's second name, Matthew Levi, or perhaps that Matthew is a Levite from the tribe of Levi (see comments on 10:31–32). If the latter were the case, he would be especially hated by his countrymen as one who should have been pursuing a religious vocation, but instead chose a dishonest one.

**Left everything and followed him (5:28).** Though hated for their duplicity with the Romans, tax collectors made a good living. To leave such a lucrative career was a major sacrifice.

**Held a great banquet (5:29).** That Levi had the resources for such a banquet confirms his financial success. It was common in the ancient world to repay honor with honor, so Levi holds a banquet for Jesus in his home. He also wants to introduce his friends and former colleagues to Jesus.

**The teachers of the law who belonged to their sect (5:30).** Literally, "their scribes." This refers to those teachers of the law (or "scribes") who are also Pharisees (see comments on 5:17).

**Why do you eat and drink with . . . sinners (5:30).** Table fellowship had great significance in the ancient world, meaning acceptance of those with whom you dined (see comments on 14:8–9). In Judaism a scrupulous Pharisee would not eat at the home of a common Israelite (those known as *ʿam ha-'aretz*, "people of the land"), since he could not be sure that the food was ceremonially clean or that it had been properly tithed (*m. Dem.* 2:2). To avoid ceremonial defilement, a guest at the home of a Pharisee would be required to wear a ritually clean garment provided by the host (*m. Dem.* 2:3). The Pharisees expect Jesus, a respected rabbi, to act in the same exclusive manner.

**I have not come to call the righteous, but sinners to repentance (5:32).** Although a guest, Jesus now functions as the host of the banquet, inviting the outcasts to dine with him.[133]

## Jesus Questioned About Fasting (5:33–39)

The religious leaders' dismay that Jesus dined with sinners provokes a further question as to why Jesus and his disciples do not fast like other good Jews. Jesus replies with an analogy about God's providing a joyful wedding banquet for his people (the time of salvation) where he himself is the bridegroom. Is it appropriate for his disciples, the guests at the wedding, to fast during such a celebration? Of course not. Now is the time to celebrate the great salvation God is accomplishing through Jesus.

But a time will come when the bridegroom will be taken away, and fasting will then be appropriate (5:35). Jesus thus hints for the first time at his rejection and "departure" (cf. 9:31, 51) and the sorrow this will cause to his followers.

Jesus' wedding feast analogy is followed by three metaphors that further elaborate the significance of his coming. The point of all three is the inevitable clash between old and new, which his ministry will provoke. The first two analogies (the patch and the wineskins) demonstrate the inevitable clash between traditional Jewish expectations and the new thing God is accomplishing in Jesus. Jesus' ministry is more than a reformation of Judaism; it is the dawn of God's final salvation. The old is gone (i.e., "fulfilled"), the new has arrived. The third analogy (unique to Luke) is about the power and resilience of traditional beliefs in Judaism. The traditions and exclusiveness of Judaism will provide strong opposition to the advance of the "new" and inclusive gospel proclaimed by the early church.

**Fast and pray (5:33).** Fasting was a common practice in Judaism, and pious Jews fasted twice a week, on Mondays and Thursdays.[134] Fasting is often associated with prayer. The point here is not that Jesus and his disciples do not pray, but that they do not fast as an essential part of their prayer life. In the Old Testament, fasting is associated with times of spiritual preparation and repentance.[135] Yet fasting as a means to self-righteousness is rejected by the prophets.[136] For more on fasting see comments on 18:12.

**Can you make the guests of the bridegroom fast . . . ? (5:34).** Weddings were times of extravagant festivities and celebration, lasting an entire week (Judg. 14:17) or even two (Tobit 8:20; 10:7). Though wedding customs of this day are not fully known, certain features seem clear. The bridegroom went out to receive his bride from her parent's home and bring her to his own, with friends and family joining in the joyful procession (Matt. 25:1–13). This was followed by the marriage feast, and eventually the consummation of the marriage in the bridal chamber. Mourning or fasting was unthinkable during such a joyful time of celebration.[137]

**He told them this parable (5:36).** Luke uses the term *parabolē* for various figures of speech, including proverbs (4:23), metaphors, and more extended stories. Here the term refers to three similitudes, or extended metaphors.

**Wineskins (5:37).** Skins of animals were scraped of their hair and sewn together to contain liquids. The process of wine fermentation would force the expansion of the skins.

## Lord of the Sabbath (6:1–11)

The opposition to Jesus that began with the healing of the paralytic and the call of Levi continues in a series of controversies concerning the Sabbath. When the Pharisees accuse Jesus and his disciples of breaking the Sabbath commandment (Ex. 20:8–11; Deut. 5:14), he responds by defining the true meaning of keeping God's laws. It is not meticulously following a set of rules and regulations, but rather a life oriented towards loving others and pleasing God.

**To pick some heads of grain, rub them in their hands (6:1).** The Old Testament law allowed one to pluck ears of grain and eat them while walking through a field, so long as one did not use a sickle

*right* ▶

HEADS OF WHEAT

(Deut. 23:25). Rubbing the grain separated the kernel from the chaff.

**What is unlawful on the Sabbath (6:2).** The disciples are not being accused of stealing (see previous comment), but of working on the Sabbath by harvesting the grain. Exodus 34:21 forbade work on the Sabbath, noting that "even during the plowing season and harvest you must rest."[138] Later rabbinic tradition took this command and elaborated on it with detailed lists of what constituted work. The Mishnah lists not only activities like reaping, threshing, and winnowing, but even such minutia as tying a knot or sewing two stitches.[139]

**What David did . . . consecrated bread (6:3–4).** In 1 Samuel 21, while fleeing from Saul, David came to the sanctuary at Nob, a town northeast of Jerusalem. The tabernacle had apparently been set up at Nob after the destruction of Shiloh (1 Sam. 4:2–4; Jer. 7:12). There David requested and received from Ahimelech the priest the consecrated "bread of the Presence." This bread was set out weekly as a sacrifice to the Lord and was consumed by the priests when new bread was set out.[140] Later Jewish sources sought to downplay David's violation. Josephus mentions only that David received provisions, not that he took the consecrated bread.[141] Some rabbinic sources claim that it was not really the consecrated bread, or that it was old bread that had already been removed from the table.[142] Jesus treats it as a real violation of the law, but points out that the meeting of human needs constitutes a higher law, overriding the ceremonial requirement.

**The Son of Man is Lord of the Sabbath (6:5).** This statement probably represents a play on words. Since the Hebrew idiom "son of man" in the Old Testament means a "human being," the saying can be taken to mean that the Sabbath was made for people and so people have priority or authority over it. Yet in the context of Jesus' ministry and Luke's Gospel, "Son of Man" must here carry its full messianic sense as the exalted king and Lord of all (see Dan. 7:13 and comments on Luke 5:24; 9:26). If human beings have priority over the Sabbath, how much more is the Son of Man "Lord of the Sabbath." He instituted it, so he has the authority to abrogate it, redefine it, or reinterpret its significance.

**A man was there whose right hand was shriveled (6:6).** The Greek word translated "shriveled" (*xēros*) can mean "dried" or "withered." The hand may have been paralyzed and been suffering from atrophy.

**A reason to accuse Jesus . . . if he would heal on the Sabbath (6:7).** The rabbis debated whether it was justified to offer medical help to someone on the Sabbath. In general they concluded that it was allowed only in extreme emergencies or when a life was in danger. The Mishnah says that "whenever there is doubt whether life is in danger this overrides the Sabbath."[143] A midwife could work on the Sabbath, since birth could not be delayed. Circumcision could also be performed since this was a sacred act and did not profane the Sabbath.[144] In the present case, this man's life is not in immediate danger, so the teachers of the law and the Pharisees view his healing as a Sabbath violation (cf. 13:14).

**They watched him closely (6:7).** In contexts like this the Greek term *paratēreō* carries sinister connotations: to spy on, watch maliciously, lie in wait for.[145] The secretive and malicious motives of the Pharisees are contrasted with the sincerity of Jesus' public act, as he brings the man forward for all to see.

**But they were furious (6:11).** The Greek reads literally, "they were filled with madness [or, mindless fury, *anoia*]." The impression is that these Jewish leaders are at their wits' end and do not know what to do.[146] The reference to destroying a life in 6:9 takes on heavy irony here, as the Pharisees break the Sabbath by plotting against Jesus' life. The real Sabbath violation is not Jesus' healing, but the uncaring and hypocritical attitude of the Pharisees.

**PALESTINE**

Showing the distances people came to hear Jesus when he gave his sermon on the plain.

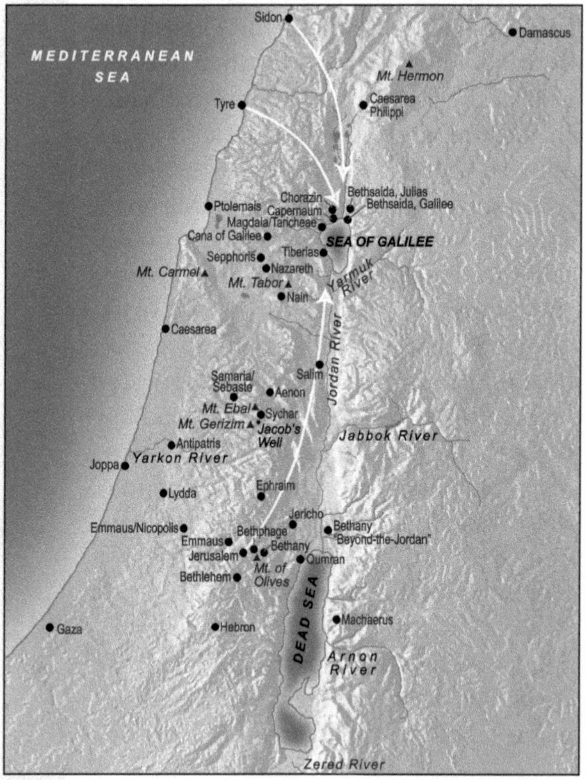

## The Twelve Apostles (6:12–16)

Jesus knows that the shortness of his ministry means he will need to select others to take his message of salvation to the ends of the earth. Only Luke among the Synoptics notes that Jesus spends a full night in prayer before this crucial decision (see comments on 3:21).[147]

**Jesus went out to a mountainside to pray (6:12).** This is also the hill on which Jesus gives his great sermon (see 6:17). Luke's reference to "a mountainside" is vague and the location is uncertain. It has traditionally been identified with the "Mount of Beatitudes" at Tabgha, a mile and a half from Capernaum. Others identify the location as the Horns of Hattim near Tiberias.[148]

**Designated apostles (6:13).** The term *apostolos* means "one who is sent." In the New Testament this word takes on the technical sense of one commissioned by Jesus to preach the good news of salvation. The number twelve is also significant, modeled as it is after the twelve tribes of Israel. Jesus in some sense views this new community as the righteous remnant of Israel, the reconstitution of God's people. Later, at the Last Supper narrative Jesus will assign a place of authority for these twelve, sitting on thrones and judging the twelve tribes of Israel (22:30; cf. Matt. 19:28).

**Matthew . . . Simon . . . the Zealot (6:15).** Though Luke does not explicitly identify Matthew with Levi, this identification seems likely (see comments on 5:27). If this is the case, the contrast between Matthew the tax collector and Simon the Zealot is striking. While tax collectors were viewed as Roman sympathizers and traitors to the cause of Jewish independence, the Zealots were freedom fighters who actively worked to overthrow the Romans. The Zealots provoked the Jewish revolt against Rome in A.D. 66–74, which resulted in the destruction of Jerusalem.

**Judas son of James (6:16).** Sometimes called "Jude" to distinguish him from Judas Iscariot, this disciple is probably to be identified with Thaddaeus in the corresponding lists of disciples in Matthew 10:3 and Mark 3:18. He is also to be distinguished from Jude, the brother of James (and probably the half brother of Jesus), who authored the letter of Jude.

**Judas Iscariot (6:16).** The background to the name "Iscariot" is debated, but probably means "a man of Kerioth." Kerioth-Hezron was a village of Judea about twelve miles south of Hebron.[149]

## The Great Sermon (6:17–49): Introduction (6:17–19)

Jesus has been proclaiming the message of the kingdom of God. Now in a sermon addressed especially to his disciples, he defines the radical values that should characterize those anticipating life in God's kingdom (6:20).

Is this sermon the same as Matthew's Sermon on the Mount (Matt. 5–7)? While there are many similarities, there are also many differences. Matthew's sermon is placed much earlier in the Galilean ministry and precedes the calling of the Twelve. In addition to the many differences in wording, Matthew's sermon is much longer and much of its material appears elsewhere in Luke's Gospel.[150] Despite these differences, the many agreements in content and order render it likely that these are two versions of the same sermon. Both begin with the Beatitudes and end with the account of wise and foolish builders. Both include Jesus' teaching on love for enemies, judging others, and a tree known by its fruit.

The timing of the sermon in Matthew's Gospel is not really a problem since Matthew frequently follows a topical rather than a chronological order. He appears to have moved the sermon forward to serve as Jesus' inaugural address. While some have contrasted the setting of the sermons—Matthew's Sermon on the *Mount* versus Luke's Sermon on the *Plain*—such a dichotomy is unnecessary. Luke does not speak of a plain but of a "level place" to which Jesus descends after a night of prayer on the mountain (6:12, 17). The implication is that Jesus is seeking a level place or plateau where he can teach.

**REFLECTIONS**

**BECAUSE OF THE SHORTNESS OF** his ministry Jesus knows he has to train others who can take forward his message of salvation to the ends of the earth. Jesus' example reminds us that disciples are made not by reading books or teaching the masses, but by investing ourselves in people and reproducing the life of Christ in them.

**KERIOTH-HEZRON**

A village about twelve miles south of Hebron and the possible home of Judas. These are the remains of a Byzantine church.

## Blessings and Woes (6:20–26)

In the "Beatitudes" Jesus announces that God's values are often radically different from the world's. God will bless those who pursue the ethics of his kingdom and choose to put him first over the things of this world. While Matthew has nine beatitudes, Luke has four, balancing these with four "woes." These woes fit the common Lukan theme of indictment of the rich and powerful for their independence of God and their oppression of the poor. This "rich versus poor" theme also appears in Luke's blessings, which do not contain the spiritual qualifications found in Matthew. It is not "blessed are the poor *in spirit*" (Matt. 5:3, italics added), but simply "blessed are you who are poor" (Luke 6:20). This is not to suggest that Luke's beatitudes lack spiritual dimensions. It is because of their allegiance to the Son of Man that the "poor" are oppressed (6:23). But Luke realizes that social and economical realities go hand in hand with spiritual ones. The physically poor *are* spiritually advantaged because their poverty fosters reliance on God. The physically rich *are* spiritually disadvantaged, because their wealth represents a danger and a hindrance to putting God first (cf. 12:13–21; 16:19–31).

**Poor (6:20).** Like Matthew, Luke has more in mind than physical poverty. The Greek expression *hoi ptōchoi* ("the poor") probably has behind it the Hebrew term *ʿānāwîm*, which originally referred to the physical poor, but came to be used of the righteous remnant of Israel who suffer oppression and poverty because of their status as God's people. The "poor" are those who trust in God for their salvation. They stand over against the arrogant rich, who mock God's name and oppress his people (see comments on 1:46–55). Isaiah 49:13 says that "the LORD comforts his people and will have compassion on his afflicted ones [*ʾānāwîm*]."[151]

**Who hunger . . . who weep (6:21).** See the comments on 1:52–53. In the Old Testament God often promises to satisfy the hungry[152] and to bring comfort and joy to his people.[153] There may be an

**POSSIBLE LOCATION OF THE SERMON ON THE MOUNT**

The Sea of Galilee at Tabgha. The "Mount of Beatitudes" is in the background.

### Blessings and Woes

There are few parallels in the Old Testament and Judaism for lists of beatitudes and woes. Somewhat parallel are the lists of blessings and cursings found in Deuteronomy 27–28, which were to be pronounced from Mount Gerizim and Mount Ebal after the Israelites crossed the Jordan into the Promised Land. In wisdom literature, blessings and woes mark out the way to a life oriented toward God.[A-17] Sirach pronounces three woes (*ouai*) on those who are timid and fainthearted in their commitment to God (Sir. 2:12–14) and sets out ten characteristics of the one who is "blessed" (*makarios;* Sir. 25:7–10). Blessing, he says, comes to those who rejoice in their children, who live with a sensible wife, who do not sin with the tongue, who find a friend, etc.

Closer similarities to the blessings and woes of Luke may be found in prophetic and eschatological contexts of the Old Testament and Judaism. Prophetic woes are pronounced against nations and individuals who oppress God's people and profane his name.[A-18] Blessings, by contrast, come to God's people when they wait patiently and expectantly for his salvation.[A-19] Perhaps the closest parallel to Jesus' beatitudes is found in Tobit 13:14: "Happy [*makarios*] also are all people who grieve with you because of your afflictions; for they will rejoice with you and witness all your glory forever" (NRSV).

allusion here to the messianic banquet, when "the LORD Almighty will prepare a feast of rich food for all peoples. . . . [He] will wipe away the tears from all faces . . ." (Isa. 25:6–8). The eschatological banquet feast is a common theme in Luke (see comments on Luke 13:29; 14:15).

**When men hate you . . . because of the Son of Man (6:22).** This verse echoes Isaiah 66:5, which speaks of those "who hate you, and exclude you because of my name." Some commentators have identified this exclusion with formal expulsion from the synagogue, which the early Jewish Christians often experienced (see comments on John 9:22). This is possible, but Jesus' words probably refer more generally to all kinds of rejection and slander.

**When all men speak well of you (6:26).** False prophets were often popular because they spoke what the people and the leaders wanted to hear.[154] Note especially Micah 2:11: "If a liar and deceiver comes and says, 'I will prophesy for you plenty of wine and beer,' he would be just the prophet for this people!"

## Love for Enemies (6:27–36)

Jesus commands his followers to a radical new ethic: to love one's enemies. Though the advice to repay good for evil is not without precedent in the ancient world (see "Love Your Enemies"), Jesus sets this as the normative standard of behavior for his followers. Only in this way can they reflect the character of their Lord. Love here is not a feeling or an emotion, but a concrete action.

**Strikes you on one cheek, turn to him the other (6:29).** The blow here is probably an insulting slap with the back of the hand. Contrary to the Old Testament laws of retaliation (e.g., "life for life, eye for eye, tooth for tooth," Deut. 19:21), Christians are to seek no retribution.

**If someone takes your cloak . . . your tunic (6:29).** This next example goes beyond nonretaliation to radical self-giving. The "cloak" here is a *himation*, a robe-like outer garment, whereas the tunic (*chitōn*) is the garment worn next to the skin. The taking could be an act of theft or perhaps a legal action, where a creditor would take the debtor's cloak as a pledge.[155] Exodus 22:25–27 commands that a cloak taken for such a pledge be returned by sunset so that the poor will have protection against the cold. Jesus' exhortation thus calls not only for radical self-sacrifice towards one's enemies but also for complete reliance on God.

**Do to others as you would have them do to you (6:31).** The so-called Golden Rule is not unique to Jesus, for it appears in various forms in the ancient world. Leviticus 19:18 says to "love your neighbor as yourself." The philosopher Seneca wrote: "Let us show our generosity in the same manner that we would with to have it bestowed on us."[156] The negative version appears in Tobit 4:15 ("And what you hate, do not do to anyone," NRSV) and is also attributed to Rabbi Hillel, a near contemporary of Jesus: "What is hateful to you, do not do to anyone else; that is the whole Law, all else is commentary."[157]

**If you love those who love you (6:32).** The concept of reciprocity, or doing good in order to receive something back, was the norm in the ancient world.[158] A benefactor providing funds for a public project, for example, expected to receive appropriate honors in return. F. W. Danker cites a decree passed by the people of Dionysopolis honoring a man named Akornion for his beneficence to the city:

## ▸ Love Your Enemies

Conventional wisdom tells us to love our friends and to hate our enemies. The Greek writer Lysias wrote: "I considered it established that one should do harm to one's enemies and be of service to one's friends."[A-20] Though this quotation represents the conventional wisdom of the day, advice to love one's enemies was not unheard of in the ancient world. Exodus 23:4–5 enjoins God's people to give help to an enemy whose ox or donkey has been lost or has stumbled under its load. According to Proverbs 25:21 we are to provide food or water to an enemy who is hungry or thirsty. In the Qumran scrolls we find similar advice: "I shall not repay anyone with an evil reward; with goodness I shall pursue the man. For to God belongs the judgment of every living being."[A-21]

Such ideas were sometimes expressed in the pagan world. A Babylonian wisdom text reads: "Do not return evil to the man who disputes with you; requite with kindness your evil-doer."[A-22] The Roman philosopher Seneca (c. 4 B.C.–A.D. 65) wrote: "If you wish to imitate the gods, do good deeds also to the ungrateful; for the sun also goes up upon the evil."[A-23] See also comments on Luke 10:29.

Yet only with Jesus does this command become the fundamental standard of behavior for God's people—the reflection of God's love for us. In the Greek world such commands are usually intended to gain power over one's enemies or to shame them. The same Dead Sea Scroll that calls the sectarians to withhold vengeance also enjoins them "to detest all the sons of darkness."[A-24] Withholding personal vengeance merely allows God time to exact a vengeance that is much better.[A-25]

> Therefore, in order that all might know that the People honor such wonderful human beings who prove to be their benefactors, be it resolved . . . that Akornion . . . be crowned annually at the Dionysia with a golden crown, and that the most advantageous place in the agora be allotted him for the erection of his statue.[159]

The theme of doing good in order to receive something in return is common both in Greco-Roman and Jewish thought. Sirach 12:1–2 reads: "If you do good, know to whom you do it, and you will be thanked for your good deeds. Do good to the devout, and you will be repaid—if not by them, certainly by the Most High." Jesus calls his followers to a higher standard of practicing good deeds without expecting anything in return.

**Lend to them without expecting to get anything back (6:34–35).** The Old Testament forbade charging interest to fellow Jews, so lending was viewed as an act of kindness and charity.[160] Yet for some it became a way to build "credit" for a time when you might be the one in need. Since the law required debts to be cancelled every seventh (Sabbath) year, the rich would be reluctant to loan to the poor as the Sabbath year drew near (see Deut. 15:9). Jesus says that such reciprocal or self-centered loans are no better than the dealings of "sinners." Christian "lending" should be equivalent to self-sacrificial giving, expecting nothing in return.

REFLECTIONS

**CONVENTIONAL WISDOM TELLS** us to love our friends and to hate our enemies. But in his great sermon Jesus calls on his followers to a radical new value: to love even their enemies, even those who hate, curse, and persecute them. It is this kind of love, demonstrated by God through his Son Jesus Christ, that is capable of breaking down the barriers of anger and hate in our world.

## Judging Others (6:37–42)

Jesus elaborates on his command to do good to others by showing how it relates to forgiveness and judgment. We must not judge or condemn others, but rather forgive them just as we desire to be forgiven. Jesus' command not to judge or condemn does not mean that we never confront sin. Rather, what Jesus condemns is hypocritical judgment.

**Good measure, pressed down . . . will be poured into your lap (6:38).** The image here relates to the purchase of grain. A generous seller not only fills up the measuring container for the customer, but then presses down the grain and shakes the container to make room for even more. He then tops it off until it overflows into the customer's lap. The "lap" (*kolpos*) may refer to the folds of the garment at the waist, which could serve as a large pocket for the grain.[161]

**For with the measure you use, it will be measured to you (6:38).** The Mishnah provides similar advice: "With the measure a man metes, it shall be measured to him again."[162] Grain contracts sometime stipulated that the same instrument—that of the purchaser—must be used to measure both the grain and the payment.[163]

**Can a blind man lead a blind man? (6:39).** This is a common proverbial image found in both Greek and Jewish sources.[164]

**A student is not above his teacher (6:40).** Before the widespread availability of books, a teacher was the only resource for a student or disciple, so his knowledge could go no further than that which he was taught. The kind of forgiveness believers show will be picked up by those who follow them.

**The speck . . . the plank in your own eye (6:41).** Similar proverbs appear in Greek literature.[165] The "plank" (*dokos*) here probably refers to a large beam rather than a board or two-by-four, making the exaggerated image even more striking.

**You hypocrite (6:42).** The Greek term *hypocritēs* is a colorful one and was often used of a play-actor in a drama. Metaphorically it came to designate one who pretended to be something one was not. By New Testament times the term was often used of a deceiver or hypocrite.[166]

## A Tree and Its Fruit (6:43–45)

The reference to hypocrisy in 6:42 is now developed with several illustrations from nature. Just as good trees produce good fruit and bad trees bad, so those whose hearts are right with God produce good deeds.

**Bad tree . . . [bad] fruit (6:43).** The term "bad" (*sapros*) originally meant "decayed" or "rotten" and so is an appropriate term for "bad" fruit. It could also mean anything of inferior quality, thus designating both the tree and its fruit.

**Figs . . . grapes (6:44).** Olives, figs, and grapes were the most common agricultural products in Palestine, so the image would have been a common one for Jesus' hearers.

## The Wise and Foolish Builders (6:46–49)

Jesus' reference to the good deeds that flow from a good heart (6:45) transitions naturally into a saying about putting his words into practice (6:46) and an illustration of the consequences that will follow (6:47–49). Those who hear his words and practice them are like a man who builds his house on a firm foundation that will survive through life's storms. Those, however, who merely play lip-service to Jesus, calling him "Lord" but not doing what he says, are building on a weak spiritual foundation that will collapse when the storms of life strike.

**Who hears my words and does not put them into practice (6:49).** Jesus' saying is similar to Ezekiel 33:31–33: "With their mouths they express devotion. . . . For they hear your words but do not put them into practice."

**He is like a man building a house (6:48–49).** Ezekiel uses a similar image of a devastating storm to describe the fate of false prophets who deceive God's people (Ezek. 13:13–14).

## The Faith of the Centurion (7:1–10)

Following his account of Jesus' sermon, Luke narrates a series of episodes illustrating responses to Jesus' person and message. In the first a group of Jewish elders come to Jesus with a request from a certain centurion to heal his dying servant. The story demonstrates not only the power and potential of faith, but also the inclusive nature of the gospel message. Though Jesus came especially for the "lost sheep of Israel" (Matt. 15:24), he often finds greater faith among those out-

◀ *left*

**CENTURION**

The typical dress of a Roman centurion.

side of Israel's fold. For Luke the episode foreshadows the mission to the Gentiles in Acts. Its parallel is the story of the centurion Cornelius, whose conversion confirms God's purpose and plan to bring salvation to the Gentiles (Acts 10).

**A centurion's (7:2).** The centurion was the mainstay of the Roman army, commanding a "century" of approximately one hundred soldiers. A Roman legion was made up of sixty centuries. As veteran soldiers, centurions maintained discipline and commanded great respect. They were paid about fifteen times as much as an ordinary soldier.

Since Roman troops were not stationed in Galilee until A.D. 44,[167] this individual may have served under Herod Antipas, tetrarch of Galilee (see 3:1), performing police or customs services. Conversely, he may have been a retired Roman soldier living in Galilee. In either case, his support for the Jewish community suggests he is a "God-fearer" like Cornelius (Acts 10:2), a Gentile who worships the God of Israel but has not undergone full conversion.

**Some elders of the Jews (7:3).** These are apparently local community leaders.[168] In Matthew's parallel account the centurion himself approaches Jesus. This can be explained from Matthew's tendency to abbreviate and telescope his narratives. It is indeed the centurion's request (see 7:3), even if it is brought by others.

**He loves our nation and has built our synagogue (7:5).** There is inscriptional evidence for Gentile support for synagogues,[169] and in at least one case, for the erection of a Jewish "place of prayer" (*proseuchē*) by a Gentile.[170] Gentiles who showed kindness toward Jewish communities were highly respected and honored.

This story has as its background the Roman system of patronage, whereby a patron provided protection or favors for a "client," who in turn pledged loyalty and service. The centurion has served as a patron for the Jewish community, providing his own resources and perhaps

**GALILEE**

Showing the location of Capernaum and the probable location of the village of Nain.

▼

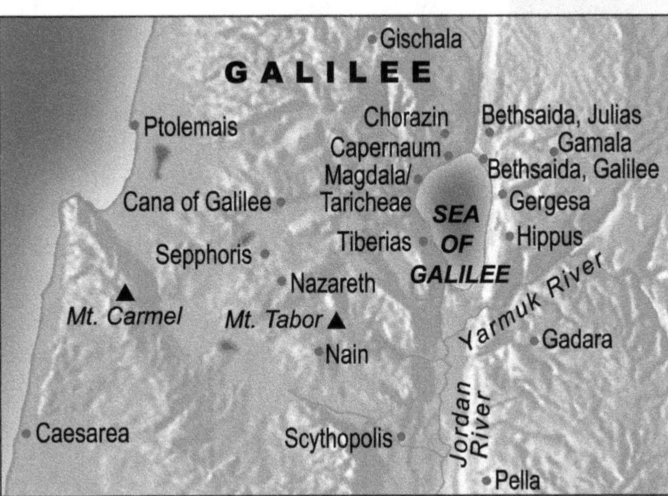

imperial influence for the building of a synagogue. The Jewish elders seek to repay him by serving as his brokers, approaching Jesus with his request.[171]

**I do not deserve to have you come under my roof (7:6).** According to Jewish tradition, entering the home of a Gentile rendered a Jew ceremonially unclean (see Acts 10:28; 11:12). The Mishnah says that "the dwelling places of Gentiles are unclean."[172] The centurion thus shows respect for Jewish sensibilities. Yet there is more to the statement than this. By recognizing Jesus' superiority, the centurion identifies himself as the subordinate "client" seeking a favor from Jesus, who now fulfills the role of the patron.

**But say the word, and my servant will be healed (7:7).** The Roman army was renowned for its discipline and organization. As a soldier commanding authority, this centurion recognizes in Jesus one with even greater authority. The authority of God's word to heal appears in Psalm 107:20.

**I have not found such great faith even in Israel (7:9).** This is not only extraordinary praise for a Gentile, but probably contains an implicit indictment of Israel for her lack of faith.

**The men . . . returned . . . and found the servant well (7:10).** An account of healing over distance appears in the Babylonian Talmud.[173] When the son of Rabbi Gamaliel falls ill, he sends two disciples to Rabbi Hanina ben Dosa to pray for him. Rabbi ben Dosa prays and tells Gamaliel's disciples, "Go, for his fever has left him." When the men return, they find the fever left the boy at the hour that ben Dosa prayed.

## Jesus Raises a Widow's Son (7:11–17)

Jesus' extraordinary authority to heal over distance in the account of the centurion's servant (7:1–10) is now exceeded as he raises a young man from the dead. The story is important because it provides an illustrative example of Jesus' identity in response to the questions raised by John the Baptist. It not only demonstrates Jesus' messianic authority, but also shows his compassion for the grieving mother.

The story has important parallels in the accounts of Elijah, who raised the only son of the widow of Zarephath (1 Kings 17:17–24), and Elisha, who raised the Shunammite's son (2 Kings 4:18–37). The former account, to which Luke has already referred (4:25–26), has particularly close verbal parallels.

Though rare, similar accounts of miracles are not wholly absent from other ancient literature. Perhaps the closest parallel appears in an account from the life of Apollonius, a Neo-Platonic teacher and wonder-worker who lived about the time of Jesus. An account of his life was composed in the third century A.D. by Philostratos. In the story, Apollonius is in Rome when he comes across the funeral of a girl who has died on the day of her wedding. Apollonius stops the funeral procession, touches the girl, and whispers some "spell" over her. The girl awakens and is restored to the grieving bridegroom. Philostratos, describing the account almost two hundred years later, wonders whether the resuscitation was authentic or whether Apollonius saw some spark of life in the girl and revived her.[174]

**A town called Nain (7:11).** Though the location is uncertain, Nain was probably at the site of the modern town of Nein, six miles southeast of Nazareth.

**A dead person was being carried out (7:12).** According to Jewish burial customs a body was anointed with spices, wrapped in cloth, and laid on a plank or in a coffin. The funeral procession, accompanied by mourners, proceeded outside the city gate to the family burial site. Burial took place soon after death to avoid decomposition.[175]

**She was a widow (7:12).** Widows are viewed throughout Scripture as the most vulnerable members of society, those for whom God has special concern.[176] For a widow to lose the only son left to support her would be a terrible loss. In the Old Testament the death of an only son is the epitome of great sorrow.[177]

**A large crowd from the town was with her (7:12).** A large number of mourners revealed the great love for the deceased and the severity of the loss. Rabbinic writings said that if the procession was small, one should interrupt the study of Torah to participate (so as to supply a sufficient number of mourners), but if the procession was already large enough, one should continue studying.[178]

**He went up and touched the coffin (7:14).** The term *soros* (NIV "coffin") can refer to either a coffin or a bier (a funeral plank) on which the body was placed. The latter is probably intended here. Touching a bier or coffin would render a person ceremonially unclean (Num. 19:11, 16). Jesus' authority reverses the direction of defilement, "cleansing" the corpse through his power over death.

**The dead man sat up (7:15).** The episode is not a "resurrection," since in Jewish and Christian thought the resurrection occurs at the end of time, when believers receive glorified bodies. Jesus' own resurrection is the "firstfruits" of this end-time resurrection (1 Cor. 15:20). This and similar Gospel miracles are better termed "resuscitations," the restoration of mortal life to an individual who has died. True resurrection is to eternal life.

*bottom left*

**NAIN**

The modern village of Nein in the plain of Jezreel where the ancient town once stood.

*bottom right*

**TOWN GATE**

The city gate at the tel of Megiddo.

## Jesus and John the Baptist (7:18–35)

As John the Baptist languished in prison (put there by Herod Antipas, see 3:19–20), he begins to have doubts about Jesus' identity. These are evidently brought on by reports concerning the nature of Jesus' ministry. Why is Jesus not fulfilling the messianic task of overthrowing the Roman oppressors and establishing God's kingdom? John sends his disciples to ask Jesus whether he is indeed the "one who was to come" (the Messiah).

Jesus' response is meant to redirect John's expectations. He points to his healing and preaching, alluding to passages in Isaiah that concern the messianic age. When Jesus turns and speaks to the crowd concerning John, he declares that John is the greatest of all the prophets—indeed, the greatest person who ever lived (7:28). This is because he is the messenger of God's end-time salvation, the forerunner of the Messiah (Mal. 3:1). Yet in an odd twist Jesus adds that the one who is *least* in the kingdom of God is greater than John. No one who came before, not even John, can compare with those who now have the privilege of living in the age of salvation, the age of the Spirit.

In a brief aside (7:29–35), Luke points out that while "all the people," even tax collectors, submitted to John's baptism of repentance and so were ready to accept Jesus' message of the kingdom, the religious leaders rejected John and so rejected God's purpose for them (7:29–30). Jesus likens the present situation to children playing make-believe games in the marketplace. One group plays a flute and calls the other to a game of joyful dance, probably a wedding feast. When the other children sulk and refuse to play, the first group switches to a dirge and calls on them to play a funeral game instead (appropriate for the sulkers!). Jesus compares the sulking children to the present generation. When John came with his solemn call for mourning and repentance (analogous to the dirge), the religious leaders accused him of being demon-possessed (i.e., of being a madman). When Jesus came with his joyful announcement of God's kingdom and free forgiveness for sinners (analogous to a joyful wedding ceremony), he is accused of partying with the wrong crowd. God's way, personified here as wisdom, is proven right or "justified" by her offspring, that is, those tax collectors and sinners who are joyfully receiving God's salvation.

**John's disciples (7:18).** See comments on 5:33.

**The one who was to come (7:19).** "The Coming One" is treated by John's disciples as a title for the Messiah. The same verb (*erchomai*) appears in Zechariah 9:9 (LXX): "See, your king *comes* to you, righteous and having salvation. . . ." The Qumran scrolls speak of the "coming" of the Messiah of righteousness, the shoot of David.[179] For more on the Messiah see comments on Luke 1:32–33; 2:11; see also "Messianic Expectation in Jesus' Day."

**The blind receive sight . . . and the good news is preached to the poor (7:22).** These phrases allude to various passages in Isaiah, which refer to God's end-time reversal of the effects of the Fall. The messianic age has arrived.[180] In his sermon at Nazareth Jesus has already cited Isaiah 61:1 and the preaching of "good news" to the poor to define the nature of his ministry. Jesus' present mission is not to conquer the Romans, but to conquer the forces of sin and Satan.

**Leprosy (7:22).** See comments on 5:12.

**Blessed is the man who does not fall away on account of me (7:23).** Jesus pronounces a blessing on those who are able to set aside their personal agendas and expectations in favor of God's greater plan. The Greek term *skandalizō* means "to cause to stumble or fall." A messiah who came with healing and reconciliation rather than with conquest over the Romans was a major obstacle to Jewish belief. Paul says elsewhere that a crucified Messiah is a "stumbling block" (*skandalon*) to Jews (1 Cor. 1:23). See Isaiah 8:14 for the Old Testament background to this image.

**A reed swayed by the wind? (7:24).** The image here is proverbial, referring to something fragile, undependable, and easily swayed. In 1 Kings 14:15 Israel is described as a reed that is easily uprooted. Isaiah 36:6 says that Egypt is like a "splintered reed" that pierces a man's hand when he tries to lean on it as a staff (cf. 2 Kings 18:21). John is a man of conviction, not a spineless "yes-man." He is in prison because he boldly spoke the truth against Herod Antipas.

**"I will send my messenger ahead of you" (7:27).** The quotation here combines language from Exodus 23:20 and Malachi 3:1. This latter text is linked to Malachi 4:5, where the "messenger" is identified as Elijah the prophet, who will be sent by God before the great Day of the Lord. These Malachi passages, together with Isaiah 40:3, are identified with John the Baptist throughout the Gospels.[181] Though John denied that he was Elijah incarnate (John 1:21–23), he came "in the spirit and power of Elijah" (Luke 1:17) to fulfill the task of forerunner of the Messiah. For more on Jewish expectations related to the coming of Elijah see 1:17; 3:4–5.

**Among those born of women (7:28).** This is an Old Testament expression meaning "among human beings."[182]

**Even the tax collectors (7:29).** On tax collectors see comments on 3:12.

**Pharisees and experts in the law (7:30).** For Pharisees see "The Pharisees" at 5:17. For the "experts in the law," see comments on 5:17 and "Scribes."

**We played the flute for you (7:32).** The children are probably playing a game of "wedding," where dancing and great celebration take place (see 5:34). The Greek historian Herodotus (5th cent. B.C.) recounts a similar proverb of obstinance and rejection. Fishes in the sea refuse to come to dry land to dance for a flute player. He then catches them in a net and scolds them for dancing (=wriggling) now rather than when he played for them.[183]

**John the Baptist came neither eating bread nor drinking wine (7:33).** "Bread" (*artos*) here probably means "food" and refers to an ascetic life of fasting and self-

**ANCIENT FLUTE**

A flute made of bone excavated in the City of David.

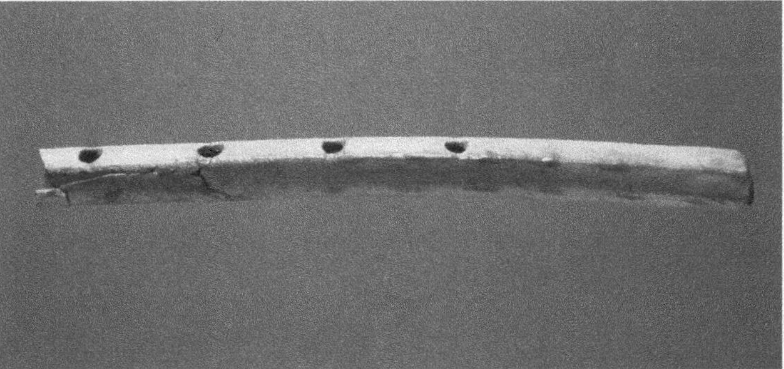

denial. In Luke's birth narrative John is described as a Nazirite from birth, who will not drink wine or other alcoholic beverages (see 1:15). According to Mark 1:6, John lived off the land, eating locusts and honey.

**Here is a glutton and a drunkard (7:34).** These accusations against Jesus are similar to the description of a rebellious son in Deuteronomy 21:20 (whose punishment was stoning!). While John lived a life of asceticism, Jesus spends time with tax collectors and sinners, even attending their banquets (Luke 5:27–32). The separatist Pharisees reject this behavior and accuse Jesus of being a sinner himself. Yet for Jesus these events represent God's celebration at the finding of lost sinners (see 15:23–25, 32). His arrival as the bridegroom means it is time to celebrate, not time to mourn (see 5:33–39).

**Wisdom . . . all her children (7:35).** In the Old Testament and in Judaism, "wisdom" is often personified as a woman, an agent of God who calls human beings to a life of wisdom and godliness.[184] Wisdom's "children" are those who follow her guidance (see Prov. 8:32; Sir. 4:11). The children here are the "sinners" and tax collectors who have responded to the calls of Jesus and John.

## Jesus Anointed by a Sinful Woman (7:36–50)

Jesus' conclusion in the previous episode—that "wisdom is proved right by all her children"—is now illustrated with a touching story of a repentant sinner, one of the precious "children of wisdom" being transformed by the grace of God in Jesus' ministry. Jesus is dining at the home of a certain Pharisee named Simon when a notorious sinner enters and attempts to anoint him with expensive perfume. The Pharisee is aghast that a respected rabbi and supposed prophet like Jesus allows such a woman to touch him. Jesus turns the tables on Simon with a parable illustrating the appropriate response to the free gift of grace offered to sinners. Those, like this woman, who have been forgiven much, respond by loving much. The self-righteous Pharisees see no need to repent because they don't think they have done anything wrong. They respond not with love, but with indifference and rejection to God's offer of forgiveness through Jesus.

**One of the Pharisees invited Jesus to have dinner with him (7:36).** The invitation indicates that Simon views Jesus as a social equal, that is, a respected rabbi. Simon's attitude will change, however, when Jesus "defiles" himself by allowing this sinful woman to touch him.[185]

**Reclined at the table (7:36).** The reclining position indicates that this is a banquet.[186] Guests normally reclined on mats or couches around a short table, with their legs extended behind them (cf. John 13:23–25).

**A woman who had lived a sinful life (7:37).** Life was far more public in the first century than it is today, and at a dinner party such as this one, interested (but uninvited) observers were allowed to stand on the sidelines and listen to the conversation of influential guests. This woman, probably a prostitute, is despised not because she "crashes" the party, but because her sinful lifestyle brings defilement to the gathering. The religious elite would never socialize with or even touch such a person. This makes her actions toward Jesus particularly offensive to those present.

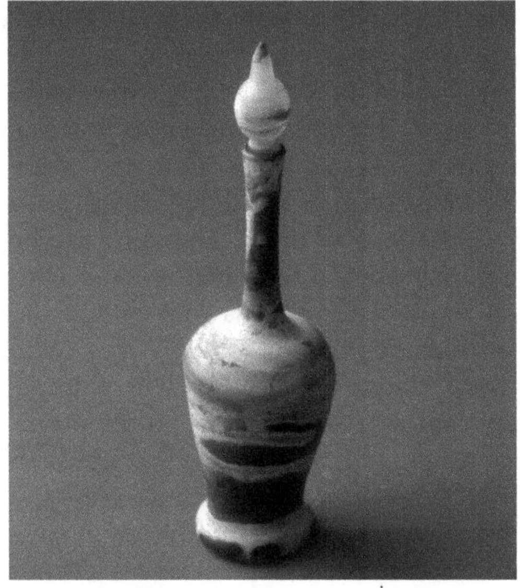

◀ *left*

ALABASTER JAR

**An alabaster jar of perfume (7:37).** The term *alabastros* probably refers to a flask carved from alabaster with a long neck that was broken off when the contents were used.[187] Such flasks were used for fine perfumes and ointments. The Greek *myron*, translated "perfume" in the NIV, is a general term that can mean "ointment" or "perfume." If this is nard, as in Mark 14:3 and John 12:3, it would have cost as much as three hundred denarii, a year's wages for a day laborer.[188] The purchase of such a gift represents an extraordinary sacrifice.

**As she stood behind him at his feet weeping (7:38).** The woman is probably trying to anoint Jesus' head, but she cannot reach him because of the manner in which the guests are reclining. Anointing the head was an act of respect given to an honored guest (cf. Ps. 23:5). She has brought no towel, so when her tears of gratitude fall on Jesus' feet, she wipes them with her hair. She then emotionally kisses and anoints his feet with the perfume she has brought for his head. The whole scene reveals a spontaneous and dramatic expression of gratitude.

**She wiped them with her hair, kissed them (7:38).** It was considered a sign of disgrace and shame for a woman to unbind her hair in the presence of men.[189] The action suggests that this woman is so overwhelmed with the presence of Jesus and her gratitude toward him that she completely forgets her surroundings. Kissing the feet indicates reverence and gratitude.[190]

**Two men owed money (7:41).** Heavy indebtedness was common in first-century Palestine, caused by several factors. Wealthy landowners leased land to poor peasants and then demanded a large percentage of the profits. This together with demands for tithes, taxes, and a variety of tolls kept constant pressure on farmers. It has been estimated that between 35 to 40 percent of total agricultural production went for taxes.[191] During times of drought or famine, a small farmer could easily lose everything to a rich overlord. (Major famines hit Palestine in 25 B.C. and again in A.D. 46.) The resentment provoked by such indebtedness is evident from an event described by Josephus, where, at the beginning of the Jewish War against Rome in A.D. 66–73, the rebels burned the debt archives.[192]

**Five hundred denarii . . . fifty (7:41).** A denarius was a Roman coin equivalent to about a day's wages for a laborer. The

◀

DENARIUS

A silver denarius depicting Alexander the Great.

## REFLECTIONS

**THE PEOPLE OF JESUS' DAY WOULD** have assumed that the religious-minded Pharisees had the greatest love for God. Yet Jesus here praises not a pious Pharisee but a notorious sinner for her great love. The story reminds us that loving God does not mean "doing religious things" to earn our way to him, but gratefully accepting the free gift of salvation offered through his Son Jesus Christ.

borrowers' debts are therefore equivalent to about two year's versus two month's wages.

**Which of them will love him more? (7:42).** There is no specific verb "to thank" in Aramaic (the language Jesus usually spoke), so the verb love (*agapaō*) here expresses the manner in which gratitude is expressed.[193]

**Water for my feet . . . a kiss . . . oil on my head (7:44–46).** There is no evidence that these are actions a host was expected to perform. While Simon could have graciously had a servant wash Jesus' feet, this was not a requirement of hospitality.[194] He was certainly not expected to perform this action himself as host (cf. John 13). Similarly, while a kiss was a common form of greeting,[195] it was not a necessary social grace. The same can be said for anointing a guest's head with olive oil. The point is that Simon did nothing exceptional for Jesus, but acted with relative indifference. The woman, by contrast, went far beyond the norms of hospitality: washing his feet not with water and a towel, but with her tears and her hair; kissing him not on the cheek, but on his feet; and anointing his feet not with (inexpensive) olive oil, but with costly perfume.

A TYPICAL VILLAGE
The village of Yata, near Hebron, which preserves the appearance of typical villages in ancient Judea.

## Jesus' Itinerant Ministry and the Women Who Supported Him (8:1–3)

In a short note, Luke summarizes Jesus' itinerant teaching ministry. He is traveling through the towns and villages of Galilee (cf. 4:43) proclaiming the "good news of the kingdom of God"—a message defined in the Nazareth sermon (4:18–21) and worked out in the episodes since. In addition to the twelve disciples, Luke mentions some women who travel with him and support his ministry financially. These references are significant. Jesus shatters the societal conception of the inferiority of women, raising them to the status of disciples (unheard of in Judaism) and to a place of spiritual equality.

**Mary (called Magdalene) from whom seven demons had come out (8:2).** Magdalene means an inhabitant of Magdala, a town on the western shore of the Sea of Galilee, a few miles north of Tiberias. Mary will play a prominent role as a witness to Jesus' burial and resurrection.[196] For more on multiple demonic possession and exorcism, see comments on 8:26–39.

**Joanna the wife of Cuza, the manager of Herod's household (8:3).** The Greek term *epitropos* can refer to a business manager (cf. Matt. 20:8, "foreman"), a child guardian (Gal. 4:2), or even a governor or procurator.[197] The sense here is probably the manager of Herod's estate. The reference confirms that Jesus' ministry is reaching even the upper echelons of society. This Herod is Herod Antipas, son of Herod the Great (see Luke 3:1).

**Susanna (8:3).** Nothing else is known about this woman.

**These women were helping to support them (8:3).** Literally, the text reads: "They were serving them from their possessions." These are women of some substance and means. It was not uncommon for wealthy patrons to support traveling teachers in the Greco-Roman world. What is uncommon is that these women travel with Jesus, a respected rabbi, and are treated as his disciples. Rabbis of this day did not have women disciples.

## The Parable of the Sower (8:4–15)

In one of his most famous parables, Jesus uses a farming metaphor to describe various responses to his announcement of the kingdom of God. While traditionally called the parable of the sower, this is really the parable of the soils, since the emphasis is on the reception of the seed and the resulting crop that is produced. The parable is puzzling to Jesus' disciples, so they ask for an explanation. Jesus first responds by noting the twofold reason he tells parables. The first is *to reveal* the truth to those who have "ears to hear" (8:8), that is, those who are willing to respond to God's call. The second reason is just the opposite, *to conceal* the message from those who reject the message because of the hardness of their hearts. Jesus concludes by explaining the meaning of the parable in terms of the responses of different individuals to the "word of God," that is, Jesus' proclamation of the kingdom of God.

**A farmer went out to sow his seed (8:5).** Jesus here uses a common image immediately recognizable to people in an agrarian society. Sowing took place in the late fall or early winter, during the rainy season. A farmer walked along with a bag of seed over his shoulder, scattering the seed in the field. Though the evidence is debated, it seems that sowing was generally done prior to plowing.[198] The Jewish book of *Jubilees* (second century B.C.) speaks of crows stealing the grain "before they plowed in the seed."[199] The farmer scattered seed more or less indiscriminately, expecting to come back later to plow it in.

**Some fell along the path (8:5).** These are the right-of-ways, either alongside or

ROCKY SOIL

A modern Palestinian plowing in rocky soil.

through the midst of the field. People walking along crush the seed into the path, and the birds then devour it.

**Some fell on rock (8:6).** "Rock" (*petra*) here probably refers to bedrock covered by a thin layer of soil. Without sufficient soil, the plants cannot take in enough moisture.

**A hundred times more than was sown (8:8).** The average yield for grain in Palestine has been estimated at a seven to fifteenfold increase, although Genesis 26:12 speaks of Isaac receiving a hundredfold increase "because the LORD blessed him." The yields mentioned in this verse are therefore extraordinary, but not outlandish.[200]

**He who has ears to hear, let him hear (8:8).** The same phrase is used at 14:35. Ezekiel speaks of Israel as a rebellious people who have "eyes to see but do not see and ears to hear but do not hear" (Ezek. 12:2). Jesus' call for a response prepares the way for his quoting Isaiah 6:9 in verse 10 (cf. Ezek. 3:27).

**The secrets of the kingdom of God (8:10).** The "secret" or "mystery" (*mystērion*) refers here to the as-of-yet unrevealed plan of God in establishing his kingdom. In Daniel the Aramaic term *rāz* (LXX *mystērion*) refers to the "mystery" of Nebuchadnezzar's dream that Daniel reveals—a mystery concerning the coming kingdom of God that would crush all other kingdoms and would endure forever.[201] The Qumran scrolls sometimes use the expression "mysteries of God" to refer to God's secret purposes now being revealed to his chosen ones.[202] To the Teacher of Righteousness, the community's original leader, "the mysteries . . . of the prophets" have been revealed.[203]

**"Though seeing, they may not see" (8:10).** This is an abbreviated quotation from Isaiah 6:9, which Mark quotes more fully (Mark 4:12). In its Old Testament context the passage refers to the certainty of coming judgment on Israel. Israel's rebellion had reached the point that her fate was sealed. God would blind her eyes until his discipline was complete. The agent of judgment in Isaiah's day was the Assyrian army, which would bring devastation to Israel.

Isaiah 6:9 was an important proof text throughout the New Testament concerning Israel's rejection of the gospel: "Though seeing, they may not see; though hearing, they may not understand."[204] The text points to God's active blinding of the eyes and closing of the ears against those who obstinately refuse to repent and believe.

**This is the meaning of the parable (8:11).** The apocryphal book of 2 Esdras (*4 Ezra*; c. A.D. 100) has a similar parable, though its origin may be later than Jesus' words:

> For just as the farmer sows many seeds in the ground and plants a multitude of seedlings, and yet not all that have been sown will come up in due season, and not all that were planted will take root; so also those who have been sown in the world will not all be saved.[205]

**The seed is the word of God (8:11).** Similar imagery appears in 2 Esdras (*4 Ezra*) 9:31–32, where it is said that the law was "sown" in Israel, but those who received it perished because they did not keep it. Jesus proclaims God's message—the announcement of the kingdom of God—but many do not receive it.

**The devil comes and takes away the word (8:12).** Birds sometimes appear in

Judaism as symbols of evil.[206] In the *Apocalypse of Abraham* (first to second century A.D.), an unclean bird harassing Abraham is identified as Azazel, the chief of the fallen angels.[207]

**But they have no root . . . they fall away (8:13).** Not having root indicates a lack of spiritual depth and stability. Sirach 40:15 reads: "The children of the ungodly put out few branches; they are unhealthy roots on sheer rock." With no soil to support the plants and little moisture to utilize, this soil "falls away" in times of testing.

**A noble and good heart (8:15).** The Greek expression *kalos kai agathos* (the terms are near synonyms) is a common Greek expression for someone with an honorable character.[208] While Mark says simply that these individuals hear the word and accept it, Luke explains the nature of the good soil for his Hellenistic audience.

## A Lamp on a Stand (8:16–18)

Jesus continues with a second parable or analogy, this one comparing the proclamation of the kingdom to a lamp that gives forth light. A lamp is of no use if its light is obscured. Similarly, the good news of the kingdom must be proclaimed for all to hear. The lamp serves two functions. (1) It provides light for those who enter the room (8:16). Jesus' proclamation illuminates the truth of the gospel for those who will hear it. (2) It reveals things that are previously concealed (8:17). The message of the gospel demands a response and so lays bare the thoughts and intentions of people's hearts (cf. 2:35).

Luke 8:18 summarizes the need for a response to both parables. Those who "have" are followers who respond to his kingdom announcement and are receiving the "secrets" of the kingdom. Those who "do not have" are the ones who reject his call and so lose not only future blessings, but also what they *think* they already have. The religious leaders opposing Jesus think they have a special status before God. Even this supposed status will be taken from them.

**Lights a lamp (8:16).** This is probably a small oval lamp filled with olive oil (see photo), which would be set in an alcove to give light to the room.

**Hides it in a jar (8:16).** The Greek verb *kalyptō* can mean "to cover up, hide." The "jar" is the general term *skeuos*, used of various kinds of containers. This is why some versions speak of covering the light with a container (NASB; NKJV; CEV) rather than placing it inside. Covering the light would snuff it out, while hiding it would obscure its light. Since the second image (placing it under a bed) suggests obscuring the light, this latter sense is probably intended.

**Whoever has will be given more (8:18).** Old Testament wisdom literature confirms that those who are already wise seek and receive even greater wisdom. Proverbs 9:9 says, "Instruct a wise man and he will be wiser still; teach a righteous man and he will add to his learning" (cf. 1:2–6).

## Jesus' Mother and Brothers (8:19–21)

The issue of the spiritual "haves" and the "have-nots" in verse 18 leads directly to a statement by Jesus concerning his true spiritual family. Jesus' teaching is set up by the announcement that his mother and brothers have arrived and are waiting outside the house for him. He replies,

"My mother and brothers are those who hear God's word and put it into practice." Jesus' statement is not meant to repudiate or reject his physical family, but rather to demonstrate the priority of spiritual relationships over physical ones.

**Your mother and brothers (8:20).** See "The Family of Jesus."

## Jesus Calms the Storm (8:22–25)

In the previous parables and teaching, Luke has been illustrating Jesus' call to hear and respond to his message. In a series of miracle stories, Luke now turns to address the issue of Jesus' identity, setting the stage for Peter's confession in 9:20 and the confession of the Father in 9:35.

While Jesus' authority over nature is the controlling theme of this episode, there is an important subtheme related to the disciples' lack of faith. Jesus' calm in the face of the storm (he remains asleep!) is starkly contrasted with the disciples' terror and panic as they cry out, "We're going to drown!" Jesus' response, "Where is your faith?" is a call to these

### ▸ The Family of Jesus

According to the Gospels, Jesus had four brothers, James, Joseph, Judas and Simon, and an undisclosed number of sisters.[A-26] His brothers did not believe in him during his public ministry (John 2:12; 7:3, 5), but appear with Mary among the first believers in Jerusalem following the resurrection (Acts 1:14). Since his earthly father, Joseph, is never mentioned during Jesus' public ministry, it is likely that he had died before Jesus began to preach. Jesus' brother James plays a central leadership role in the Jerusalem church.[A-27] Independent confirmation of the conversion and leadership role of Jesus' brothers is provided by Paul, who identifies them as itinerant preachers (1 Cor. 9:5), calls James one of the "pillars" of the Jerusalem church (Gal. 1:19; 2:9, 12), and refers to a resurrection appearance to James (1 Cor. 15:7). Two New Testament letters, James and Jude, have traditionally been ascribed to these brothers of Jesus.

There is a lively debate concerning the actual relationship of these "brothers" to Jesus. There are three main possibilities. (1) Roman Catholic theologians have traditionally followed the interpretation of Jerome that these are not Jesus' brothers, but rather his cousins. This is usually suggested to protect the perpetual virginity of Mary. This view is unlikely, since Greek has a distinct word for cousin (*anepsios*, Col. 4:10).[A-28] (2) A second view is that these are children from a previous marriage of Joseph.[A-29] One problem with this is that no mention of these children is made in the birth narratives of Matthew or Luke. (3) The most likely explanation is that these are the brothers of Jesus born to Mary and Joseph after the birth of Jesus. Matthew 1:25 suggests that Mary and Joseph had normal sexual relations after Jesus was born.

Little is known of Jesus' brothers from extrabiblical material. Josephus reports the stoning of James, Jesus' brother, under the high priest Ananias.[A-30] The early church father Julius Africanus is quoted by the church historian Eusebius as saying that the relatives of Jesus spread the gospel throughout Palestine, starting in Nazareth and Cochaba (in Transjordan).[A-31] Hegesippus, also cited by Eusebius, relates a story about the grandsons of Jude, who were summoned to Rome by the emperor Domitian. Domitian feared that as members of the royal line of David they might be politically dangerous. When Domitian found that they were merely poor farmers and were looking for a heavenly rather than earthly kingdom, he dismissed them and ordered the persecution of the church to stop.[A-32] The historical veracity of this account is uncertain.

disciples (and all disciples) to greater faith in his sovereign control through the great storms of life.

**A squall came down on the lake (8:23).** The Sea of Galilee, lying in a basin seven hundred feet below sea level and surrounded by mountains, is particularly susceptible to sudden violent storms. With two large valleys open on the west (Wadi Hamam and the Beit Netopha Valley), cold westerly winds can descend quickly, turning the placid lake into a raging sea, with waves up to seven feet. In the winter sudden easterly winds can blow up to six- or seven-foot waves.[209] Luke is not exaggerating when he says the disciples are in great danger.

**He . . . rebuked the wind and the raging waters (8:24).** The "rebuke" does not mean that the wind and the sea are represented as demonic forces, but rather that Jesus is able to command even the forces of nature. God is described in the Old Testament as "rebuking" the sea, a demonstration of his sovereign control over all of nature.[210]

**The storm subsided (8:24).** While the Hellenistic world of Jesus' day sometimes attributed authority over the sea and wind to kings and wise men,[211] there are no actual accounts where a human figure exercises such power to calm a storm. The closest parallels in Jewish sources relate to the calming of a storm in answer to prayer. The Jerusalem Talmud (fourth century A.D.) records a story with parallels to the Jonah account, where a young Jewish boy is traveling with a boatload of Gentiles when a great storm strikes. After their cries to their pagan idols fail, they call out to the Jewish boy to pray to his god. He prays to the Lord and the storm ceases.[212] Unlike the present account, there is no indication of personal authority and power over nature.

**In fear and amazement (8:25).** See the similar reaction to the calming of the storm in Jonah 1:16. Fear and awe is the natural reaction to the powerful presence and work of God (see comments on 1:12; 5:8).

**Who is this? He commands even the winds and the water (8:25).** In the Psalms, the Lord is celebrated as the master of the storm and sea.[213]

REFLECTIONS

**JESUS' EXTRAORDINARY AUTHORITY** to calm a storm with a word reminds us that he is sovereign over all of life's circumstances and that he cares for our every need. In what difficulties in life do you need to trust the Lord of life's storms?

## The Healing of a Demon-Possessed Man (8:26–39)

As Jesus arrives on the other side of the lake with his disciples, a demonized man approaches him. The story illustrates Jesus' authority over the forces of evil and provides one more part of the answer to the disciple's question, "Who is this?" (8:25). Jesus, the powerful Son of God, enters and overwhelms the dominion of evil. The account also contrasts various responses to Jesus' authority: terror and destruction within the demonic realm, fear and rejection from the people of Gerasa, but salvation and proclamation for the healed man.

The closest Hellenistic parallel to the present story appears in the third century A.D. *Life of Apollonius of Tyana*, written by Philostratus.[214] Common features include a dialogue between Apollonius and the demon before the exorcism, an authoritative command by Apollonius to the demon (as opposed to a series of incantations or rituals), an obvious "return to his own self" by the man after the exorcism, and an attempt by the healed man to become a disciple after the exorcism.

**Region of the Gerasenes (8:26).** While Luke identifies this place as "across the lake from Galilee," its specific location has presented problems for scholars. The Gerasenes were inhabitants of the city of Gerasa (modern Jerash), a city of Decapolis located over thirty miles southeast of Galilee. This is much too far away for the story.[215] Related to this is a major textual problem, with some ancient manuscripts reading either "Gadarenes" or "Gergesenes." Gadara was another city of Decapolis, but it was only six miles southeast of the lake. Matthew seems to identify this as the location of the events (Matt. 8:28). The third possibility, Gergesa, is identified by the early church writer Origen as an old city on the shores of Galilee. It has been identified by many as modern Khersa on the eastern side of the lake.

Though any conclusion must be tentative because of the many unknowns, there are various ways to resolve the issue without denying the historicity of the passage. (1) The original reading may have referred to Gergesa, but later scribes mistook this obscure location for either Gerasa or Gadara. (2) The reading may have been Gadarenes, but with reference

**GALILEE**

The "region of the Gerasenes" was located on the eastern shore of the Sea of Galilee.

**GERASENE?**

Traditional site of the region of the Gerasenes.

to the broader "region" of the Gadarenes, which stretched to the shores of the lake. (3) The reading Gerasenes may be authentic, but it may refer not to the city of Decapolis, but to an otherwise unknown (similarly sounding?) location on the eastern shore of Galilee.

**A demon-possessed man (8:27).** See "Demonization and Exorcism in the First Century."

**Lived in the tombs (8:27).** Contact with the dead rendered a Jew ceremonially unclean (Num. 19:11, 14, 16; Ezek. 39:11–15). Apostate Israel is described in Isaiah 65:3–4 as a people "who sit among the graves and spend their nights keeping secret vigil; who eat the flesh of pigs." In the intertestamental Jewish book of *Jubilees* (second century B.C.), Gentiles are viewed as unclean because they "slaughter their sacrifices to the dead, and

## Demonization and Exorcism in the First Century

Demonization and exorcism were not uncommon in the first century, appearing both in Judaism and in the greater Hellenistic world. The New Testament itself testifies to Jewish exorcists other than Jesus and the apostles. Jesus points out in Luke 11:19 that the disciples of the Pharisees practiced exorcism, and in Acts 19 seven sons of a Jewish priest named Sceva attempt to cast out demons in Jesus' name (but fail miserably!).[A-33] Luke 9:49 (par. Mark 9:38) speaks of a man outside the band of disciples who is casting out demons in Jesus' name. This last example is somewhat different since this man appears to be a true follower of Jesus.

Demonic oppression of sorts appears in the Old Testament account of King Saul, who was tormented by an "evil spirit from the LORD" (1 Sam. 16:14). Later Jewish traditions trace exorcist techniques back to King Solomon. Jewish writers evidently interpreted Old Testament statements about Solomon's great wisdom (cf. 1 Kings 4:29–34) to include knowledge of exorcist techniques and the magical arts. The first-century Jewish historian Josephus writes:

> Now so great was the prudence and wisdom which God granted Solomon that he surpassed the ancients. . . . And God granted him knowledge of the art used against demons for the benefit and healing of men. He also composed incantations by which illnesses are relieved, and left behind forms of exorcisms with which those possessed by demons drive them out, never to return.[A-34]

A whole body of literature arose around Solomon's exploits. The *Testament of Solomon* (first to third century A.D.) recounts how Solomon used a magic ring to control demons tormenting a young boy, even coercing them to help him build the temple. This document illustrates a growing syncretism between pagan magic and Jewish traditions.

First-century exorcists—both Hellenistic and Jewish—used a variety of techniques, including rituals, incantations and spells, potions or herbs of various kinds, and rings or other magical objects. The magical papyri are full of incantations to ward off evil spirits.[A-35] Following his statement about Solomon (cited above), Josephus describes an exorcism he witnessed in which a man named Eleazar used a ring containing a magical root to draw out a demon through the nostrils of a demonized man.

Jesus' exorcisms contrast sharply with these examples. No incantations or magical objects are used. There is no sense that the power is in the technique or the words that are used. Jesus rather commands the demons from his own authority and they immediately submit. The exorcisms are not meant as showy demonstrations of his magical arts, but to confirm the in-breaking of the kingdom of God in his words and deeds. When the Lord's Messiah arrives, the forces of Satan are confronted and overcome.

to demons they bow down. And they eat in tombs."[216]

**Had not worn clothes (8:27).** Demonization often resulted in wildness of appearance and lack of personal care. The Talmud describes features of demon-possession as going out alone at night, sleeping in a graveyard, ripping one's clothes, and losing what is given to them.[217]

**Evil spirit (8:29).** Literally, "unclean spirit." This fits the whole context of ceremonial defilement. The tombs, the pigs, and the evil spirits all bring uncleanness. Jesus' presence and power brings purification to this defiled scene.

**What is your name? (8:30).** It was popularly believed that the knowledge of a demon's name gave a person control over it (see comments on 4:34 and references there). This cannot be a factor here, however, since Jesus already demonstrates complete mastery over these demons.[218]

**Legion (8:30).** A legion of Roman soldiers consisted of approximately six thousand men. As Luke points out, the number is meant to signify "many."

**The Abyss (8:31).** The Greek word means "bottomless" or "very deep" and came to be used of the place of captivity of evil spirits or fallen angels.[219] In Revelation 20:1–3 Satan is seized and sealed up in the Abyss for a thousand years. Matthew 25:41 speaks of the place of "eternal fire prepared for the devil and his angels."

**A large herd of pigs (8:32).** According to the Old Testament law, pigs were unclean animals.[220] The transfer of demons or disease into animals appears elsewhere in Hellenistic literature.[221]

**Sitting at Jesus' feet (8:35).** This is the position of a disciple, a point made explicit by the man's desire to follow Jesus (8:38).

## A Dead Girl and a Sick Woman (8:40–56)

This double miracle is the third in a series of extraordinary acts leading up to Peter's confession in 9:20. As Jesus has demonstrated power over nature (8:22–25) and over the demonic realm (8:26–37), so now he reveals his authority over disease and death. This episode once again emphasizes Jesus' authority, but also highlights his compassion. On the human side, this story commends the importance of a response of faith.

**A ruler of the synagogue (8:41).** This administrative officer maintained the synagogue and organized the worship services.[222] Acts 13:15 speaks of "synagogue rulers" in the plural at Pisidian Antioch, suggesting perhaps a committee of elders.

**His only daughter (8:42).** See comments on 7:11–17. The loss of an only child represents a special tragedy. The Old Testament often speaks of the tragedy of losing an only son who could have carried on the family name,[223] but Judges 11:30–40 speaks of the tragedy of the loss of an only daughter.

**Subject to bleeding for twelve years (8:43).** The nature of this condition is not specified, but it may have been some kind of menstrual disorder. Such a condition not only damaged her health but rendered her ceremonially unclean, limiting her participation in Israel's religious life.[224]

**The edge of his cloak (8:44).** The word for "edge" (*kraspedon*) is used in the LXX of the "tassels" Israelites were to wear on the four corners of their robes; this may be the sense here.[225] It could also mean simply "hem" or "edge" (see Deut. 22:12, LXX).

**Daughter (8:48).** This is the only time in the Gospels Jesus addresses someone with this affectionate term. It indicates the tenderness with which Jesus speaks to her.

**Your faith has healed you. Go in peace (8:48).** Jesus said the same thing to the sinful woman who anointed his feet (7:50). "Peace" indicates the state of spiritual wholeness captured in the Hebrew word *shalom*.

**All the people were wailing and mourning for her (8:52).** It was important in Jewish culture to have a large group of mourners to demonstrate the great sadness at the loss of a loved one. These would have included not only family and friends, but also professional mourners (see comments on 7:12).

**"My child, get up!" (8:54).** Mark records the actual Aramaic phrase that Jesus used, "Talitha koum!" The impact of those words must have forever resonated in the disciples' ears. Luke provides only the Greek since the Aramaic carried no meaning for his Hellenistic readers.

**She is not dead but asleep (8:52).** "Asleep" here indicates the temporary nature of her condition, since Jesus is about to reverse it. The fact that the girl is in fact dead and not comatose is clear from Luke's explanation of the mourners' laughter: "knowing that she was dead." "Sleep" is often used in the New Testament of the temporary nature of a believer's death.[226]

**Her spirit returned (8:55).** As in the case of the son of the widow of Nain, this is a resuscitation rather than a true resurrection (see comments on 7:15). The girl's spirit returns to her mortal body. "Spirit" here may mean merely "life force," or may refer to her immaterial spirit distinct from her body.[227] It is sometimes said that Hebraic thought was monist rather than dualist, and that life returned only at the resurrection of the body. Dualist perspectives, however, appear in some Jewish sources.[228]

## Jesus Sends Out the Twelve (9:1–9)

A new phase of Jesus' ministry begins in chapter 9 as Jesus sends out the twelve "apostles" (6:13; 9:10) on a mission of their own. Up to this point, the disciples have been portrayed primarily as observers, accompanying Jesus as he preaches and heals. Now he gives them the authority and power to do just what he has been doing: casting out demons, healing the sick,

TUNIC

An Egyptian (Coptic) tunic.

and proclaiming the message of the kingdom of God. The mission of the Twelve foreshadows the apostolic mission in Acts, where the apostles continue Jesus' work through the presence and power of the Holy Spirit.[229]

**The Twelve (9:1).** This designation becomes a technical term for the twelve "apostles" Jesus chose from among his larger band of disciples (see comments on 6:12–16). The term *apostolos* (6:13; 9:10) means "one sent out" with a delegated task. As a preview of the apostolic mission in Acts, this passage illustrates the role these apostles will fulfill. The number twelve represents the twelve tribes of Israel. The apostles are not only the foundation of the church, but also represent the righteous remnant of Israel. In Luke 10:1–16 Jesus will send out seventy-two more, a number that probably signifies the evangelization of the Gentile nations.

**Take nothing . . . no staff, no bag, no bread, no money, no extra tunic (9:3).** A staff was used not only as a walking aid, but also to ward off attackers. The bag here could be a beggar's bag to receive alms, but more likely refers to a knapsack to carry one's meager possessions (see 10:4; 22:35). Since no possessions are carried, no bag is required. The tunic was a shirt or undergarment worn next to the skin (see 3:11; 6:29).

Various suggestions have been offered for the reason for these prohibitions. (1) The Mishnah prohibits a man going onto the temple Mount "with his staff or his sandal or his wallet, or with the dust upon his feet."[230] Jesus may be saying that the task of the disciples is a sacred one and so they must leave behind anything that could defile them. While the "dust off your feet" comment in 9:5 provides some circumstantial evidence for this view, Jesus gives no indication that these items are associated with ceremonial uncleanness. (2) Others have suggested that the commands are meant to distance the Christian missionaries from the wandering Hellenistic philosophers of the Cynic tradition, who carried a purse or wallet to receive financial support.[231] This explanation, however, fits better with the later missionary movement than the historical context of Jesus' ministry. The fact that the injunctions are later altered in light of changing circumstances (22:35–38) suggests that Luke does not see these as established guidelines for the church's (later) missionary activities. (3) The simplest explanation is probably the best. The injunctions are meant to encourage traveling light and without encumbrance, living in complete dependence on God. While the principle is universal, the details are meant specifically for this mission of the Twelve.

**Shake the dust off your feet (9:5).** (Cf. 10:11). This is a formal act of separation, leaving the town to the judgment it deserves for rejecting the gospel (see the judgment pronounced against Korazin, Bethsaida, and Capernaum in 10:13–15; cf. Acts 18:6). In rabbinic traditions, the action indicated that the place was heathen and had no status among God's people.[232] This appears to be the sense in Acts 13:51, where Paul and Barnabas "shook the dust from their feet" against the Jews of Pisidian Antioch.

**Herod the tetrarch (9:7).** This is Herod Antipas, one of the sons of Herod the Great (see comments on 3:1; 3:19–20).

**That Elijah had appeared (9:8).** For expectations related to Elijah, see comments on 1:17; 3:4–5; 7:27.

**I beheaded John (9:9).** See Mark 6:14–29 and "Josephus on John the Baptist" at Luke 3:19–20.

## Jesus Feeds the Five Thousand (9:10–17)

The feeding of the five thousand is the only miracle that appears in all four Gospels. Like the calming of the sea (8:22–25), this dramatic nature miracle provides one more clue to the answer of the question posed by Herod, "Who ... is this?" (9:9). The answer will come in the confession of Peter that follows (9:20).

Important to the background of the passage are (1) the miraculous feeding of the people of Israel with manna in the desert (Ex. 16; Num. 11; cf. John 6:14–40); (2) Elisha's feeding of a hundred men with barley loaves and grain (2 Kings 4:42–44); and, perhaps most important, (3) the "messianic banquet," God's eschatological promise to feed and shepherd his people (Isa. 25:6–8; 65:13–14). The messianic banquet is an important theme for Luke, which will recur again and again during his travel narrative.[233]

The miracle reveals not only Jesus' power over nature, but also his ability to care for and sustain his people. The extra food left over confirms the abundant nature of God's blessings and sustenance.

**A town called Bethsaida (9:10).** Bethsaida was located on the northern shore of the Sea of Galilee, east of the Jordan River. It was the hometown of Peter and Andrew (John 1:44) as well as the disciple Philip (12:21).

**In groups of about fifty each (9:14).** It has been suggested that the people are organized in ranks like an army and that some of the people present may have thought Jesus was organizing them as a messianic army.[234] John's version of the account, in which the people wish to make Jesus king after the miracle (John 6:15), may lend itself to this interpretation. But there is no indication of this in the Synoptic accounts, either in Jesus' actions or in the interpretation of the Gospel writers. The word for "group" (*klisia*) is used elsewhere with reference to people gathered for a meal, not for battle.[235]

**Looking up to heaven, he gave thanks (9:16).** The Mishnah provides an example of an ancient prayer of thanksgiving before a meal: "Blessed art thou ... who bringest forth bread from the earth."[236] Jesus may have prayed something like this on this occasion. Lifting one's eyes to heaven was a common posture for prayer.[237]

**Taking the five loaves ... he gave thanks and broke them (9:16).** This passage has clear verbal parallels with the institution of the Lord's Supper (22:19), which itself has strong links to the Old Testament imagery of the messianic banquet.

**Twelve basketfuls ... were left over (9:17).** The reference to leftover provisions is another parallel to 2 Kings 4:43, where the Lord promises that "they will eat and have some left over." The number twelve may symbolically point to the twelve tribes of Israel. Food is provided for all God's people.

## Peter's Confession of Christ (9:18–27)

Luke's Gospel reaches a climax in 9:20 when Peter, after witnessing the powerful words and deeds of Jesus, confesses

Jesus to be the Christ. The confession represents an important first stage in Jesus' self-revelation. What the angel Gabriel had prophesied about Jesus (1:33–35) and what his miracles have revealed is now recognized and proclaimed by Peter as representative of the disciples. The question by Herod, "Who . . . is this?" (9:7–9) now finds its answer.

The passage represents a key turning point in Luke's narrative, as Jesus radically clarifies the role of the Messiah. His present task is not to conquer the Roman legions, but to suffer and die for his people (9:21–22). In light of his own suffering role, Jesus calls his followers to cross-bearing discipleship (9:23–26). The path to true life comes not through self-preservation, but through a daily willingness to sacrifice one's life for Jesus. Those who are not ashamed of the Son of Man in the present age will be given life and glory in the age to come.

**Some say John the Baptist; others say Elijah (9:19).** For expectations related to Elijah in Judaism, see comments on 1:17; 3:4–5.

**The Christ of God (9:20).** The word "Christ" (*christos*) is a Greek translation of the Hebrew word "Messiah" (*māšiaḥ*), meaning "anointed one." Kings, priests, and prophets were anointed with oil as a sign that they were consecrated to God and set apart for his work.[238] Luke's phrase "the Christ of God" (i.e., "God's Anointed One") recalls the Old Testament phrase, the "LORD's Anointed"—a designation applied to Israel's king, especially David (cf. 2:26). It eventually became a title, the "Messiah," for the coming deliverer from David's line (see comments on 1:32–33; 2:11; see also "Messianic Expectation in Jesus' Day"). In Jesus' day the title had strong political connotations.

**The Son of Man must suffer many things (9:22).** The suffering role of the "Servant of the Lord" is set out in Isaiah 52:13–53:12. There is little evidence, however, that the Jews of Jesus' day recognized this passage as referring to the Messiah.[239] Their messianic expectations focused instead on a powerful and triumphant king who would overthrow the Romans and reign in righteousness on David's throne (see *Pss. Sol.* 17–18; see comments on Luke 1:32–33; 2:11).

**The elders, chief priests and teachers of the law (9:22).** Though Israel only had one "high priest" (*archiereus*, see comments on 3:2), the plural of this term—translated as "chief priests" in the NIV—was used of the upper echelons of the priestly class, especially those who served on the Sanhedrin, the Jewish high court.[240] "Elders" probably refers to the lay nobility who served together with them.[241] (For "teachers of the law," see comments on 5:17 and "Scribes.")

**On the third day (9:22).** "The third day" may allude to Hosea 6:2, a reference to Israel's national restoration by God. As the Messiah, Jesus both represents and brings restoration to God's people.

**Take up his cross daily (9:23).** This is not merely an image of self-denial, but of violent death by execution. The term *stauros* ("cross") originally meant a stake set in an upright position. Persians, Greeks, and Romans used stakes both as instruments of execution and as a means of exposing an executed body to shame and humiliation (and as a warning to others). The Romans raised crucifixion to an art form, and it became a favorite method of torture and capital punishment.[242] Roman prisoners bound for crucifixion were forced to carry the horizontal cross beam (the *patibulum*) to the place of execution (cf. 23:26). This cross beam would then be affixed to a permanent upright beam, while ropes or nails in the wrists and feet were used to fasten the victim to the wood (see "Crucifixion" at 23:33 [cf. 14:27]). Jesus is here referring to a life of total commitment to him, even to the point of suffering and martyrdom.

**The Son of Man . . . when he comes in his glory (9:26).** On the title "Son of Man," see comments on 5:24. The allusion here is to Daniel 7:13–14, where an exalted messianic figure is described as "one like a son of man" who comes on the clouds of heaven and is given authority, glory, and an eternal kingdom. In Daniel, this figure appears to be identified not only with the "saints of the Most High" (7:18, cf. v. 27), but also as an individual Messiah (7:13–14). This is similar to the "Servant of the LORD" in Isaiah 40–55, who is identified both with corporate Israel (Isa. 44:1; 49:3) and with an individual (Isa. 42:1). The key here is that the Messiah functions as representative head of his people Israel.

The Jewish apocalyptic work *1 Enoch* uses the title "Son of Man" for a messianic heavenly deliverer who saves his people and judges the wicked.[243] The portrait is clearly drawn from Daniel 7, but it is debated whether it is pre- or post-Christian and whether Jesus' hearers would have identified him with this figure.[244]

**Some . . . will not taste death before they see the kingdom of God (9:27).** This cannot refer to the *parousia* (second coming of Christ) since Jesus would have been wrong; he did not return to earth in the lifetime of the disciples. The statement refers instead to the Transfiguration, which immediately follows in Luke's narrative. The disciples are given a glimpse of the coming kingdom through the manifestation of Jesus' glory on the mountain.

## The Transfiguration (9:28–36)

At the Transfiguration, the veil over Jesus' person is lifted and Peter, James, and John (the inner circle of disciples) are given a glimpse of his true glory. The term "transfiguration" means to change form or appearance and is taken from the Latin translation of the Greek verb used in Mark 9:2 (*metamorphoō*). Two great Old Testament saints, Moses and Elijah,

MOUNT HERMON

MOUNT TABOR

appear with Jesus in "glorious splendor," confirming that Jesus' message and mission are from God and fulfill the Old Testament.

While in Matthew and Mark the Transfiguration is usually seen as a preview of the glory Jesus will have at his second coming, for Luke the greater emphasis is on the heavenly glory he will receive at his exaltation to God's right hand. Only Luke among the Synoptic Gospels mentions that the topic of Jesus' conversation with Moses and Elijah was his "departure" (*exodos*), which he was going to fulfill in Jerusalem (9:31). This term probably refers to the whole event of Jesus' death, resurrection, and ascension to God's right hand (Acts 2:33). This gives us a clue as to why this event occurs at this point in Jesus' ministry. Following Peter's confession of Jesus' messiahship (Luke 9:18–20), Jesus instructs his disciples on the true suffering role of the Messiah (9:21–22) and calls them to cross-bearing discipleship (9:23–26). The glimpse of his exaltation glory serves as encouragement and hope for the disciples during the dark days that lie ahead.

**About eight days after Jesus said this (9:28).** This statement links the Transfiguration with Jesus' words about the kingdom in 9:27. "About eight days" probably means "about a week." Mark refers to six days.

**Onto a mountain to pray (9:28).** Mountains are places of revelation in biblical tradition. Moses received God's law from the Lord on Mount Sinai/Horeb and there saw his glory (Ex. 24; 33–34). Elijah defeated the prophets of Baal on Mount Carmel (1 Kings 18) and heard God's quiet voice on Mount Horeb (ch. 19). The actual site of the Transfiguration is not named, but has been traditionally identified as Mount Tabor in southern Galilee. Others have suggested Mount Hermon because of its proximity to Caesarea Philippi, the place of Peter's confession.

**His face changed (9:29).** This recalls the face of Moses, which glowed from God's glory when he came down from Mount Sinai (Ex. 34:29). Paul points out that while Moses' glory faded, the glory we will receive through Christ is eternal (2 Cor. 3:7–18).

**His clothes became as bright as a flash of lightning (9:29).** Angelic and other heavenly beings are often described in Jewish apocalyptic and early Christian literature in terms of brightness and white clothing.[245]

**Moses and Elijah (9:30).** Why these two? They may signify the Law and the Prophets respectively, and so confirm Jesus' fulfillment of the Old Testament Scriptures. Both men also received mountaintop revelations of God (see comments on 9:28) and were known for their powerful miracles. Jesus' miracles often recall their works (e.g., Moses recalled in the feeding of the five thousand; Elijah recalled in the raising of the widow's son). Both men's lives also ended unusually. Elijah did not die, but was taken to heaven in a fiery chariot (2 Kings 2). Moses died alone on Mount Nebo and was buried by God himself (Deut. 34:6).

**They spoke about his departure (9:31).** "Departure" is the Greek word *exodos*, a term that can refer euphemistically to death.[246] The same word is used in the

LXX of the exodus from Egypt.[247] As Moses led the first Exodus, so Jesus, the new Moses, will lead a second one. God's end-time salvation is often described in the Old Testament prophets as a new and greater exodus.[248]

**Let us put up three shelters (9:33).** Scholars have puzzled over the significance of Peter's statement. The Greek word for "shelter" is *skēnē,* the word used in the LXX for the tabernacle, Israel's portable place of worship in the desert (Ex. 25:9). It is also used of the temporary huts or booths assembled during the Old Testament Feast of Tabernacles.[249] Since the tabernacle represented God's presence with his people, Peter may be wishing to celebrate God's intervention in the events he is witnessing. Another possibility is that he is hoping to prolong the experience by providing shelters for Moses, Elijah, and Jesus.

**A cloud appeared and enveloped them (9:34).** Clouds are often symbols of God's presence in the Old Testament and Judaism.[250] The closest Old Testament parallel appears in Exodus 24:16, when God's voice calls to Moses "from within the cloud" at Mount Sinai (cf. 16:10; 19:9).

**They were afraid as they entered the cloud (9:34).** The fear of the disciples parallels the fear of the Israelites at Mount Sinai.[251] Fear is the common reaction to a heavenly visitation or an act of divine power.[252]

**This is my Son, whom I have chosen (9:35).** The phrase "This is my Son" alludes to Psalm 2:7, identifying Jesus not only as uniquely related to the Father, but also as the Messiah from David's line.[253] The phrase "whom I have chosen" reflects Isaiah 42:1, where the messianic Servant of the Lord is called "my chosen one."[254] As at his baptism, Jesus is identified here as both the Messiah and the suffering Servant. The title "Chosen One" will be used again of Jesus in Luke 23:35.

**Listen to him (9:35).** This probably alludes to Deuteronomy 18:15, where Moses prophesied that God would one day raise up a prophet like himself within Israel and warned, "You must listen to him" (cf. Acts 3:22; 7:37). Jesus is the "prophet like Moses," who speaks God's word for the dawning age of salvation.

**REFLECTIONS**

**AT HIS TRANSFIGURATION JESUS** reveals to his disciples the awesome glory that was his before he came to earth and the glory to which he will return after his death and resurrection. This glimpse of the real Jesus is intended to encourage the disciples during the dark days that lie ahead. Such a glimpse into Jesus' real glory should inspire us to live on a higher plane in the face of life's difficulties.

## The Healing of a Boy With an Evil Spirit (9:37–45)

The episode that follows the Transfiguration presents further proof of the identity of Jesus revealed on the mountain. As Jesus and the three disciples are coming down the mountain, a crowd meets them. The disciples who remain behind have been unable to help a man whose son is suffering from epileptic-like symptoms caused by a demon. Jesus reacts strongly by rebuking this "unbelieving and perverse generation." The statement is probably directed not only at the disciples, but also at the crowd and the boy's father. All are lacking faith in the power of God to intervene. Jesus takes control of the situation by rebuking the demon and healing the boy. Characteristic of Luke, the crowd responds in amazement at the greatness of God manifested through Jesus' works.

As the crowd stands amazed at Jesus' power, he turns to his disciples and instructs them a second time on the suffering role of the Christ. Despite his acts of power, his present path is not one of conquest, but one of suffering and sacrifice. The disciples are unable to understand Jesus' words, however, not only because they are still looking for a conquering Messiah, but also because this understanding "was hidden from them" (9:45). The comprehension of the significance of the true role of the Messiah will come only through divine revelation (for this same theme see 24:16, 25–27, 30–32).

**For he is my only child (9:38).** The Old Testament often speaks of the tragedy of losing an only son who would receive the inheritance and carry on the family name.[255]

**It throws him into convulsions so that he foams at the mouth (9:39).** The symptoms here are similar to epilepsy, but this does not rule out demonization as the ultimate cause. Demons are often described as inflicting actual illnesses, including muteness (11:14), lameness (13:11), and madness (8:29). Nor are illnesses like epilepsy always considered demonic (see Matt. 4:24).

**O unbelieving and perverse generation (9:41).** This phrase echoes Deuteronomy 32:20, which refers to Israel's unfaithfulness and disobedience in the desert. Though the Israelites experienced the awesome power of God, they still demonstrated a lack of faith.

## Who Will Be the Greatest? (9:46–50)

The disciples' failure to grasp the significance of Jesus' suffering role is now illustrated by a series of episodes revealing their pride and self-serving attitude. In the first, Jesus points out that true greatness is found in a humble heart of servanthood and love for others, which welcomes the most vulnerable members of society. Welcoming (or honoring) the weak and vulnerable is the same as welcoming Jesus, since they are special recipients of his grace. Welcoming Jesus, in turn, is the same as welcoming the Father, since Jesus is the Father's Son and representative (cf. 9:35). Jesus sums up by noting that "he who is least among you all . . . is the greatest" (9:48). "Least" here means not social inferiority, but those willing to take a lower place in order to lift up and encourage others.

In the second episode, the disciple John informs Jesus that he has tried to prevent a man from driving out demons in Jesus' name, since the man was not one of the Twelve. Jesus says not to stop the man, since "whoever is not against you is for you." The cause of advancing the kingdom takes precedence over individual status and privilege. The man casting out demons is viewed as no different from the disciples themselves, since all are merely servants and instruments to accomplish God's work.

**Took a little child (9:47).** Status and position were of supreme importance in first-century culture. Each member of family and society knew his or her position in this hierarchy. Though children were certainly loved and cared for by their parents, they had essentially no social status.[256]

**Whoever welcomes this little child (9:48).** People of position and status were "welcomed," that is, treated with honor and respect as social equals or superiors. Here Jesus, the disciple's honored master and teacher, shockingly places a child on the same social status as himself.

**Driving out demons (9:49).** See comments on 8:26–39 and "Demonization and Exorcism in the First Century."

**We tried to stop him (9:49).** This episode has an interesting parallel in the life of Moses. When two elders (Eldad and Medad) begin prophesying apart from the seventy elders appointed by Moses, Joshua calls on Moses to stop them. Moses replies, "I wish that all the LORD's people were prophets and that the LORD would put his Spirit on them!" (Num. 11:24–30).

**Whoever is not against you is for you (9:50).** This statement is proverbial, appearing in a similar form in Cicero.[257] There the philosopher pleads with Caesar on behalf of a client by pointing out that "while we considered all who were not on our side to be our opponents, you held all those who were not against you to be your adherents."[258] Since the statement is proverbial, we would expect it to be a general rather than an absolute truth; in fact, Jesus cites the inverse statement in 11:23: "He who is not with me is against me."

## Samaritan Opposition (9:51–56)

At 9:51, Jesus' Galilean ministry comes to a close and a section begins that has been called Luke's "Travel Narrative" or "Journey to Jerusalem." Luke tells us at this point that "Jesus resolutely set out for Jerusalem" (lit., "set his face to go to Jerusalem") in order to fulfill the role of the suffering Messiah (see 13:31–35). Luke takes ten full chapters to treat a period that Mark covers in a single chapter.

The journey to Jerusalem begins with a story of opposition from a certain Samaritan village. It continues the theme of the disciples' pride and self-importance found in 9:46–50 and alludes to the theme of God's love for all people, regardless of ethnic or cultural background.

When Jesus sends messengers ahead to prepare a Samaritan village for his visit, the Samaritans refuse to welcome him (see 9:48) because he is traveling toward Jerusalem. When James and John ask whether they should call down fire from heaven to destroy the village, Jesus rebukes them. The episode forms a fitting introduction to a travel narrative in

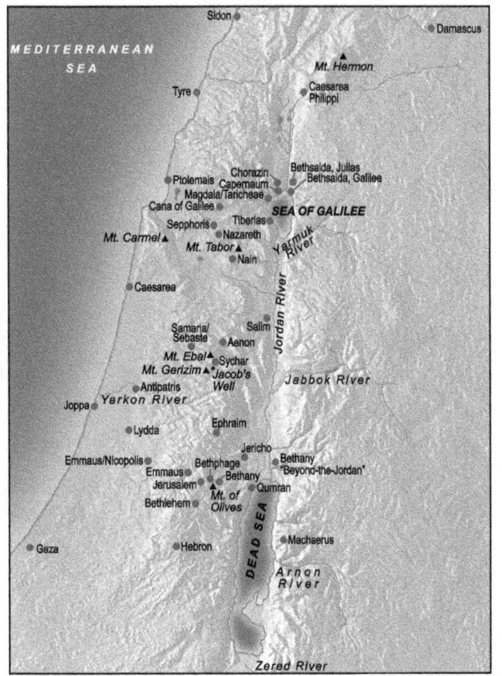


**GALILEE, SAMARIA, AND JUDEA**

The region around Mount Gerizim was the location of many Samaritan villages.

which God's love for the outcast is on center stage. Despite their past animosity toward God's people, even despised Samaritans are offered the free gift of salvation that Jesus brings (see Acts 8:4–25).

**To be taken up to heaven (9:51).** The Greek here is literally "for his taking up" or "his ascension" (*analēmpsis*), with no specific reference to "heaven." *Analēmpsis* is occasionally used of death in Jewish literature, and this sense may be present here.[259] More likely, however, the meaning is similar to the term *exodos* in 9:31 and refers to the whole event of Jesus' death, resurrection, and ascension to heaven.

**To get things ready for him (9:52).** Jesus is seeking hospitality or at least accommodations in this Samaritan village. While some pilgrims may have purchased provisions from the Samaritans, most probably carried sufficient supplies for their journey. Many pious Jews

**SEBASTE**

A Hellenistic tower is in the foreground and the Roman theater is in the background. ▶

*right* ▶

**MODERN SAMARITANS**

Men seated around a table at mealtime.

## ▶ Samaria

Samaria was the region located between Judea and Galilee, west of the Jordan River. According to the Old Testament, the Samaritans arose as a race from the population of foreign colonists settled by the Assyrians following their conquest of the northern kingdom of Israel. Samaritan religion was syncretistic, with elements both of pagan and Israelite worship (2 Kings 17:24–41). There was much animosity between Jews and Samaritans, initially sparked when the Jews returning from Babylon resisted Samaritan attempts to aid in the construction of the temple (Ezra 4). The Samaritans eventually built their own temple on Mount Gerizim (see John 4:21), developed their own liturgy, and used as their Scriptures only the Pentateuch, the first five books of the Old Testament. The hatred between the two peoples became particularly intense during the period of the Maccabees, when the Hasmonean priest-king John Hyrcanus marched against Samaria and destroyed the temple on Mount Gerizim (c. 128 B.C.).[A-36]

It was a three-day journey through Samaria from Galilee to Jerusalem.[A-37] Contrary to the popular view that Jewish pilgrims commonly went *around* Samaria, Josephus says the usual custom was to pass *through* Samaria. (The route through Perea to bypass Samaria would mean passing through Gentile territory, which was equally distasteful to pious Jews.[A-38]) But Josephus also cites an example where Jewish pilgrims were attacked by a Samaritan village, and certainly some Jews would have bypassed Samaria.[A-39] Relations between Jews and Samaritans were always tense and often hostile.[A-40] viewed receiving hospitality from the Samaritans as scandalous.

**Because he was heading for Jerusalem (9:53).** From the Samaritan perspective, Jesus' intention is to worship at the temple in Jerusalem, a rival to their worship on Mount Gerizim.

**To call fire down from heaven (9:54).** Elijah had called down fire from heaven to consume two companies of troops sent against him by Ahaziah, the king of Samaria (2 Kings 1:1–17). Though "Samaria" in that case refers to the capital of the northern kingdom of Israel rather than the Samaritans of the New Testament, James and John may have connected the two. Elijah also called down fire from heaven to consume his sacrifice in the contest against the priests of Baal on Mount Carmel (1 Kings 18:38). The symbol is one of divine judgment against the enemies of God. In their misplaced zeal James and John seek divine retribution against those who oppose God's messenger.

## The Cost of Following Jesus (9:57–62)

The key Christological theme of the Travel Narrative—that Jesus is heading to Jerusalem to suffer and die—has its corollary in the willingness of a disciple to suffer for the master. The present account introduces this prominent theme. Three men approach Jesus, all with aspirations of discipleship. All three of Jesus' responses point to the radical nature of commitment to him and the extreme cost a disciple must be willing to pay.

**Foxes have holes and birds of the air have nests (9:58).** A similar proverb appears in Plutarch, who cites Tiberius Gracchus: "The wild beasts roam over Italy and each one has his own hole and lair, but those who fight and die for Italy have only the light and the air as their portions."[260] Jesus' singular devotion to his task means that he has no permanent home to provide security.

**First let me go and bury my father (9:59).** Respect for parents was of utmost importance in Jewish society. To "honor your father and your mother" is among the greatest commandments.[261] Equally important was providing a proper burial for a loved one, a responsibility that took priority over even the study of the Law. The Talmud makes the surprising statement that "he who is confronted by a dead relative is freed from reciting the Shema, from the Eighteen Benedictions, and from all the commandments stated in the Torah."[262] Though this text is late, its spirit permeates earlier documents.[263] According to the Old Testament, even priests, who would normally be defiled by touching a dead body, could bury immediate family members (Lev. 21:1–3). It was especially the eldest son's responsibilities to make such arrangements (Tobit 6:15).

**Let the dead bury their own dead (9:60).** Jesus probably means to let those who are *spiritually* dead bury the *physically* dead. Some commentators have sought to soften Jesus' words by suggesting that the man is requesting a long delay until his father dies (which could take years), or that he is referring to the reburial of bones in a common family grave (a "gathering to the fathers") after the flesh has rotted off the bones (which could take a year).[264] It seems more likely, however, that the man's father has already died or is near death. Jesus' reply is meant to be truly radical and countercultural.

**First let me go back and say good-by to my family (9:61).** The statement echoes Elisha's request when he was called to be Elijah's successor (1 Kings 19:19–20). Jesus responds by playing off this same Old Testament text, since Elisha was plowing in his family's field when Elijah met him: "No one who puts his hand to the plow and looks back is fit for service in the kingdom of God" (Luke 9:62). The farmer must keep looking forward in order to plow a straight furrow. Likewise, a disciple constantly distracted by past associations cannot provide effective service for the kingdom of God. Jesus demands an even more rigorous commitment from his disciples than Elijah and an even more dramatic break with family.

**No one who puts his hand to the plow (9:61–62).** See comments above related to 1 Kings 19:19–20. A similar proverb appears in Hesiod, *Works and Days* 443, who speaks of "one who will attend to his work and drive a straight furrow and is past the age for gaping after his fellows, but will keep his mind on his work."[265]

PLOW

## Jesus Sends Out the Seventy-Two (10:1–24)

Jesus had previously sent out his twelve apostles to preach and to heal (9:1–6). Now he sends out a larger group of seventy (or seventy-two) disciples. While the earlier mission of the Twelve represents the gospel going to Israel, this one points to the mission to the Gentiles (see comments on 10:1). The actual target of the mission, however, remains the towns of Israel.

Jesus first calls his followers to prayer (10:2). The potential abundance of the harvest, the paucity of workers, and the dangers of the task mean that God's power and help are essential for the task. He also warns of the dangers of the task.

After their return the disciples announce with joy that even the demons have submitted to them. Jesus responds by affirming that Satan is being defeated through their actions (10:18–20). By defeating Satan, the in-breaking power of the kingdom is providing free and unhindered access to God's presence.

Jesus' joy at the spiritual success of his disciples and at the reception of the message of the kingdom results in a prayer of praise to the Father (10:21–22), the theme of which is God's self-revelation through the Son. Finally, Jesus turns to the disciples and describes the blessing and privilege they have so as to see and hear God's revelation through the Son (10:23–24). For centuries prophets and kings longed to experience the fulfillment of God's promises (cf. 1 Peter 1:10–12). The disciples now have that privilege.

**Seventy-two (10:1).** The number probably symbolically represents the nations of the world. There are seventy names listed in the table of nations in the Hebrew text of Genesis 10, and seventy-two names listed in the Septuagint, the Greek Old Testament (LXX). This difference in numbers could account for the textual problem in Luke, where some manuscripts read "seventy" and others "seventy-two" (10:1, 17). Luke may have written "seventy-two" and later scribes altered his text to agree with the Hebrew text of Genesis 10.

**Sent them two by two (10:1).** Going out in twos provides support and security. It is also in line with the Old Testament need for two witnesses to provide valid testimony in court (Num. 35:30; Deut. 19:15).

**The harvest is plentiful (10:2).** The final gathering of God's people is described with harvest imagery in Isaiah 27:12, suggesting the eschatological significance of Jesus' words. This is the end-time gathering of God's people. The harvest image also conveys a sense of urgency, since crops must be gathered in a timely fashion when they are ripe. The disciples are participating in a unique window of opportunity.

**Like lambs among wolves (10:3).** This is an image of danger and vulnerability. In the Old Testament Israel's unrighteous leaders are described as ravenous wolves devouring the poor and helpless among God's people.[266] Israel is also described in Jewish literature as sheep living among wolves (*Pss. Sol.* 8:23, 30). A rabbinic conversation dated to the late first century reads, "Hadrian said to R. Jehoshua [c. A.D. 90]: 'There is something great about the sheep [Israel] that can persist among 70 wolves [the nations].' He replied: 'Great is the Shepherd who delivers it and watches over it and destroys them [the wolves] before them [Israel].' "[267]

**Do not greet anyone (10:4).** A similar command was given by Elisha to his servant Gehazi in 2 Kings 4:29, when he sent him to place his staff on the face of the Shunammite's dead son. The key there, as here, is the urgency of the task.

**"Peace to this house" . . . a man of peace (10:5–6).** The offer of peace here is more than a greeting. It suggests spiritual wholeness and so represents the offer of the kingdom of God (see 10:10–11). A "man of peace" (lit., "son of peace") is one whose heart is ready to welcome the kingdom.

**For the worker deserves his wages (10:7).** Paul quotes this proverb in 1 Timothy 5:18.[268] In the former Paul

GALILEE

The map shows the relative locations of Chorazin, Bethsaida, Tyre, and Sidon.

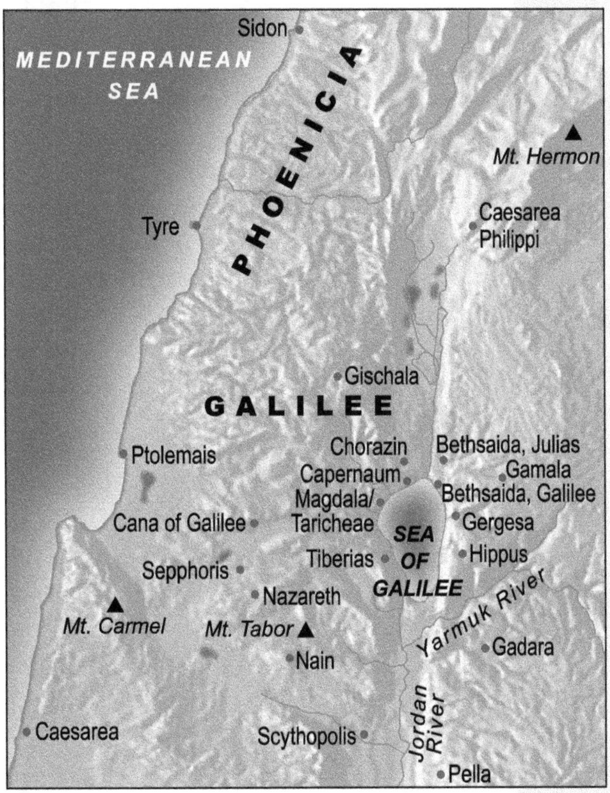

identifies this as the teaching of Jesus and in the latter as "Scripture." This may suggest that Jesus' recorded words were already being treated as authoritative Scripture in Paul's day.

**Heal the sick. . . . The kingdom of God is near you (10:9).** In Isaiah, the healing of the sick is a sign of the dawn of the new age, the arrival of the kingdom of God.[269] The phrase "is near you" can mean temporal or spatial nearness. Jesus may be saying that the kingdom is about to arrive or that it is already in some sense present in his own person, words, and deeds.

**The dust . . . wipe off (10:11).** See comments on 9:5.

**More bearable on that day for Sodom (10:12).** God destroyed Sodom and Gomorrah with fire and brimstone (NIV "burning sulfur") because of their grievous sin (Gen. 18:16–19:29). Their sin and destruction became proverbial already in the Old Testament[270] and are recalled repeatedly in later Jewish tradition. The Mishnah says, "The men of Sodom have no share in the world to come, for it is written, *Now the men of Sodom were wicked and sinners against the Lord exceedingly.*"[271] Yet the sin (and hence the judgment) is even greater for those who reject God's present offer of salvation (see 17:26–30).

**Woe to you Korazin . . . Bethsaida (10:13).** Korazin has been identified with Khirbet Korazim, three miles north of Tell Hum, the probable site of Capernaum. It is the northernmost city bordering the Sea of Galilee.[272] On Bethsaida see comments on 9:10.

**Tyre and Sidon (10:13–14).** These were Phoenician (and hence, pagan) cities located on the Mediterranean coast northwest of Galilee (see 6:17). Judgment oracles like those pronounced here are made against Tyre and Sidon in the Old Testament (Isa. 23; Ezek. 28).[273] As bad as Tyre and Sidon were, they would have repented if they had seen the miracles performed in Korazin and Bethsaida.

**Sitting in sackcloth and ashes (10:13).** "Sackcloth" (*sakkos*) was the material used to make sacks and was normally made of goats' hair. It is often identified in the Old Testament as a garment of mourning and is sometimes associated with ashes.[274] The symbolism of sitting in or being covered with ashes reflects one's utter devastation (Job 2:8), as though one's life were a burned-down house.

**Capernaum . . . you will go down to the depths (10:15).** Jesus made Capernaum his base of operations (see comments on 4:31; cf. Mark 2:1), yet many rejected him there. Jesus' statement alludes to the judgment against the prideful king of Babylon in Isaiah 14, a text traditionally associated with the fall of Lucifer, or Satan, from heaven (see next note).[275] Though the prideful king thinks he will "ascend to heaven," he will instead be "brought down to the grave [*sheol*]" (Isa. 14:13–15). Similarly, while prideful Capernaum thinks she will be "lifted up" because of Jesus' presence there, her disbelief and rejection of him means she will "go down to the depths." "Depths" here is *hadēs*, the equivalent of the Hebrew *Sheol* of Isaiah 14:14 (LXX *hadēs*). While Isaiah may be referring to physical death, both terms were increasingly used with reference to the place of punishment for the wicked dead (see Luke 16:23).

**"I saw Satan fall like lightning from heaven" (10:18).** Jesus again alludes to

Isaiah 14:12 (see previous note), linking it explicitly with Satan's fall from heaven (for "Satan" see Luke 4:2). Jesus may be referring to an original fall of Satan, which he saw in his preincarnate state. More likely, he is drawing on the traditional image of Satan's fall to describe his defeat in the present exorcisms of the disciples. Similar imagery related to Satan's defeat appears in John 12:31; Revelation 12:7–17; 20:1–3, 10.

**Trample on snakes and scorpions (10:19).** Snakes and scorpions were symbols of extreme danger in the Old Testament and Judaism.[276] "Trampling" snakes is evidence of divine protection in Psalm 91:13. The more difficult question is whether these snakes and scorpions represent natural dangers or are symbols for evil spirits. If the latter, a striking parallel appears in the pseudepigraphic *Testament of Levi* 18:12, where the messianic high priest is described as one who will "grant to his children the authority to trample on wicked spirits." Demonic forces are described like scorpions in Revelation 9:3–4, and Satan is the wicked serpent who will ultimately be crushed by the "seed" of the woman.[277] Both views are possible, but the force of the text seems to suggest victory over both natural dangers ("snakes and scorpions") and supernatural ones ("the power of the enemy" = Satan).

**Your names are written in heaven (10:20).** Jesus is here referring to the common image of a book in heaven that records the names of the righteous. It is found throughout the Old Testament, the New Testament, and Jewish literature.[278] The background is the common practice of ancient cities and kingdoms to keep lists of citizens' names.

**Lord of heaven and earth (10:21).** This is a Jewish way of addressing God, acknowledging him as the sole Creator of all things.[279]

**Hidden . . . from the wise . . . revealed . . . to little children (10:21).** In the Old Testament God's wisdom is said to confound the wise (Isa. 29:14). Paul cites this Isaiah text when he points out that in the cross God has made foolish the wisdom of the world.[280] The term *nēpios* ("little child") refers to a child older than an infant, but probably not more than three or four. The image conveys both spiritual need and simple faith in God. Small children are immature and in need of guidance, but their simple faith makes them open to such instruction (cf. Ps. 19:7; 116:6).

**No one knows who the Son is except the Father (10:22).** The intimacy of relationship between the Father and the Son has parallels to the personification of wisdom in the Old Testament and Judaism. Job 28:21, 23 says that while wisdom "is hidden from the eyes of every living thing . . . God understands the way to it and he alone knows where it dwells." The apocryphal book of Baruch similarly speaks of God's knowledge and revelation of wisdom: "But the one who knows all things knows her [Wisdom], he found her by his understanding . . . and gave her to his servant Jacob."[281]

**Blessed (10:23).** For beatitudes see comments on 6:20–22.

**Blessed are the eyes that see. . . . For . . . many prophets and kings wanted to see what you see . . . (10:23–24).** Jesus' statement carries a strong eschatological flavor, reflecting the messianic hopes of Judaism. In the *Psalms of Solomon* (first century B.C.), the psalmist beseeches God to raise up the "Son of David" Messiah to deliver Israel from her enemies, and then reflects: "Blessed are those born in those days to see the good fortune of Israel which God will bring to pass."[282]

## The Parable of the Good Samaritan (10:25–37)

This famous parable of Jesus teaches that authentic spiritual life is defined not by ethnic or national heritage, but by love for God and for others. When a "lawyer," an expert in the Mosaic Law, asks Jesus, "And who is my neighbor?" whom he is commanded to love, the man probably intends to limit the scope of his neighborly love and so justify his antipathy toward his enemies. Jesus, however, shatters the common conception of a neighbor by telling a parable in which a despised Samaritan turns out to be the true neighbor because he reaches out in love and self-sacrifice to his enemy.

**An expert in the law (10:25).** The term here is *nomikos*, "lawyer," and is essentially the same office as a "scribe" (*grammateus*). These were experts in the Old Testament law (see comments on 5:17; 7:30).

**"What must I do to inherit eternal life?" (10:25).** The same question will be posed later by the rich ruler (18:18–23; cf. Mark 10:17–22). It appears to be a common one in rabbinic dialogue. Rabbi Eliezer (c. A.D. 90) is reported to have been asked by his pupils, "Rabbi, teach us the ways of life so that by them we may attain to the life of the future world."[283] Eternal life as the reward for God's people is promised in Daniel 12:2 and appears frequently in later Jewish literature.[284]

**"Love the Lord your God . . ." and, "Love your neighbor as yourself" (10:27).** The same two Old Testament texts (Deut. 6:5 and Lev. 19:18) are identified in Mark 12:28–34 as the first and second greatest commands. Both commandments occupied a prominent place in Jewish thought, and there is some evidence that they were linked together already before Jesus' time.[285] The command to love God was constantly before the Jews as they recited the daily prayer known as the *Shema*: "Hear, O Israel: The LORD our God, the LORD is one. Love the LORD your God with all your heart and with all your soul and with all your strength" (Deut. 6:4–5).

**You have answered correctly (10:28).** Jesus is not suggesting that salvation is by works. Rather, authentic acts of love arise from an attitude of faith. Through his parable, Jesus will expose the man's failure to truly love his neighbor. As in the case of David's sin, the parable will serve to catch the man in his shortcomings.[286]

**And who is my neighbor? (10:29).** A "neighbor" would normally have been identified as a fellow Israelite, though in Leviticus 19:34 this is extended to resident aliens living in Israel. It would not commonly include Samaritans or Gentiles. Indeed, the community at Qumran explicitly called for love for the "sons of light" (=members of the community) and hate for the "sons of darkness."[287] In the Wisdom of Jesus Ben Sirach, the author writes,

> *If you do good, know to whom you*
> *do it. . . .*
> *Give to the devout, but do not help*
> *the sinner.*
> *Do good to the humble, but do not*
> *give to the ungodly;*

*hold back their bread, and do not give*
*it to them,*
*for by means of it they might*
*subdue you;*
*then you will receive twice as*
*much evil*
*for all the good you have done*
*to them.*
*For the Most High also hates sinners*
*and will inflict punishment on*
*the ungodly.*
*Give to the one who is good, but do*
*not help the sinner.*[288]

While exhortations to love one's enemies were not unheard of in the ancient world (see Luke 6:27–28), conventional wisdom called for love for one's friends and hate for one's enemies. Sirach reveals Israel's distrust and hatred for the Samaritans and other surrounding nations when he writes: "Two nations my soul detests, and the third is not even a people: Those who live in Seir, and the Philistines, and the foolish people that live in Shechem" (Sir. 50:25–26). Seir is a designation for the Edomites (or Idumeans), the descendants of Esau southeast of Israel. The Philistines were the coastal peoples to the east. Shechem was the center of the northern kingdom of Israel and a euphemism for Samaria in Sirach's time. As a "half-breed" race with a perverted form of worship, the "foolish" Samaritans are not even to be reckoned as a real people (see comments on Luke 9:52).

**Going down from Jerusalem to Jericho (10:30).** This is a stark and desolate seventeen-mile road, dropping from over 2,500 feet above sea level in Jerusalem to approximately 800 feet below sea level at Jericho.[289] It was a dangerous place, and robbers often lay in wait for unprotected travelers.

**A priest . . . a Levite . . . passed by on the other side (10:31–32).** The Levites were the descendants of Levi, one of the twelve sons of Jacob (by Leah). Unlike the other tribes of Israel, they were not given a tribal allotment in the land (Num. 35:2–3; Deut. 18:1; Josh. 14:3), but were rather consecrated as

**ROAD FROM JERUSALEM TO JERICHO**

The road followed this gorge, known as the Wadi Kelt. St. George's Monastery is visible in this photo.

JERUSALEM TO JERICHO

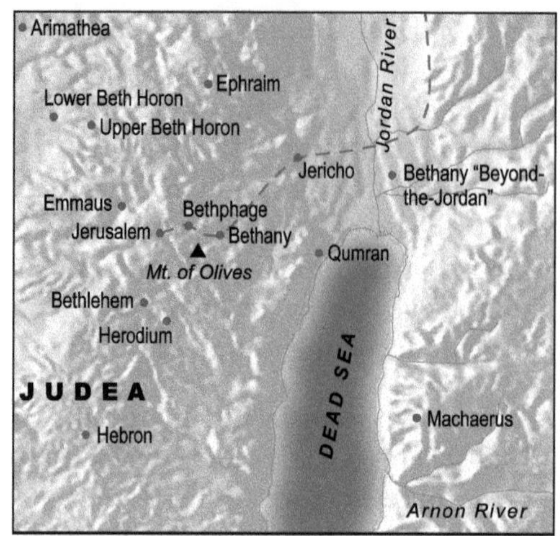


God's special tribe in place of the firstborn of all the Israelites (Num. 3:41, 45; 8:18). Their role was to assist the priests in the service of the tabernacle (Num. 18:4) and later the temple. Levites are mentioned only three times in the New Testament.[290]

The priests were also Levites, but were more specifically descendants of Aaron, the brother of Moses and first priest of Israel (Ex. 28:1–3). They were entrusted with the religious oversight of the nation, including teaching the law (Lev. 10:11; Deut. 17:18), administering the temple and the sacrificial system, and inspecting uncleanness, especially leprosy, in the people (Lev. 13–14).

Touching a dead body rendered priests and Levites ceremonially unclean and so unable to fulfill temple commitments (Lev. 21–22). The two who passed by may have suspected the man was dead. For the priest, however, this is a poor excuse, since he is specifically said to be "going down" the road and so presumably traveling *away* from Jerusalem after his temple service. Many priests were also members of the aristocratic elite and so would not associate with commoners. Jewish hearers may therefore have expected such snobbery from these two. Perhaps they would have expected a local rabbi or a respected Pharisee to come along next and help the man . . . .But a Samaritan?

**Pouring on oil and wine (10:34).** Both oil and wine had medicinal value (Isa. 1:6; *m. Šabb.* 19:2). The oil soothed and the wine served as a disinfectant.

**Took him to an inn (10:34).** The term *pandocheion* refers to a public lodging place, run by an "innkeeper" (*pandocheus,* 10:35), where a traveler might rent a room. See comments on 2:7 for the distinction between this and the so-called "inn" (*katalyma*) of the nativity story.

**Two silver coins (10:35).** The Greek says "two denarii." A denarius was equivalent to a day's wages for a laborer.

### REFLECTIONS

**LOVING GOD AND LOVING YOUR** neighbor are the two greatest commandments. But who is your neighbor? When Jesus was asked this question, he told a story that shocked his hearers. A true neighbor is one who is willing to look past the differences that traditionally divide people and to love others unconditionally and without prejudice. Who would God have you to reach out to today?

## At the Home of Martha and Mary (10:38–42)

The account of Jesus' visit to the home of Martha and Mary demonstrates the importance of learning from Jesus and being in relationship with him. Such a relationship takes priority even over service. When Martha complains to Jesus that her sister Mary is neglecting her household duties and leaving all the work to her, Jesus gently corrects her. While Martha is occupied with things, Mary is occupied with Jesus. She has chosen the better, which "will not be taken away from her." The "better" is the privilege of learning at Jesus' feet as a faithful disciple.

**A village where a woman named Martha opened her home to him (10:38).** We learn from John's Gospel that Mary, Martha, and their brother, Lazarus, are good friends of Jesus.[291] They live in Bethany, a few miles east of Jerusalem (see Luke 19:29). The invitation to Jesus is identified specifically with Martha, the matron of the home.

**Mary, who sat at the Lord's feet (10:39).** To sit at the feet of a respected rabbi was the position of a disciple. In Acts 22:3 Paul says he was instructed "at the feet of Gamaliel" (NRSV), a leading rabbi of Jerusalem (cf. Luke 8:35). The Mishnah speaks of a similar position: "Let thy house be a meeting-house for the Sages and sit amid the dust of their feet and drink in their words with thirst."[292] Mary's initiative in taking this position is particularly shocking, since rabbis did not have women disciples. Girls did not even receive a formal education; they were taught only in household duties like sewing and weaving.[293] In the Mishnah it is said that "if any man give his daughter a knowledge of the Law it is as though he taught her lechery."[294]

**Martha was distracted by all the preparations (10:40).** Literally, "distracted by much service [*diakonia*]." Jewish society placed a high value on hospitality, and a woman's honor and reputation depended on her ability to manage her household well.[295] Since service was a woman's highest calling, Martha's complaint against Mary would be seen as legitimate. Yet for Jesus all her hard work is a mere distraction compared to Mary's desire to sit at Jesus' feet as a disciple and learn from him. Jesus shatters cultural expectations by affirming the status of a woman as his disciple.

## Jesus' Teaching on Prayer (11:1–13)

Luke here presents various teachings of Jesus on prayer, stressing dependence and trust in God. When his disciples ask him to teach them to pray, Jesus gives them a simple model prayer that sums up the essence of effective communication with God (11:1–4).

Jesus follows this model prayer with a parable about prayer (11:5–8). The parable of the persistent neighbor has been interpreted in two different ways. Some have argued that it is similar to the parable of the unjust judge (18:1–8), teaching God's desire for his people to be bold and persistent in prayer.

For others the parable is not about persistence (the borrower only asks once) or about boldness (what the man does is a cultural necessity, not a bold action), but about issues of honor and shame.[296] It must be understood in the context of Palestinian peasant society, where hospitality was the highest of values and the obligation of the entire community. The man who receives the traveler does not have enough food to provide the necessary level of hospitality, so he *must* go to a neighbor. This is expected behavior. While the sleeping neighbor has no *desire* to help because of the inconvenience involved, *not* helping would be unthinkable, an act of shame. Jesus concludes that while the sleeper may not get up because of friendship (notice he does not address the borrower as "friend"), he will get up to retain honor for himself and for the community. In this case, the parable teaches that God will surely answer prayers because it is a question of his honor and glory.

Whether the parable is about persistence in prayer or about God's honor, the proverb that follows turns to the petitioner's responsibility to pray and the certainty that God will answer (11:9–10). It is a natural transition from this proverb to Jesus' analogy of a father granting the request of a son. Fathers naturally desire to meet the needs of their children with good gifts. If this is true of sinful human beings, how much more will it be true of our loving heavenly Father, who gives us the greatest gift of all, the Holy Spirit (11:11–13).

**Father (11:2).** The Greek address *pater* almost certainly has behind it the Aramaic *Abba*, the term of intimacy that Jesus used to address God (Mark 14:36) and that he encouraged his disciples to use.[297] While it has been commonly said that *Abba* is a children's term meaning "daddy," this is not quite right, since Jewish adults also addressed their parents in this way. *Abba* was, however, a term of considerable intimacy. While Jews would sometimes refer to God as "our heavenly Father," they rarely if ever addressed him as "my father" or "father" (*Abba*).[298] Jesus calls his followers to a new intimacy with God through his unique relationship with the Father.

**Hallowed be your name, your kingdom come (11:2).** The petition means "cause your name to be honored." It points both to God's ultimate victory at the establishment of his kingdom, but also to the present, as God's people "hallow" his name through righteous living. "Your name" was a Jewish expression for "you" and a way of avoiding the holy name of God. There are interesting parallels to the Jewish prayer in Aramaic known as the *Qaddish* ("holy"), recited after the sermon in synagogue services:

*Exalted and hallowed be his*
*great name*
*in the world which he created*
*according to his will.*
*May he let his kingdom rule*
*in your lifetime and in your days*
*and in the lifetime*
*of the whole house of Israel speedily*
*and soon.*
*Praised be his great name from*
*eternity to eternity.*
*And to this, say: Amen.*[299]

**Give us each day our daily bread (11:3).** "Bread" here means "food" (cf. 7:33; 2 Thess. 3:8). The word translated "daily" (*epiousion*) is a rare Greek word with an uncertain meaning. It can mean (1) "necessary for existence," (2) "for today," or (3) "for the coming day." The reference recalls God's daily provision of manna for Israel in the desert (Ex. 16), as well as God's daily sustenance of his people (Prov. 30:8).

**Forgive us our sins, for we also forgive (11:4).** The idea that forgiven people should be willing to forgive was a common one in Judaism. Sirach 28:2 reads: "Forgive your neighbor the wrong he has done, and then your sins will be pardoned when you pray."

**Lead us not into temptation (11:4).** This phrase has caused difficulties since God does not tempt his people (James 1:13). One solution is that the word "temptation" (*peirasmos*) can also mean "trial" or "testing." Some have argued that this is a technical term for the eschatological "hour of trial" of the tribulation period (Rev. 3:10). Yet such a specific case would be odd in Jesus' general teaching on prayer. The term can mean testing in general, and there are certainly Old Testament examples where God tests his people.[300] Yet it would be unusual for Jesus to encourage prayer for the removal of all tests of faith. It seems best to retain the translation "temptation," not in the sense of "do not tempt us," but rather in terms of active protection from temptation (something like, "Protect us from the tempting power of sin"). Jesus says something similar in Luke 22:40, 46: "Pray that you will not fall into temptation." A prayer in the Babylonian Talmud reads, "Bring me not into the power of sin, nor into the power of guilt, nor into the power of temptation."[301]

**At midnight . . . a friend of mine on a journey (11:5–6).** While Bedouins in the desert often traveled by night to avoid the heat of the night, such travel was uncommon in Palestine. The friend's arrival is something unusual and inconvenient for those who must provide hospitality.[302]

**Lend me three loaves of bread (11:5).** It is debated among scholars whether bread was baked daily or less often in Palestinian villages. The latter seems more likely, with village women cooperating in the baking.[303] Everyone in the village knew who had baked most recently. Though some of the day's bread may have been left in the borrower's house, to feed a guest a broken loaf would have been an insult.

**I have nothing to set before him (11:6).** As in Middle Eastern culture today, hospitality was of critical importance in first-century Palestine and involved the whole community. Both the host who received a late night guest and the man already in bed would have been obligated to provide the best for the traveler. Jesus' hearers would have considered the "hassles" of getting up and unbolting the door a minor inconvenience compared to the scandal of not providing adequate hospitality.

**The door is already locked, and my children are with me in bed (11:7).** This is a peasant home where the whole family sleeps in a single room on mats on the floor. A wooden or iron bar through rings secures the door. To get up and unbolt it would disturb the whole family.

**Because of the man's boldness (11:8).** The Greek term *anaideia* normally carries the negative sense of "shamelessness." This is interpreted in the NIV positively in the sense of "boldness" or persistence and is applied to the borrower who is at the door. The Greek is ambiguous, however, and may refer to the sleeper, whose "shamelessness" would be revealed if he *failed* to provide bread for hospitality.[304] Bailey takes a similar approach, claiming that the term here means "avoidance of shame" and that the sleeper gets up so as to avoid the shame that would come to him if he did not provide hospitality.[305]

**A fish . . . a snake . . . an egg . . . a scorpion (11:11–12).** Fish bear a general resemblance to snakes in their slimy appearance. The parallel between eggs and scorpions may be because the latter roll themselves into balls[306] (see comments on 10:19 for snakes and scorpions as symbols of danger and evil).

**If you then, though you are evil . . . how much more (11:13).** This is a common rabbinic "lesser to greater" (*qal wāḥômer*) argument.

## Jesus and Beelzebub (11:14–28)

This episode begins a series of controversies between Jesus and the religious leaders that will run through the rest of chapter 11. It will climax in 11:54 with their growing opposition and desire to trap him in his words.

The first controversy arises from Jesus' exorcism of a mute man. When some of Jesus' opponents accuse him of casting out demons by the power of Beelzebub, he answers with two arguments. (1) He points out how foolish it would be for Satan to cast out his own demonic forces, since a house or kingdom divided against itself cannot stand (11:17–18). (2) He notes that their accusation would indict their own followers, who also claim to perform exorcisms (11:19).

Jesus then goes on the offensive. Since his exorcisms are the work of God and not Satan, they reveal the presence and power of God's kingdom (11:20). Satan is like a strong man whose castle is being disarmed and overpowered by Jesus, the stronger man (11:20–23). Jesus then warns of the danger of exorcism without the inward spiritual renewal that comes with the kingdom of God (11:24–26).

Jesus' teaching on exorcism is followed by a short episode in which a woman in the crowd shouts an acclamation of praise for Jesus. Jesus, however, directs the praise away from himself and toward the message of the kingdom of God: "Blessed rather are those who hear the word of God and obey it" (11:27–28). True spiritual blessings come not through the acclamation of others, but through obedience to God's Word.

**A demon that was mute (11:14).** For the link between disease and demonic possession see comments on 4:39. In Isaiah

### ▸ Beelzebub, the Prince of Demons

The Greek text actually reads *beelzeboul* (in some manuscripts) and *beezeboul* (other manuscripts). The spelling *beelzebub*, which appears in the NIV, comes from the Latin version (and the KJV), which has assimilated the text to 2 Kings 1:2, 3, 6. The historical background to the name is disputed. The prefix "Beel-" comes from the Canaanite god Baal (meaning "lord"), and Baal-Zebul probably means either "Baal, the Prince," or "Baal of the Exalted Abode."[A-41] The Israelites seem to have mocked this name, changing it to Baal-Zebub (Gk. *beelzeboub*), meaning "lord of the flies" (see Judg. 10:6; 2 Kings 1:2, 3, 6).[A-42]

Whatever its origin, the name Beelzeboul eventually came to be used in Judaism for the "prince of demons," the highest ranking angel in heaven prior to his fall.[A-43] The literature of Judaism contains a variety of names for the chief of demons. The book of *Jubilees* refers to the chief of the spirits as Mastema, a Hebrew term presumably meaning "hostility."[A-44] In the apocryphal book of Tobit the head of the demons is Asmodeus (Tobit 3:8, 17), and in *1 Enoch* 6:1 Semyaz is the leader of the fallen angels (cf. *1 Enoch* 8:7). Belial, or Beliar, meaning "the worthless one," is one of the most common names for Satan in the Dead Sea Scrolls and elsewhere in Judaism.[A-45] The New Testament refers to Satan by a variety of names, including the devil, the evil one (Matt. 6:13; 13:19), the father of lies (John 8:44), the god of this age (2 Cor. 4:4), the ruler of the kingdom of the air (Eph. 2:2), the dragon (Rev. 12:9), and the ancient serpent (12:9).

35:6, the healing of those who are mute is a sign of God's end-time salvation. For demons and demonization see comments on Luke 4:31–37; 8:26–39.

**Asking for a sign from heaven (11:16).** It is not clear what kind of a sign they are requesting. Signs from heaven in the Old Testament include the sun standing still (Josh. 10:13), the provision of manna from heaven (Ex. 16), and the turning back of the sun for Hezekiah.[307] There are also eschatological signs in the heavens predicted in the Old Testament.[308]

**Any kingdom divided against itself will be ruined (11:17).** Throughout history, civil war has weakened and destroyed nations from within. A first-century Jewish hearer would certainly think of the civil war that divided Israel and Judah (1 Kings 12), resulting in weakness and eventual destruction. More recently, the Roman occupation of Palestine took place during a period of division and conflict within the Hasmonean dynasty.

**By whom do your followers (11:19).** Lit., "your sons." The "sons" of the Pharisees, like the "sons of the prophets" (e.g., 2 Kings 2:3, RSV), were disciples or followers of the Pharisees. For Jewish exorcisms see the texts cited in "Demonization and Exorcism in the First Century" at Luke 8:26–39.

**I drive out demons by the finger of God (11:20).** While Matthew has "the Spirit of God," Luke has "the finger of God." The two expressions mean essentially the same thing—God's power—but Luke's reference alludes back to Exodus 8:19, where Pharaoh's magicians recognize the "finger of God" in Moses' miracles. The Ten Commandments are also said to have been inscribed by God's finger (Ex. 31:18; Deut. 9:10), and in Psalm 8:3 the heavens are said to be the work of God's fingers. Anthropomorphic images, especially the "hand" of God or the "arm" of God, are common in the Old Testament.

**When a strong man, fully armed, guards his own house (11:21).** While Mark's parallel presents an image of household robbery (Mark 3:27), the picture here is one of warfare, with two lords battling over a castle estate. Through his exorcisms, Jesus is disarming Satan and taking the spoils (=people bound by him) from his castle. The reference to "dividing the spoils" may be an allusion to Isaiah 53:12 and the ultimate victory of the Suffering Servant of the Lord.

**He who is not with me is against me (11:23).** This picks up the battle image of the previous verses. In Joshua 5:13, Joshua meets the commander of the Lord's army and, unaware of his identity, asks, "Are you for us or for our enemies?"

**He who does not gather with me, scatters (11:23).** This second image is probably related to the gathering of sheep. In the Old Testament, Israel is often identified as a flock and the Lord as their shepherd.[309]

**Takes seven other spirits (11:26).** The number "seven" may indicate completeness or may simply emphasize the greater power now controlling the man. There are verbal parallels in the "seven spirits" that are before the throne of God in Revelation 1:4; 3:1; 4:5; 5:6 and in the "seven angels" who stand before the glory of the Lord.[310]

**Blessed is the mother who gave you birth (11:27).** The Greek says literally, "Blessed is the womb that bore you and breasts at which you nursed," a figure of speech known as synecdoche, whereby a part of something is used for the whole. The NIV replaces "womb" and "breasts" with the thing signified, "mother." For a similar statement about Mary see 1:42.

It was common both in Greco-Roman and Jewish society to praise a child by congratulating the mother. The first-century Roman satirist Petronius writes, "How blessed is the mother who bore such an one as you."[311] The famous Rabbi Johannan ben Zakkai is said to have praised his student Joshua ben Hananiah with the statement, "Happy is she that bare him."[312]

## The Sign of Jonah (11:29–32)

In 11:16 some responded to Jesus' miracles by asking for a sign from heaven. Jesus now answers by declaring that only one more sign will be given to this wicked generation, the "sign of Jonah" (11:29–30). In Matthew's Gospel this sign is identified with Jesus' resurrection (Matt. 12:40). For Luke, the stress seems to be on Jonah's preaching and call for repentance (see Luke 11:32). At the final judgment, those who *did* respond to God's word—the Queen of Sheba and the people of Nineveh—will condemn the present generation for rejecting a greater witness than Solomon or Jonah.

**JONAH AND THE FISH**

A Byzantine era pottery sherd.

**A wicked generation (11:29).** See comments on 9:41.

**Jonah (11:30).** Jonah, the son of Amittai, is mentioned in 2 Kings 14:25 as well as the book of Jonah. He was from Gath Hepher in Zebulun and ministered from about 800–750 BC, predicting the restoration of Israel's borders during the reign of Jeroboam II. Jonah is best known, of course, from the book of Jonah, where he rejected God's call to preach his impending judgment against wicked Nineveh, the great city of the Assyrian empire (Jonah 1:1–2). When Jonah fled on a ship bound for Tarshish (probably a city in Spain), God pursued him with a storm. Jonah ended up in the belly of a great fish, where he repented and was spit up on dry land. Jonah finally fulfilled God's call to preach to Nineveh. When the city repented, however, Jonah was not pleased, for his hopes were placed on its destruction. The book ends with God's rebuke to Jonah (and implicitly, to the nation Israel) for his lack of compassion for a lost world.

**The Queen of the South (11:31).** This is the queen of Sheba, mentioned in 1 Kings 10:1–29 (cf. 2 Chron. 9:1–12), who traveled a great distance (the "ends of the earth" is hyperbole) to hear Solomon's wisdom. Sheba was located in southern Arabia.

**Solomon's wisdom (11:31).** In 1 Kings 3 Solomon asks for a discerning heart to rule God's people well. The Lord was pleased with this request and granted him not only wisdom, but also riches, power, and long life (1 Kings 3:10–15). Solomon's wisdom is said to be greater than all the kings of the earth (4:29–34; 10:23–24) and far surpassed the queen's expectations (10:6–9).

**The men of Nineveh . . . repented (11:32).** Nineveh's notorious wickedness is identified in the book of Jonah as the reason for her impending judgment.[313] The city's extraordinary conversion through the preaching of Jonah stands in stark contrast to Israel's failure to respond to Jesus' even more powerful words and deeds.

## The Lamp of the Body (11:33–36)

Jesus' teaching on hearing and responding to God's word continues with two analogies related to light and darkness. In the first, Jesus' kingdom proclamation is like light from a lamp that must shine forth for all to see. The second analogy takes this meaning forward with reference to the person receiving the light. Just as external light must be taken in by the eye in order to benefit the body, so Jesus' teaching must be appropriated by the person.

**No one lights a lamp (11:33).** See 8:16 for a similar lamp image.

**In a place where it will be hidden (11:33).** This phrase translates the Greek word *kryptē*, which indicates a dark and hidden place. It was commonly used of cellars, crypts, and vaults.[314] Since Palestinian homes did not usually have cellars, Luke may be referring to a hidden alcove or wall recess.

◀ LAMP

**Your eye is the lamp of your body (11:34).** Some Greek writers considered the eye to be a source of light that shone outward to illuminate objects.[315] While this could be the sense intended here, more likely Jesus means that the eye is the lamp *for* the body, that is, it lets light *in* so that the person can see.

**When your eyes are good . . . when they are bad (11:34).** The word translated "good" is the Greek word *haplous*, which means literally "single" or "simple." It can be used of eyes in the sense of "healthy" or "sound," but can also carry moral connotations of goodness or generosity. There is probably a play on words here, since *ponēros* can mean either "unhealthy" or "evil."

**Light . . . darkness (11:34).** Light and darkness were common symbols for good and evil in both Greek and Hebrew literature.[316] The Qumran community, which produced the Dead Sea Scrolls, considered themselves to be the "sons of light" at spiritual war against the "sons of darkness" (cf. 16:8).

## Six Woes (11:37–54)

The references to those who receive the light and those who reject it transitions naturally into an indictment by Jesus of the Pharisees, who are rejecting his message of the kingdom of God. The whole passage has the tone of the Old Testament prophets, who rebuked the nation of Israel for her wickedness and hypocrisy (e.g., Isa. 1). The context is a banquet setting with a Pharisee. When he is surprised that Jesus does not wash in the traditional manner, Jesus responds by noting the hypocrisy of the Pharisees. Though they "clean the outside of the cup"—an external show of religiosity—inside they are full of greed and wickedness. Jesus then launches into a series of six "woes" against the hypocrisy and pride of the Jewish religious leaders. They respond with fierce opposition, seeking to trap Jesus through his words.

**A Pharisee (11:37).** See comments on 5:17.

**Reclined at the table (11:37).** The reclining position may indicate a banquet setting or a Sabbath meal.[317] Jews normally ate two meals a day, a mid-morning and a mid-afternoon meal. Three meals were eaten on the Sabbath.[318] The word Luke uses in verse 38 (*ariston*) normally indicates the mid-morning meal.

**TOMB OF THE PROPHETS**

This tomb on the Mount of Olives contains over 30 burial shafts (*kokhim*). A medieval Jewish tradition claims this tomb was the burial place of Haggai, Zecharaiah, and Malachi.

**Jesus did not first wash (11:38).** This is a ceremonial washing of the hands before the meal (see Mark 7:1–5 for a fuller description). The Pharisees had developed detailed regulations concerning the amount of water to be used, the kinds of vessels from which to pour, and the manner of pouring.[319] Such minutia was not commanded in the Old Testament.

**You Pharisees clean the outside of the cup (11:39).** The Old Testament law refers to occasions where a cup was to be cleaned or destroyed when something ceremonially unclean fell in it (Lev. 11:33) or if someone unclean touched it (Lev. 15:12). The Pharisees set out detailed regulations to govern the cleaning of vessels of various kinds.[320] Jesus' point is that the Pharisees are concerned with "externals" while ignoring the real matters of the heart.

**Greed (11:39).** This is a strong Greek word (*harpagē*), which can mean violent greed, robbery, extortion, or plunder.

**Give what is inside the dish to the poor (11:41).** The Greek literally says, "Give as alms what is inside. . . ." Giving alms to the poor was a sign of great piety in Judaism since it reflected God's mercy and care for the poor. The apocryphal book of Tobit says, "Prayer with fasting is good, but better than both is almsgiving with righteousness. . . . For almsgiving saves from death and purges away every sin. Those who give alms will enjoy a full life."[321]

**Woe to you (11:42).** For "woes" see comments on 6:20–26.

**A tenth of your mint, rue . . . herbs (11:42).** Tithing of crops and livestock was commanded in the Old Testament, and the Mishnah discusses tithing requirements in great detail.[322] Interestingly, *m. Šebiᶜit* 9:1 lists "rue" as one of the herbs that is exempt from tithing. Jesus' point is that the Pharisees are meticulous in the small things, but then ignore the truly important things, like justice and love for God. God's demand for justice is a leading theme among the prophets.[323]

**The most important seats in the synagogues (11:43).** These are the places of honor near the front, where the leading elders sit.

**Greetings in the marketplaces (11:43).** These are not simple greetings, but honorary greetings of an inferior to a superior. Later Jewish literature speaks of the need to greet first a teacher of the Mosaic law.[324]

**Unmarked graves (11:44).** Touching a grave rendered a Jew ceremonially unclean because of the corpse inside (cf. Num. 5:2). If a grave was unmarked someone might accidentally touch it (cf. the "whitewashed tombs" of Matt. 23:27). Jesus' point is that while the Pharisees consider themselves to be pure, they are defiling everyone with whom they come in contact.

**Experts in the law (11:45).** Luke uses the term *nomikos* ("lawyer") here. See comments on 5:17 for their close association with the Pharisees.

**Tombs for the prophets (11:47).** It was common during this time to build tombs in honor of the prophets and other Old Testament figures. David's tomb is mentioned in Acts 2:29–30.

**Your forefathers who killed them (11:47).** Israel's persecution of the prophets is a common theme in the Old Testament.[325]

**God in his wisdom said (11:49).** The Greek says literally, "The wisdom of God said. . . ." Wisdom is often personified in the Old Testament and in Judaism, speaking God's word and imparting his wisdom to humanity.[326] The reference here could be to Jesus, who is God's wisdom incarnate, or to God himself (the NIV takes the latter interpretation). The quote that follows ("I will send them prophets . . .") is not from any known source.

**This generation will be held responsible for the blood (11:50).** The sense of corporate and accumulated guilt is a common theme in the Old Testament and in Judaism. Later generations suffer for the sins of their ancestors.[327] The language here echoes the Old Testament requirements for the death penalty for murder. Blood must be atoned for with blood.[328] In the Old Testament God promises to avenge the blood of his righteous servants.[329]

**The blood of Abel to the blood of Zechariah (11:51).** The murder of Abel by his brother Cain is recorded in Genesis 4:8. The stoning of Zechariah son of Jehoiada appears in 2 Chronicles 24:20–22 and was expanded upon in later Jewish tradition.[330] In the Hebrew canon, Chronicles is placed at the very end, as part of the section called the Writings. Jesus is thus saying, "from the first murder in the first book to the last murder in the last."

**The key to knowledge (11:52).** The "key" here may refer to access to the kingdom of God (see Matt. 16:19; 23:13) or perhaps to the "house of wisdom" of

Proverbs 9:1–4.[331] Though the scribes are to provide the people with access to God's Word, instead they are obscuring it from them.

## Warnings and Encouragements (12:1–12)

After describing Jesus' confrontation with the religious leaders in chapter 11, Luke turns in chapter 12 to his instruction for the coming time of crisis. Jesus' popularity is high as a crowd of thousands gathers to hear him. Yet his teaching is directed primarily to his disciples (12:1), since his greatest focus now is to train them as he journeys to Jerusalem.

**The yeast of the Pharisees (12:1).** The background here is the Passover command to the Jews to remove all yeast from their homes and not to eat unleavened bread for seven days (Ex. 12:14–20). Yeast became a symbol in Judaism for the permeating power of sin (cf. 1 Cor. 5:6).[332]

**There is nothing concealed that will not be disclosed (12:2).** Proverbs 15:3 says, "The eyes of the LORD are everywhere, keeping watch on the wicked and the good." The reference here is to eschatological judgment. Since God sees and knows all things, every human deed will be righteously judged.[333]

**Do not be afraid of those who kill the body (12:4).** Such is the appropriate attitude for a martyr, whose focus is on heavenly realities. In *4 Maccabees*, a first-century Jewish text about the martyrdom of a man named Eleazar and his seven sons during the Maccabean period, the statement is made, "Let us not fear him who thinks he is killing us. . . . For if we so die, Abraham and Isaac and Jacob will welcome us, and all the fathers will praise us."[334]

**To throw you into hell (12:5).** The word "hell" is the Greek term *geenna*, a transliteration of the Hebrew Gehenna. It means "the Valley of (the son[s] of) Hinnom," a ravine running along the southwestern edge of Jerusalem (also called Topheth in the Old Testament). The valley became notorious as a place where the sons and daughters of Judah were offered as burnt sacrifices to the god Baal Molech.[335] Later it was used as a place to burn rubbish (Jer. 19:2, 10–13). The continually burning fire and stench provided an appropriate metaphor for the place of fiery judgment prepared for the wicked. God's judgment is already associated with fire in the Old Testament (Deut. 32:22), and a fiery place of torment for the wicked appears in Jewish and Christian literature.[336]

**Five sparrows sold for two pennies (12:6).** The word for penny here is *assarion*, a Roman copper coin worth only one-sixteenth of a denarius (see 7:41). The sparrow was one of the cheapest things sold in the marketplace and may have been eaten by the poor.[337] If God remembers even

HINNOM VALLEY

"Gehenna" was located along the west and south sides of Jerusalem.

these "worthless" birds, how much more does he care for human beings.

**The very hairs of your head are all numbered (12:7).** Like the sparrow image in verse 6, this is a "from the lesser to the greater" (*qal wāḥômer*) style of Jewish argument. If God knows such insignificant details, how much more does he care for the important things. A similar image appears in the Old Testament, where "not a hair" being damaged means complete protection from harm.[338]

**The Son of Man will also acknowledge him (12:8).** The image here is of the throne room of God on the Day of Judgment. The reference to the Son of Man recalls the judgment scene in Daniel 7:7–14. For background on the Son of Man, see comments on Luke 5:24; 9:26.

**Before the angels of God (12:8).** When the throne room of God is described in Scripture, angelic attendants are present (see Isa. 6:1–4; Rev. 4:6–11). They are gathered here for the Day of Judgment.

**Anyone who blasphemes against the Holy Spirit (12:10).** Though blasphemy against the Spirit is not mentioned in the Old Testament, it does contain references to rebellion against and grieving the Spirit of God in the context of Israel's failure in the desert (Ps. 106:32–33; Isa. 63:10). The reference here (as in Mark 3:29) appears to be final rejection of the Spirit's revelation through Jesus, resulting in the certainty of judgment. This is because the Holy Spirit provides the authenticating evidence of the truth. It is turning to the darkness in the face of the greatest light.

**Synagogues, rulers and authorities (12:11).** Synagogues served as both administrative and worship centers in first-century Judaism, so the early Jewish Christians received trials and sentences there (cf. the disciples before the Sanhedrin in Acts 4:1–22; 5:17–42; 6:12–15). "Rulers and authorities" probably refer to Roman and other Gentile authorities (see Luke 21:12).

## The Parable of the Rich Fool (12:13–21)

The parable of the rich fool demonstrates the dangers of covetousness and of not recognizing that our resources are merely gifts from God to be used for his service. A striking parallel appears in the book of Sirach:

> One becomes rich through diligence and self-denial, and the reward allotted to him is this: when he says, "I have found rest, and now I shall feast on my goods!" he does not know how long it will be until he leaves them to others and dies. (Sir. 11:18–19)

**Teacher (12:13).** Rabbis of that day often served as mediators for disputes, particularly those that involved the interpretation of the Mosaic law.

**Divide the inheritance with me (12:13).** The Old Testament laws of inheritance are set out in Numbers 27:1–11 and Deuteronomy 21:15–17. Rabbinic expansions of these laws appear in the Mishnah.[339] The firstborn son was to receive a double portion of the inheritance (Deut. 21:17). It is this "birthright" that Jacob purchased from Esau in Genesis 25:29–34. Since the man here assumes he is in the right (he does not ask Jesus to mediate, but rather tells him what to do!), he is probably a younger son asking for the share he deserves according to the law. Jesus' response concerning the insignificance of possessions would have been shocking in a society where inheritance and land rights were of great social importance.

**Be on your guard against all kinds of greed (12:15).** Commands and warnings against greed and covetousness are common in the Old Testament,[340] in Judaism,[341] and in the early church.[342] The *Testament of Judah* 19:1 (second century B.C.) reads, "My children, love of money leads to idolatry, because once they are led astray by money, they designate as gods those who are not gods. It makes anyone who has it go out of his mind."

The pseudepigraphic work *1 Enoch* speaks of the ultimate destruction of those who accumulate wealth:

*Woe unto you who gain silver and*
*gold by unjust means;*
*you will then say, "We have grown*
*rich and accumulated goods,*
*we have acquired everything that we*
*have desired.*
*So now let us do whatever we like;*
*for we have gathered silver,*
*we have filled our treasuries (with*
*money) like water.*
*And many are the laborers in our*
*houses."*
*Your lies flow like water.*
*For your wealth shall not endure*
*but it shall take off from you quickly*
*for you have acquired it all unjustly,*
*and you shall be given over to a great*
*curse.* (1 Enoch *97:8–10)*

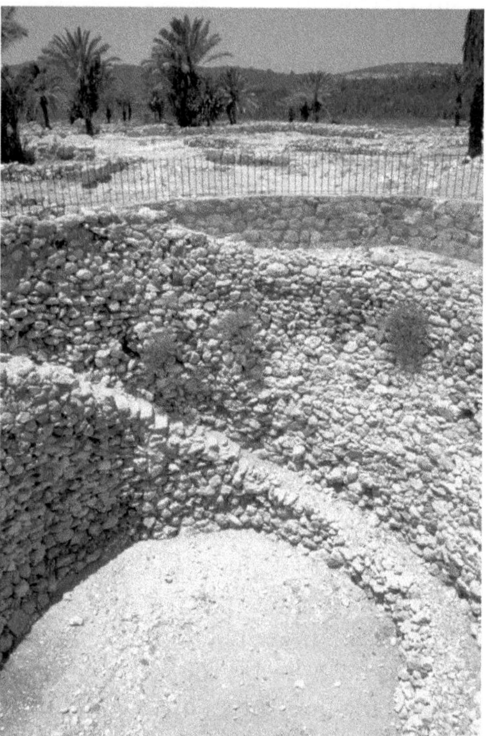

**GRAIN STORAGE BIN**

The underground grain storage bin at Megiddo.

**Take life easy; eat, drink and be merry (12:19).** This was a common expression in both Jewish and Greek literature, indicating a carefree, sensuous lifestyle.[343] It was characteristic of the Greek Epicurean lifestyle, which sought comfort and pleasure above everything else in life.

**You fool! (12:20).** The Greek term for "fool" (*aphrōn*) is a strong one. In this context it indicates not only stupidity, but moral and spiritual deficiency. The term is used in the LXX in Psalm 14:1 (13:1 LXX): "The fool (*aphrōn*) said in his heart, 'There is no God'" (cf. Ps. 53:1 [52:2 LXX]).

**Your life will be demanded from you (12:20).** The term translated "life" here is *psychē*, which can mean life, soul, or self (cf. 12:19). The meaning here is the whole person—physical as well as spiritual destruction. There is an ironic play on words between 12:19 and 20. The man selfishly speaks to his "soul" (=himself), and it is this very soul that he loses. See 9:24: "For whoever wants to save his life (*psychē*) will lose it. . . ."

**Then who will get what you have prepared for yourself? (12:20).** The Old Testament speaks of the futility of storing up wealth that will only go to others who have not worked for it.[344]

## Do Not Worry (12:22–34)

Jesus' negative illustration about the dangers of greed (12:13–21) is now balanced with positive instruction on how to live a life of trust and dependence on God, free from worry and anxiety. Using a rabbinic "from the lesser to the greater" style of argument, Jesus demonstrates that since God feeds the birds of the air and beautifully clothes the flowers of the field, he will surely care for his own children. Since God has already given us his eternal kingdom, the best one can do is to sell temporal earthly possessions and to give them to the poor.

**Consider the ravens . . . God feeds them (12:24).** In antiquity ravens were considered careless creatures that even failed to return to their own nests.[345] For the Israelites they were unclean birds, forbidden to be eaten and so of little value (Lev. 11:15; Deut. 14:14). Yet the Old Testament says that God cares for them and provides them with food: "He provides food for the cattle and for the young ravens when they call" (Ps. 147:9; cf. Job 38:41).

**Add a single hour to his life (12:25).** The Greek here is odd, reading literally "add a single cubit to his length." A cubit (*pēchys*) was a unit of measure of about eighteen inches (the length from the elbow to the end of the hand). The term for "length" (*hēlikia*) can mean either "life span" or "height." While the text could mean "add eighteen inches to his height," this would be odd, since the point is that this is a very little thing! More likely, a person's life is here portrayed as striding forward (in time). Jesus says, "By worrying you cannot add a single step on the road of life."

**Consider how the lilies grow (12:27).** The "lily" here has been identified with various flowers, including the white lily, the Easter daisy, the autumn crocus, and others.[346] Perhaps the most interesting suggestion is that it is the purple anemone, which is then contrasted with the royal purple of Solomon's robes.[347]

**Even Solomon in all his splendor (12:27).** Solomon's extraordinary riches are described in 1 Kings 10:4–23 and 2 Chronicles 9:13–21.

**Here today, and tomorrow is thrown into the fire (12:28).** The temporal and fleeting nature of plants is a common Old Testament image.[348] Dried grass was used to kindle fires.

**The pagan world (12:30).** The Greek here reads "the nations of the world," a reference to the Gentile world. Remember that Jesus is speaking to a Jewish

LILIES ON THE MOUNT OF BEATITUDES

audience, which viewed Gentiles as antagonistic to God's kingdom values.

**But seek his kingdom (12:31).** On the kingdom of God, see comments on 4:43; 17:20. Seeking God's kingdom means focusing one's life on things that have eternal value rather than on material things.

**Do not be afraid, little flock (12:32).** God's people are often identified as his flock in the Old Testament (see comments on 11:23).[349] Since God is a protecting shepherd, they have nothing to fear (on Old Testament commands not to fear, see comments on 1:12).

**To give you the kingdom (12:32).** On eschatological rulership by God's people, see comments on 22:30.

**Give to the poor (12:33).** Literally, "give as alms" (for the importance of almsgiving see Tobit 4:8–11 and comments on Luke 11:41). The command is not to make oneself destitute, but to recognize that all of our possessions are to be used for God's purposes.

**A treasure in heaven (12:33).** Various Jewish texts speak of good works (such as almsgiving) as a means of storing up true treasures.[350] Sirach says, "Lose your silver for the sake of a brother or a friend, and do not let it rust under a stone and be lost. Lay up your treasure according to the commandments of the Most High, and it will profit you more than gold" (Sir. 29:10–11).

**REFLECTIONS**

**IN TODAY'S BUSY WORLD, IT'S EASY** to let worry and anxiety control our lives and affect our relationships. Jesus calls on his followers to simple trust and dependence on their heavenly Father. The answer to anxiety is a deep-seated trust and dependence on God, and a focus on his kingdom and purpose in this world. In the end, this is all that really matters.

## Watchfulness (12:35–48)

Jesus' call for an eternal perspective on material possessions in 12:22–34 now transitions naturally into a call for good stewardship and readiness for the return of the Son of Man. Jesus draws four analogies, all related to a Middle Eastern household where a master had many servants to manage his affairs.

**Dressed ready for service (12:35).** Literally, "let your waist be girded." The reference is to long garments that were drawn up around the waist and tucked in so that the servant could move around freely and quickly. In Exodus 12:11 the Passover was to be eaten with "your cloak tucked into your belt" (KJV, "your loins girded"), so that the Israelites could leave Egypt quickly.[351]

**Keep your lamps burning (12:35).** Having a lamp burning was a sign of vigilance, as with the continually burning lamp outside the curtain of the tabernacle (Ex. 27:20–21; Lev. 24:2).

**A wedding banquet (12:36).** Wedding banquets were times of extravagant festivities and celebration, lasting an entire week (Judg. 14:17) or even two (Tobit 8:20; 10:7). See comments on 5:34 for more details.

**He will dress himself to serve (12:37).** The image of a master putting on servants' clothes and serving is a shocking one; it recalls Jesus' washing the disciples' feet in John 13. The scene here is probably meant to represent the messianic banquet, when "the LORD Almighty will prepare a feast of rich food for all peoples" (Isa. 25:6; cf. 65:13–14), and when God's servants will receive their just reward (see comments on Luke 13:29; 14:15).

**Second or third watch of the night (12:38).** Jewish sources divide the night into three watches (6–10; 10–2; 2–6; see Judg. 7:19) and Roman sources into four (6–9; 9–12; 12–3; 3–6; see Mark 13:35).[352] In either case, this is meant to signify the dead of night.

**Thief . . . broken into (12:39).** The verb for "broken into" means to "dig through."[353] Thieves would dig through the sun-dried brick wall of a house to break into it.

**The Son of Man will come (12:40).** See comments on 5:24; 9:26.

**Faithful and wise manager (12:42).** The manager or steward (*oikonomos*) here is a chief servant who is left in charge of the household while the master is away. Such stewards often had significant authority over the master's business, household staff, and personal affairs.

**He will put him in charge of all his possessions (12:44).** Because of the servant's faithfulness, he is placed in an even greater position of authority, perhaps as second only to the master (cf. the role of Joseph in Gen. 39:8–9). Slaves in both Roman and Jewish society could rise to positions of great prestige and authority, managing their masters' large estates.

**To eat and drink and get drunk (12:45).** Gluttony, excessive revelry, and drunkenness are all viewed in Scripture as destructive and irresponsible behavior.[354] The same is true in Jewish literature.[355]

**Cut him to pieces (12:46).** The Greek term here (*dichotomeō*) is a strong one and means to cut in two or dismember.[356] Such horrible punishment was not uncommon in the ancient world,[357] but commentators are divided as to whether it is here to be taken literally or figuratively. The next phrase, "assign him a place with the unbelievers," does not solve the problem, since this can mean social ostracism or the lack of a proper burial among God's people. Whether a literal or figurative image, there is the further question of the intended application. Spiritually speaking, is this an allusion to hell or to being cut off from the community of faith? The former seems more likely in light of the previous parable of the rich fool.

**Does not do what his master wants (12:47).** Sins of ignorance are less severe and so deserving of less punishment than intentional sins. This is true in the Old Testament (Num. 15:22–26; Ps. 19:13), in Judaism (1QS 7.3; 8.22, 24; CD 10:3; *m. Šabb.* 78:1), and in the New Testament (Luke 23:34).

**From everyone who has been given much, much will be demanded (12:48).** Higher standards are demanded of those who have been given greater gifts and abilities. Wisdom of Solomon 6:6, 8 reads: "For the lowliest may be pardoned in mercy, but the mighty will be mightily tested. . . . A strict enquiry is in store for the mighty." See also James 3:1, where teachers "will be judged more strictly."

## Not Peace but Division (12:49–53)

Jesus' instructions on the need for good stewardship before his return (12:35–48) now lead to a discussion of the profound seriousness of his present ministry. He is engaged in a cosmic war that will climax in his sacrificial death (his "baptism") and will ultimately bring fiery judgment on the earth (12:49–50). This war mentality means that sides must be taken. It will divide even family members, with parents and children standing on opposite sides of the spiritual battlefield. Wartime means wholehearted commitment to the cause, no matter what the price.

**To bring fire on the earth (12:49).** Fire is a common symbol of God's judgment in the Old Testament and Judaism[358] and is used this way by Luke elsewhere (3:16–17; 9:54; 17:29; see comments on 3:16). Here the image may be both judging the wicked and purifying the righteous.[359] Jesus' coming provokes a time of crisis and decision.

**A baptism (12:50).** "Baptism" here is not Christian baptism but rather the judgment of God that Jesus will receive at his crucifixion. In the Old Testament God's judgment is often described as an overwhelming deluge or flood.[360]

**Family divided against each other (12:52).** The division of close friends and families indicates great crisis in a nation, such as civil war. The passage recalls Micah's description of the social disintegration in Israel leading up to the Assyrian conquest, when "a man's enemies are the members of his own household" (Mic. 7:6). The rabbis interpreted this Old Testament passage with reference to the great time of crisis before the coming of the Messiah, when "children shall shame the elders, and the elders shall rise up before the children."[361] Similar images appear elsewhere in Jewish literature.[362]

## Interpreting the Times (12:54–59)

Addressing the crowds again, Jesus continues the theme of eschatological crisis and preparation that runs through this section. He points out that although they know how to read the signs of the changing weather, they have failed to recognize the clear signs of the kingdom of God in his ministry. The second saying of Jesus may seem to have little connection to the first. He encourages his hearers to settle their disputes before going to court, thus avoiding debtor's prison. While the parable may concern the need for reconciliation in personal relationships, more likely it allegorically portrays the need to get right with God before the final judgment.

**A cloud rising in the west (12:54).** In Palestine a cloud from the west usually contained moisture from the Mediterranean Sea and so indicated rain (see 1 Kings 18:44).

**The south wind blows (12:55).** The sirocco or khamsin wind blowing in from the southern or southeastern desert meant hot weather.[363] Such a scorching wind could even wither crops (Gen. 41:6; Isa. 40:7).

**The magistrate . . . the judge . . . turn you over to the officer (12:58).** The scene envisioned is a civil case involving an unpaid debt. The "magistrate" (or ruler, *archōn*) is the same individual as the judge (*kritēs*) who hears the case. The "officer" (*praktōr*) refers to the constable or bailiff in charge of a debtor's prison. See James 2:6 for a similar image.

**The last penny (12:59).** The "penny" (*lepton*) was the smallest coin available, worth about half a quadrans (Mark 12:42), or 1/128th of a denarius. A denarius was a day's wages for a laborer (Luke 7:41; 12:6). Thus, the lepton was worth less than five minutes of a ten-hour work day (see 21:2 for the widow's *lepta*).

◀ *left*

**PENNIES**

A pile of copper *lepta*.

## Repent or Perish (13:1–9)

Jesus' teaching on the need for eschatological preparation (12:54–59) continues with a call for repentance (13:1–5) and a parable on the need to produce the fruit of repentance (13:6–9). The teaching is evoked when some in the crowd ask Jesus to comment on a brutal police action taken by the governor Pilate against some Galileans in the temple precincts. Though the specific incident is unknown, it is in line with Pilate's character (see comments on 13:1). Evidently the questioners believed the popular misconception that personal tragedy was always the result of individual sins. Jesus rejects that idea and stresses that *all* people are sinners who need to repent before God.

**Whose blood Pilate had mixed with their sacrifices (13:1).** Though this incident is unknown, Josephus recounts several times when Pilate faced protests from the Jews and sometimes resorted to bloody oppression. In A.D. 26 Pilate brought effigies of Roman emperors into Jerusalem. Viewing these as idols (Ex. 20:4), a large number of Jews marched in protest to Pilate's headquarters in Caesarea. After they had petitioned him for six days, Pilate surrounded them with his soldiers and threatened a massacre. The Jews threw themselves on the ground and said they would rather accept death than let their law be broken. Pilate was moved by this action and removed the images from Jerusalem.[364] Such mercy was uncharacteristic of Pilate's later oppressive techniques. On one occasion popular demonstrations broke out when Pilate used money from the temple treasury to build an aqueduct for Jerusalem. Pilate sent soldiers to surround and attack the protestors, killing many.[365] Typical of the Romans, Pilate met protest with ruthless and overwhelming force. For more on Pilate see "Pilate" at Mark 15:1.

**Were worse sinners . . . were more guilty . . . ? (13:2, 4).** It was popularly held that tragedy was the result of personal sins. Job's friend Eliphaz asks rhetorically, "Who, being innocent, has ever perished?" (Job 4:7).[366]

**Eighteen who died when the tower in Siloam (13:4).** This incident is otherwise unattested. The pool of Siloam was a reservoir in the southeastern corner of Jerusalem.[367] This tower may have been part of the fortifications of the southern or eastern walls of Jerusalem, or perhaps was part of an aqueduct that Pilate built to improve Jerusalem's water supply.[368]

**A fig tree (13:6).** In the Old Testament Israel is sometimes compared to a fig tree or an unfruitful vine or vineyard.[369] Micah 7:1–2 presents an image similar to this one, where God seeks for figs (=righteous people) but finds none.[370]

**Planted in his vineyard (13:6).** It was common to plant figs and other kinds of trees in vineyards, though the law forbade planting two kinds of crops together (Lev. 19:19; Deut. 22:9). Healthy vineyards and fig trees are common images in the Old Testament for success and prosperity and their destruction serves as a symbol of judgment.[371]

**For three years (13:7).** Fig trees bear annually, so the farmer had already demonstrated great patience.

**Cut it down! (13:7, 9).** A cut-down tree or a stump was a common symbol of judgment (Isa. 6:13; 9:10).[372]

**Leave it alone for one more year (13:8).** There is an interesting parallel in an Aramaic rabbinic text. When an owner is about to dig up an unfruitful palm tree, the tree itself speaks and asks him to grant it one more year. The owner refuses saying, "You miserable tree! You did not bear your own fruit, so how could you bear other fruit?"[373]

**Dig around it and fertilize it (13:8).** Digging around the plant would allow more moisture to reach the roots and also provide space for fertilizer. The Greek for "fertilize" is to "throw manure" around it. For similar statements of God's care for his vineyard, see Isaiah 5:1–2; Mark 12:1.

## A Crippled Woman Healed on the Sabbath (13:10–17)

Jesus' teaching that has occupied most of chapters 11–13 is now interrupted with a healing miracle, returning to the Sabbath-controversy theme developed earlier in Luke.[374] While teaching in a Sabbath synagogue service, Jesus heals a woman who has been crippled by an evil spirit for eighteen years. The ruler of the synagogue objects, citing the Old Testament prohibition against work on the Sabbath (Ex. 20:9–11; Deut. 5:13). Jesus responds by rebuking the religious leaders for their hypocrisy. They selfishly take care of the needs of their animals on the Sabbath, but then object to meeting the greater spiritual and physical needs of a human being.

**Sabbath . . . teaching in one of the synagogues (13:10).** Visiting rabbis were often asked to give the sermon or homily for the synagogue service. For the order of a Jewish synagogue service see the introduction to 4:14–30.

**A woman was there (13:11).** Though women were excluded from much of Israel's religious life, including access to the inner temple court, they participated in synagogue worship.[375]

**Crippled by a spirit (13:11).** The Greek says literally, "having a spirit of weakness." Luke explains that the condition caused her to be stooped over, a condition many commentators have identified as *spondylitis ankylopoietica*.[376] Verse 16 indicates that this was caused by demonic oppression of some sort. Demons are often described as inflicting actual illnesses, including epilepsy (9:39), muteness (11:14), lameness (here), and madness (8:29). Yet such illnesses are not always considered demonic (see Matt. 4:24). Elsewhere Luke distinguishes between Jesus' healings and his exorcisms.[377] For demons and demonization see comments on 4:31–37; 8:26–39.

**Synagogue ruler (13:14).** This administrative officer maintained the synagogue and organized the worship services.[378]

**There are six days for work (13:14).** This verse alludes to the prohibition to work on the Sabbath in Exodus 20:9–11 (cf. Deut. 5:13). Notice that the synagogue ruler does not address Jesus directly, perhaps to avoid a direct confrontation or to respect his position.

**Be healed on those days, not on the Sabbath (13:14).** The rabbis debated whether it was justified to offer medical help to someone on the Sabbath. It was generally concluded that it was allowed only in extreme emergencies or when a life was in danger.[379] Since this woman's life is not in immediate danger, the synagogue ruler considers this a Sabbath violation (see comments on 6:1–11).

**Untie his ox or donkey . . . lead it out to give it water (13:15).** The Mishnah allows that animals can go out on the Sabbath, but restricts the burdens they can carry.[380] While restricting the kinds of knots that could be tied on the Sabbath, the rabbis allowed animals to be tied to prevent straying.[381] They also found ways to water their animals without breaking the limits of Sabbath travel (Sabbath travel was limited to two thousand cubits, about six-tenths of a mile, from home; *m. ʿErub.* 4:3).[382] They would build a crude structure around a public well, converting it into a private residence. Since the well was now a "home," animals could be taken there for watering, provided "the greater part of a cow shall be within [the enclosure] when it drinks."[383] Jesus points out the hypocrisy of taking such measures to protect one's property while objecting to an act of human compassion.

**Then should not this woman . . . be set free on the Sabbath. . . ? (13:16).** This is a rabbinic "from the lesser to the greater" (*qal wāḥômer*) style argument. If an animal can be helped on the Sabbath, how much more a human being. The contrast is heightened by a Greek wordplay, since the verb for "set free" is the same word used for untying an animal in 13:15 (*luō*).

**His opponents were humiliated (13:17).** In both Greek and rabbinic rhetorical debate, a wise and skillful orator was one who could baffle and silence his opponents.[384] Luke makes it clear that Jesus has won this one.

## The Parables of the Mustard Seed and the Yeast (13:18–21)

The reference to the defeat of Satan in the woman who was healed (13:10–17) recalls for the reader the in-breaking power of the kingdom of God in Jesus' ministry. Jesus now provides two short parables to reveal the nature of God's kingdom. While the traditional Jewish expectation envisioned a dramatic and cataclysmic event that would bring in the kingdom, these parables suggest a gradual but overwhelming growth, permeating and transforming the hearts of people throughout the world (see also comments on Mark 4:26–29).

**The kingdom of God (13:18).** See comments on 4:43; 17:20.

**A mustard seed (13:19).** The mustard seed was used proverbially in Judaism of something very small.[385] It normally grows into a bush of about four feet, but can reach ten feet or more.[386]

**Planted in his garden (13:19).** The Mishnah indicates that the mustard seed was not cultivated in gardens, but rather in fields (*m. Kil.* 3:2). It is uncertain whether this was true in first-century Palestine, however, so its effect on the parables' interpretation is doubtful.

**Became a tree (13:19).** This is a somewhat surprising image, since the mustard "tree" is really a bush (contrast the mighty cedars in the next note). This may be meant to give the parable an unexpected twist (the bush becomes a great tree!) in line with the theme of the "mysteries" of the kingdom in Matthew 13.[387] On the other hand, since mustard is a large bush, it may rightly be called a "tree." The Greek naturalist Theophrastus in fact notes that mustard grows into a "tree" (*dendron*).[388]

▸ MUSTARD PLANTS

**The birds of the air perched in its branches (13:19).** The picture is one of peace and security that the tree provides for birds. Such an image appears repeatedly in the Old Testament.[389] While some have argued that the birds represent evil influence permeating the kingdom, there is nothing in the present context or the Old Testament background to suggest this.

**Yeast (13:21).** While yeast is often used in Scripture as a negative image (see comments on 12:1), here it probably functions positively. Yeast was used every day for baking bread, a staple of life, so it was certainly not universally viewed as something evil. As in the mustard seed parable, the sense is that the kingdom starts small and grows large. The additional sense here is that it quietly permeates the entire world.

**A large amount of flour (13:21).** The "large amount" here in the Greek is "three *sata*." A *saton* was a unit of dry measure equal to about three gallons (approx. twenty pounds).[390]

## The Narrow Door (13:22–30)

After reminding his readers that Jesus is journeying to Jerusalem where God's salvation will be achieved, Luke records a question posed by one of Jesus' followers about whether many or few will be saved. Jesus responds with two related analogies, the first portraying salvation as a narrow door through which many will try but fail to enter, and the second about a banquet at the home of a wealthy owner. When the time for this banquet arrives, the owner shuts the door and late arrivals are refused entrance. The analogy is a transparent reference to Jesus' ministry. Jesus is issuing an urgent call to Israel to respond in repentance and enter the kingdom. Those who refuse will be shut out of the messianic banquet.

**Are only a few people going to be saved? (13:23).** This question was sometimes discussed in Jewish literature. 2 Esdras (*4 Ezra*) 8:1–3 reads: "The Most High made this world for the sake of many, but the world to come for the sake of only a few. . . . Many have been created, but only a few shall be saved."[391]

It was a common belief among the Jews that all Israelites would be saved. The Mishnah says, "All Israelites have a share in the world to come," citing Isaiah 60:21 as the proof text. The only exceptions are those who deny the resurrection, who deny the divine origin of the Law, who read heretical books, who utter charms, who pronounce the divine name YHWH, and Epicureans (*m. Sanh.* 10:1). "Epicureans" here does not refer to the Greek philosophy of Epicurus, but was a common designation for Jews and Gentiles who opposed the teachings of the rabbis.[392]

**Enter through the narrow door (13:24).** In Matthew 7:13 Jesus speaks of a narrow gate and a narrow road, images that are similar to the "way of life" and the "way of death" of Jeremiah 21:8 (cf. Deut. 30:15). Somewhat similar imagery appears in 2 Esdras (*4 Ezra*) 7:3–14, where a narrow strait to a vast sea and a narrow gate to a large city symbolize the difficulties the righteous suffer in life, which will ultimately open into a broad place of blessings and inheritance. The key difference is that in Jesus' words the narrow door does not symbolize life's difficulties but the exclusivity of salvation found in him.

**Closes the door (13:25).** The shutting of the door indicates both the authority of the owner and the lost opportunity for those shut out.[393]

**I don't know you (13:25).** In the Old Testament "knowing" often means God's sovereign choice to have a saving relationship with another. In Amos 3:2 God says to Israel: "You only have I chosen [lit., known] of all the families of the earth" (cf. Isa. 63:16; Jer. 1:5). Here the sense is a refusal to acknowledge a relationship (cf. Isa. 63:16). Some commentators have seen parallels here to Jewish texts on excommunication from the synagogue.[394]

**Where you come from (13:25).** A person's identity was closely associated with his or her place and people of origin. To

A NARROW DOOR

refuse to acknowledge origin was to refuse to acknowledge identity.[395]

**Away from me, all you evildoers! (13:27).** These words allude to Psalm 6:8, where a righteous sufferer cries out to his persecutors to depart from him.

**Weeping there, and gnashing of teeth (13:28).** This combination appears repeatedly in Matthew.[396] Weeping in this context is a symbol of both mourning and torment. Judith 16:17 reads: "Woe to the nations that rise up against my people! The Lord Almighty will take vengeance on them in the day of judgment; he will send fire and worms into their flesh; they shall weep in pain forever." In the Old Testament gnashing or grinding the teeth is a sign of anger (Ps. 35:16; 37:12)[397] and perhaps, as here, rejection and judgment (112:10).

**Abraham, Isaac and Jacob (13:28).** As the recipients of God's covenant, these three patriarchs symbolized Israel's national identity. God delivered the Israelites in the Exodus when he "remembered his covenant with Abraham, with Isaac and with Jacob."[398] Their names appear together throughout the Old Testament and Jewish literature.[399]

**People will come from east and west and north and south (13:29).** It is a common Old Testament image that when the kingdom is established, the Gentile nations will stream to Jerusalem to worship God (Isa. 2:2; 55:5).[400] Isaiah 25:6–9 provides the closest parallel since it combines this image with that of the messianic banquet (see next comment). While in Judaism the point is often the subjugation of the nations to Israel's authority (*Pss. Sol.* 17:30–31; cf. Isa. 45:14), here Jesus indicates that the Gentiles will be full participants in the blessings of the kingdom—even to the exclusion of many Israelites. For more on this theme see 14:15; 17:20.

**The feast in the kingdom of God (13:29).** This refers to the messianic banquet, a symbol of God's eschatological blessings for his people. The imagery has its roots in the promise of Isaiah 25:6: "On this mountain [Mount Zion] the LORD Almighty will prepare a feast of rich food for all peoples, a banquet of aged wine—the best of meats and the finest of wines."[401] The emphasis is on God's eternal and bountiful sustenance for his people (Ps. 22:26; 23:5).[402] The Qumran scrolls give detailed rules for seating and procedure at the banquet.[403] See also 14:15.

**REFLECTIONS**

**IT IS OFTEN SAID THAT ALL ROADS** lead to God and that everyone must find his or her own way. But Jesus teaches that the door to God's presence is a narrow one and that salvation belongs only to those who personally know him. Yet paradoxically, this "exclusive" gospel is also fully inclusive, and those from every corner of the earth will participate in it. Salvation does not come to those with an outward show of religiosity, but to all who lean wholly on God's saving grace.

## Jesus' Sorrow for Jerusalem (13:31–35)

In this passage Jesus receives a warning from some Pharisees that Herod Antipas is seeking to kill him. Jesus takes the opportunity to reaffirm his resolve to complete his God-ordained mission in Jerusalem and to pronounce judgment against the nation.

Throughout his Gospel Luke stresses Jesus' role as a prophet. This passage brings out key aspects of his prophetic identity.[404] Jesus will suffer the fate of the prophets, that is, rejection and martyrdom in Jerusalem (13:33). As a prophet he speaks for God, expressing his heart of compassion for the nation. Though Jerusalem (representing Israel) rejects his messengers, God still loves her and longs to gather her under his wings as a hen gathers her chicks (13:34). Finally, he prophetically pronounces impending judgment against her (13:35).

**Herod (13:31).** This is Herod Antipas, one of Herod the Great's sons (see comments on 3:1, 19–20). Since Herod ruled over Galilee and Perea, this event probably takes place in one of these two regions.

**Go tell that fox (13:32).** Today the fox is viewed as clever and sly; this is one of the qualities attributed to it by the Greeks and in later rabbinic literature (often with negative connotations of deception and cunning).[405] In other Jewish contexts, however, the fox is viewed as an insignificant creature (Neh. 4:3) or as a destroyer. Ezekiel identifies false prophets as prowling "jackals among ruins."[406] Jesus' comment may contain a variety of these connotations. It was certainly not intended as a compliment. It is significant that while Herod is a fox who preys on chicks, Jesus is the hen who protects them (see comments on 13:34).[407]

◀ *left*

COIN MINTED DURING THE REIGN OF HEROD ANTIPAS

**Today and tomorrow, and on the third day (13:32).** This is probably not a reference to three literal days, but rather to Jesus' continuing journey. The "third day" may perhaps be an allusion to Jesus' resurrection, when he will complete his messianic task.

**No prophet can die outside Jerusalem (13:33).** See 11:47 for this theme. Since Jerusalem was the center of Israel's religious life, this statement would have shocked Jesus' listeners.[408]

**Stone those sent to you (13:34).** Stoning was the prescribed method of capital punishment in the Old Testament law (Lev. 20:2; Num. 15:35), but here Israel stones God's messengers! The stoning of a prophet appears in 2 Chronicles 24:21, where Zechariah son of Jehoiada the priest is murdered in the courtyard of the temple (see comments on Luke 11:51).

**Hen gathers her chicks (13:34).** The Old Testament frequently speaks of the protection found in the shelter of God's wings (Deut. 32:11 [an eagle's wings]).[409]

**Your house is left to you desolate (13:35).** The "house" here may refer to the temple or more generally to Jerusalem. Jesus is no doubt speaking of the destruction of Jerusalem in A.D. 70 (see comments on 21:6). Jeremiah similarly prophesied the desolation of Jerusalem and the temple ("this house") in the Babylonian conquest.[410]

**Blessed is he who comes in the name of the Lord (13:35).** This comes from Psalm 118:26. Psalm 118 was one of the "Hallel" (praise) psalms (Ps. 113–118) used liturgically by pilgrims at various Jewish feasts (especially Tabernacles and Passover). There is some evidence that the psalm was interpreted with reference to the Messiah in later Judaism, though whether this was true of Jesus' day is uncertain.[411]

## Jesus at a Pharisee's House (14:1–14)

In this passage and the next (14:15–24) a cluster of Jesus' teaching is set in the context of a meal at the home of a prominent Pharisee (cf. 7:36; 11:37). The key themes are criticism of the Pharisees for their pride and hypocrisy and affirmation of God's love for the lowly and outcast. Humility and love should characterize the people of the kingdom.

**The house of a prominent Pharisee (14:1).** Literally, "one of the leaders of the Pharisees." For Pharisees see comments on 5:17. Though the Jewish high court, the Sanhedrin, was made up mostly of Sadducees, some prominent Pharisees like Gamaliel were also members (Acts 5:34).

**A man suffering from dropsy (14:2).** Dropsy (Gk. *hydrōpikos*), medically known as edema, is an excessive accumulation of serous fluid in tissue spaces or a body cavity, causing excessive swelling.[412] It is not a disease but rather a symptom and usually points to a more serious condition. It is not clear whether the man was an invited guest, whether he was "planted" by the Pharisees to provoke Jesus to heal, or whether he was an uninvited guest who came in seeking Jesus (see comments on 7:37 for such uninvited observers).

**Is it lawful to heal on the Sabbath . . . ? (14:3).** The rabbis debated this question, generally concluding that it was allowed only in extreme emergencies or when a life was in danger (see comments on 6:7). Here they refuse to answer, perhaps because their traditions are unclear or because they realize that if they say "no," Jesus will attack their lack of compassion (as he did at 13:15–17; cf. 6:9).

**A son or an ox that falls into a well on the Sabbath day (14:5).** See Deuteronomy 5:14 for the Sabbath commandment related to household members and livestock. Rabbinic writings debate the kind of help that may be given to animals on the Sabbath.[413] The Qumran scrolls explicitly say that "no one should help an animal give birth on the sabbath day. And if he makes it fall into a well or a pit, he should not take it out on the sabbath" (CD 11:13–14). Human beings may be rescued, but one must not use a ladder, a rope, or other implement to save them (!) (CD 11:16–17; see comments on Luke 13:15 for the elaborate rabbinic means of circumventing the Sabbath prohibitions in order to care for animals).

**A wedding feast (14:8).** Weddings were major social events, lasting a week or more (see comments on 5:34).

**Do not take the place of honor (14:8).** Jesus' words here are a commentary on Proverbs 25:6–7: "Do not exalt yourself in the king's presence, and do not claim a place among great men; it is better for him to say to you, 'Come up here,' than for him to humiliate you before a nobleman." Similar advice appears in rabbinic writings.[414] The Greek writer Theophrastus (c. 372–287 B.C.), a pupil of Aristotle, gives as one of the traits of an arrogant man that he seeks the place of honor beside the host.[415]

**Then, humiliated . . . the least important place (14:9).** Honor and shame were pivotal values of the ancient Mediterranean world. A family's honor in the community determined whom they could marry, what functions they could attend, where they could live, and with whom they could do business.[416] The public shame of moving from the first seat to the last in front of one's colleagues would be a humiliation almost worse than death.

**He who humbles himself will be exalted (14:11).** Jesus encourages his followers not to seek honor but to serve others in humility. While similar proverbial wisdom appears in Sirach 3:18 ("The greater you are, the more you must humble yourself; so you will find favor in the sight of the Lord"), Jesus' words have more in common with the eschatological tone of Ezekiel, who predicted that in the wake of God's judgment, "The lowly will be exalted and the exalted will be brought low" (Ezek. 21:26).

**A luncheon or dinner . . . a banquet (14:12–13).** The terms in 14:12 refer to the two daily meals: the *ariston*, a late morning meal, and the *deipnon*, a late afternoon meal (see comments on 11:37). The "banquet" (*dochē*) in 14:13 is a more formal dinner party or reception. The use of this term with reference to the social outcasts makes Jesus' image even more striking.

**They may invite you back (14:12).** Since giving and receiving such invitations

## Banquets, Meals, and Social Status

Meals were important social rituals in the ancient world, and one would normally eat only with those of his or her own social class. One's place at the table was determined by social status, and the places beside the host represented the highest status. This was true both in Greco-Roman and Jewish society. Roman sources describe meals where guests of different social status are seated in different rooms and are even served different food and wine depending on their social rank.[A-46] Various writers criticize such behavior as elitist. Martial describes an incident where a host alone eats choice food while his guests look on:

> Tell me, what madness is this? While the throng of invited guests looks on, you, Caecilianus, alone devour the mushrooms! What prayer shall I make suitable to such a belly and gorge? May you eat such a mushroom as Claudius ate [i.e., a poisonous one]![A-47]

In another humorous passage Martial criticizes the different quality of food served to guests:

> Since I am asked to dinner . . . why is not the same dinner served to me as to you? You take oysters fattened in the Lucrine lake, I suck a mussel through a hole in the shell; you get mushrooms, I take hog funguses; you tackle turbot, but I brill. Golden with fat, a turtle-dove gorges you with its bloated rump; there is set before me a magpie that has died in its cage. Why do I dine without you, although Ponticus, I am dining with you?[A-48]

While affirming the inclusive nature of the gospel, the early church still struggled against traditional and societal pressures to maintain such social distinctions (see 1 Cor. 11:17–34). See comments on Luke 5:30 for the exclusive table fellowship of the Pharisees.

determined one's social status, "accepting a dinner invitation normally obligated the guest to return the favor."[417]

**Invite the poor, the crippled (14:13).** It was uncommon to eat with someone of a lower social status. Such fraternization could risk one's social standing with friends and colleagues. See also comments on 14:15–24.

**The resurrection of the righteous (14:14).** The first clear reference to the resurrection of the righteous appears at Daniel 12:2, and it was a common theme in Jewish literature.[418] Josephus points out that the Pharisees believed that the righteous would be rewarded with the resurrection, while the wicked would be detained in everlasting prison.[419]

**REFLECTIONS**

**WE TEND NATURALLY TO STRIVE** for recognition and esteem from others. But Jesus says that those who seek self-glorification will ultimately find themselves humbled, while those who put others first will be exalted. The highest calling of a Christian is to look out for others first, encouraging them to be all that God would have them to be.

## The Parable of the Great Banquet (14:15–24)

This parable is set in the same meal context as the previous passage. It reflects what is happening in Jesus' ministry. While the religious elite are refusing to accept Jesus' preaching of the kingdom (his invitation to the messianic banquet), spiritual outsiders—the poor, sinners, Samaritans, and (in Acts) the Gentiles—are responding with faith and repentance. This passage recalls Jesus' teaching on exclusion from the messianic banquet in 13:28–30 and once again plays out the theme of eschatological reversal.[420]

An interesting parallel to this story appears in the Jerusalem Talmud. When a village tax collector named Bar Ma'jan dies, the whole town comes out to mourn. A poor holy man, a teacher of the law, also dies, but he is not properly mourned. When the holy man's friend bemoans this injustice, he is informed in a dream that the tax collector's honor came because of a single good deed. He had invited the city officials to a banquet, and when they failed to come, he gave orders that the poor should be invited so that the food would not be wasted. The story has a very different moral, however, as Bar Ma'jan's fate in the afterlife is contrasted with that of the holy man. The holy man's friend has a dream in which he sees his friend in Paradise beside streams of flowing water, but Bar Ma'jan standing beside a river unable to reach the water. Though the banquet scene is similar to the present parable, Bar Ma'jan's fate is more like the rich man in the parable of the rich man and Lazarus (see comments on 16:19–31).[421]

**The feast in the kingdom of God (14:15).** This refers to the end-time messianic banquet predicted by Isaiah: "On this mountain [Zion] the LORD Almighty will prepare a feast of rich food for all peoples . . ." (Isa. 25:6; see comments on Luke 13:29). While Isaiah makes it clear that the messianic banquet is for "all peoples," there was a tendency in Judaism to reject the notion that Gentiles would be included. The Targum (an Aramaic paraphrase of Scripture) on Isaiah 25 dramatically alters the original meaning:

> Yahweh of Hosts will make for all the people in this mountain a meal; and though they suppose it is an honour, it will be a shame for them, and great plagues, plagues from which they will be unable to escape, plagues whereby they will come to their end.[422]

Isaiah spoke of the salvation of the Gentiles; the Targum now speaks of their destruction! Though the Targum is difficult to date, the tendency to emphasize the Gentiles' judgment over their salvation was common in Judaism. The first-century B.C. *Psalms of Solomon* offers a prayer that the Messiah will "purge Jerusalem from gentiles" and "will destroy the unlawful nations with the word of his mouth. At his warning the nations will flee from his presence."[423] Jesus is about to radically alter this exclusive view of messianic salvation.

**Preparing a great banquet and invited many guests (14:16).** This would be a major social event in the life of a Middle Eastern village, with all those of social status attending.

**He sent his servant (14:17).** It seems to have been common practice in both Hellenistic and Jewish society to issue an original invitation and then to send a servant to summon the guests when the banquet was prepared (see Est. 6:14).[424] This custom is still practiced today in traditional Middle Eastern contexts and is intended to allow the host to calculate the correct amount of (freshly butchered) meat to prepare.[425] Once the invitation has been accepted, not to show up is an insult as well as a financial burden to the host. The passage is not about a last minute invitation that is impossible to accept, but a shameful refusal to come after sending in an RSVP.

**All alike began to make excuses (14:18).** From a Middle Eastern perspective, none of the excuses is legitimate and all would be insulting to the host.

**I have just bought a field, and I must go and see it (14:18).** Bailey argues that this is a bold-faced lie since "no one buys a field in the Middle East without knowing every square foot of it like the palm of his hand," including things like anticipated rainfall, trees, paths, stone walls, and so forth.[426] Fertile land was scarce and of premium value. Its history of ownership and productive value would be known well before the sale. While Bailey's insistence that the man is lying may be an exaggeration (commentators have pointed to some late rabbinic evidence for post-purchase inspections of land[427]), there is no doubt that the excuse is a great insult to the host. In a culture where personal relationships are of supreme importance, the guest essentially says that a field is more important than their relationship.

**I have just bought five yoke of oxen (14:19).** A "yoke" is a pair or team of oxen. Like the previous excuse, this one is inadequate and insulting since oxen were tested before purchase rather than

YOKED OXEN

after. The prospective buyer needed to know the animals' strength and ability to work as a team before beginning negotiations. Bailey points out that teams of oxen are sold in the Middle East in two ways. Either a small field beside the marketplace is used by prospective buyers to test the team, or a farmer invites buyers to his farm on a given day to watch the animals work.[428] Again the invited guest has placed property above friendship.

**I just got married, so I can't come (14:20).** While some have seen more legitimacy in this excuse, it too is unnecessary and insulting. (1) The excuse cannot mean that the marriage is presently taking place, since no host would schedule a major banquet at the same time as a wedding. Everyone in the village would be at the latter event.[429] (2) While the language of the verse suggests a recent marriage, it does not say the wedding has *just* taken place (the word "just" is not in the Greek). After all, the invitee accepted the original invitation to the banquet (see 14:17), something he would not have done if his wedding were imminent. (3) While men were exempt from military service for their first year of marriage (Deut. 20:7; 24:5), this does not apply here, since this is not a distant war but a village social event. Though women were often excluded from such occasions (and that is the assumption here), the man would be absent from his new wife for only a few hours. (4) Bailey also points out that Middle Eastern men are reluctant to discuss their women in formal settings.[430] It was considered crude and unbecoming to use his sexual relationship as an excuse. (5) Finally, unlike the first two invitees, this man does not even ask to be excused, but rudely announces that he is not coming.

**The poor, the crippled, the blind and the lame (14:21).** The new invitation reflects Jesus' ministry to the outcasts of Israel. The Old Testament promised eschatological blessings to the poor and handicapped (see comments on 4:18; 7:22).[431] Just as "blemished" animals could not be offered as sacrifices in Israel (Lev. 22:19–22), so priests who were blind, lame, or crippled were excluded from full participation in Israel's worship (Lev. 21:17–23). The Qumran scrolls are particularly relevant to the present context since they explicitly exclude the "lame, blind, deaf, dumb or defiled in his flesh" from the messianic banquet.[432] Jesus came to heal the broken and to invite all to the banquet.

**The roads and country lanes (14:23).** While the poor and handicapped were from the host's community ("the streets and alleys of the town," 14:21), the call now goes to those outside the community. While the former represent the outcasts within Israel, the latter probably portrays the mission to the Gentiles in Acts.

## The Cost of Being a Disciple (14:25–35)

Jesus sets out the extraordinarily high cost of discipleship. Commitment to him must far exceed devotion to family or to self (14:26–27). In light of such demands, everyone should weigh the cost carefully before making such a commitment (14:28–33). Just as salt is useless if it loses its saltiness, so a disciple without full commitment is useless to the kingdom of God (14:34).

**Hate his father and mother (14:26).** (Cf. Matthew 6:24; John 12:25.) This is obvious hyperbole since elsewhere Jesus says we must love even our enemies (Matt.

5:44; Luke 6:27, 35). The point is that love for family must seem like hate by comparison to devotion to Jesus. There are biblical examples where Hebrew or Greek words for "hate" mean to reject in favor of a greater love.[433]

**Carry his cross (14:27).** Roman prisoners bound for crucifixion were forced to carry the horizontal cross beam (the *patibulum*) to the place of execution (cf. 23:26). See comments on crucifixion at 9:23 and "Crucifixion" at 23:33. The image reflects not just self-denial, but humiliation and sacrificial death.

**To build a tower (14:28).** Towers were used as protective fortifications for cities as well as for private homes, land, or vineyards.[434] See 13:4 for the collapse of a poorly built tower, perhaps because financial corners were cut.

**Everyone who sees it will ridicule him (14:29).** In a society where honor and shame were pivotal values (see 11:5–8; 14:9), an uncompleted tower would serve as a monument of shame.

**Estimate the cost (14:28).** It is common sense to count the cost before a major project. Similar advice appears in Greek and Jewish literature. The Stoic philosopher Epictetus (A.D. 50–130) wrote: "Reckon, sir, first what the task is, then your own nature, what you are able to carry."[435]

**A king is about to go to war (14:31).** The phrase "go to war" means to engage an enemy on the battlefield (1 Macc. 4:34; 2 Macc. 8:23). History is full of examples of kings who lost battles because they miscalculated the strength of the opposition. Proverbs 20:18 reads: "Make plans by seeking advice; if you wage war, obtain guidance." The Jewish philosopher Philo draws on similar proverbial wisdom when he writes:

> Virtue's nature is most peaceable; she is careful, so they say, to test her own strength before the conflict, so if she is able to contend to the end she will take the field; but if she finds her strength too weak, she may shrink from entering the contest at all.[436]

**Salt is good (14:34).** Salt in the ancient world was used for various purposes: as flavoring, as a preservative, as a fertilizer, as weed killer, and as a catalyst in certain kinds of ovens.[437] The functions envisioned here are flavoring (14:34), fertilizing ("for the soil," 14:35), and weed-killing ("for the manure pile," 14:35).

**Loses its saltiness (14:34).** Sodium chloride (table salt) cannot actually lose its saltiness. Indeed, a later rabbinic story attributed to Rabbi Joshua ben Hananiah (c. A.D. 90) seems to intentionally refute Jesus' words when it points out that just as a mule (a sterile offspring of a donkey and a horse) cannot bear young, so salt cannot lose its saltiness.[438] There are several possible explanations for Jesus' words. He may be indicating an absurdity ("If salt were to lose its saltiness, which it obviously can't . . ."). More likely, however, his statement refers to the kind of salt found around the Dead Sea, which is a mixture of sodium chloride and other compounds. When water evaporates from this mixture, the sodium chloride crystallizes first and may be removed. What is left are gypsum and other impurities, that is, "salt" that has lost its saltiness.[439]

**Fit neither for the soil nor for the manure pile (14:35).** Though flavoring and preserving were the most important functions of salt, it was secondarily used to fertilize soil and to spread on manure piles. On the latter it killed weeds and slowed down the fermentation process.[440]

**He who has ears to hear (14:35).** See comments on 8:8.

## The Parable of the Lost Sheep (15:1–7)

Luke 15 contains three parables that concern things that are lost and then found: a sheep, a coin, and a son. The parables symbolically depict the central theme of Luke's Gospel, God's love for his lost children and the joy he experiences when they return.

**Tax collectors (15:1).** See comments on 3:12.

**Pharisees and the teachers of the law (15:2).** See comments on 5:17.

**Eats with them (15:2).** Table fellowship with common people and especially "sinners" was frowned upon by the scrupulous Pharisees. A later rabbinic saying reads, "Let not a man associate with the wicked, even to bring him near to the law."[441] See comments on 5:30; 14:7.

**One of you has a hundred sheep (15:4).** On the social status of shepherds in the first century see comments on 2:8. In the Old Testament, Israel is often identified as a flock and the Lord as their shepherd; for references see 11:23. A hundred sheep was an average flock for a herdsman of modest means.[442]

**Does he not leave the ninety-nine in the open country. . . ? (15:4).** This is not an irresponsible act. Shepherds generally worked in teams, so this man likely left the flock with one of his companions.[443] "In the open country" (lit., "in the wilderness") means that the shepherd delayed taking the rest home until he found the lost sheep.

**He joyfully puts it on his shoulders (15:5).** God is portrayed as carrying his people as sheep in Psalm 28:9 and Isaiah 40:11. See comments on the Lord as a shepherd at Luke 2:8.

## The Parable of the Lost Coin (15:8–10)

As with the previous parable, the key themes here are the intense effort to find what is lost and the joy experienced when it is found. God longs for his children to return to him.

**Ten silver coins (15:8).** The coin here is the Greek *drachmē*, approximately equivalent to a Roman denarius, worth about a day's wages. Some have suggested this is part of the woman's dowry and may have been worn as a headdress bedecked with coins or on a necklace (giving the coin special value to her).[444] This is speculative since the parable doesn't even mention her marriage. In any case, the woman's relative poverty makes the coin a major loss.

**Sweep the house (15:8).** The coin could have fallen in the many crevices on a stone floor. By sweeping, she may hope to hear the coin rattle.[445]

## The Parable of the Lost Son (15:11–31)

The parable of the lost (or prodigal) son brings the three parables on things lost to a climax. The parable has two principal parts. The first concerns the departure and reconciliation of the prodigal (15:11–24). As with the previous two parables, the finding of the lost symbolizes Jesus' ministry to the outcasts and sinners in Israel. God longs for and rejoices at the restoration of his lost children. In the second part (15:25–32), the older brother represents the religious leaders in Israel, who refuse to join Jesus in welcoming sinners and rejoicing at their restoration to God's family.

**Father, give me my share of the estate (15:12).** An inheritance was not normally distributed until a father's death; thus, to ask for it early would be a great insult to the father. It would be like saying, "I wish you were dead."[446] Upon receiving such a disgraceful request a father would be expected to beat his son or perhaps cut off his inheritance. Ben Sirach warns against giving one's inheritance while still alive, lest you be left destitute: "For it is better that your children should ask from you than that you should look to the hand of your children." The appropriate time to distribute it is "in the hour of death" (Sir. 33:20–24). While the Mishnah allowed for a father to legally divide his property before his death, the right to dispose of it did not pass to the heirs until he died. Until that time, the father retained control and did with it as he wished.[447] What is extraordinary here is that the younger son demands and receives the actual property, which he squanders, canceling any further claims to inheritance. The older son receives his inheritance ("he divided his property between *them*"), but it appropriately remains under the control of the father.[448] Jesus' readers would have been horrified first that the younger son would ask for the division, but then that he would demand power over it immediately. They would be equally shocked that a father would allow himself to be treated in this way.

**Got together all he had (15:13).** The Greek verb here (*synagō*) has the sense "to turn into cash."[449] The son callously sells off the family inheritance.

**A distant country . . . squandered his wealth in wild living (15:13).** The verb translated "squandered" normally means to scatter; the image is of throwing one's possessions to the wind.[450] The adverb translated "wild living" (*asōtōs*) suggests both reckless and immoral behavior.[451] The Jews considered the loss of family property to Gentiles a particularly grievous offense and grounds for excommunication.[452]

**To feed pigs (15:15).** Pigs were unclean animals for Jews (Lev. 11:7; Deut. 14:8) and to tend them was viewed as despicable work. The Talmud says, "Cursed is the man who raises swine and cursed is the man who teaches his son Greek philosophy."[453]

**The pods that the pigs were eating (15:16).** Most commentators consider these to be carob pods (*ceratonia siliqua*), which were used for animal feed and eaten only by very poor people.[454] A rabbinic saying reads: "When the Israelites are reduced to carob pods, then they repent."[455] This young man has sunk to the lowest possible state, working for a Gentile, tending pigs, and longing to eat their slop.

**When he came to his senses (15:17).** A later rabbinic proverb reflects the sentiments of the son: "When a son abroad goes barefoot [becomes destitute], then he remembers the comfort of his father's house."[456]

**I have sinned against heaven (15:18, 21).** "Heaven" is a Jewish expression for God, a way to avoid using the divine name.

**His father . . . ran to his son (15:20).** The scene is striking since even today, a distinguished Middle Eastern patriarch in robes does not run, but always walks in a slow and dignified manner. Running was viewed as humiliating and degrading.[457] The man's unrestrained joy and affection—even to the point of humiliation before others—reveals God's overwhelming love and grace for the lost sinner and the joy experienced when a person repents.

**The best robe . . . a ring . . . sandals (15:22).** These items represent full reinstatement into the family. The best robe was probably the father's own, since the patriarch had the finest robe in the house.[458] For the robe as a symbol of honor and royal authority see Esther 6:6–11. There may also be eschatological significance here since glorified believers are said to receive white robes (Rev. 6:11; 7:9, 13). The ring may be a signet ring, indicating membership and authority in the family (cf. Gen. 41:42; Est. 3:10; 8:2). Sandals distinguished sons from servants.

**REFLECTIONS**

**THE PARABLE OF THE PRODIGAL** son illustrates God's grace and forgiveness for us as sinners. Though we have turned from God and squandered our inheritance, he is always ready to welcome us back with open arms. Since God has forgiven us in this way, we must reflect our Father's character and welcome those who return to him.

**Bring the fattened calf (15:23).** A fattened calf was selected and fed for a special occasion such as a wedding feast. Bailey claims that the choice of a calf over a goat or a sheep indicates that the whole village is to be invited, confirming the father's desire to reconcile his son to the community.[459]

**The older brother became angry (15:28).** According to Middle Eastern custom, the oldest son should have been the key reconciler between the father and his rebellious sibling. Moreover, to refuse to join in a banquet given by his father would be viewed as a great public insult. Instead of confronting the father privately later, he dishonors him by arguing while the guests are present.[460] His failure to use an honorific title ("my father" or "sir") in 15:29 also demonstrates a disrespectful attitude.

**This son of yours . . . squandered your property with prostitutes (15:30).** The older brother attempts to represent his brother as the rebellious son of Deuteronomy 21:18–21, who should by law be stoned. He also refuses to identify him as "my brother."

## The Parable of the Shrewd Manager (16:1–15)

Whereas chapter 15 concerns parables about God's love for the lost, chapter 16 concerns the spiritual dangers of their counterparts, the wealthy and powerful. The parable of the shrewd manager is an encouragement to use worldly wealth shrewdly for eternal purposes (16:9). Though this general moral is clear, the parable itself is one of Jesus' most puzzling.

The primary problem facing interpreters is that Jesus appears to condone the steward's seemingly dishonest behavior. Various explanations have been suggested. (1) The traditional one is that though the manager acted dishonestly, Jesus' application relates only to the manager's shrewdness, not to his dishonesty. (2) Other interpretations seek to justify the manager's actions, claiming that while he originally acted dishonestly in squandering his master's resources (16:1), he is now acting justly in reducing the clients' debts (16:2–8). (a) Some suggest he is removing the master's interest charges, forbidden by the Old Testament law.[461] (b) Others think that he is removing his own exorbitant commission.[462]

Whichever interpretation is correct, Jesus' sayings that follow draw application from the parable. (1) God's people should act with discernment and shrewdness in the management of their resources (16:8b). (2) Worldly wealth (lit., "unrighteous mammon") should be used to make friends who will provide access to "eternal dwellings" (16:9). The plural "friends" here may refer to God the Father and Jesus or perhaps God and the angels. (3) Those who are faithful with a little will be entrusted with much (16:10). (4) No one can serve two masters (16:13). The manager appropriately chooses a secure future with his "friends" (=God) over his worldly wealth, which will be lost anyway when he loses his position. (5) Finally, the Pharisees—described by Luke as "lovers of money"—scoff at Jesus' criticism of worldly wealth. Jesus condemns their self-justification and pronounces their worldly value system detestable in God's sight (16:14–15).

**A rich man whose manager (16:1).** The rich man here may be an absentee landlord and the servant his estate manager (*oikonomos*). This situation was common in Galilee, with its large landed estates and many peasant tenant farmers (see 20:9–19). Managers of this kind had significant financial and administrative authority.

**Give an account of your management (16:2).** The owner is asking for a written statement of financial accounts, probably for the benefit of his successor.

**To dig . . . to beg (16:3).** Manual labor was viewed as a lower manner of life than that of a scholar or other "white-collar" worker.[463] Begging was considered a shameful life. Sirach says, "It is better to die than to beg."[464]

**His master's debtors (16:5).** These may be either independent merchants or perhaps the owner's tenant farmers. If the latter, their debts are the portions of the crops owed to the landlord. The former may be suggested by the large value of their debts and the fact that they are portrayed as capable of employing a manager (16:4).

**Eight hundred gallons of olive oil . . . a thousand bushels of wheat (16:6–7).** The large debt suggests relatively wealthy businessmen. The actual measurements are 100 "baths" (a bath was about 8 gallons of olive oil) and 100 "cors" (a cor was about 10 bushels) of wheat. The former would have been worth about 1,000 denarii or about three years' wages for a day laborer; the latter,

2,500 denarii or about eight years' wages.[465] The reduction of debt in each case (from 100 to 50 baths and from 100 to 80 cors, respectively) would have been roughly the same, worth about 500 denarii.

**The master commended the dishonest manager (16:8).** Since the owner is now in good graces with his clients (who assume the manager's actions were at the owner's command), he will not reverse the transactions, which would bring shame on himself and accusations of miserliness. Instead, he accepts the loss and wryly commends the manager's cleverness.[466] On the values of shame and honor see comments on 11:5–8; 14:9.

**People of this world . . . people of the light (16:8).** Lit., "sons of this age . . . sons of light." The children of the light are those who will enter God's glorious kingdom. The community at Qumran considered themselves the "sons of light," God's eschatological community opposing the forces of darkness[467] (see also John 12:36; 1 Thess. 5:5).

**Worldly wealth (16:9, 11).** This is a good translation for the literal "mammon of unrighteousness" (KJV), which does not mean "wealth gained dishonestly." Mammon is an Aramaic term that refers to possessions of all kinds. "Unrighteousness" (*adikia*) here carries the sense "of this world" in contrast to "of God's kingdom."[468]

**When it is gone . . . you will be welcomed (16:9).** An old Egyptian proverb says, "Satisfy thy clients with what has accrued to thee. . . . If misfortunes occur among those [now] favored, it is the clients who [still] say: 'Welcome!'"[469] Old Testament wisdom literature speaks of the fleeting nature of riches (Prov. 23:5; 27:24; cf. Isa. 10:3).

**Whoever can be trusted with very little (16:10).** There are rabbinic parallels to this principle. One notes that God "does not give a big thing to a man until He has tested him in a small matter; and afterwards He promotes him to a great thing." The illustration is then given of Moses and David, who were faithful with sheep and so were given leadership over the nation.[470]

**No servant can serve two masters (16:13).** Some have claimed that behind this verse is the fact that slaves in the ancient world could not be owned by more than one person. But this is not the case (see Acts 16:19).[471] The saying means rather that complete devotion to more than one master is impossible. The temptation will always be to love and serve one more than the other.

**Pharisees, who loved money (16:14).** While the Sadducees—the religious aristocracy—were especially known for their love of wealth,[472] the Pharisees are sometimes accused of greed and hypocrisy in Jewish literature.[473]

## Additional Teachings (16:16–18)

This passage sums up the theme of promise and fulfillment that runs as a thread throughout Luke-Acts. Jesus affirms that John the Baptist stands at the crossroads of the two ages. Though the last of the old covenant prophets, he is also the herald of the Messiah and the dawning kingdom of God. John's relationship to the two covenants then sparks a statement about the continuing validity of the Old Testament law. This does not mean that each individual command must continue to be obeyed (many were unique for Israel), but that the Old Testament remains God's Word because it prophetically points to the Christ. Luke views the Old Testament primarily as "promise" rather than "law."

Jesus' statement about divorce seems at first sight unrelated to the context. Luke probably includes it here to show that in the new covenant age, Jesus' authoritative teaching sets the new standard, both explaining and fulfilling the Old Testament law.

**The Law and the Prophets (16:16).** This is a way of referring to the Old Testament, which in the Hebrew canon was divided into three sections, the Law (*Torah*), the Prophets (*Neviʾim*), and the Writings (*Ketuʾbim*). The Hebrew canon is known as the *Tanak*, from the first letter of each of these names (cf. 16:29; 24:27, 44).

**John (16:16).** See comments on 1:5–25; 7:18–35, especially verses 24–28, and "John the Baptist and the Community at Qumran" and "Josephus on John the Baptist."

**Easier for heaven and earth to disappear (16:17).** "Heaven and earth," conjoined like this, are symbols of permanence, but only temporal permanence. At the end of history, the present heavens and earth will be destroyed and replaced by a new heaven and earth (Job 14:12; Ps. 102:26).[474] God's Word, however, endures forever (Ps. 119:89, 160; cf. Luke 21:33).[475]

**The least stroke of a pen (16:17).** The Greek word *keraia* (lit., "horn") means a "hook" or "projection" and was used of a short stroke or a part of a letter of the alphabet.[476] In the Hebrew alphabet certain letters are distinguished by very short strokes, as with the difference between the *resh* (ר) and the *daleth* (ד).

**Anyone who divorces his wife (16:18).** The Old Testament recognized the reality of divorce, even if it did not explicitly sanction it (Deut. 24:1–4). The rabbis debated legitimate grounds. The conservative school of Shammai allowed a man to divorce his wife only in the case of unfaithfulness, while the more liberal school of Hillel accepted almost any reason, including the ruining of a meal. Rabbi Akiba is even cited as saying that divorce was allowed if the man "found another fairer than she" (*m. Gitt.* 9:10), giving as justification Deuteronomy 24:1, "[if she] becomes displeasing to him." Jesus reacts strongly against such a casual attitude toward the law and points to the inviolable nature of marriage: To break a marriage vow and marry another constitutes adultery. God hates divorce (Mal. 2:16).[477]

## The Rich Man and Lazarus (16:19–31)

This parable repeats a theme found throughout Luke's Gospel, the great eschatological reversal that comes with the kingdom of God. Lazarus represents the humble and contrite poor who will be made rich, while the rich man represents the arrogant wealthy who will be left destitute. The twin morals of the story are: (1) Those who value riches more than God will be rejected (cf. 12:13–21); and (2) God demands a heart of love and justice for the poor and lowly (cf. 14:12–14). The final part of the parable introduces a third theme relating more directly to Jesus' ministry (16:27–31). When in Hades, the rich man's request for water is rejected, and he begs that Lazarus be sent to his five living brothers to spare them the same fate. Abraham denies the request, pointing out that they already have the Scriptures to show them the truth. Even if someone were to rise from the dead they would not believe. The statement is a veiled reference to the religious leaders, who are presently rejecting the scriptural prophecies concerning Jesus the Messiah and who will continue to reject him even when he rises from the dead.

Stories of justice attained in the afterlife appear occasionally in ancient literature. A Jewish parallel, the story of Bar Ma'jan, has been described in the introduction to the parable of the great banquet (14:15–24). In a first-century Egyptian parallel, a man named Setme views two burials, one of a very rich man and one of a poor man. While the rich man's is conducted with much pomp and a great crowd of mourners, the poor man is wrapped in a mat and carried out alone. When Setme announces how much more blessed it is to be rich, his son Si-osire says he hopes his father will have an afterlife like the poor man. Setme expresses dismay at this remark, so his son (who has been reincarnated) takes him to the underworld and shows him both men. Because of his good deeds, the poor man is living in royal splendor, while the rich man, whose evil deeds outweighed his good, is in gruesome torment.[478]

**Dressed in purple and fine linen (16:19).** Purple was the color of royalty. The term probably refers to an outer robe made of fine wool dyed with Phoenician purple, an expensive dye made from murex, a type of mollusk. Fine linen probably refers to his undergarments—the best underwear money could buy.

**At his gate was laid a beggar named Lazarus (16:20).** The reference to a "gate" suggests that the rich man owns a large estate. "Lazarus" is an abbreviated form of Eleazar and appropriately means "God helps."[479]

**Covered with sores . . . longing to eat what fell (16:20–21).** The picture is one of absolute degradation. A later rabbinic

**RICH MAN'S HOUSE**

Remains of a Herodian-era home discovered in Jerusalem.

proverb says, "There are three whose life is no life: he who depends on the table of another, he who is ruled by his wife, and he whose body is burdened with sufferings."[480] Lazarus has two out of three. From society's perspective, he has "no life" at all.

**Even the dogs came and licked his sores (16:21).** The Jews viewed dogs as detestable animals and dangerous scavengers, not lovable pets (1 Kings 14:11; 21:19, 23).[481]

**Angels carried him to Abraham's side (16:22).** Literally, "to Abraham's chest or bosom." The phrase probably alludes to a feast (perhaps even the messianic banquet, see comments on 13:28–29; 14:15), where guests reclined beside one another around a table (see John 13:23). The place beside the host was the position of highest honor (see 14:7). Pious Jews expected to join Abraham and the patriarchs at the messianic banquet (see 13:28).

**In hell (16:23).** See comments on 10:15; 12:5. The Greek here is *hadēs* (the parallel to the Hebrew *Sheol*), which can refer (1) to the grave or death itself (the place of both the righteous and unrighteous; see Acts 2:27); or (2) to the place of the wicked dead. Here it carries this second sense. *Hadēs* is sometimes viewed as an interim place of torment, ultimately to be thrown into the lake of fire (Rev. 20:13–14).

**I am in agony in this fire (16:24).** Torment and fire are associated with the judgment of the wicked both in Judaism and in early Christianity[482] (see comments on 12:5).

**A great chasm has been fixed (16:26).** The permanence of divine judgment and reward was commonly taught in Judaism. Second Esdras (*4 Ezra*) 7:104 reads, "The day of judgment is decisive and displays to all the seal of truth" (cf. Rev. 20:10).

**Moses and the Prophets (16:29).** This is the same as "the Law and the Prophets" (16:16), identifying the five books of the Law by their traditional author.[483] The Qumran scrolls use a similar designation.[484]

**If they do not listen to Moses and the Prophets (16:31).** Despite the Old Testament's repeated instruction to care for the poor and outcast, Israel's rich and powerful often oppressed them.[485]

## Sin, Faith, Duty (17:1–10)

This section is directed to Jesus' disciples (17:1) and contains various teachings on the characteristics of true discipleship: forgiveness, faith, and servanthood.

**A millstone tied around his neck (17:2).** This would be a large round stone with a hole in its center, pulled by an animal

MILLSTONE

An olive press with a millstone in the center.

to grind grain. It would weigh hundreds of pounds and so would cause certain drowning.

**If your brother sins, rebuke him . . . forgive him . . . seven times (17:3–4).** "Seven times" is not an exact number, but means "many times" a day, as in Psalm 119:164. The principle of rebuke and forgiveness appears in Leviticus 19:17–18 as well as in Jewish texts.[486] Yet none emphasizes such unlimited forgiveness (cf. Matt. 18:21–22).

**As small as a mustard seed (17:6).** The mustard seed was used proverbially in Judaism of something very small (see comments on 13:19).[487]

**Mulberry tree, "Be uprooted and planted in the sea" (17:6).** This tree has been identified as the black mulberry, which has a vast root system enabling it to live up to six hundred years.[488] To uproot it required a major effort. To "plant it in the sea" is an odd and paradoxical image, since the roots could not be established in water. The point is that faith can do the impossible.

**Would he say to the servant " . . . sit down to eat"? (17:7).** "Servant" here is *doulos*, a bondservant or slave. A master would never think of eating with his slaves. For the shocking image of a master serving in this way see 12:37; for social status at meals see 14:7.

**We have only done our duty (17:10).** Similar expressions of humility and service owed to God appear in Jewish writings. Rabbi ben Zakkai is cited in the Mishnah as saying, "If you have wrought much in the Law claim not merit for yourself, for to this end you were created."[489] Similarly, Antigonus of Soko said, "Be not like slaves that minister to the master for the sake of receiving a bounty."[490] The believer owes all to God without expectations of reward.

## Ten Healed of Leprosy (17:11–19)

When Jesus heals ten men with leprosy, only one returns to thank him, and this one is a hated Samaritan. The episode not only demonstrates Jesus' compassion, but also symbolizes what is happening in Jesus' ministry: The religious leaders reject the gospel while "outsiders" (sinners, tax collectors, and Samaritans) joyfully receive it with a heart of gratitude.

**Samaria (17:11).** On Samaria and the hatred and distrust between Jews and Samaritans see comments on 9:52; 10:29; John 4:4–42.

**Ten men who had leprosy (17:12).** Biblical leprosy was not the same as modern leprosy (Hansen's disease), but a variety of diseases that may have included psoriasis, lupus, ringworm, and others (see comments on 5:12). Lepers were required to keep their distance from people and to cry out "Unclean! Unclean!" when approached (Lev. 13:45–46). Because of this social ostracism, lepers sought out others with the disease, even those with whom they would not normally associate.

**Go, show yourselves to the priests (17:14).** The Old Testament set out strict guidelines in Leviticus 13–14 for the examination and isolation of leprosy (see Lev. 13–14). It was the job of the priests to diagnose leprosy and to declare healed lepers "clean" (see comments on 5:12, 14).

**He was a Samaritan (17:16).** It would have been shocking to Jesus' Jewish audience that only the despised Samaritan returned with a grateful heart. See 2 Kings 5 for an Old Testament account of a non-Jew healed of leprosy and Jesus' reference to this episode in Luke 4:27.

**Your faith has made you well (17:19).** The Greek says, "Your faith has saved you." While the Greek verb *sōzō* is often used by Luke of healings, here there is probably the added dimension of spiritual healing. While all ten were healed, only one was "saved."

REFLECTIONS

**WHEN JESUS HEALED TEN MEN** with leprosy, only one saw fit to come back and thank him. Astonishingly, he was a despised Samaritan, the least likely of the ten to return. From this story we learn that a grateful heart is one that recognizes God's undeserved favor poured out for us and responds with faith and obedience.

## The Coming of the Kingdom of God (17:20–37)

Jesus' teaching here concerns the nature of the kingdom, both in its present and future manifestations. The first part is directed at the Pharisees (17:20–21) and responds to the traditional Jewish expectation of a dramatic and cataclysmic arrival of the kingdom of God. Jesus teaches that the kingdom of God will not come (at first) in a outward visible form, but rather through his healings, exorcisms, and authoritative teaching (see 4:18–19; 7:22–23).

Turning next to his disciples, Jesus affirms that the kingdom *will come* in a dramatic and cataclysmic manner, when he—the Son of Man—returns. But first he must be rejected by his own people, suffer, and die. During the interim period that follows, his disciples need not look for hidden signs or chase rumors of his coming, for his return will be evident to all (17:22–25). It will be a time of great judgment against those who have turned from God (17:26–29). In light of these coming events, God's people must stay focused on his priorities, forsaking all to follow him. Jesus gives additional teaching on the end times in the Olivet Discourse in chapter 21.

**The Pharisees (17:20).** For Pharisees see comments on 5:17 and next comment.

**When the kingdom of God would come (17:20).** The Pharisees had a strong expectation for the reestablishment of God's kingdom on earth through the Davidic Messiah. The *Psalms of Solomon*, a first-century B.C. document arising from Pharisaic circles, beseeches God to raise up his Messiah, the Son of David, to rule over Israel, to destroy her enemies, and to establish a glorious and righteous kingdom.[491] Jesus has been proclaiming the kingdom of God, and the Pharisees want to see a physical manifestation of its power and glory. For more on the kingdom of God see comments on 4:43.

**With your careful observation (17:20).** This Greek phrase is better translated "with premonitory signs" or "with signs predicting its arrival." Jesus is referring to the dramatic heavenly signs common in the apocalyptic literature of his day.[492] Jesus does not say these signs will not occur in the future (see 21:25; Acts

2:19–20), but that the Pharisees are missing the present manifestation of the kingdom in Jesus' ministry.

**Days of the Son of Man (17:22).** The "days of the Messiah" was a rabbinic way of referring to the time when the Messiah would come and establish his glorious kingdom on earth.[493] For more on the kingdom of God see comments on 4:43; for background to the Son of Man title see comments on 5:24; 9:26.

**Men will tell you, "There he is!" (17:23).** Jesus warns against following false messiahs. Messianic expectations were high in first-century Palestine, and at various times individuals arose claiming to be God's agent of deliverance, a prophet, or a messiah. In Acts 5, Rabbi Gamaliel speaks of two such messianic pretenders: Theudas, who "claimed to be somebody" (i.e., a messiah), and Judas the Galilean, who led a revolt against the Romans (Acts 5:36–37). Similarly, in 21:38 Paul is suspected by the commander of the Roman temple guard of being a certain Egyptian who led four thousand Jews to the Mount of Olives in a messianic action.

Josephus, with his pro-Roman sympathies, speaks of such prophets and messiahs as dangerous criminals bent on leading the nation to destruction.[494] In one episode a group of these "wicked" men deceived the people by claiming divine inspiration and leading them into the desert to await a sign of God's deliverance. The procurator Felix responded by sending troops to destroy and disperse them.[495] Such Roman police actions were not uncommon (cf. 13:1).

**The Son of Man in his day (17:24, 30).** The "day" of the Son of Man here and in 17:30 probably alludes to the Old Testament "day of the LORD," the great and final time of judgment for all the earth (Isa. 13:6).[496]

**He must suffer many things (17:25).** See comments on 9:22.

**The days of Noah . . . the days of Lot (17:26–28).** (Cf. Genesis 6–9 [Noah]; 18:16–19:29 [Lot].) The generations of Noah and Lot are often identified together in Judaism as symbols of great wickedness and examples of God's judgment.[497] Sirach 16:7–8 reads: "He did not forgive the ancient giants who revolted in their might. He did not spare the neighbors of Lot, whom he loathed on account of their arrogance." The Mishnah says neither the "generation of the Flood" nor "the men of Sodom" have any share in the world to come.[498] (Cf. comments on 10:12.)

**The day the Son of Man is revealed (17:30).** Some Jewish texts speak of the Messiah as hidden by God and waiting to be revealed at the end time.[499]

**On the roof (17:31).** The flat roofs of Palestine were used as living space and usually had external staircases. The idea is that there will be no time to go inside to retrieve possessions.

*right* ▶

**SOD ROOF**

A house in Beit Guvrin.

**Remember Lot's wife (17:32).** Lot's wife became a pillar of salt when she looked back at the destruction of Sodom (Gen. 19:26)—an example of unbelief in later Judaism. Wisdom of Solomon 10:7 speaks of "a pillar of salt standing as a monument to an unbelieving soul."

**One will be taken and the other left (17:34–35).** The image is of separation, one to salvation and one to judgment.

**Where there is a dead body, there the vultures will gather (17:37).** Jesus' puzzling response to the disciples' question, "Where, Lord?" seems to mean that the place of judgment will be as evident to all (and as gruesome) as a dead body around which vultures gather (17:37).

## The Parable of the Persistent Widow (18:1–8)

Jesus' discussion of the end times and coming judgment (17:20–37) naturally raises the issue of trials and perseverance. Jesus tells a parable about a widow who through perseverance eventually receives justice from an uncaring and unjust judge. The theme develops through a rabbinic style "lesser to greater" (*qal wāḥômer*) argument. If this woman's persistence resulted in justice from an evil judge, how much more will our persistent prayers be answered by our loving heavenly Father.

**A judge who neither feared God (18:2).** Judges in Israel were supposed to be God's representatives, administering justice to those who most needed it. When King Jehoshaphat appointed judges in Judah, he instructed them: "Consider carefully what you do, because you are not judging for man but for the LORD . . . for with the LORD our God there is no injustice or partiality or bribery" (2 Chron. 19:6–7). The judge in the parable is the opposite of the model judge. Edersheim claims that judges in Jerusalem were so corrupt they were referred to as *Dayyaney Gezeloth* (Robber-Judges) rather than by their real title, *Dayyaney Gezeroth* (Judges of Prohibitions).[500]

**A widow (18:3).** Widows are viewed throughout Scripture as the most vulnerable and helpless members of society, for whom God has special concern. The Old Testament warns that God will avenge those who withhold justice from the widow and the fatherless.[501] The same is true later on in Judaism.[502]

**Grant me justice against my adversary (18:3).** The widow may be facing a creditor trying to take her land or property. The law is evidently on her side since she only asks for justice.[503]

**Wear me out with her coming (18:5).** "Wear me out" carries the literal sense of "strike the eye" or give someone a black eye. The figurative sense intended here is to "wear down with persistence," as one boxer wears down another.

**Will not God bring about justice . . . who cry out to him (18:7).** God's vindication of the widow and fatherless when they cry out to him is a common theme in the Old Testament and Judaism (see comments on 18:3). Sirach 35:17–21 says that God

> *will not ignore the supplication of*
> *the orphan,*
> *or the widow when she pours out*
> *her complaint. . . .*
> *The prayer of the humble pierces the*
> *clouds,*

*and it will not rest until it reaches its goal;*
*it will not desist until the Most High responds.*

**Will he find faith on the earth? (18:8).** Jewish writings often portray the time of distress before the dawn of the messianic age as one of lawlessness and apostasy (see comments on 21:23).[504] This verse connects the parable to the eschatological theme of 17:20–37.

REFLECTIONS

THE STORY OF THE PERSISTENT widow reminds us of the power and potential of prayer. If this woman's persistent requests to an unjust judge results in an answer, how much more will our prayers of faith to our loving heavenly Father be answered.

## Parable of the Pharisee and the Tax Collector (18:9–14)

This parable illustrates the need for a humble and contrite heart before God. In the parable forgiveness comes not to the proud and self-righteous Pharisee, who thinks that his good deeds have earned him a right standing before God, but to the tax collector, who recognizes his own sinfulness and prays for mercy. The parable probably shocks Jesus' listeners, who consider the Pharisees' pious and upright, but the tax collectors wicked sinners.

**A Pharisee (18:10).** For background on the Pharisees see comments on 5:17. The Pharisees were admired by the common folk for their piety and devotion to the Mosaic Law. Our contemporary equation of Pharisaism with hypocrisy would not have been made by a first-century Jew.

**A tax collector (18:10).** See comments on 3:12. The tax collectors were among the most despised members of Jewish society because of their reputation for embezzlement and their complicity with the Roman oppressors. The Mishnah prohibits even receiving alms from a tax collector at his office, since the money is presumed to have been gained illegally.[505] If a tax collector entered a house, all that was in it became unclean.[506] The very presence of a tax collector in the temple, the house of God, was viewed as an act of defilement.

**God, I thank you that I am not like other men (18:11).** The Pharisee's prayer has an external air of humility since thanksgiving is given to God. Psalm 26 is conceptually similar, as David speaks of his "blameless" life and his separation from sinners. The difference is one of heart attitude. David had a pure heart (Ps. 26:2); this Pharisee has a heart of pride, praying "about himself" (Luke 18:11) and seeking self-glorification. Similar prayers of self-congratulation appear in later Jewish literature (though there are also examples reflecting greater humility). One, recorded in the Jerusalem Talmud (c. A.D. 400) and attributed to a first-century rabbi, reads:

> I give thanks before thee O Lord my God, and God of my fathers, that thou has appointed my portion with those who sit in the College and the Synagogue, and hast not appointed my lot in the theatres and circuses. . . . I labour to inherit Paradise and they labour to inherit the pit of destruction.[507]

**I fast twice a week and give a tenth of all I get (18:12).** Both fasting and tithing were signs of piety in Judaism. Fasting was required only on the Day of Atonement (Lev. 16:29–31), but pious Jews fasted twice a week, on Mondays and Thursdays.[508] For more on fasting see comments on Luke 5:33. On tithing and almsgiving see comments on 11:41–42. The problem here is not the man's accomplishments (which are impressive), but his self-righteousness and attitude of superiority.

**Beat his breast (18:13).** Beating the breast was a sign of mourning and/or repentance.[509]

**God, have mercy on me, a sinner (18:13).** Like the prayer of the Pharisee (see comments on 18:11), this one has conceptual parallels in the Psalms. In Psalm 51, David prays, "Have mercy on me, O God.... For I know my transgressions, and my sin is always before me."[510] God longs to forgive and welcome back the repentant sinner (see Luke 15:11–32).

**Everyone who exalts himself (18:14).** See comments on 14:11.

## The Little Children and Jesus (18:15–17)

The reference to the humble who will be exalted (18:14) transitions naturally into a passage about people bringing their children to be blessed by Jesus. When the disciples try to turn them away, Jesus says not to hinder them because the kingdom of God belongs to "such as these." The point is that receiving the kingdom of God takes childlike faith and dependence on God.

**Bringing babies ... children (18:15–16).** The word for "baby" (*brephos*) usually means an infant, but it can refer to a child old enough to understand Scripture (see 2 Tim. 3:15). The use of the more general term *paidia* ("children") in verse 16 confirms that various ages are present.

**To have him touch them (18:15).** The people are probably requesting a blessing from this respected rabbi.[511]

**They rebuked them (18:15).** Children had essentially no social status in the ancient world, so the disciples consider this an intrusion on Jesus' valuable time. For the status of children, see comments on 9:47–48.

## The Rich Ruler (18:18–30)

This story illustrates the need for absolute commitment to Jesus and the impossibility of earning salvation through human achievement. Just as it is impossible for a camel to pass through a needle's eye, so *no one* can be saved through human effort or riches. Faith in God alone saves.

**A certain ruler (18:18).** Luke does not specify what kind of a ruler this is. He may have been a synagogue official or a secular city official. The latter is more likely since Luke does not identify him with the teachers of the law or the Pharisees.

**What must I do to inherit eternal life? (18:18).** The same question was posed earlier by a teacher of the law (10:27) and concerns immortal life in God's presence received at the final resurrection—a common topic in rabbinic discussions. On eternal life see comments on 10:27.

**No one is good—except God alone (18:19).** While the Old Testament frequently refers to God's goodness (Ps. 34:8; 106:1), the point here is moral perfection, a doctrine also taught in the Old Testament and Judaism.[512]

**You know the commandments: "Do not commit adultery . . ." (18:20).** Jesus cites, though not in biblical order, the fifth through the ninth of the Ten Commandments.[513] These are commands relate to relationships with other human beings.

**All these I have kept since I was a boy (18:21).** It was not uncommon for pious Jews to claim complete adherence to the Old Testament law.[514] Paul says he was "faultless" before his conversion (Phil. 3:6). Luke describes Zechariah and Elizabeth as upright, "observing all the Lord's commandments and regulations blamelessly" (Luke 1:6).

**Treasure in heaven (18:22).** See comments on 12:33.

**How hard it is for the rich to enter the kingdom of God! (18:24).** Since wealth is sometimes viewed in the Old Testament and Judaism as evidence of God's blessing, it was popularly believed that the rich were favored by God.[515] Yet the Old Testament and Judaism also repeatedly warn against the dangers of trusting in riches instead of God.[516]

**A camel to go through the eye of a needle (18:25).** Some commentators have tried to soften Jesus' hyperbole by claiming that there was a small gate in Jerusalem known as the "Needle's Eye." Camels could pass through it only by unloading and stooping down low. But there is no archaeological or literary evidence that such a gate existed in the first century. Others have claimed that the word *kamēlos* (camel) was originally *kamilos*, a ship's cable or rope, and that the idea was passing a rope through a needle's eye. Again this is unlikely since there is no manuscript evidence for this reading. In fact, both these "solutions" miss Jesus' point, which is the *impossibility* of a rich man being saved *by trusting in his riches.* It is only through faith in God that anyone can be saved. Jesus explicitly says, "What is *impossible* with men is possible with God" (18:27, italics added).

## Jesus Again Predicts His Death (18:31–34)

Jesus has explicitly predicted his death three times in Luke's Gospel (9:22, 44–45; 17:25) and has alluded to it at least three other times (5:35; 12:49–50; 13:32–33). Now, as the Journey to Jerusalem draws to a close (see introductory comments to 9:51–19:44), Jesus again predicts the suffering, death, and resurrection that await him in Jerusalem. As before, the disciples fail to grasp its significance (cf. 9:45).

**Everything that is written by the prophets (18:31).** The premier passage on the suffering of the Messiah is Isaiah 52:13–53:12, where the Suffering Servant offers up his life for the sins of his people. Jesus may also be thinking of Old Testament passages like Psalm 16 (Acts 2:25–28), Psalm 2 (Acts 4:25–26), Psalm 118:22 (Luke 20:17), and Isaiah 50:4–9 (see comments on Luke 18:32). The Jews of Jesus' day did not interpret Isaiah 53 with reference to a suffering Messiah, focusing instead on the Old Testament portrait of a conquering, victorious king (Isa. 11, etc.; see comments on 9:22).

**The Son of Man (18:31).** See comments on 5:24; 9:26.

**Mock him . . . spit on him, flog him (18:32).** The verse probably alludes to the suffering of the Servant of the Lord in Isaiah 50:4–9, the third of Isaiah's Servant Songs: "I offered my back to those who beat me, my cheeks to those who pulled out my beard; I did not hide my face from mocking and spitting" (Isa. 50:6; cf. John 19:1).

## A Blind Beggar Receives His Sight (18:35–43)

The account of the healing of the blind man outside Jericho functions on various levels in Luke's Gospel. While another example of Jesus' compassionate heart, it also sets the stage for the Messiah's entrance into Jerusalem. Healing the blind recalls Isaiah's promise of the signs of the new age and points back to Jesus' use of these texts to define his ministry.[517] The reader is reminded that in Jesus the age of salvation is dawning. Further, the blind man's cry to Jesus as "Son of David" recalls Gabriel's announcement to Mary that Jesus is the promised Messiah from David's line, who will reign forever on his throne (1:32–33; cf. 2:11). Israel's Savior and King is about to enter Jerusalem. Finally, the blind man's simple faith and subsequent healing pick up the Journey-to-Jerusalem theme that the humble outcasts of Israel are the recipients of God's mercy and salvation.

**Begging (18:35).** With little in the way of social welfare in the first century, those who could not work were forced to beg (see comments on 16:3 for the shamefulness of begging). Giving alms to a beggar was considered a righteous deed in Judaism (see comments on 11:41).

**Son of David, have mercy on me! (18:38, 39).** "Son of David" became a favorite title in Judaism for the Messiah from David's line, who would defeat Israel's enemies and reign forever in justice and righteousness on David's throne.[518] Its background is found in the Davidic covenant of 2 Samuel 7:12–16.[519] For the messianic hope in the first century see Luke 1:32–33; 9:20; see also "Messianic Expectation in Jesus' Day."

## Zacchaeus the Tax Collector (19:1–10)

The story of Zacchaeus together with the parable of the ten minas (19:11–27) bring Luke's Journey to Jerusalem to a close (9:51–19:44). This episode is a fitting conclusion to a section that has sometimes been called "The Gospel to the Outcast." Zacchaeus is the ultimate of Israel's outcasts, not just a hated tax collector, but a *chief* tax collector, the worst among the worst. Yet manifesting God's grace, Jesus reaches out and offers salvation even to him. The "today" of salvation announced in the Nazareth sermon (4:21) now arrives in Zacchaeus's home (19:9). Many commentators consider 19:10 to be the best summarizing and epitomizing verse of Luke's Gospel: "For the Son of Man came to seek and to save what was lost."

**Jericho (19:1).** See "Jericho."

**A chief tax collector (19:2).** Both the Romans and local authorities imposed various taxes, tolls, and customs in Palestine. The Romans often leased the right to collect taxes to individuals, who then hired underlings to collect the taxes. Although the term "chief tax collector" (*architelōnēs*) is unique to this passage, it probably indicates that Zacchaeus is responsible for a broader region—perhaps the custom on goods passing between Perea and Judea—

**JERICHO**

*(top)* The Old Testament era tel is in the foreground. Jebel Quruntul (the Mount of Temptation) is in the background. *(bottom left)* Roman era Jericho: excavations at Herod's palace. *(bottom right)* Roman era Jericho: the remains of Herod's palace.

## ▸ Jericho

Jericho is located in an oasis in the Judean desert eighteen miles northwest of Jerusalem.[A-49] A winding desert road, familiar to Luke's readers from the parable of the good Samaritan (10:30), connects the two cities. In Jesus' day there were two Jerichos, the uninhabited city of the Old Testament and a new city located about a mile to the south. Since Mark says Jesus healed the man while leaving Jericho (10:46), some commentators think Jesus was between the two cities, leaving old Jericho (Mark) and approaching new Jericho (Luke). Another possibility is that Luke has rearranged the account to place the healing before the Zacchaeus episode in Jericho.

Archaeologists consider Jericho to be the oldest continuously inhabited city on earth, with settlements dating back to 8,000 B.C.[A-50] At 820 feet below sea level, it is also the world's lowest city.

with subordinates working for him.[520] It is not surprising, therefore, that Luke identifies him as a wealthy individual.

Tax collectors were despised in Israel because they were viewed as extortionists and Roman collaborators (see comments on 3:12; 18:10). The Jewish Mishnah goes so far as to say it is permissible to lie to tax collectors to protect one's property![521]

**A sycamore-fig tree (19:4).** This is evidently not the European sycamore, but the *ficus sycōorus,* also known as the "fig-mulberry." It is something like an oak with a short trunk and wide branches, making it easy to climb.[522]

**The guest of a "sinner" (19:7).** Table fellowship carried great social significance in the ancient world. For a religious-minded Pharisee to eat with a notorious sinner brought ceremonial defilement and social ostracism (see comments on 5:30; 14:7).

**I give half of my possessions to the poor (19:8).** Though almsgiving was a sign of great piety in Judaism (see comments on 11:41), later rabbis considered it unwise to give away more than twenty percent of one's goods, lest one become a burden to others.[523] Zacchaeus takes the radical step of giving away half.

◀ *left*

SYCAMORE TREE IN THE JORDAN VALLEY

## REFLECTIONS

**THOUGH THE STORY OF ZACCHAEUS** is often viewed as a cute children's story, it is in fact one of the most important stories in the whole Bible, since it reveals the heart of Jesus' mission and God's purpose for the world. Jesus came quintessentially to "seek and to save what was lost." Those who love God will share his passion to bring his wondrous salvation to a lost world.

**I will pay back four times the amount (19:8).** Normal restitution in the Old Testament for a wrong committed was to add one-fifth or 20 percent to the value of the goods lost.[524] The penalty for outright theft of an animal was much more severe, requiring restitution of four (2 Sam. 12:6) or five times (Ex. 22:1) the value of the animal. Similar penalties appear in Roman sources and in the Qumran scrolls.[525] Later Judaism seems to have softened this penalty, and the Mishnah only requires restitution equivalent to the loss.[526] By contrast Zacchaeus treats his ill-gotten wealth as theft and promises a full fourfold restitution (see comments on Luke 3:12; 18:10 for the Jewish presumption that a tax collector's wealth was illegally gained).

**A son of Abraham (19:9).** The Jews were proud of their status as children of Abraham (see 3:8) and treated this as reason enough for God's blessing. But a tax collector was viewed as having forfeited his rights as Abraham's offspring.

**To seek and to save what was lost (19:10).** This is a major theme in Luke's Gospel and reflects the image of a shepherd seeking his lost sheep (see comments on 11:23). It recalls especially the image in Ezekiel 34 of God as shepherd of his nation Israel.

## The Parable of the Ten Minas (19:11–27)

The parable of the ten minas teaches the need for Jesus' disciples to practice good stewardship during his absence. Servants who are faithful with the resources Jesus has given them will be rewarded at his return with greater privilege and responsibility. Those who exercise poor stewardship will suffer loss (see 1 Cor. 3:14–15).

A second point of the parable (not found in Matthew's similar parable of the talents, see Matt. 25:14–30) is to explain why the kingdom of God does not appear physically on earth at Jesus' entrance into Jerusalem (Luke 19:28–40). In his narrative introduction Luke says Jesus told the parable "because he was near Jerusalem and the people thought that the kingdom of God was going to appear at once" (19:11). The nobleman in the parable goes away "to a distant country" to be appointed king, later to return with reward and judgment (19:12). The point is that Jesus will receive his royal authority not now in Jerusalem, but in heaven at his exaltation to God's right hand (see Acts 2:32–36). He will then return in the future to assume his throne, to reward his faithful stewards, and to judge those who rejected his kingship (19:14, 17, 27).

**The kingdom of God was going to appear at once (19:11).** Most Jewish expectations envisioned an earthly kingdom with Jerusalem as its center.[527] While not rejecting this expectation, Jesus makes it clear that the present manifestation of the kingdom will take on a different form (cf. Acts 1:6–8).

**Went to a distant country to have himself appointed king (19:12).** Since Rome ruled Palestine as a vassal kingdom, it was necessary to gain favor in the capital to consolidate one's kingship. Herod the Great, Archelaus (see 19:14), Herod Antipas, Herod Philip, and Herod Agrippa I all spent time in Rome to gain approval for their reigns.[528]

**Ten minas (19:13).** A mina was equivalent to one hundred drachmas; one drachma was approximately a day's wages. Each servant is thus given several month's wages and told to invest it appropriately to turn a profit.

**But his subjects hated him and sent a delegation after him (19:14).** This would recall for Jesus' hearers the story of Archelaus, the son of Herod the Great. When protests broke out after the death of Herod, Archelaus used his soldiers to violently restore order, killing over three thousand Jews at a Passover demonstration. The Jews responded by sending a fifty-man delegation to Rome to plead against his kingship. The emperor Caesar Augustus compromised by giving Archelaus half of Herod's kingdom (dividing the other half between his brothers Philip and Antipas; see comments on 3:1) and the title *ethnarch* instead of king. Augustus ruled that if Archelaus governed wisely, he would later appoint him king.[529] Instead, Archelaus ruled poorly and was deposed in A.D. 6.

**Take charge of ten cities . . . five cities (19:17, 19).** In the parable this refers to servants who have proven faithful in lesser administrative roles being appointed to regional governorships. A rabbinic proverb affirms the principle: "Run to fulfill the lightest duty even as the weightiest . . . for the reward of a duty [done] is a duty [to be done]."[530] In the application of the parable the authority given to the servants coincides with the eschatological rule promised to God's faithful servants. Such rule by the saints appears in both Jewish and early Christian literature.[531]

**Laid away in a piece of cloth (19:20).** The rabbis speak of this as a careless and irresponsible way to guard money.[532] The servant is not only unfaithful, he is also foolhardy. Even hiding money in the ground was considered safer (cf. Matt. 25:18, 25).

**Put my money on deposit . . . collected it with interest (19:23).** The servant is chastised for not bothering to (lit.) "put the money on the table," that is, to loan it to money lenders in order to receive interest. Because wealth in the ancient world tended to be concentrated in the hands of few, high interest rates could be charged and large profits made. The Mishnah says that an individual is not personally liable for money lost by a money lender.[533]

**To everyone who has, more will be given (19:26).** See comments on 8:18.

**Those enemies . . . kill them in front of me (19:27).** Jesus' hearers understood this image since it was a common practice in the ancient world for kings to eliminate their enemies and rivals when they ascended to the throne (see 1 Kings 2:13–46).[534] The application of the parable is the final judgment against those who ultimately reject Jesus as Savior and King.

## The Triumphal Entry (19:28–44)

Jesus' approach to Jerusalem (19:28–40) and his lament over the city (19:41–44) together set the stage for the climactic events that will occur there. On the one side there is rejoicing as Jesus publicly reveals his messiahship. Yet there is also a tragic side as he weeps over the city and predicts her destruction. Jerusalem has refused to recognize and acknowledge her Messiah and so faces judgment.

Though Luke does not explicitly cite Zechariah 9:9–10 (cf. Matt. 21:5), there is little doubt that Jesus' actions point to the prophet's portrait of the humble and righteous king, bringing salvation and peace:

> *Rejoice greatly, O Daughter of Zion!*
> *Shout, Daughter of Jerusalem!*
> *See, your king comes to you,*
> *righteous and having salvation,*
> *gentle and riding on a donkey,*
> *on a colt, the foal of a donkey. . . .*
> *He will proclaim peace to the nations.*
> *His rule will extend from sea to sea*
> *and from the River to the ends of*
> *the earth.* (Zech. 9:9–10)

THE AREA AROUND JERUSALEM

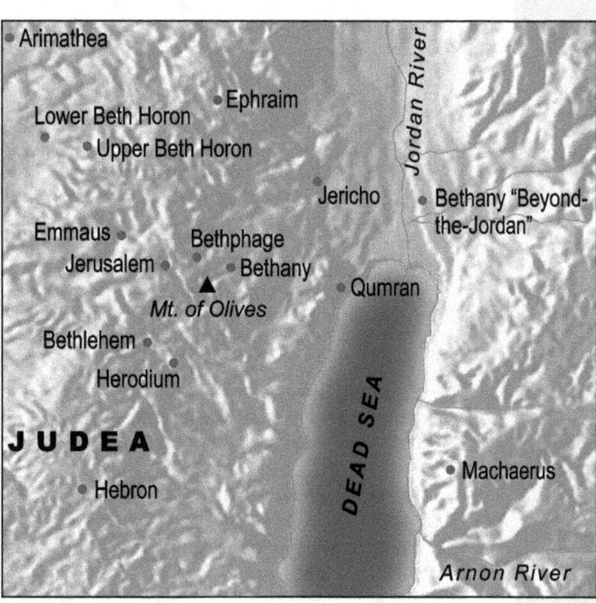

**PASSION WEEK**

Bethany, the Mount of Olives, and Jerusalem

**4. Clearing of the temple**
**MONDAY**
Mt 21:10—17
Mk 11:15—18
Lk 19:45—48

The next day he returned to the temple and found the court of the Gentiles full of traders and money changers making a large profit as they gave out Jewish coins in exchange for "pagan" money. Jesus drove them out and overturned their tables.

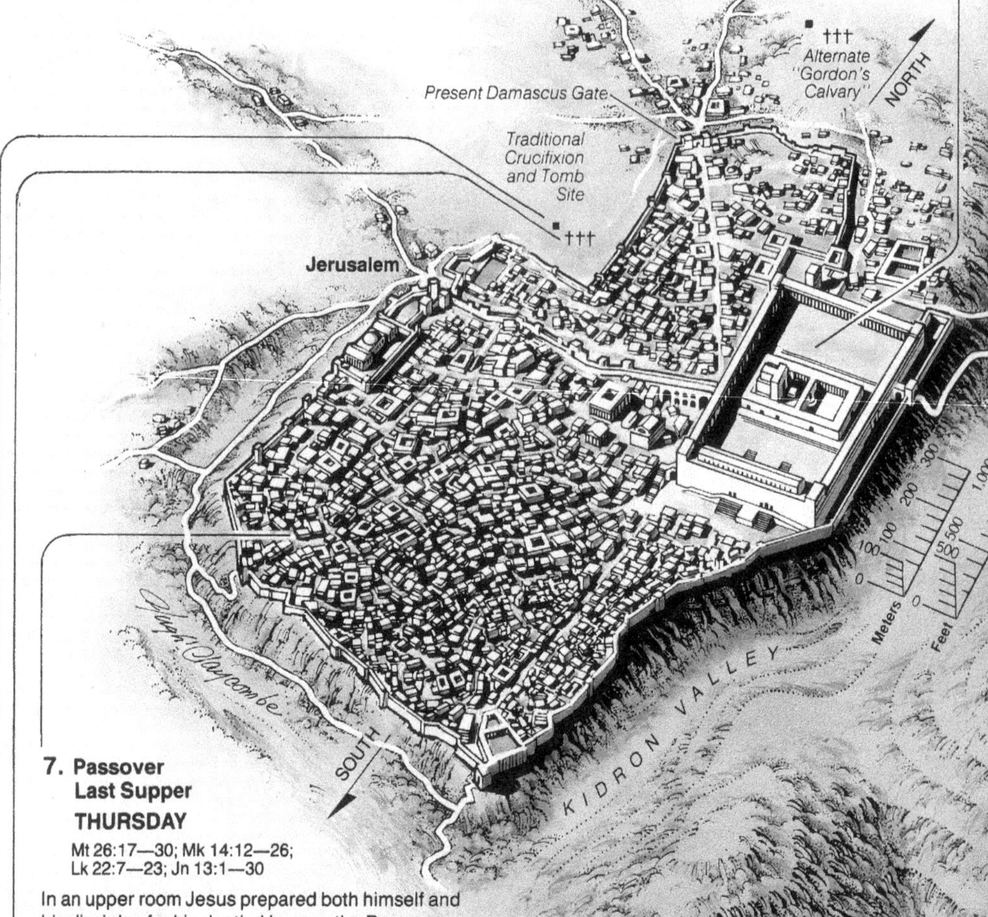


**7. Passover Last Supper**
**THURSDAY**
Mt 26:17—30; Mk 14:12—26; Lk 22:7—23; Jn 13:1—30

In an upper room Jesus prepared both himself and his disciples for his death. He gave the Passover meal a new meaning. The loaf of bread and cup of wine represented his body soon to be sacrificed and his blood soon to be shed. And so he instituted the "Lord's Supper." After singing a hymn they went to the Garden of Gethsemane, where Jesus prayed in agony, knowing what lay ahead for him.

**8. Crucifixion—FRIDAY** Mt 27:1—66; Mk 15:1—47; Lk 22:66—23:56; Jn 18:28—19:37
Following betrayal, arrest, desertion, false trials, denial, condemnation, beatings and mockery, Jesus was required to carry his cross to "The Place of the Skull," where he was crucified with two other prisoners.

**9. In the tomb**
Jesus' body was placed in the tomb before 6:00 P.M. Friday night, when the Sabbath began and all work stopped, and it lay in the tomb throughout the Sabbath.

**10. Resurrection—SUNDAY** Mt 28:1—13; Mk 16:1—20; Lk 24:1—49; Jn 20:1—31
Early in the morning, women went to the tomb and found that the stone closing the tomb's entrance had been rolled back. An angel told them Jesus was alive and gave them a message. Jesus appeared to Mary Magdalene in the garden, to Peter, to two disciples on the road to Emmaus, and later that day to all the disciples but Thomas. His resurrection was established as a fact.

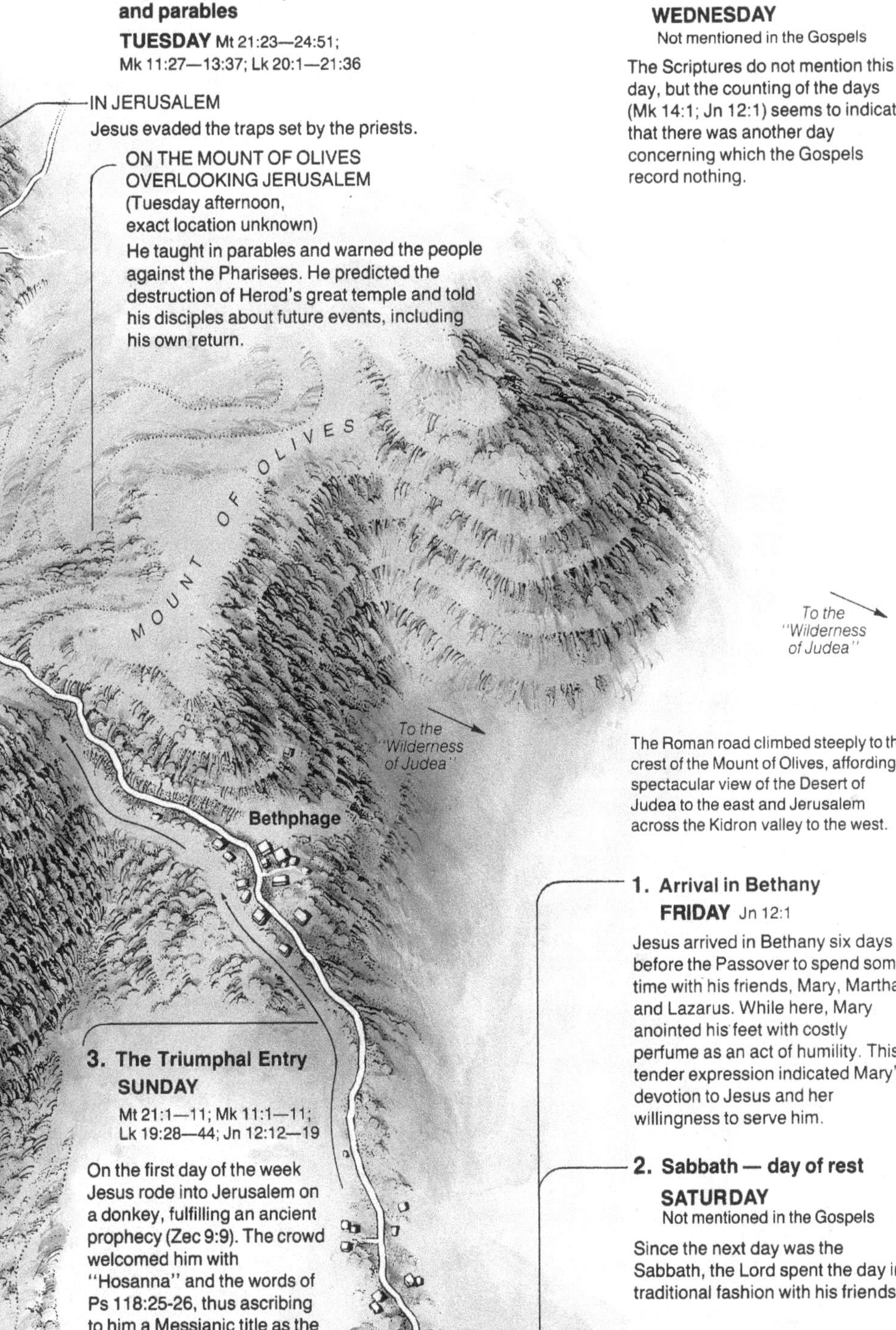


**5. Day of controversy and parables**

**TUESDAY** Mt 21:23—24:51; Mk 11:27—13:37; Lk 20:1—21:36

IN JERUSALEM

Jesus evaded the traps set by the priests.

ON THE MOUNT OF OLIVES OVERLOOKING JERUSALEM (Tuesday afternoon, exact location unknown)

He taught in parables and warned the people against the Pharisees. He predicted the destruction of Herod's great temple and told his disciples about future events, including his own return.

**6. Day of rest**

**WEDNESDAY**

Not mentioned in the Gospels

The Scriptures do not mention this day, but the counting of the days (Mk 14:1; Jn 12:1) seems to indicate that there was another day concerning which the Gospels record nothing.

The Roman road climbed steeply to the crest of the Mount of Olives, affording a spectacular view of the Desert of Judea to the east and Jerusalem across the Kidron valley to the west.

**1. Arrival in Bethany**

**FRIDAY** Jn 12:1

Jesus arrived in Bethany six days before the Passover to spend some time with his friends, Mary, Martha and Lazarus. While here, Mary anointed his feet with costly perfume as an act of humility. This tender expression indicated Mary's devotion to Jesus and her willingness to serve him.

**2. Sabbath — day of rest**

**SATURDAY**

Not mentioned in the Gospels

Since the next day was the Sabbath, the Lord spent the day in traditional fashion with his friends.

**3. The Triumphal Entry**

**SUNDAY**

Mt 21:1—11; Mk 11:1—11; Lk 19:28—44; Jn 12:12—19

On the first day of the week Jesus rode into Jerusalem on a donkey, fulfilling an ancient prophecy (Zec 9:9). The crowd welcomed him with "Hosanna" and the words of Ps 118:25-26, thus ascribing to him a Messianic title as the agent of the Lord, the coming King of Israel.

**Bethphage and Bethany (19:29).** Bethany (meaning "House of Ananiah") was a village located on the road from Jericho about two miles east of Jerusalem, on the eastern slope of the Mount of Olives. It was the home of Lazarus and his sisters, Mary and Martha.[535] The location of Bethphage is uncertain, though it was probably near Bethany on the same road.

**The Mount of Olives (19:29).** The Mount of Olives (2,660 feet above sea level) overlooks Jerusalem and the temple mount from the east. The prophet Zechariah predicted that when Messiah came, he would appear on the Mount of Olives (Zech. 14:4). Though Zechariah describes a scene of cataclysmic judgment—a description of Jesus' second coming—the mountain's eschatological significance contributes to the messianic imagery found here. It is significant that Jesus ascends from the Mount of Olives in Acts 1 with the promise to return "in the same way" (Acts 1:11).

**You will find a colt tied there (19:30).** The "colt" here is the offspring of a donkey, not a horse (cf. Zech. 9:9; Matt. 21:2). The use of the colt certainly alludes to Zechariah 9:9–10, but may also relate to Solomon's coronation (1 Kings 1:32–40) and/or the messianic figure from Judah's line predicted in Genesis 49:9–11 (who tethers his colt to a vine). Together these background texts give the scene a strong royal and messianic flavor.

Some commentators point out that animals were often kept for the benefit of travelers who might borrow or hire them. While this may be the case, a more likely background is the right of a king or other person of authority to borrow an animal needed for immediate service.[536] While it is possible that Jesus arranged earlier to borrow the colt, the point here seems to be his divine knowledge and foresight (19:32).

**Which no one has ever ridden (19:30).** An unridden colt points to its purity—fitting for a king. The Old Testament sometimes demands animals that have never been worked or yoked to provide pure sacrifices (Num. 19:2; Deut. 21:3) or to carry the ark of the covenant (1 Sam. 6:7).

**People spread their cloaks on the road (19:36).** The spreading of garments indicates homage to a person of high rank and recalls the royal greeting to Jehu in 2 Kings 9:13.[537] Luke omits the reference to palm branches found in Matthew and Mark, probably because his Gentile audience would not have recognized these as symbols of Jewish nationalism. Palm branches, praise, hymns, and songs are associated with the entrance of Simon Maccabeus into Jerusalem after his victory over the Syrians.[538]

**Blessed is the king who comes in the name of the Lord! (19:38).** The phrase is drawn from Psalm 118:26, with the addi-

A ROAD ON THE MOUNT OF OLIVES

Jerusalem is visible in the distance.

tion of "the king" for "he." This links the psalm to Zechariah 9:9 and brings out its messianic significance. In its original context Psalm 118 probably celebrated the return of a Davidic king from victory in battle (Ps. 118:10–118) and his ascent to the temple to worship (118:19–29). In Judaism it became one of the Hallel Psalms (Ps. 113–18), used liturgically by pilgrims at the Feast of Tabernacles and Passover. For the disciples the psalm clearly carried messianic significance (cf. Luke 13:35).[539]

**The stones will cry out (19:40).** The personification of creation recalls Isaiah 55:12, where the mountains and hills "burst into song" and the trees of the field "clap their hands," rejoicing at God's deliverance. There may also be an allusion to Habakkuk 2:11, where the prophet announces that "the stones of the wall will cry out" in judgment against Babylon. Jesus will soon pronounce judgment against Jerusalem, predicting her destruction (Luke 19:43–44).

**He wept over it (19:41).** Jesus' judgment oracle and tears of lament recall the Old Testament prophets, who often wept over Israel's sins and impending judgment.[540] Jeremiah has been called the "weeping prophet."

**Your enemies will build an embankment against you (19:43).** Jesus predicts the destruction of Jerusalem by the Romans, which took place in A.D. 70. Josephus describes the walls and embankments built by the Roman general Titus (son of Emperor Vespasian) to besiege the city and prevent the escape of its inhabitants.[541]

**Dash you to the ground, you and your children (19:44).** Josephus portrays in great detail the terrible and gruesome suffering of the inhabitants of Jerusalem during the three-year siege of the city.[542] Many died by a terrible famine. Others were killed by desperate bandits within the city. Thousands were slaughtered by the Romans when they breached the walls.[543] Josephus claims that eleven hundred thousand perished during the siege and ninety-seven thousand were taken captive.[544] Though the number is almost certainly grossly exaggerated (it may have been between one-quarter and one-half million), these numbers reveal the horrible sufferings the city will experience (see 21:23 for more details).

**Not leave one stone on another (19:44).** See 21:6. This image is one of total devastation, but should not be taken too literally. According to Josephus, Titus demolished the entire city but left some of the important towers and part of the west wall standing to use as a garrison for his troops. The city as a whole was leveled to the ground, "as to leave future visitors to the spot no ground for believing that it had ever been inhabited."[545]

## Jesus at the Temple (19:45–48)

Upon entering the temple, Jesus drives out those selling animals and other goods to pilgrims for sacrifices. By "cleansing" the temple, Jesus symbolically acts out the judgment he has just predicted (19:41–44). His actions provoke outrage among the leadership, who plot to kill him. Yet his popularity among the people prevents a public arrest.

**Those who were selling (19:45).** Pilgrims coming to Jerusalem had to purchase animals and other products for sacrifices (animals, birds, wine, oil, flour, etc.; *m. Šeqal.* 4:8).[546] These sellers were located

MODERN JERUSALEM FROM THE MOUNT OF OLIVES

in the Court of the Gentiles. Luke does not specifically mention the money changers (see Matt. 21:12; Mark 11:15), who exchanged local currencies for the Tyrian shekel required for the temple tax.[547] Jesus' actions against the temple would have been viewed as disruptive to the sacrificial system and thus blasphemous by the Jerusalem leadership.

**"My house will be a house of prayer" . . . "a den of robbers" (19:46).** This is a combination of Old Testament citations from Isaiah 56:7 and Jeremiah 7:11. The former speaks of a future restoration of the temple, when the Gentile nations will stream to Jerusalem and the temple will be called "a house of prayer for all nations." The latter is an indictment against Israel for her injustice and unrighteousness. The nation has turned God's temple, which bears his name, into "a den [or cave] of robbers." As in the present context (19:41–44), Jeremiah also includes an oracle of judgment, predicting the temple's destruction (Jer. 7:14).

THE JERUSALEM TEMPLE

The Court of the Gentiles is the spacious area surrounding the temple proper.

**Chief priests, the teachers of the law and the leaders among the people (19:47).** These probably represent the three groups comprising the Sanhedrin. The chief priests were the upper echelon of the Jewish priesthood (see comments on 9:22); the teachers of the law were "scribes" or experts in the Mosaic law—mostly Pharisees (see comments on 5:17). The "leaders among the people" were probably the lay nobility in Jerusalem, the "elders" of 9:22; 20:1.[548]

## The Authority of Jesus Questioned (20:1–8)

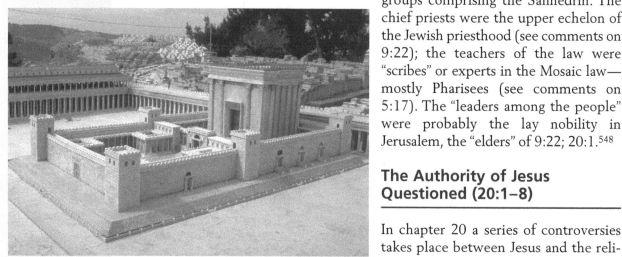

In chapter 20 a series of controversies takes place between Jesus and the religious leaders in Jerusalem—controversies that will result in the plot to seize him.

**The temple courts (20:1).** For this term see comments on 2:27.

**The chief priests and the teachers of the law, together with the elders (20:1).** This was probably an official delegation from the Sanhedrin (see comments on 19:47).

**John's baptism—was it from heaven (20:4).** "From heaven" means "from God," a Jewish expression to avoid using the divine name. Counter-questions were a common rabbinic method of argumentation.

Jesus turns the question to one of *prophetic* authority. In the period of the united monarchy there was a separation of powers between the Davidic king, who oversaw secular affairs, and the Aaronic priests, who oversaw religious affairs. Yet everyone recognized that God could raise up a prophet as his mouthpiece to indict both king and priest of corruption and sin. First Maccabees 14:41 says that the Maccabean ruler Simon "should be their leader and high priest forever, until a trustworthy prophet should arise." If these leaders admit that John was a prophet—as the people believe (Luke 20:6)—they should submit to his indictment of their corrupt leadership.

**The people will stone us (20:6).** Stoning was the prescribed Old Testament punishment for blasphemy (Lev. 24:14), idolatry (Lev. 20:2; Deut. 13:10), and other sins of defiance against God. To knowingly reject God's prophet was surely a capital offence.

## The Parable of the Tenants (20:9–19)

Jesus now tells a parable that allegorically depicts his controversy with Israel's leadership. The parable draws imagery from Isaiah's song of the vineyard (Isa. 5:1–7), where the vineyard represents Israel and the owner God. When the vineyard fails to produce fruit, the owner takes away its protection and allows invaders—the Assyrians in Isaiah's context—to overwhelm and destroy it. It is a parable of impending judgment. Here Jesus expands on Isaiah's imagery with a new parable. God is again the owner and the vineyard Israel, but the main characters are now tenant farmers, representing Israel's corrupt leadership. When the owner sends servants (=the prophets) to receive the produce of the vineyard, the tenants beat and abuse them, sending them away empty-handed. Finally, the owner sends his own son (=Jesus), whom the farmers murder, thinking they will now inherit the vineyard. Jesus concludes by asking, "What then will the owner . . . do to them?" The answer is obvious: "He will come and kill those tenants and give the vineyard to others" (Luke 20:16). Israel's rejection of her

**VINEYARD**

A vineyard near the tel of Lachish.

Messiah will result in her destruction, and Israel's salvation blessings will pass on to others.

The people, who certainly knew Isaiah's parable, gasp in response, "May this never be!" Jesus replies by pointing to the Old Testament prophecy of Psalm 118:22. Though the rejected stone, Jesus will be vindicated as the cornerstone of God's new building. The teachers of the law and the chief priests also understand the parable and look for a way to destroy Jesus. Again, however, his popularity prevents a public arrest.

**Rented it to some farmers (20:9).** Wealthy landowners often leased land to poor farmers, so the portrait here was familiar to Jesus' hearers. There were many such estates with absentee landlords in Palestine, especially in Galilee.

**Some of the fruit of the vineyard (20:10).** Rent to the landlord was normally paid through a percentage of the grapes produced.

**He sent a servant . . . the tenants beat him (20:10).** The Old Testament speaks of God's repeated sending of prophets to call Israel to repentance and Israel's frequent mistreatment and even murder of them (see comments on 3:19–20; 11:47).[549]

**My son, whom I love (20:13).** The Messiah was expected to have a unique father-son relationship with God (see comments on 1:32–33).[550] Though it is debated whether "Son of God" was a common messianic title in the first century, Jesus' hearers may have recognized a messianic allusion here.[551] As in the divine voice at Jesus' baptism (see comments on 3:22), there may also be an Isaac typology ("whom I love" = Gen. 22:2).

**They threw him out of the vineyard and killed him (20:15).** While Mark speaks of the tenants killing the master's son and throwing the body out of the vineyard—a reference to the shame associated with an unburied corpse (see Mark 12:8)—Luke emphasizes first his rejection ("they threw him out") and then his murder. The present rejection of the Messiah will result in his death.

**The stone the builders rejected has become the capstone (20:17).** The disciples shouted Psalm 118:25–26 as Jesus approached Jerusalem (Luke 19:38; cf. 13:35). Now Jesus cites Psalm 118:22 to refer to his rejection. The meaning of "capstone" (*kephalē gōnias;* lit., "head of the corner") is debated, but probably refers to the "cornerstone" used at the corner of a building to support two adjoining walls. Such stones were essential to maintain the integrity of the structure.[552] The stone metaphor was a common one among the early Christians, who used a catena of texts to explain Jesus' rejection and vindication (see also next comment).[553]

*right* ▶

**CAPSTONE**

A huge lintel stone at Nimrud.

**Everyone who falls on that stone . . . but he on whom it falls (20:18).** The second and third stone images are about judgment and allude respectively to Isaiah 8:14–15 and Daniel 2:34, 44–45. In the former text, the Lord Almighty identifies himself as a sanctuary for those who fear him, but a "stone that causes men to stumble" for unrepentant Israel. In the latter, God's kingdom is apocalyptically portrayed as a stone "[not made with] human hands," which crushes the other kingdoms of the world and endures forever. Jesus, the rejected stone, will triumph in judgment over those who have rejected him (see comments on 2:34).

## Paying Taxes to Caesar (20:20–26)

Conflict and controversy continue as the religious leaders send spies to catch Jesus in a compromising statement. They ask him a clever "no-win" question: Should we pay taxes to Caesar? The beauty of Jesus' response is its disarming ambiguity. On the surface it affirms Roman authority, encouraging obedience to the government while maintaining spiritual allegiance to God. Yet for those most opposed to Rome, it could be interpreted to mean "since everything belongs to God, nothing belongs to Caesar." Jesus' opponents are astonished and silenced by his answer.

**Spies, who pretended to be honest (20:20).** The term "spy" (*enkathetos*) means someone hired to lie in wait and so indicates the desire of Jesus' enemies to trap him.[554] "Honest" (*dikaios*, "righteous, innocent") probably here means pious and sincere observers of the Mosaic law.

**We know that you speak and teach what is right . . . the way of God (20:21).** The spies seek to gain Jesus' confidence through flattery. The Old Testament repeatedly warns against the danger of flattering lips (Ps. 5:9; 12:2–3).[555] The spies affirm that Jesus teaches the "way of God," an expression that means obedience to God's law, living the righteous life he desires (Deut. 8:6; 10:12).[556]

**Is it right . . . to pay taxes to Caesar . . . ? (20:22).** This refers especially to the poll tax paid directly to Rome, not to local customs or property taxes. The Jews hated Roman rule with its heavy burden of taxation. Josephus describes how, under the governorship of Coponius (A.D. 6–10), the insurrectionist Judas of Galilee "incited his countrymen to revolt, upbraiding them as cowards for consenting to pay tribute to the Romans and tolerating mortal masters, after having God for their Lord."[557]

**Show me a denarius. Whose portrait and inscription are on it? (20:24).** While there were many coins in circulation in the Roman empire, Jesus requests a Roman denarius (worth about a day's wages). The coin bore the image of the emperor Tiberius (cf. 3:1), with the inscription "Tiberius Caesar, Augustus, son of the divine Augustus." Both the image and the acclamation of deity were abhorrent to the Jews (see Ex. 20:3–5, 23). There is great irony in the fact that Jesus' "pious" inquisitors themselves carry and trade Roman coins bearing idolatrous images and blasphemous inscriptions.

**DENARIUS**

A silver denarius with the image of the emperor Tiberius.

**Give to Caesar what is Caesar's (20:25).** Ecclesiastes 8:2 enjoins obedience to the king, and the New Testament repeatedly commands submission to governmental authorities.[558] God's establishment of and sovereignty over all the kings of the earth is also an important Old Testament theme.[559]

## The Resurrection and Marriage (20:27–39)

Another attempt to discredit Jesus now comes from some Sadducees, who pose a question about levirate marriage (see comments on 20:28).[560]

**Sadducees (20:27).** See "The Sadducees."

**Who say there is no resurrection (20:27).** The clearest Old Testament reference to the resurrection is Daniel 12:2, but it is alluded to elsewhere.[561] Since the Sadducees viewed only the Torah (first five books of the Old Testament) as authoritative, they rejected any proof texts from the Writings and the Prophets.

**Moses wrote . . . if a man's brother dies (20:28).** The Old Testament law of levirate marriage required the brother of a deceased man to bear children with the dead man's wife in order to preserve the latter's genealogical line (Deut. 25:5–10). Old Testament examples appear in Genesis 38:8 and Ruth 4:1–12. Extensive rules relating to the practice are discussed in the Mishnaic tract *Yebamot* ("sisters-in-law").

**Now there were seven brothers (20:29).** An interesting parallel appears in the apocryphal book of Tobit (fourth or third century B.C.), where seven husbands of a young woman named Sarah die before giving her children (all killed by the evil demon Asmodeus). The grief-stricken woman eventually finds solace through her marriage to Tobit's son Tobias, the closest relative in a levirate marriage.[562]

**For they are like the angels (20:36).** Jesus did not say that believers become angels (a popular misconception), but that their glorified state will be like that of angels. Angels and human beings are distinct creations of God (Heb. 1–2).[563] The Jewish apocalyptic work *1 Enoch* develops a midrash around the account of the "sons of God" in Genesis 6. Though created not to marry, some of the angels sinned by taking wives for themselves from the daughters of man, producing giants as offspring.[564]

**In the account of the bush, even Moses showed (20:37).** Since the Sadducees viewed only the Pentateuch (Genesis to Deuteronomy) as authoritative, Jesus appeals to the account of the burning bush in Exodus 3 for proof of the resurrection. Jesus' argument may seem odd to modern ears, but it was a common rabbinic method. In a second-century rabbinic text, Rabbi Simeon ben Eleazar says:

> On the following basis I proved that the versions of Scripture of the Samaritans are forgeries, for they maintained that the dead do not live. I said to them, "Lo, Scripture says, ' . . . that person shall be utterly cut off; his iniquity shall be upon him.' "

The Samaritans had their own version of the Pentateuch, and they, like the Sadducees, did not believe in the resurrection. The rabbi here uses the future sense of the phrase "shall be upon him" (Num. 15:31, RSV) to prove that this person will face a future judgment, so there must be a resurrection.[565]

**He is not the God of the dead (20:38).** This expression of God's ongoing relationship with his people has an interesting parallel in *4 Maccabees*, where it is said of the Maccabean martyrs that "those who die for the sake of God live to God, as do Abraham and Isaac and Jacob and all the patriarchs" (*4 Macc.* 16:25; cf. 7:19).

**Some of the teachers of the law responded, "Well said, teacher!" (20:39).** Most teachers of the law were Pharisees (see 5:17), who, contrary to the Sadducees, agreed with Jesus' teaching on the resurrection.

**No one dared to ask him any more questions (20:40).** The ability to silence an opponent was viewed in Hellenistic culture as one of the marks of a wise man and a skilled orator (cf. Wisd. Sol. 8:12).

## Whose Son Is the Christ? (20:41–44)

The controversies and debates in Jerusalem conclude with three episodes in which Jesus challenges or rebukes the religious leaders. These include the question about David's son (20:41–44), a rebuke of the teachers of the law (20:45–47), and the account of the widow's offering (21:1–4). In the first Jesus asks how the rabbis can call the Messiah the "Son of David," when David himself calls him "Lord" in Psalm 110. The title "son" implies subordination, so how can he be David's Lord? Jesus' point is that his messianic identity exceeds traditional Jewish expectations of an earthly, conquering king.

**The Christ is the Son of David (20:41).** The title "Son of David," which appears here and in 18:38–39, was a favorite title for the Messiah in rabbinic Judaism. It first appears in the first century B.C. *Psalms of Solomon* (17:21), where it carries strong political connotations (see "Messianic Expectation in Jesus' Day"). Its roots are to be found in the promise to David that God would raise up his offspring after him who would reign forever on his throne (2 Sam. 7:11–16). For more on traditional messianic expectations see comments on Luke 1:32–33; 9:20. For the related title "shoot of David," see comments on 1:78–79.

### The Sadducees

The origin of the Sadducees is uncertain, but they appear to have arisen from the priestly families of the Jerusalem aristocracy who supported the Hasmonean dynasty during the period of Hebrew independence (c. 164–63 B.C.). In New Testament times, they controlled the priesthood and most political affairs, dominating the Sanhedrin (Acts 5:17). According to Josephus, they only considered the Pentateuch (the Torah) fully authoritative, denying the oral traditions of the Pharisees. As a result they denied the immortality of the soul and the resurrection of the body, no doubt claiming that these were later accretions to the Torah. They also emphasized human free will over divine predestination, in contrast to the Pharisees and (especially) the Essenes.[A-51] Luke further notes in Acts that the Sadducees did not believe in angels or spirits (Acts 23:8), which may mean the kinds of angelic orders and hierarchies characteristic of apocalyptic Judaism. Since the Sadducean power base was the priesthood and the temple, the destruction of Jerusalem in A.D. 70 ended their political influence, and the group disappeared from history.

**David himself declares . . . "'The Lord said to my Lord . . .'" (20:42).** Jesus identifies the speaker in Psalm 110 as David, who addresses the Messiah as "my Lord" and speaks of his enthronement at God's right hand. Surprisingly, first-century Judaism does not seem to have interpreted Psalm 110 messianically, though some have argued that the messianic interpretation was suppressed by later rabbis opposing its use as a messianic proof text by Christians. It is among the most frequently cited Old Testament texts in the New Testament.[566]

## Denouncing the Teachers of the Law (20:45–47)

In this episode, Jesus warns his disciples against the hypocrisy of the teachers of the law. Though making an outward show of religiosity in the public arena, they act with injustice and exploit the poor. God will judge such hypocrisy. The passage is similar to the woes pronounced against the teachers of the law and the Pharisees in 11:37–54.

**Teachers of the law (20:46).** See comments on 5:17 and "Scribes."

**THE "HOUSE OF DAVID" INSCRIPTION**

A ninth-century B.C. Aramaic inscription found in Dan mentioning the battle of Ben Hadad, king of Aram, against "the house of David."

**Flowing robes (20:46).** This probably refers to long robes with tassels used to distinguish the office of the teacher of the law.

**Greeted in the marketplaces . . . important seats in the synagogues (20:46).** See comments on 11:43.

**Places of honor at banquets (20:46).** Meals carried great social significance in the ancient world, with guests seated according to their social status. See comments on 5:30; 14:7.

**They devour widows' houses (20:47).** This may refer to exploiting the estate of widows for whom they had been appointed guardians,[567] or perhaps the abuse of a widow's hospitality, a charge leveled at the Jerusalem aristocracy in the *Testament of Moses* 7:6.[568] Widows are viewed throughout Scripture as the most vulnerable and helpless members of society. God will judge those who oppress them. See comments on 18:3 for Old Testament and Jewish references.

## The Widow's Offering (21:1–4)

The episode of the widow's sacrificial offering stands in contrast to the greed of the teachers of the law (see previous passage). While they exploit others for gain, she gives self-sacrificially from her poverty.

**The temple treasury (21:1).** The term *gazophylakion* refers either to one of various treasury rooms located in the temple[569] or to a chest or receptacle used to receive the money. The Mishnah speaks of thirteen shofar-chests (trumpet-shaped receptacles) located in the temple, which were used to collect various kinds of offerings.[570] Since people are "throwing" (*ballō*; NIV, "putting") money into the *gazophylakion*, this latter sense seems more likely. The former sense is evident in John 8:20, where Jesus is said to have been teaching in the *gazophylakion*.

**A poor widow (21:2).** Widows were often the poorest and most helpless members of society. See comments on 18:3.

**Two very small copper coins (21:2).** The copper coin here is a *lepton*, the smallest coin in circulation in Palestine (see 12:59). It was worth one-half a quadrans (Mark 12:42), or 1/128 of a denarius (the wage of a day laborer). A common laborer would earn one *lepton* in about four minutes of a ten-hour work day. Since this is "all [this widow] had to live on" (Luke 21:4), the woman is indeed very poor.

**This poor widow has put in more (21:3).** There are Jewish and Greek parallels to the maxim that generosity is relative to a person's wealth. Aristotle wrote that "one's generosity is to be evaluated in terms of one's resources. . . . People who are truly generous give in proportion to what they actually have. It is possible, therefore, that a person who gives but little out of small resources is more generous than another."[571]

## Signs of the End of the Age (21:5–38)

With the time of his departure rapidly approaching, Jesus instructs his disciples on the cataclysmic events to come for Jerusalem and the signs that will accompany his return. In the first part of the discourse, Jesus speaks of signs that, though often interpreted eschatologically, are *not* indications of the imminent end (21:8–24). These include the appearance of false christs (21:8), catastrophic events like wars, earthquakes, and famines (21:9–11), widespread persecution of believers (21:12–19), and the horrific destruction of Jerusalem (21:20–24). For Luke Jerusalem's destruction serves as a preview and "type" of the final day of God's judgment; but it must be distinguished from it. A key transition occurs in 21:24, when Jesus predicts that "Jerusalem will be trampled on by the Gentiles *until the times of the Gentiles are fulfilled*" (italics added). The discourse then turns to the events that will follow the "times of the Gentiles" and will herald the end.[572]

**The temple was adorned with beautiful stones and with gifts dedicated to God (21:5).** Herod the Great's greatest building project was his restoration of the temple in Jerusalem. The extraordinary beauty of the place astounded everyone who saw it. A later rabbinic proverb reads, "He who has not seen the temple of Herod has never seen a beautiful building in his life."[573] Josephus gives a detailed description of the buildings and ornaments and remarks that the exterior of the building lacked nothing that could astound a person. The sun reflecting off the massive gold plates on the building "radiated so fiery a flash that persons straining to look at it were compelled to avert their eyes as from solar rays." Massive white stones twenty-five cubits long (37.5 feet), with some as much as forty-five cubits long (67.5 feet), were used in the construction. These gave the building a brilliant white appearance so that to approaching strangers the temple looked like a snow-covered mountain.[574] The

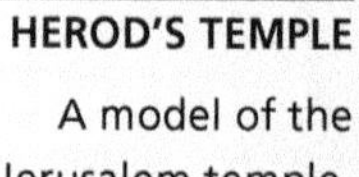

HEROD'S TEMPLE
A model of the Jerusalem temple.

"gifts dedicated to God" (*anathēma*) are probably offerings given by worshipers in fulfillment of vows.

**Not one stone will be left on another (21:6).** This image indicates total devastation, but should not be read over-literally (see comments on 19:44). Jesus was not the only one to predict the destruction of Jerusalem. Josephus describes a man named Jesus son of Ananus, who, for four years before the Jewish revolt and then for three years during it, wandered the city crying, "Woe to Jerusalem!" Though whipped first by the Jewish leadership and then by the Roman procurator Albinus, for seven years he continued his mournful cry. He was eventually killed during the siege of Jerusalem by a stone from a Roman catapult.[575]

**Many will come in my name, claiming, "I am he" (21:8).** Messianic and prophetic claims were not uncommon in the first century (see comments on 17:23). Josephus blames an incorrect interpretation of "an ambiguous oracle" from the sacred writings about one who would become "ruler of the world" (a reference to Isaiah 9?) for the disastrous Jewish revolt of A.D. 66–74. Josephus denies the messianic significance of this prophecy and claims it concerned the establishment of Vespasian as Roman emperor.[576]

**Wars and revolutions ... great earthquakes, famines and pestilences (21:9–11).** Cataclysmic events, whether human conflicts like war and revolution[577] or "natural" disasters like earthquakes are often associated in the Old Testament and Judaism with God's judgment.[578] The judgments of the Day of the Lord are marked by earthquakes and other cosmic disturbances.[579] Apocalyptic Judaism drew strongly on this imagery. In the third vision of 2 Esdras (also *4 Ezra*), Ezra asks the Lord when the signs he has been showing him will take place. The Lord responds:

> Measure carefully in your mind, and when you see that some of the predicted signs have occurred, then you will know that it is the very time when the Most High is about to visit the world that he has made. So when

> there shall appear in the world earthquakes, tumult of peoples, intrigues of nations, wavering of leaders, confusion of princes, then you will know that it was of these that the Most High spoke from the days that were of old, from the beginning.[580]

Jesus responds against overzealous apocalyptic fervor by pointing out that these events are typical of human history and should not be confused with the end.

**Great signs from heaven (21:11).** Cosmic signs are also common in prophetic and apocalyptic literature as portents of God's judgment (see comments on 21:25).

**Deliver you to synagogues (21:12).** (Cf. 12:10.) In first-century Judaism the elders of the synagogue were administrative as well as religious leaders, and the synagogue served not only as a place of worship, but also for public gatherings, including judicial hearings.[581] The judicial hearings and sentences that led to Paul's five lashings by the Jews (2 Cor. 11:24) probably took place in local synagogues.

**I will give you words and wisdom (21:15).** These words recall God's promise to Moses (Ex. 4:12, 15) and Jeremiah (Jer. 1:9) that he would put his words in their mouths.[582]

**Betrayed even by parents, brothers, relatives and friends (21:16).** (Cf. Micah 7:6.) In the tight-knit Diaspora Jewish communities, acceptance of Jesus as Messiah could result in excommunication and even stoning.[583] Such social disintegration was viewed by the rabbis as a sign of the end of the age (see comments on 12:52–53).[584]

**Not a hair of your head will perish (21:18).** This is an idiom meaning complete protection.[585] In light of the reference to martyrdom in 21:16 and to "gaining life" in 21:19, this probably means spiritual rather than physical deliverance.[586]

**When you see Jerusalem being surrounded by armies (21:20).** The horrific siege of Jerusalem by the Romans and its accompanying famine is described by Josephus in great detail in books 5–6 of

*bottom left*

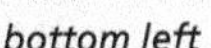

**ARCH OF TITUS**

The arch depicts the captives of Jerusalem in the aftermath of the Jewish war in A.D. 70.

*bottom right*

**JUDEA CAPTA COIN**

An imperial bronze coin commemorating the Roman victory over the Jews in A.D. 70. It is inscribed with the words, "captive Judea" (*IVDEA CAPTA*).

his *Jewish War* (see comments on 19:44; 21:23).

**Let those who are in Judea flee to the mountains (21:21).** Normally, people in the countryside would flee to the fortified cities for protection. Yet Jerusalem will be the wrong place to be during this siege (see comments on 21:23). The early church historian Eusebius records that, in response to this oracle, Christians in Judea fled to the city of Pella in Decapolis during the Jewish revolt.[587]

**Punishment in fulfillment of all that has been written (21:22).** The Old Testament repeatedly speaks of judgment against Jerusalem for her sins.[588] While many of these prophecies speak of Jerusalem's destruction by the Babylonians in 586 B.C., Jesus saw them as prophetic previews for the destruction of A.D. 70.

**How dreadful . . . for pregnant women and nursing mothers! (21:23).** The siege and famine in Jerusalem were particularly traumatic for those with children. Josephus describes one gruesome episode where a starving woman, whose food was repeatedly stolen by certain city defenders, killed and cooked her own infant. She ate half and, when the guards arrived and demanded the food they smelled cooking, offered the other half to them. In horror they fled from the house. When this report went out to the city, "those who were starving longed for death, and considered blessed those who were already dead, because they had not lived long enough either to hear or to see such evils."[589]

**STANDARD OF THE 10TH ROMAN LEGION**

This was a key Roman army in the Jewish war.

**Jerusalem will be trampled on by the Gentiles (21:24).** Israel's darkest times were when foreign nations conquered and occupied the holy city of Jerusalem, whether at the Babylonian captivity (Jer. 25:10–11), during the Maccabean period, or now with the Romans.[590] The author of 1 Maccabees deplores the time when "Jerusalem was uninhabited like a wilderness. . . . The sanctuary was trampled down, and aliens held the citadel; it was a lodging place for the Gentiles. Joy was taken from Jacob" (1 Macc. 3:45).

**The times of the Gentiles (21:24).** This is a period of world domination by the Gentiles that precedes the return of the Messiah. Daniel's prophecies of a great statue (Dan. 2) and beasts from the sea (Dan. 7) envision a period of world domination by the Gentiles before the establishment of the kingdom of God (2:44; 7:27).

**Signs in the sun, moon and stars . . . the heavenly bodies will be shaken (21:25–26).** Cosmic signs and disturbances are common in prophetic and apocalyptic literature as evidence of God's judgment and the end of the age (Isa. 13:9–10; 34:4).[591] Ancient peoples viewed heavenly signs as omens of good or evil. Josephus describes a star shaped like a sword and a comet that appeared over Jerusalem as a sign of her coming destruction.[592] Heavenly armies were also seen running through the clouds and surrounding the city.[593]

**Nations will be in anguish and perplexity. . . . Men will faint (21:25–26).** It was widely held in Judaism that the time leading up to the end, sometimes called the "messianic woes" or the "birth pains of the Messiah," would be a period of great distress and tribulation.[594] The War Scroll at Qumran says, "It will be a time of suffering for all the people redeemed by God. Of all their sufferings, none will be like this, from its haste until eternal redemption is fulfilled" (see comments on 21:9–11).[595]

**The Son of Man coming in a cloud with power and great glory (21:27).** This image is taken from Daniel 7:13, 14, where an exalted messianic figure is described as "one like a son of man," who comes on the clouds of heaven and is given authority, glory, and an eternal kingdom. The apocalyptic work *1 Enoch* develops this image with reference to the Messiah (see comments on 5:24; 9:26).

**Look at the fig tree and all the trees (21:29).** The fig tree here represents a nature analogy and is not a symbol for Israel (contrast 13:6). Fig trees are bare in the winter, so the first signs of leaves are evidence that summer is near. The signs Jesus has been describing will herald the return of the Son of Man.

**This generation (21:32).** The Greek term *genea* normally means "generation," that is, people living at a particular time. Some have suggested that the word instead should be translated "race" and that the saying means the nation Israel will survive until the return of Christ.[596] Although possible, this is an unusual use of *genea*. If the reference is to the disciples' own generation, either Jesus' prediction was wrong (since he did not return in the first century) or else the events of A.D. 70 in some way fulfilled the prophecy (the Son of Man "came" in judgment). Perhaps the best explanation is that "this generation" refers not to the disciples' generation, but to a (later) generation alive when the signs begin to take place.

**Heaven and earth will pass away (21:33).** See comments on 16:17.

**To stand before the Son of Man (21:36).** To "stand before" in this context means to stand confident of approval and vindication. In *1 Enoch* 62:8–9 the "elect ones" stand before the Son of Man in glory, while the wicked fall on their faces and flee from his presence in shame.

## Judas Agrees to Betray Jesus (22:1–6)

The climax of this Gospel is now reached with Luke's account of Jesus' Passion (chs. 22–23). It begins with Judas's agreement to betray Jesus (22:1–6) and includes the Last Supper (22:7–38), Jesus' arrest on the Mount of Olives (22:47–53), Peter's denial (22:54–62), Jesus' trials before the Sanhedrin, Pilate, and Herod (22:63–23:25), the crucifixion (23:26–49), and

### REFLECTIONS

**THE THEME THAT RECURS OVER AND OVER IN JESUS'** great Olivet Discourse is the need to be ready and prepared for the Lord's return. While biblical scholars may debate the details of how end-time events will play out on the stage of human history, two themes permeate biblical prophecy. The first is that God is sovereign over world events. He will bring them to their appropriate conclusion. The second is that the Christian must persevere in righteousness, always ready for the Master's return.

the burial (23:50–56). The primary theme is Jesus as the innocent and righteous servant who remains faithful to God's calling.

**The Feast of Unleavened Bread, called the Passover (22:1).** Passover was celebrated on the fifteenth of Nisan (March/April) and was followed by the seven-day Feast of Unleavened Bread.[597] See "Passover and the Feast of Unleavened Bread" at 2:41. The two festivals were often linked together and called "Passover."[598] Large crowds of pilgrims gathered in Jerusalem for this festival season.

**Chief priests and the teachers of the law (22:2).** See comments on 9:22. Jesus is viewed as a threat to the power of both the chief priests, who administer the temple and control the Sanhedrin, and the teachers of the law, who lead the local synagogue communities.

**Satan entered Judas, called Iscariot (22:3).** For Old Testament and Jewish background on Satan see comments on 4:2; 10:18; cf. 11:15. A similar statement appears in the Jewish work *Martyrdom and Ascension of Isaiah* (second century B.C. to fourth century A.D.), where Beliar (=Satan) "dwelt in the heart of king Manasseh," prompting him to arrest and eventually execute Isaiah by sawing him in half (3:11; 5:1). For similar activity by Satan see comments on John 13:2; Acts 5:3. On the name "Iscariot" see comments on 6:16.

## The Last Supper (22:7–38)

In the Last Supper narrative, Jesus interprets his death as the sacrifice that will establish the new covenant predicted in Jeremiah 31. Jesus calls on his disciples to take the bread and the cup together as a remembrance of what he will accomplish for them. In the discourse that follows the supper, Jesus predicts his betrayal and once again calls his disciples to true servant leadership. He also affirms their leadership role in the kingdom. Yet such leadership will not come easily. The crisis they are about to face will be far more severe than anything they have encountered.

**The day of Unleavened Bread on which the Passover lamb had to be sacrificed (22:7).** Passover lambs were sacrificed in the temple on the late afternoon of Nisan (March/April) 14. The Passover (Nisan 15) began at sunset. Each family was to have one lamb, though a small family could share one with neighbors. The lamb was to be roasted and eaten with bitter herbs and unleavened bread.[599] The bitter herbs symbolized the bitterness of their slavery in Egypt and the unleavened bread the haste with which they left Egypt (see "Passover and the Feast of Unleavened Bread" at 2:41).[600]

**A man carrying a jar of water (22:10).** This man—probably a servant of the household—would stand out since

*right* ▶

**STORAGE JARS**

These large jars were found in Ekron and could have been used for storing water, oil, or wine.

women normally carried water jars (Gen. 24:11; John 4:7).[601] Though it is possible that Jesus had prearranged for this room, the text seems to suggest divine foreknowledge (see 1 Sam. 10:2–8 for a similar Old Testament story).

**The guest room (22:11).** The word used here (*katalyma*) is the same one used for the crowded "inn" where Joseph and Mary could find no room (see 2:7). It here means a guest room in a private residence. In 22:12 it is described as a "large upper room, all furnished" (22:12). The furnishings would have included the couches or cushions on which the guests reclined.

**Jesus and his apostles reclined at the table (22:14).** The Passover was originally to be eaten standing in readiness to flee Egypt, "with your cloak tucked into your belt, your sandals on your feet and your staff in your hand" (Ex. 12:11). Yet by Jesus' day, "even the poorest in Israel must not eat unless he sits down to the table."[602] This was because standing was the position of a slave, an inappropriate posture for celebrating freedom from slavery in Egypt!

**After taking the cup, he gave thanks (22:17).** The traditional Passover celebration used four cups of wine: (1) the first with an opening benediction over the Passover day; (2) the second after the explanation of the Passover and the singing of the first part of the Hallel (Ps. 113–114); (3) the third following the meal of unleavened bread, lamb, and bitter herbs; (4) the fourth following the concluding portion of the Hallel.[603] Luke refers to two cups (22:17, 20), but it is debated by scholars which two these were. It seems likely that the second cup in 22:20 is the third Passover cup (see below). This one is probably the first since it accompanies Jesus' introduction to the meal.

**He took bread . . . "This is my body . . ." (22:19).** Jesus inaugurates a new Passover by confirming that his body, symbolized by the bread, is the fulfillment and replacement for the Passover lamb (see 1 Cor. 5:7). His death will provide deliverance for God's people.

**This cup is the new covenant in my blood (22:20).** This is probably the third Passover cup, after the meal (see comments on 22:17). Covenants in the Old Testament were ratified with a blood sacrifice (Gen. 15:9–10; Ex. 24:8). Jesus' death will inaugurate the new covenant predicted by Jeremiah (Jer. 31:31–34).

**The hand of him who is going to betray me is with mine on the table (22:21).** Sharing a meal indicated a relationship of friendship and trust, so the note of betrayal is shocking. Jesus' words recall Psalm 41:9: "Even my close friend, whom I trusted, he who shared my bread, has lifted up his heel against me" (cf. John 13:18).

**Kings of the Gentiles lord it over them . . . call themselves Benefactors (22:25).** Ancient Near Eastern kings usually exercised absolute authority over their subjects, taking exalted titles and even claiming to be gods. The Jews could relate well to Jesus' words, having suffered much under despots like Antiochus Epiphanes (see 1 Macc. 1–6). A "benefactor" (*euergetēs*) was one who bestowed gifts on his subjects to gain loyalty and praise.[604] The title was taken by many rulers, though often it "would conceal tyranny under extravagant expenditure."[605]

**Who is greater, the one who is at the table (22:27).** See comments on 12:37; 17:7.

**Eat and drink at my table . . . sit on thrones, judging the twelve tribes of Israel (22:30).** Eating and drinking here points to the messianic banquet (see comments on 13:29; 14:15).[606] The image of God's people reigning and judging appears in Daniel 7:9, 14, 27; Matthew 19:28; 1 Corinthians 6:2–3. On the foundational role of the apostles see Ephesians 2:20; Revelation 21:14.

**Satan has asked to sift you as wheat (22:31).** Satan is the "accuser" of God's people (see comments on 4:2; 10:18; 11:15). As he gained permission to test Job (Job 1:12; 2:6), so now he will test Peter and the other apostles (in the Greek "you" is plural in Luke 22:31, but singular in 22:32). Wheat was sifted through a sieve to separate the grain from chaff and other foreign matter (Isa. 30:28; Amos 9:9). Sirach 27:4 reads: "When a sieve is shaken, the refuse appears; so do a person's faults when he speaks."

**I am ready to go with you to prison and to death (22:33).** Peter will be jailed several times in Acts (Acts 4:3; 5:18; 12:1–19). According to church tradition he suffered martyrdom in Rome by being crucified upside down.[607]

**Before the rooster crows today (22:34).** Some have suggested that this does not refer to an actual rooster, but to the bugle call marking the third division of the Roman night, called *gallicinium* in Latin and *alektorophōnia* ("cockcrow") in Greek.[608] The context, however, suggests Jesus meant an actual rooster. Although the Mishnah says it was forbidden to raise chickens in the holy city of Jerusalem, this is likely a later idealization rather than a first-century reality.[609]

**Purse, bag or sandals (22:35).** See comments on 9:3; 10:3–4.

**It is written: "And he was numbered with the transgressors" (22:37).** Jesus quotes Isaiah 53:12, from Isaiah's fourth Servant Song, about the suffering of the Messiah (see comments on 9:22; 18:31). To be "numbered" with transgressors means to be considered a criminal and alludes to the two criminals crucified with Jesus (23:32–33).

**See, Lord, here are two swords. . . . "That is enough" (22:38).** It is perhaps not surprising that the disciples were carrying two swords since opposition was growing and since at least one of Jesus' disciples had a Zealot background (see 6:15). Josephus mentions that the Essenes commonly carried weapons for defense against thieves.[610] Jesus' response may mean, "Two swords is enough," but more likely his comment is negative, indicating the disciples have misunderstood his meaning: "Enough of this silly talk!"

## REFLECTIONS

**WHEN JESUS' DISCIPLES ARGUE** among themselves as to who is the greatest, Jesus teaches them the true meaning of greatness. Greatness comes from a humble heart of servanthood. It is epitomized in Jesus' self-sacrificial death on the cross. If Jesus served us in this way, how ought we to serve others?

## Jesus Prays on the Mount of Olives (22:39–46)

Following the Last Supper, Jesus and his disciples go to the Mount of Olives. There Jesus agonizes in prayer over his coming ordeal. Both Jesus' true humanity and his willing obedience are evident as he prays, "Father, if you are willing, take this cup from me; yet not my will, but yours be done." By contrast, the weakness of the disciples is evident as they fall asleep, failing to obey Jesus' call to watchfulness and prayer.

**The Mount of Olives (22:39).** See comments on 19:29.

**Take this cup from me (22:42).** Drinking a cup was a common metaphor for experiencing a traumatic event (cf. Mark 10:38). In the Old Testament it is often associated with the outpouring of God's judgment.[611] This sense is probably present here since on the cross Jesus will receive God's judgment against humanity's sin.

**An angel from heaven . . . strengthened him (22:43).** Angels appear as servants for aid and encouragement in both the Old Testament and Judaism.[612]

**Sweat was like drops of blood (22:44).** Luke does not say that Jesus sweated blood, but that his sweat was *like* (*hōsei*) drops of blood—that is, it fell profusely. While there are references to blood-red sweat in ancient literature[613] and medical claims of this possibility,[614] it is not necessary to appeal to them here.

◀ *left*

GARDEN OF GETHSEMANE

## Jesus Arrested (22:47–53)

Judas, having arranged earlier to betray Jesus (see 21:37–22:6), suddenly appears with a crowd to arrest him. In a brief attempt to defend Jesus, one of the disciples (identified as Peter by John) strikes the servant of the high priest with a sword, cutting off his ear. Jesus' sovereign control is particularly evident in Luke, who alone recounts that Jesus heals the man's ear and prohibits further resistance. He then rebukes the leaders for treating him like an insurrectionist when they could have openly arrested him at any time. Yet the present time of darkness is a fitting metaphor for their sinister act.

**He approached Jesus to kiss him (22:47).** The kiss was (and is) a common Middle

COURTYARD

The church of St. Peter in Gallicantu. One tradition regards this as the area for the home of the high priest Caiaphas.

▼

Eastern greeting between friends and those with a special bond (Gen. 29:13; 33:4).[615] It can also indicate homage and respect (Job 31:27; Ps. 2:12) and was probably the common greeting between disciple and rabbi. In 2 Samuel 20:9, as here, it is used in an act of treachery.

**Should we strike with our swords? (22:49).** See comments on 22:38.

**The chief priests, the officers of the temple guard, and the elders (22:52).** See comments on 22:2. The chief priests and the elders represent the religious and lay leadership of the Sanhedrin. The officers of the temple guard are the Sanhedrin's police force.

**Am I leading a rebellion. . . ? (22:52).** The Greek says literally, "as against a thief." Josephus uses the term *lēstēs* of revolutionaries opposing the Roman authorities.[616] To patriotic Jews they were freedom fighters; to the Romans they were common criminals.

## Peter Disowns Jesus (22:54–62)

**The house of the high priest (22:54).** This may be either the house of Caiaphas, the actual high priest, or Annas, his father-in-law, whom Luke also calls high priest (see comments on 3:2). John reports that Jesus was first taken to Annas and then to Caiaphas (John 18:13, 24).

**A fire in the middle of the courtyard (22:55).** Large homes were built around an open courtyard. While the leaders go in the house, the servants and perhaps guards stay in the courtyard.

**For he is a Galilean (22:59).** Peter's accent must have given him away as a Galilean (see comments on Matt. 26:73). For an Old Testament example see Judges 12:6, where Ephraimites are identified because they pronounce "Shibboleth" as "Sibboleth."

**The rooster crowed (22:60).** See comments on 22:34.

## The Guards Mock Jesus (22:63–65).

**The men who were guarding Jesus (22:63).** These are members of the Jewish temple guard used in the arrest of Jesus (see comments on 22:52).

**Mocking and beating him . . . "Prophesy! Who hit you?" (22:63–64).** See comments on 18:32. The abuse of Jesus recalls the suffering of the righteous servant in Isaiah 50:6; 53:3–5. That those considered false prophets were subject to such treatment by the Jewish authorities is clear in the case of Jesus son of Ananus (see comments on 21:6).

right ▶

**HIGH PRIESTLY GARMENTS**

An illustration of Aaron from a 16th century German manuscript.

## Trial Before the Sanhedrin (22:66–71)

Jesus' hearing before the full Sanhedrin occurs at daybreak on Friday morning. The purpose is to gather evidence to bring charges of messianic claims against Jesus before the governor. Scholars have noted that Jesus' trial as reported in the Gospels violates various regulations concerning judicial protocol set forth in the Mishnah (*m. Sanh.*; for details see "The So-Called Illegalities of Jesus' Trial" at Mark 14). Some have used these "illegalities" to point out the gross disregard for justice of the Jewish authorities. Others use them to argue against the historicity of the Gospel accounts. Neither of these conclusions is warranted. The mishnaic regulations are from the late second century and present an idealized picture of the judicial system. They may not have been strictly followed, or even in force, in the first century. In the eyes of the Sanhedrin, Jesus is a false prophet and a dangerous threat to national stability. They must expedite this matter quickly to eliminate the threat to their position and authority.

**The council of the elders (22:66).** This refers to the Sanhedrin, the Jewish high court. See "The Sanhedrin."

**From now on, the Son of Man will be seated at the right hand of the mighty God (22:69).** This phrase combines the image of the Son of Man from Daniel 7 (see comments on 5:24; 9:26) with the exaltation of the Messiah in Psalm 110:1–2 (see comments on 20:42).

**Are you then the Son of God? (22:70).** The Sanhedrin is probably not asking whether Jesus is claiming deity, but whether he is the Messiah. The Old Testament promised that the Messiah would have a special father-son relationship with God.[617] It is debated whether "Son of God" was a common messianic title in first-century Judaism (see comments on 1:35; 4:41).

## Trial Before Pilate and Herod (23:1–25)

Having affirmed Jesus' guilt in their eyes, the Sanhedrin now takes him to the Roman prefect, Pilate, to obtain a capital

### ▸ The Sanhedrin

Though later rabbis traced its origin to the appointment of seventy elders by Moses in Numbers 11:16 (*m. Sanh.* 1:6), there is little evidence for a formal council until the Greek period (third century B.C.).[A-52] The Sanhedrin was originally made up of the Jerusalem nobility, both lay leaders and priests, with the hereditary high priest as its head. In the time of Jesus the Sadducees (the party of the aristocracy and the priesthood) still controlled the Sanhedrin (see Acts 5:17), though leading Pharisees and scribes had also gained a prominent place (cf. Acts 23:7). Luke's reference to the "chief priests" and "teachers of the law" (Luke 22:66) probably refers respectively to these Sadducean and Pharisaic power blocks.

The authority and jurisdiction of the Sanhedrin waxed and waned depending on the political situation. Josephus reports that Herod the Great consolidated his reign by ordering the execution of the whole Sanhedrin, and he held the council in tight check during his reign. Under the Roman governors, the Sanhedrin exerted greater influence, with wide-ranging judicial and administrative jurisdiction.[A-53] sentence. The charges against Jesus here take a more political tone: misleading the nation, opposing Roman taxes (a blatantly false accusation; cf. 20:20–26), and claiming to be Christ, a king. Luke's central theme of this Roman phase of the trial is Jesus' innocence. Both Pilate and Herod find no guilt in Jesus (23:4, 14–15, 22). Later, the repentant criminal on the cross and the centurion on duty also affirm his innocence (23:41, 47). Jesus is the righteous and innocent suffering servant.

**Led him off to Pilate (23:1).** According to John 18:31, the Sanhedrin did not have the right to administer capital punishment, so they had to bring Jesus before Pilate. This judicial limitation is confirmed by later rabbinic tradition and by Josephus, who reports that the high priest Ananus was deposed for orchestrating the execution of Jesus' half-brother James during the interim period between the Roman governors Festus and Albinus.[618]

The seat of Roman government in Judea was at Caesarea on the Mediterranean coast, but Pilate was usually in Jerusalem to maintain order during the festival. He resided either at the fortress of Antonia overlooking the Temple Mount, or at the Herodian palace on the western wall in the upper city (see map of Jerusalem). For more on Pilate see comments on 13:1; also Mark 15:1.

**THE PONTIUS PILATE INSCRIPTION**

A Roman era stone slab discovered in Caesarea that names Pontius Pilate.

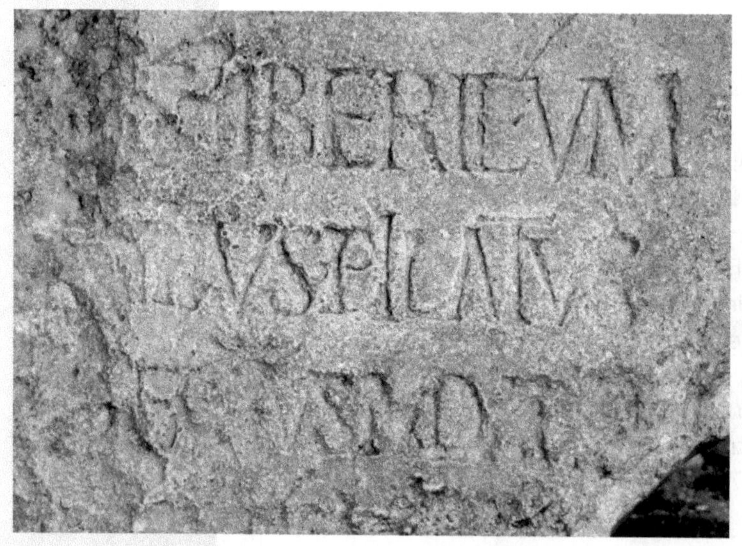

**And they began to accuse him (23:2).** The Romans had two main judicial systems, jury courts (which tried cases involving formal statutes of state law—the *ordo*) and more informal police courts (adjudicated by a magistrate). These latter were the norm in the Roman provinces, where local governors would hear charges, conduct examinations (*cognitio*), and pronounce sentences.[619] Jesus' trial before Pilate is a typical example of such a *cognitio*.[620]

**Opposes payment of taxes to Caesar (23:2).** This was a serious charge. Twenty-five years earlier Judas of Galilee provoked an insurrection in Judea over the issue of Roman taxation.[621]

**Christ, a king . . . "Are you the king of the Jews?" (23:2–3).** While the Jewish religious title "Christ" (Greek) or "Messiah" (Hebrew) would have carried little significance for Pilate, the claim of "king" would represent a threat to Roman authority.

**Yes, it is as you say (23:3).** The Greek here (lit., "You have said so") is more ambiguous than the NIV translation suggests, but probably indicates a qualified affirmation. In any case, Pilate looks at Jesus and judges that he is not a political threat.

**Jesus was under Herod's jurisdiction (23:7).** See comments on 3:1; 3:19–20. Herod Antipas ruled as tetrarch over

Galilee and Perea from the death of his father Herod the Great in A.D. 4 until A.D. 39. He appears in the Gospels as the executor of John the Baptist (3:19–20) and as a distant but curious spectator of Jesus' ministry (9:7–9; 13:31–32). Like his father, he sought to present himself as a faithful Jew. His coins, like those of Herod the Great, did not bear an image of the emperor,[622] and, as this passage shows, he faithfully attended Jewish festivals in Jerusalem.

**He sent him to Herod (23:7).** Pilate may have wanted to avoid personal liability for a difficult decision, or perhaps he was seeking expert Jewish advice from Herod. Herod was in Jerusalem for the Passover and was probably staying in the Hasmonean palace, to the west of the temple (see map of Jerusalem).

**Jesus gave him no answer (23:9).** Isaiah 53:7 predicts the silence of the Suffering Servant before his oppressors: "As a sheep before her shearers is silent, so he did not open his mouth." Ancient writers sometimes speak of the wisdom of silence before false and hypocritical accusations. Note Sirach 20:1: "There is a rebuke that is untimely, and there is the person who is wise enough to keep silent."[623]

**Dressing him in an elegant robe (23:11).** The Greek says "bright" (*lampros*) clothing, which may mean either "white" or "regal" (cf. the purple robe used by the Roman soldiers in Mark 15:17, 20). In either case, the point is mocking Jesus' kingship.

**Herod and Pilate became friends—before this they had been enemies (23:12).** Pilate and Herod Antipas had good reasons to be suspicious of each other, since Pilate was governing the land of Antipas's father, Herod the Great. Surely Antipas hoped one day to rule it for himself. The Jewish philosopher Philo reports an incident in which Pilate

**FORTRESS OF ANTONIA**

The four towers mark the location of this palace on the northwest corner of the Temple Mount.

offended Jewish sensibilities by setting up golden shields inscribed with patrons' names in the Herodian palace in Jerusalem. Four sons of Herod the Great—including Antipas—brought charges against him before the emperor Tiberius, who ordered Pilate to remove them (see comments on 13:1 for similar actions by Pilate).[624] Incidents like these had made Pilate and Antipas enemies and rivals.

**I will punish him (23:16; cf. v. 22).** The verb translated "punish" (*paideuō*) is a mild one which can mean "discipline" or even "instruct." Here it is a euphemism for a beating, something like the English idiom "to teach him a lesson." The Romans distinguished between three kinds of beatings: *fustes, flagella,* and *verbera.* The first was the lightest and was often used as a judicial warning against further infractions. The third was the most severe and was usually given as a prelude to a more severe punishment like execution.[625] Pilate intends to give Jesus a *fustigatio* and release him. As it turned out, Jesus certainly received the *verberatio* when Pilate conceded to his crucifixion (for a description of this kind of beating see Matt. 27:26; Mark 15:15).

**PAVEMENT FROM THE FORTRESS OF ANTONIA**

The "Lithostratos"—a Roman era pavement stone found near the location of the fortress where Jesus carried his cross.

**I will . . . release him (23:16).** The other Gospels note that it was the custom of the day to release a prisoner at the Passover.[626] It is implied in Luke, since the crowd cries out to release Barabbas instead of Jesus. Though the custom is not explicitly described outside the Gospels, it fits well with the clemency practices of religious festivals in the Greco-Roman world.[627]

**Barabbas . . . thrown into prison for an insurrection in the city, and for murder (23:19; cf. v. 25).** First-century Palestine was a hotbed of revolutionary movements in the years leading up to the Jewish revolt of A.D. 66–74. Josephus describes a variety of such insurrectionists, which he calls "robbers" and "imposters."[628] Among the most vicious were the Sicarii, who would mingle with the crowds during the festivals and stab Roman sympathizers with small swords (*sicae*) hidden under their robes.[629] Josephus identifies the Zealots who occupied Masada during the Jewish War as Sicarii.[630] Though Barabbas is not explicitly called a Zealot or a Sicarii, his crimes of insurrection and murder are suggestive of this kind of revolutionary activity. Perhaps he was an associate of the two criminals crucified with Jesus (see comments on 17:23; 21:8).

**"Crucify him! Crucify him!" (23:21).** See "Crucifixion" at 23:33.

**Pilate . . . surrendered Jesus to their will (23:24–25).** Pilate was a pragmatist more interested in maintaining his own power than in justice for an individual. His tendency to capitulate under pressure is seen elsewhere in his withdrawal of Roman standards from Jerusalem and his removal of golden shields from the

Herodian palace (see comments on 13:1; 23:12).[631]

## The Crucifixion (23:26–43)

Luke's crucifixion scene shows Jesus faithfully fulfilling his calling to suffer as the servant of God. Though a victim of injustice, he is in charge of his own fate. He continues to act as a prophet, calling on the grieving women to mourn for themselves because of their coming devastation (in the fall of Jerusalem; cf. 13:34–35; 19:41–44; 21:20–21). He continues to dispense God's grace, forgiving his enemies and offering salvation to the repentant criminal.

The earliest extant Roman record of Pilate's crucifixion of Jesus is from the historian Tacitus. Writing about the persecution of Christians by Nero, he describes their founder as a certain Christus, who "suffered the extreme penalty during the reign of Tiberius at the hands of one of our procurators, Pontius Pilatus."[632] In his famous *Testimonium*, Josephus also mentions Jesus' crucifixion by Pilate.[633] Although this passage has clearly been embellished by later Christians, a recently discovered Arabic version of the *Testimonium* appears to be closer to Josephus' original:

> At this time there was a wise man who was called Jesus. And his conduct was good, and (he) was known to be virtuous. And many people from among the Jews and other nations became his disciples. Pilate condemned him to be crucified and to die. And those who had become his disciples did not abandon his discipleship. They reported that he had appeared to them three days after his crucifixion and that he was alive; accordingly, he was perhaps the Messiah concerning whom the prophets have recounted wonders.[634]

**Simon from Cyrene (23:26).** Cyrene was located in north Africa, in the Roman province of Cyrenaica (modern Libya). Simon was probably a Jewish pilgrim visiting Jerusalem during the Passover.

**Put the cross on him (23:26).** This would be the *patibulum*, or crossbeam of the cross.

**Blessed are the barren women (23:29).** In a culture where childlessness was the cause of great shame (see comments on 1:7) Jesus' words represent a shocking reversal. It is the barren who are blessed because they will not watch their children suffer and die before their eyes. See comments on 21:23 for the horrors of the siege of Jerusalem, particularly on women and children.

**They will say to the mountains, "Fall on us!" and to the hills, "Cover us!" (23:30).** This alludes to Hosea 10:8, a judgment oracle against Israel (cf. Rev. 6:16, where the same verse is cited). The image probably indicates a desire for swift death over prolonged judgment. There may also be the sense that the painful crushing of creation is like "protection" when compared to the awful wrath of God.

**For if men do these things when the tree is green . . . when it is dry (23:31).** Dry wood is sparked to life and burns more easily than freshly cut green wood. The saying probably means that if the Romans crucify an innocent man during relatively peaceful times (the green wood), how much worse will they do during the coming days of revolution (the dry). Josephus records the crucifixion of thousands of

Jews by the Romans during the siege of Jerusalem:

The soldiers out of rage and hatred amused themselves by nailing their prisoners in different postures; and so great was their number, that space could not be found for the crosses nor crosses for the bodies.[635]

**The place called the Skull (23:33).** Luke gives only the Greek term *kranion* rather than the Aramaic "Golgotha" (Matt. 27:33; Mark 15:22). "Calvary" (*calvaria*) is the Latin word for skull. The location is uncertain. It would have been outside the city (Lev. 24:14; Heb. 13:12) and located near a major road, since crucifixion was intended to be a public spectacle and a warning to others.[636] The name could refer to an outcropping of rocks shaped like a skull, or perhaps to the presence of tombs in the area. The traditional site is in an upper section of the Church of the Holy Sepulchre on the west side of Jerusalem. More recent claims have been made for Gordon's Calvary, which has a skull-like appearance and is located near the Garden Tomb. Most contemporary scholars are inclined toward the former traditional site (or remain agnostic).

**THE "WAY OF SORROWS"**

The sign marks the location of the Via Dolorosa, the road Jesus walked to the place of his crucifixion.

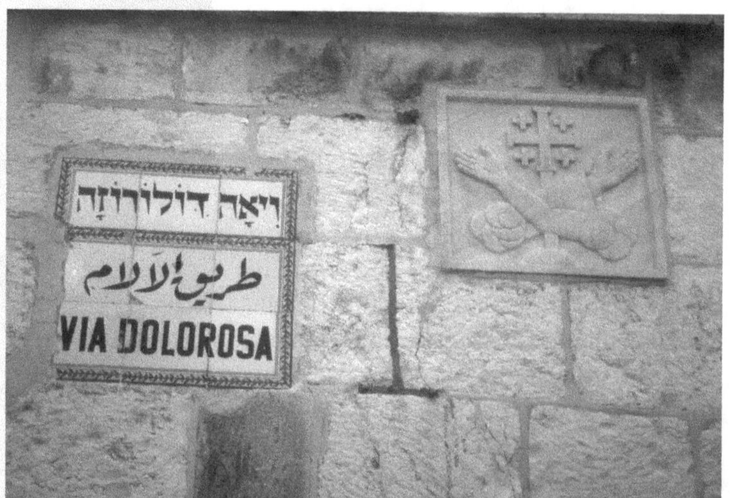


**There they crucified him (23:33).** See "Crucifixion."

**"Father, forgive them, for they do not know what they are doing" (23:34).** Jesus' prayer for the forgiveness of his executioners stands in contrast to the cries for vengeance of the Maccabean martyrs of 2 Maccabees 7:17, 19, 34–35 (cf. 7:14; *4 Macc.* 9:15):

> Keep on, and see how his mighty power will torture you and your descendants! . . . But do not think that you will go unpunished for having tried to fight against God! . . .
>
> But you, unholy wretch, you most defiled of all mortals, do not be elated in vain and puffed up by uncertain hopes, when you raise your hand against the children of heaven. You have not yet escaped the judgment of the almighty, all-seeing God.

**And they divided up his clothes by casting lots (23:34).** The language alludes to Psalm 22:18. It was a common Roman custom for executioners to divide the meager possessions of their victims. This arose from the practice of taking plunder from the battlefield.[637]

**The rulers even sneered at him. . . . The soldiers . . . mocked him (23:35–36).** The taunting and mocking, like the dividing of garments, recalls the treatment of the righteous sufferer in Psalm 22:7–8.

**The Chosen One (23:35).** See comments on 9:26, 35.

**They offered him wine vinegar (23:36).** This sour wine (*oxos*) was a favorite beverage of the lower classes and especially soldiers. It was cheaper than regular wine and relieved thirst better than water.[638]

An allusion to the righteous sufferer of Psalm 69:21 may be present.

**A written notice above him, which read: THIS IS THE KING OF THE JEWS (23:38).** It was evidently common for the Romans to hang a notice (in Latin, a *titulus*) on the cross with the name of the victim and the charge against him.[639] The title mocks Jesus' claim to messiahship.

**Today you will be with me in paradise (23:43).** "Paradise" is from a Persian word meaning "garden" and is used in the LXX and other Jewish writings for the Garden of Eden.[640] In apocalyptic Judaism it came to signify the eternal place of bliss for the righteous. 2 Esdras (*4 Ezra*) 8:52 reads:

> . . . it is for you that paradise is opened, the tree of life is planted, the age to come is prepared, plenty is provided, a city is built, rest is appointed, goodness is established and wisdom perfected beforehand.[641]

The term is used twice elsewhere in the New Testament (2 Cor. 12:4; Rev. 2:7). Jesus uses it here generally of the presence of God, which believers experience immediately at death (cf. 2 Cor. 5:8; see Luke 16:23).

▲ GARDEN TOMB (GORDON'S CALVARY)

An alternative (although unlikely) site of Jesus' tomb. The tomb is associated with the site that General Charles Gordon suggested as the location of Golgotha in 1883.

## ▸ Crucifixion

Crucifixion was used both as a means of execution and for "exposing" an executed body to shame and humiliation.[A-54] The Romans practiced a variety of forms. The main stake or *palus* generally remained at the place of execution, while the victim would be forced to carry the crossbeam or *patibulum* (see 23:26). The crossbeam was placed either on top of the *palus* (like a "T") or in the more traditional cross shape (†). The victim would be affixed to the cross with ropes or, as in the case of Jesus, with nails (John 20:25). Various positions were used to maximize torture and humiliation (see comments from Josephus at 23:31). Seneca wrote that "some hang their victims with head toward the ground, some impale their private parts, others stretch out their arms on fork-shaped gibbet."[A-55] Death was caused by loss of blood, exposure, exhaustion, and/or suffocation, as the victim tried to lift himself to breathe. Victims sometimes lingered for days in agony. Crucifixion was viewed by ancient writers as the cruelest and most barbaric of punishments[A-56] (see comments on Luke 9:23).

The bones of a crucified man named Jehohanan were discovered in 1968 at *Giv'at ha Mivtar* in the Kidron Valley northeast of the Old City, dated between A.D. 7 and 70.[A-57] He was probably a victim of one of the various insurrectionist movements of the first century.

## Jesus' Death (23:44–49)

Jesus' death in Luke picks up various themes of the Passion narrative. The nation's sin and God's coming judgment are indicated by the darkness, the tearing of the curtain, and the mourning of the people. Jesus, by contrast, stays faithful to the end, committing his spirit to God. Finally, his innocence is once again affirmed as the centurion declares him to be a "righteous" or "innocent" man (*dikaios*). Jesus dies as the faithful and righteous Servant of the Lord (Isa. 53:11).

**The sixth hour darkness came . . . until the ninth hour (23:44).** The sixth hour is twelve noon, so the darkness continued from 12:00 to 3:00 P.M. According to Mark 15:25, the crucifixion began at the third hour (9:00 A.M.). In the Old Testament darkness is related to the judgments of the Day of the Lord, and the motif of judgment is probably present here.[642] Darkness is also associated with the death of great men in both Greco-Roman and Jewish traditions.[643]

**The curtain of the temple was torn in two (23:45).** This could be either the curtain that separated the temple from the inner courtyard, or the curtain between the Holy Place and the Most Holy Place.[644] Josephus describes this latter as a magnificent Babylonian curtain of blue, scarlet, and purple, symbolically representing the universe.[645] The symbolism of tearing is probably threefold: judgment against the nation, the cessation of temple sacrifices, and a new way open for all into the presence of God (Heb. 10:19–20).

Josephus reports various signs that served as omens of the destruction of the temple (see comments on 21:25–26). One of these was the mysterious opening of the massive eastern gate of the inner court at midnight on a certain Passover. Though the gate normally took twenty men to open and shut, on this night it mysteriously opened of its own accord. While the ignorant considered this to be a positive sign—God's opening the door of happiness—the wiser men of learning recognized it as opening for the advantage of their enemies—an omen of the coming desolation.[646]

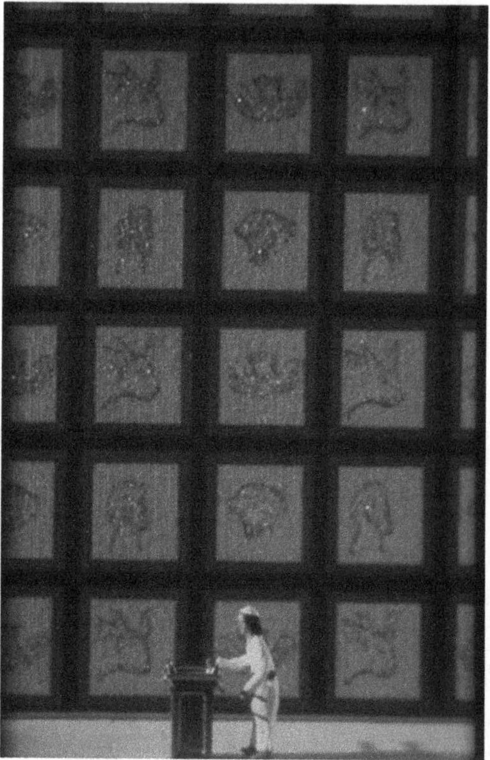

*right* ▶

**THE CURTAIN IN THE TEMPLE**

A reconstruction of the appearance of the temple veil.

### REFLECTIONS

**JESUS' WILLINGNESS TO FORGIVE EVEN HIS MURDERERS** sets a new standard of forgiveness and epitomizes Jesus' teaching about loving your enemies. Just as God loved us "while we were still sinners" (Rom. 5:8), so we ought to reach out in love and forgiveness to those who have wronged us. We are not to be overcome by evil, but to overcome evil with good (Rom. 12:21).

**Father, into your hands I commit my spirit (23:46).** Jesus' final words allude to Psalm 31:5, a psalm of a righteous sufferer crying out for deliverance from enemies who are persecuting him. The psalm is here used typologically. Jesus is the righteous sufferer par excellence.

**The centurion (23:47).** A centurion commanded a "century" of about one hundred soldiers. This man was probably in charge of the crucifixion.

**Surely this was a righteous man (23:47).** The term *dikaios* can mean either "innocent" or "righteous." Both senses are significant for Luke. Throughout the trial and crucifixion Jesus is described as an innocent sufferer. This in turn points to Isaiah 53:11, where God's "righteous [LXX *dikaios*] servant will justify many" (cf. Acts 3:14; 7:52; 22:14).

**They beat their breasts (23:48).** Beating the breast is a sign of mourning and, perhaps, repentance (see comments on 18:13).[647] In context the point seems to be that the people recognize that a great injustice has been done.

## Jesus' Burial (23:50–56)

**Joseph, a member of the Council . . . asked for Jesus' body (23:50–52).** On the basis of Deuteronomy 21:22–23, the Jews sought to bury a crucified body before nightfall, especially before the Sabbath began.[648] This sometimes clashed with the practice of the Romans, who used crucifixion as a public example to provoke fear. They often refused burial for their victims. It was probably Joseph's status as a respected member of the Sanhedrin that prompted Pilate to release Jesus' body so soon after death.

**Arimathea (23:51).** The location of Arimathea is uncertain, but may refer to Ramathaim, another name for Ramah, the birthplace of Samuel (1 Sam. 1:1, 19; 2:11). It was located east of Joppa, twenty miles northwest of Jerusalem.[649]

**Placed it in a tomb cut in the rock, one in which no one had yet been laid (23:53).** Family tombs of Jesus' day were usually caves carved into the sides of hills. In the first century the Jews practiced two-stage burial. In the first stage the corpse would be laid lengthwise in a niche cut in the wall or on a shelf carved alongside the wall. After the flesh decomposed, the bones would be either gathered together in a common pile with other family bones or placed in a small ossuary (burial box) about two feet long and one foot wide. In this way the tomb could be used for many family members over several generations.[650]

**It was Preparation Day, and the Sabbath was about to begin (23:54).** Preparation Day refers to the day before the Sabbath, which began on Friday evening at sunset. Preparations had to be completed quickly so that no work would be done on the Sabbath.

**Then they went home and prepared spices and perfumes (23:56).** Spices and oils were used to honor the dead and to keep down the stench of decomposition.

**But they rested on the Sabbath in obedience to the commandment (23:56).** The Mishnah allows the preparation of the body on the Sabbath but not its movement: "They may make ready [on the Sabbath] all that is needful for the dead, and anoint it and wash it, provided that they do not move any member of it."[651]

## RECONSTRUCTING THE TOMB OF CHRIST

Based on "Reconstructing the Tomb of Christ from Archaeological and Literary Sources" by Eugenia L. Nitoviski, Ph.D., O.C.D., University of Notre Dame

All dimensions shown here are based on studies of actual rolling stone tombs. The original tomb of Christ was destroyed by the Roman Emperor Hadrian.

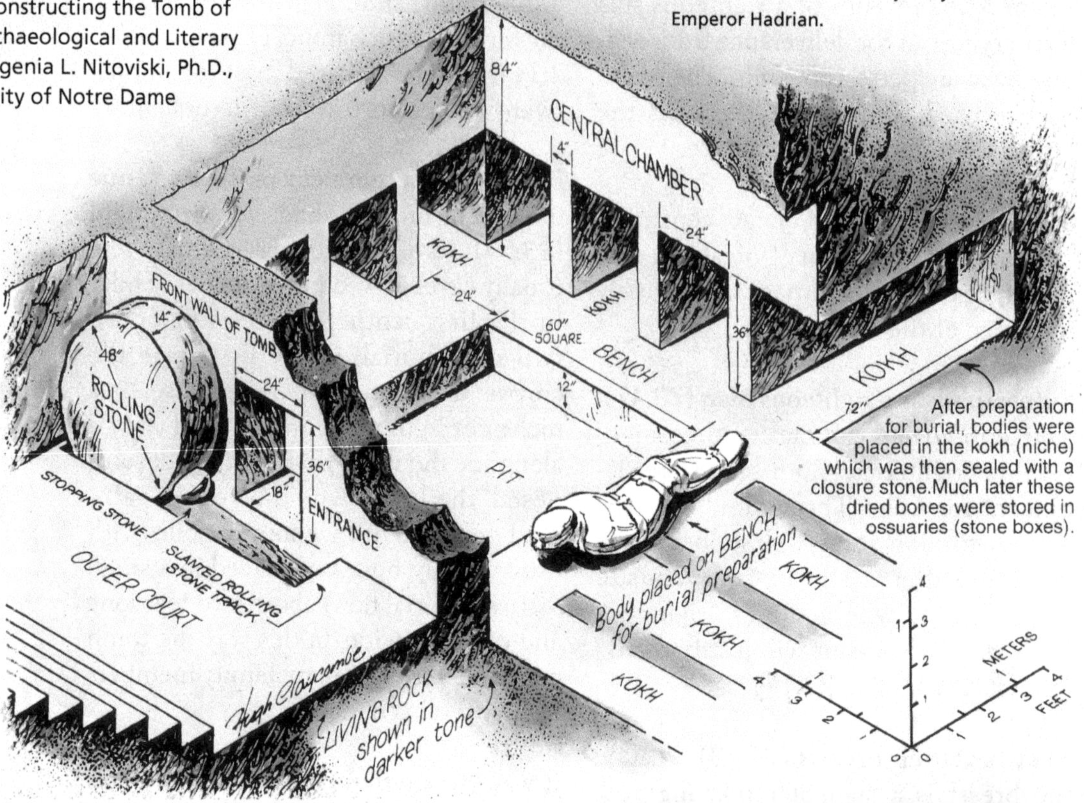

CENTRAL CHAMBER
84"
4"
24"
KOKH
24"
60" SQUARE
BENCH
12"
36"
KOKH
72"
FRONT WALL OF TOMB
14"
48"
ROLLING STONE
24"
36"
18"
ENTRANCE
PIT
STOPPING STONE
SLANTED ROLLING STONE TRACK
OUTER COURT
Body placed on BENCH for burial preparation
KOKH
KOKH
KOKH
LIVING ROCK shown in darker tone
Hugh Claycombe
METERS
FEET

After preparation for burial, bodies were placed in the kokh (niche) which was then sealed with a closure stone. Much later these dried bones were stored in ossuaries (stone boxes).

The original tomb belonging to Joseph of Arimathea was destroyed by the Roman Emperor Habrian after a.d. 135. This reconstruction is based on 61 other "rolling stone" tombs which have remained, particulary on a classic example found in Heshbon, Jordan in 1971. Joseph's tomb may not have been this extensive nor complete, being as yet unused. Affordable by wealthy familes only, these tombs were constructed according to Jewish law, the Mishnah, as follows:

> "If a man sold to his fellow a place to make a tomb (so, too, if a man received from his fellow a place in which to make hima tomb), he must make the inside of the vault four cubits by six, and open up within it eight niches, three on this side, and two oppisite [the doorway]. The niches must be four cubits long, seven handbreadths high and six wide. R. Simeon says: He must make the inside of the vault, four cubits by eight and open up within thirteen niches, four on this side, four on that side, three opposite [the doorway] and one to the right of the doorway and one to the left. He must make a courtyard at the opening of the vault, six cubits by six, space enough for the bier and its bearers; and he may open up within it two other vaults, one on either side. R. Simeon says: Four, one on each of its four sides. Rabban Simeon b. Gamaliel says: All depends on the nature of the rock." (Baba Bathra 6:8)

Tomb F.1 at Tell Hesban, Transjordan

Courtesy of the Heshbon Expedition Andrews University

These were emergency procedures to prevent the onset of decomposition before burial. Since Joseph had been able to complete burial before the Sabbath, the women appropriately rest on the Sabbath.

## The Resurrection (24:1–12)

Luke provides three accounts of resurrection appearances: the women at the tomb (24:1–12), the appearance to two disciples on the road to Emmaus (24:13–35), and the appearance to the eleven disciples in Jerusalem (24:36–49). He then concludes his Gospel with a short account of Jesus' ascension (24:50–53).

All four Gospels agree that women first discovered the empty tomb on Sunday morning and that the resurrected Jesus first appeared to women. This is particularly striking since women were not considered reliable witnesses in first-century Judaism. Josephus claims to be reporting the law of Moses when he writes:

> Put not trust in a single witness, but let there be three or at the least two, whose evidence shall be accredited by their past lives. From women let no evidence be accepted, because of the levity and temerity of their sex.[652]

While the reference to two or three witnesses comes from Deuteronomy 17:6; 19:15, the statement about women is nowhere found in the Old Testament and must come from first-century rabbinic traditions. Philo, too, claims that women are "irrational" and should not be trusted.[653] Considering this background, it is unlikely that the followers of Jesus would have *created* stories in which women were the primary witnesses to the empty tomb. Few would have believed them. This is a strong argument for the essential historicity of these accounts.

**They found the stone rolled away from the tomb (24:2).** This stone would have been a disk-shaped stone placed in a track or groove and rolled in front of the opening.[654]

**Two men in clothes that gleamed like lightning (24:4).** In the Old Testament and Judaism angels are often called "men" because of their human appearance.[655] They often appear shining and in white clothing—signs of purity and holiness (Dan. 10:5–6; cf. Luke 9:29).[656]

**In their fright the women bowed down (24:5).** Fear is a common response to the appearance of an angelic presence (see comments on 1:12).[657]

**On the third day be raised again (24:7).** The "third day" does not refer to three twenty-four hour days, but inclusively to any part of three days: Friday, Saturday, and Sunday. The "third day" may be an allusion to Hosea 6:2, a reference to Israel's national restoration.

**TOMB WITH A ROLLING STONE**

The first-century A.D. tomb of Queen Helena of Adiabene.

As the Messiah, Jesus both represents and brings restoration to God's people.

**It was Mary Magdalene, Joanna, Mary the mother of James, and the others with them (24:10).** For the first two women see comments on 8:2–3. The third name says literally "Mary of James," which could refer to James's wife, mother, or even sister. Mark 15:40 suggests "mother" is meant. This is not the mother of James and John, who appears beside this woman in Matthew 27:56. It may be the mother of James the son of Alphaeus (Luke 6:15) or of another unknown James.

**But they did not believe the women, because their words seemed to them like nonsense (24:11).** The disciples' unbelief may have been partly due to a first-century view of women (see comments on 24:1–12), but relates primarily to the strangeness of the report. In Jewish understanding the resurrection of the dead occurred not within history, but at the end of time (see comments on 8:55; 14:14; 20:27).

## On the Road to Emmaus (24:13–35)

The account of two disciples on the road to Emmaus occurs only in Luke and represents his most theologically significant contribution to the resurrection narratives. Cleopas and his companion represent the discouragement and unbelief of Jesus' followers. When they meet Jesus on the road, his identity is hidden from them. They express their profound disappointment at the tragic events in Jerusalem. While Jesus of Nazareth was clearly a great prophet, they had hoped that he might be even more—the Messiah who would redeem Israel. Yet his crucifixion dashed all such hopes. Jesus responds by rebuking them for their hardness of heart. Did not the Scriptures predict the suffering of the Messiah?

GARDEN TOMB

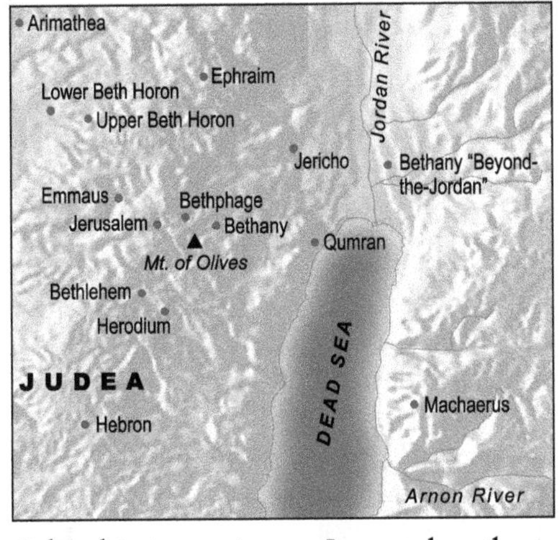


◀ *left*

**JERUSALEM AND ITS VICINITY**

Emmaus was located just northwest of Jerusalem.

School is in session as Jesus takes them through the Old Testament, showing them that all the Scriptures point to the coming of the Christ. He is the centerpoint of salvation history.

Though now equipped with the truth of Scripture, the disciples' recognition of Jesus does not occur until they invite him into their home and he breaks bread with them. Jesus meets them—as us—in personal fellowship and communion. When Jesus disappears from their presence, they joyfully rush back to Jerusalem to report their experience. There they find the apostles already announcing the same message: Jesus is risen indeed!

**Two of them . . . Cleopas (24:13, 18).** Nothing else is known about Cleopas or the identity of his companion. It may have been his wife. They are probably returning home after a Jerusalem Passover visit and probably assume the stranger walking with them is doing the same.

**A village called Emmaus, about seven miles from Jerusalem (24:13).** The location of Emmaus is uncertain, although two possible sites have been suggested.[658] (1) Josephus mentions an *Ammaous* thirty stadia (three and a half miles) from Jerusalem. In this case Luke could be describing a roundtrip distance. (2) There is an Arab village seven miles northwest of Jerusalem on the road to Lydda named El-Qubeibeh, where the Crusaders built a fort called Castellum Emmaus. While this village is the right distance from Jerusalem, no first-century evidence attaches the name "Emmaus" to it.

**But they were kept from recognizing him (24:16).** While this could have something to do with the differences in Jesus' resurrection body, the passive suggests that God intentionally prevents their recognition until the moment of revelation (see 2 Kings 6:17 for God's opening blind eyes to spiritual realities).

**"Did not the Christ have to suffer these things. . . ?" And beginning with Moses and all the Prophets . . . (24:26–27).** This is a surprising revelation since first-century Jews did not view the Messiah as a suffering figure (see comments on 9:22; 18:31).[659] "Moses and the Prophets" is a shorthand way of describing the Old Testament—the Law, the Prophets, and the Writings (see comments on 16:16, 19; 24:44). The whole Old Testament points forward to Jesus the Messiah. The early church recognized the suffering of the Messiah in passages like Psalms 2; 16; 22; 118; Isaiah 50:4–9; 52:13–53:12.[660]

**But they urged him strongly, "Stay with us . . ." (24:29).** Middle Eastern culture demanded such hospitality (see Gen. 18:3; 19:2; Judg. 19:5–9; also comments on Luke 11:1–13).

**He took bread, gave thanks, broke it (24:30).** Although in the home of these disciples, Jesus takes over the role of the host. As with so many meals in Luke, this one points forward to the messianic banquet over which the Messiah will preside (see comments on 13:29; 14:15). The breaking of bread recalls the feeding of the five thousand (9:16) and the Last Supper (22:19), both of which contain messianic-banquet imagery.

**He disappeared from their sight (24:31).** Jewish and Greco-Roman literature speaks of similar disappearances by angelic and divine figures.[661] Jesus' disappearance confirms he has received a unique and glorified resurrection body.

**Were not our hearts burning within us (24:32).** This idiom could mean that their hearts were grieved at Jesus' convicting words on the road (see Ps. 72:21 LXX), but more likely means they felt a strong urge to respond to Jesus' powerful words (see Ps. 38:4 LXX; Jer. 20:9).

**The Lord has risen and has appeared to Simon (24:34).** The Greek grammar makes it clear that this is a report coming from the Eleven, not the Emmaus disciples. A resurrection appearance to Peter is independently confirmed by Paul in 1 Corinthians 15:5.

## Jesus Appears to the Disciples (24:36–49)

While the Emmaus disciples are giving their report to the Eleven, Jesus suddenly appears before them all. There is a strong emphasis in the scene on the real and bodily resurrection of Jesus, as he lets the disciples touch him and eats before them. Jesus reveals to them how his death and resurrection were in fulfillment of Scripture—a key theme throughout Luke-Acts. The salvation he has achieved means that repentance and forgiveness of sins can now be preached in his name to all nations. They will be his witnesses, going forth in the power of the Spirit from Jerusalem to the ends of the earth.

**They were startled and frightened, thinking they saw a ghost (24:37).** Although Jewish eschatology focused on the resurrection of the body at the end of time, there was also popular belief in disembodied spirits or ghosts. As today, spiritualists and mediums consulted with the dead.[662]

**Look at my hands and my feet (24:39).** This provides indirect evidence that Jesus was nailed rather than tied to the cross.

**Touch me and see; a ghost does not have flesh and bones (24:39).** Jesus' resurrection is neither the simple resuscitation of his body nor the appearance of a disembodied spirit, but rather a true resurrection into a new and glorified body (1 Cor. 15:20–23, 35–49). It is the beginning—the firstfruits and guarantee—of the end-time resurrection of all believers.[663]

**Everything must be fulfilled that is written about me (24:44).** See comments on 24:26.

**Law of Moses, the Prophets and the Psalms (24:44).** This is a reference to the threefold division of the Hebrew Scriptures: the Law (*Torah*), the Prophets (*Neviʾim*), and the Writings (*Ketuʾbim*). The Psalms stood at the head of the Writings and here represents them (see comments on 16:16, 29; 24:27).

**This is what is written: The Christ will suffer and rise . . . repentance and forgiveness of sins will be preached in his name to all nations (24:46–47).** For Old Testament texts related to the suffering of the Christ see comments on 24:26. The resurrection is defended by the apostles in Acts from Psalms 2:7; 16:9–10; 110:1–2; and the universal proclamation of the Gospel from Isaiah 42:6; 49:6; Joel 2:28–32; Amos 9:11–12.[664]

**I am going to send you what my Father has promised (24:49).** In the Old Testament God promised the outpouring of his Spirit on his people in the end times.[665]

## The Ascension (24:50–53)

The Gospel ends with a brief account of Jesus' ascension, described in more detail in Acts 1:1–11. Luke here abbreviates events, giving the appearance that Jesus ascended on the day of his resurrection rather than forty days later, as Acts will clarify (see comments on Acts 1:3). This ascension gives closure to Luke's Gospel and sets the stage for Jesus' guidance over his church from his authoritative position at the right hand of God (cf. Acts 2:33–36).

**The vicinity of Bethany (24:50).** Bethany was located two miles east of Jerusalem on the eastern slope of the Mount of Olives. Acts 1:12 identifies the ascension with the Mount of Olives, the place where the Messiah will return in glory (Zech. 14:4).

**He lifted up his hands and blessed them (24:50).** Jesus' blessing provides closure of this Gospel and sends the disciples on their way to accomplish God's purposes. Sirach 50:20 describes a similar blessing by the high priest Simon II (219–196 B.C.) during worship at the Jerusalem temple: "Then Simon came down and raised his hands over the whole congregation of Israelites, to pronounce the blessing of the Lord with his lips, and to glory in his name." Jesus is portrayed as the authoritative mediator between God and his people.

**He left them and was taken up into heaven (24:51).** In the Old Testament Elijah ascended to heaven in a whirlwind with a fiery chariot (2 Kings 2:11; cf. 1 Macc. 2:58), and Enoch "was no more, because God took him away" (Gen. 5:24). In later Jewish traditions various Old Testament heroes ascend to heaven.[666] These are sometimes journeys to heaven to receive revelations and then return to earth (Enoch, Abraham, Isaiah, Baruch, Ezra). Other times they are permanent departures—a royal transport—at the end of life (Enoch, Moses, Elijah). Jesus' ascension is much more significant, establishing his exalted position of glory and power over all of creation.[667]

**They stayed continually at the temple (24:53).** The temple was a place of worship and prayer as well as a place of sacrifice.

## ANNOTATED BIBLIOGRAPHY

**Bailey, Kenneth E.** *Poet and Peasant* and *Through Peasant Eyes: A Literary-Cultural Approach to the Parables of Luke.* Combined edition. Grand Rapids: Eerdmans, 1983.

This is a fascinating and informative work on the Lukan parables by a biblical scholar who has spent years studying contemporary Middle Eastern peasant culture. Many unique cultural insights into the parables may be found here.

**Bock, Darrell L.** *Luke.* 2 vols. BECNT. Grand Rapids: Eerdmans; *Volume 1: 1:1–9:50,* 1994; *Volume 2: 9:51–24:53,* 1996.

This massive two-volume commentary provides extensive discussion in all key aspects of Luke's Gospel, including background, historicity, and theology. Though written in a popular and accessible style, it is well documented, with extensive references to other commentaries and background material.

**Boring, Eugene M., Klaus Berger, and Carsten Colpe, eds.** *Hellenistic Commentary to the New Testament.* Nashville: Abingdon, 1995.

This volume gathers a wide range of Hellenistic texts related to the New Testament. An excellent resource for those without easy access to the more obscure primary sources.

**Danker, Frederick W.** *Jesus and the New Age: A Commentary on St. Luke's Gospel.* 2d ed. Philadelphia: Fortress, 1988.

This commentary provides a wealth of classical and Hellenistic background. While most commentaries focus on Jewish background, Danker keeps a constant eye on the wider literature of the Greco-Roman world.

**Fitzmyer, Joseph A.** *The Gospel According to Luke: A New Translation with Introduction and Commentary.* 2 vols. AB 28, 28A. New York: Doubleday; *Luke I-IX,* 1981; *Luke X-XXIV,* 1985.

Fitzmyer's expertise in New Testament background, and especially in Aramaic and the Dead Sea Scrolls, makes this two-volume commentary a wealth of information for background material on Luke's Gospel.

**Jeremias, Joachim.** *Jerusalem in the Time of Jesus.* Translated by F. H. Cave and C. H. Cave. Philadelphia: Fortress, 1969.

This classic work by one of the foremost New Testament scholars of the twentieth century is a wealth of background material on first-century Palestinian culture and society. Caution must be exercised, however, against uncritical acceptance of later rabbinic material as necessarily applicable to Jesus' day.

**Malina, Bruce J. and Richard L. Rohrbaugh.** *Social-Science Commentary on the Synoptic Gospels.* Minneapolis: Fortress, 1992.

This volume is a unique and helpful resource for the distinct sociological background to the New Testament, particularly with references to issues like social status, honor and shame, rich and poor, etc. Such issues, while often overlooked in the past, have profound significance for the interpretation of certain texts.

**Manson, T. W.** *The Sayings of Jesus.* London: SCM, 1949.

Manson's constant eye on the rabbinic literature makes this a helpful background resource for the sayings of Jesus common to Matthew and Luke.

**Marshall, I. Howard.** *The Gospel of Luke: A Commentary on the Greek Text.* NIGTC. Grand Rapids: Eerdmans, 1978.

Marshall's careful and erudite scholarship makes this a classic commentary not only for Lukan purpose and theology, but also for background and historical material.

**Nolland, John L.** *Luke.* 3 vols. WBC 35. Dallas: Word; : 1989 (a); 1993 (b, c).

This three-volume work provides extensive bibliographical material on individual passages. An excellent research tool.

## Main Text Notes

1. Luke 2:32; 3:6; 4:25–27.
2. Col. 4:7–17; 2 Tim. 4:10–11; Philem. 23–24.
3. Josephus, *J.W.* 1.1 §§1–2.
4. For examples see J. A. Fitzmyer, *The Gospel According to Luke: A New Translation with Introduction and Commentary* (AB 28, 28A; New York: Doubleday, 1981, 1985), 1:292.
5. Cf. 1 Chron. 26:13–16; Neh. 11:1; Jonah 1:7.
6. *m. Tamid* 5:2–6:3.
7. Josephus, *Ant.* 13.10.3 §§282–3.
8. Cf. Sir. 48:10; 2 Esd. (*4 Ezra*) 6:26; Justin, *Dialogue with Trypho* 8, 49; Str-B 4:784–89, 792–98; J. Jeremias, "Ἠλίας," *TDNT*, 2:928–34.
9. Dan. 8:16; 9:21; the other is Michael: 10:13; 12:1; cf. *1 En.* 20:1–7.
10. *m. Yoma* 5.1.
11. See Jeremias, *Jerusalem*, 105–8, 206.
12. For more details see Jeremias, *Jerusalem*, 364–67.
13. See Isa. 9:6–7; 11:1–5; Jer. 23:5–6; 33:15–16; Ezek. 37:24–25.
14. Luke 1:69; 20:41–44; Acts 2:30–36; 13:23.
15. See also 4QFlor 1.11 (=4Q174); 1QSa 2.11.12 (=1Q28a); Ps. 2:7; 89:26; Isa. 7:14.
16. Matt. 16:16; 26:63; Luke 4:41; 22:70.
17. Cf. John 10:30 (and throughout John); Rom. 1:3; Gal. 4:4; Heb. 1:1–4.
18. Both cited by I. Howard Marshall, *The Gospel of Luke: A Commentary on the Greek Text* (NIGTC; Grand Rapids: Eerdmans, 1978), 80.
19. Ex. 6:6; Deut. 4:34; Ps. 44:3.
20. 1 Sam. 2:5, 7; cf. Ps. 147:6; Jer. 5:27–29.
21. Luke 1:73; 3:8; 16:24; Acts 3:25; 7:5–6.
22. See Marshall, *Gospel of Luke*, 88; John L. Nolland, *Luke* (WBC 35; Dallas: Word Books, 1989, 1993), 1:79.
23. Ezra 7:6, 28; Isa. 41:20; Ex. 9:3; Judg. 2:15; etc.
24. See Luke 1:46–55; 2:14; 2:29–32.
25. Cf. Ps. 2; 72; 89; 110; 132.
26. 1 Kings 1:48; 1 Chron. 16:36; Ps. 41:13; 68:19; 72:18; 106:48; etc.
27. Jer. 31:34; 33:8; 50:20.
28. See Isa. 11:1–5; Jer. 23:5–6; 33:15–16; Zech. 3:8; 6:12; 4QFlor 1.10–13; 4QPBless 1–5 (4Q252); 4QpIsa[a]; *Shemoneh Esreh* 14.
29. Isa. 9:2; 42:6–7; 49:6.
30. See, for example, 4QTestim 12; CD 7.18; 1QM 9.6; *T. Levi* 18.3; *T. Jud.* 24.1–6.
31. See Isa. 58:8–10; 60:1–3; Mal. 4:2.
32. Judg. 13:24–25; 1 Sam. 2:21, 26; 3:19; cf. Luke 2:40, 52.
33. See Jos. *Ant.* 18.1.1 §§3ff.; 18.2.1 §26.
34. See W. M. Ramsay, *The Bearing of Recent Discovery on the Trustworthiness of the New Testament* (4th ed.; London: Hodder & Stoughton, 1920), 275–300. Unfortunately the inscription is damaged (the name Quirinius does not appear on it), and so this proposal is highly speculative.
35. Nolland, *Luke*, 1.101.
36. 1 Sam. 17:12, 58; 20:6.
37. Ex. 13:2; Deut. 21:15–17.
38. Cf. the description of Solomon in the Wisd. Sol. 7:4.
39. See Ex. 4:24 LXX; 1 Kingdoms 1:18 LXX; Jer. 14:8 LXX.
40. The tradition that Jesus was born in a cave appears in the *Protevangelium of James* 18–19, Justin, *Dialogue with Trypho* 78:4; Origin, *Against Celsus* 1:15.
41. For the rabbinic evidence see Str-B 2:113–14.
42. John 10:11; Heb. 13:20; 1 Peter 2:25.
43. Ex. 16:7, 10; 33:18, 22; 40:34, etc.
44. See Luke 1:19; 2:10; 3:18; 4:18, 43; 7:22; 8:1; 9:6; 16:16; 20:1.
45. For the full text and references see Frederick W. Danker, *Jesus and the New Age: A Commentary on St. Luke's Gospel* (2d ed.; Philadelphia: Fortress, 1988), 54.
46. Ps. 18:46; 24:5; Isa. 17:10, etc.
47. Luke 1:47, 68–69, 71; cf. Acts 5:31; 13:23.
48. 2 Sam. 22:51; Ps. 2:2; 89:20, 38.
49. Cf. 4QFlor (4Q174) 1:13. Cf. *Pss. Sol.* 17:21–43; 18:5–9; 1QSb (1Q28b) 5:21–29; *4 Ezra* 11:1–12:39; etc.
50. For details see Marshall, *Gospel of Luke*, 112; Fitzmyer, *Luke*, 1:411, 412; Nolland, *Luke*, 1:109.
51. Ex. 13:1–15; 34:19–20; Num. 3:11–13, 40–51; 18:15–16.
52. Isa. 40:1–2; cf. 49:13; 57:18; 61:2.
53. Ps. 118:22; Isa. 8:14; 28:16.
54. Borne of Zilpah, Leah's maidservant; Gen. 30:12–13; cf. Num. 1:40, 41; Rev. 7:6.
55. 1 Cor. 7:8, 34; 1 Tim. 5:3–16; Titus 1:10.
56. Josephus, *Ant.* 18.6.6 §180.
57. Fitzmyer, *Luke*, 1:432.
58. Ibid., 1:440; *m. Nid.* 5:6; *m. ʾAbot* 5:21; *Gen. Rab.* 63:10.
59. Josephus, *Ant.* 5.10.4 §348; cf. 1 Sam. 3.
60. Moses (Josephus, *Ant.* 2.9.6 §§230–31; Philo, *Moses* 1:21); Cyrus the Great (Herodotus 1:114–15); Alexander the Great (Plutarch, *Alex.* 5); Apollonius (Philostratus, *Vita Apoll.* 1:7).
61. Josephus, *Life* 2 §9.

62. A similar neuter plural expression appears in the LXX at Gen. 41:51; Est. 7:9; Job 18:19; and in Josephus (*Ant.* 8.5.3 §145; 16.10.1 §302).
63. Deut. 21:18–21; Prov. 30:17; 2 Tim. 3:2.
64. Ex. 20:12; Deut. 5:16; Mark 7:10 pars.; 10:19 pars.; Eph. 6:2.
65. Luke 3:7–14; see also Matt. 3:1–12; Mark 1:2–8.
66. For details see Marshall, *Gospel of Luke,* 13. The other rulers mentioned here do not help to narrow the date further since their dates overlap with all of these.
67. Josephus, *Ant.* 17.11.4 §§317–20; *J.W.* 2.6.3 §§93–100.
68. Luke 23:1–24, 52; cf. Acts 3:13; 4:27; 13:28.
69. Luke 3:19–20; cf. Mark 6:17–29.
70. Josephus, *Ant.* 14.13.3 §330; 15.4.1 §92.
71. Josephus, *Ant.* 19.5.1 §275; 20.7.1 §138; *J.W.* 2.11.5 §215; 2.12.8 §247. The inscriptional evidence may be found in A. Böckh, *Corpus Inscriptionum Graecarum* (Berlin: Reimer, 1828–1877). See Fitzmyer, *Luke,* 1:457–58.
72. Josephus, *Ant.* 18.2.2 §§33–35.
73. Cf. John 18:13–14, 24; Acts 4:6.
74. BAGD, 131.
75. Ex. 30:19–20; Lev. 14:7–8, 51; 15:5–27; Num. 19:18.
76. 1QS 3:5–9; 1QS 5:13–14.
77. *b. Yebam.* 47ab.
78. 2 Chron. 7:14; Isa. 6:10; Jer. 36:3; Ezek. 18:21, 30, 32; 33:9, 14.
79. Jer. 33:8; Ezek. 34:25–26.
80. 1QS 5:13–14.
81. Josephus, *Ant.* 18.5.2 §117.
82. See K. R. Snodgrass, "Streams of Tradition Emerging from Isaiah 40:1–5 and Their Adaptation in the New Testament," *JSNT* 8 (1980): 24–45.
83. 1QS 8:12–15; 9:19–20.
84. Sir. 48:24–25.
85. See Isa. 11:15–16; 42:14–16; 43:1–3, 14–21; 48:20–21; 49:8–12; 52:11–12; 55:12–13; *Pss. Sol.* 11:2–5; 17:21–46; *4 Ezra* 13; *Tg. Lam.* 2:22.
86. The eventual destruction of evil will mean the harmlessness of snakes: "The young child [will] put his hand into the viper's nest" (Isa. 11:8).
87. 1QH 3:12–18.
88. See also John 8:33–39; Acts 7:2; Rom. 4:1.
89. *Pss. Sol.* 18:4.
90. Cf. Str-B 1.116–21; Fitzmyer, *Luke,* 1:468; *T. Levi* 15:4; cf. *m.* ʾ*Abot* 5:19.
91. Cf. O. Michel, "τελώνης," *TDNT* 8:88–105; J. R. Donahue, "Tax Collectors and Sinners: An Attempt at Identification," *CBQ* 33 (1971): 39–61.
92. For evidence of abuses see Josephus, *Ant.* 18.6.5 (§§172–78); *J.W.* 2.14.1 (§§272–76); Philo, *Embassy* 199.
93. Josephus, *Ant.* 17.8.3 §§198–99; 18.5.1 §113.
94. Cf. Str-B 1:121; 4:2, 712, 717–18; Darrell L. Bock, *Luke* (BECNT; Grand Rapids: Eerdmans, 1996), 1:320–21.
95. Isa. 32:15; Ezek. 36:26–27; Joel 2:28–32.
96. See Gen. 19:24; Isa. 29:6; Ezek. 38:22; Amos 7:4; Zeph. 1:18; 3:8; Mal. 4:1; *4 Ezra* 13:10–11, 27; *1 En.* 67:13; 90:24–27; 1QS 2:8; 4:13.
97. Luke 3:17; cf. Luke 9:54; 12:49; 17:29.
98. Cf. 1QH 8:20; 1QS 3:7–9; 4:21; *T. Isaac* 5:21–32; *T. Ab.* 12–13.
99. See 1 Kings 13:4; 18:13; 19:2; 22:26–27; 2 Kings 1:9; 6:31; 2 Chron. 24:21.
100. Jer. 18:18, 23; 26:11, 20–23; 36–38.
101. Luke 4:24; 11:47–51; 13:34; Acts 7:52.
102. Ezek. 1:1; John 1:51; Acts 7:56; 10:11; Rev. 19:11.
103. *b. Ḥag.* 15a.
104. Gen. 22:17–18; Luke 1:54–55, 72–73; 2 Sam. 7:12–16; Luke 1:32–33.
105. Philo, *Virtues* 204–5.
106. Philo, *Virtues* 205.
107. Deut. 8:3; 6:13, 16.
108. Cf. Mark 1:13; Luke 4:3, 5, 13; 8:12; 10:18; 11:18; 13:16; 22:3, 31.
109. 1 Chron. 21:1; Job 1–2; Zech. 3:1–2.
110. John 8:44; 2 Cor. 12:7; 1 Peter 5:8; Rev. 12:9; 20:2.
111. Dio Cassius, *Roman History* 62.5.3; cited by Danker, *Jesus and the New Age,* 102.
112. Josephus, *Ant.* 15.11.5 §415.
113. *Pesiq. Rab.* §36; cited by Fitzmyer, *Luke,* 1:517.
114. Cf. Matt. 4:12–17; Mark 1:14–15; 6:1–6.
115. See J. A. Sanders, "From Isaiah to Luke 4," in *Luke and Scripture: The Function of Sacred Tradition in Luke-Acts* (Minneapolis: Fortress, 1993), 46–69.
116. See J. L. Nolland, "Classical and Rabbinic Parallels to 'Physician, Heal Yourself' (Lk iv 23)," *NovT* 21 (1979):193–209.
117. See J. Blinzer, "The Jewish Punishment of Stoning in the New Testament Period," in *The Trial of Jesus* (FS C. F. D. Moule, ed. E. Bammel; London: SCM, 1970), 147–61.
118. Marshall, *Gospel of Luke,* 193.
119. Though this work postdates the New Testament, its traditions probably come from much earlier; cf. Josephus, *Ant.* 8.2.5, where Solomon's gifts of exorcism are described: *T. Sol.* 1:7.
120. H. C. Kee, "The Terminology of Mark's Exorcism Stories," *NTS* 14 (1967–1968): 232–46.
121. See, for example, the many rituals described in the *T. Sol.*

122. See H. J. Cadbury, "Lexical Notes on Luke-Acts: II. Recent Arguments for Medical Language," *JBL* 45 (1926): 190–209.
123. See Luke 9:35; 22:66–71; Acts 9:20, 22.
124. See Jer. 33:17, 22; Ezek. 37:25; Dan. 7:27; *Pss. Sol.* 17:4; *1 En.* 62:14; Str-B 2:552.
125. See *4 Ezra* 7:28–29 (400 yrs.); 12:34; *b. Sanh.* 97a, 99a; cf. Rev. 20:4–6. See Schürer, 2:536–37.
126. Josephus, *Ant.* 18.2.1 §28.
127. See E. F. Bishop, "Jesus and the Lake," *CBQ* 13 (1951): 398–414, esp. 401.
128. Lev. 13:45–46; cf. Luke 17:12, 14.
129. Marshall, *Gospel of Luke,* 213.
130. *m. Sanh.* 7:5.
131. For references see H. W. Beyer, "βλασφημέω," *TDNT,* 1:621–25.
132. Cf. Matt. 9:9–13; Mark 2:13–17.
133. Danker, *Jesus and the New Age,* 126.
134. See Luke 18:12; *Didache* 8:1; *b. Taʿan.* 12a.
135. Est. 4:16; 2 Sam. 12:23; Joel 1:14; Jonah 3:5.
136. Isa. 58:4–5; Jer. 14:12.
137. For more on first-century marriage customs see J. Jeremias, *The Parables of Jesus* (rev. ed.; trans. S. H. Hooke; New York: Scribner's, 1963), 171–75.
138. Cf. Ex. 20:8–11; Deut. 5:14.
139. Cf. *y. Šabb.* 7.9b; Str-B 1.617; *m. Šabb.* 7:2.
140. Ex. 25:30; 35:13; 40:23; Lev. 24:8–9.
141. Josephus, *Ant.* 6.12.1 §§242–243.
142. Fitzmyer, *Luke,* 1:609; Str-B 1.618–19.
143. *m. Yoma* 8:6.
144. *m. Šabb.* 18:3; 19:2.
145. BAGD, 622.
146. Marshall, *Gospel of Luke,* 236.
147. Cf. Mark 3:13–19.
148. George A. Turner, *Historical Geography of the Holy Land* (Grand Rapids: Baker, 1973), 104–6.
149. Fitzmyer, *Luke,* 1:620.
150. For a good discussion of the similarities and differences, and a general introduction to the sermon, see Bock, *Luke,* 1:931–49.
151. Cf. Ps. 149:4; Isa. 66:5.
152. See Ps. 22:26; 107:9, 36–41; 132:15; Isa. 49:10–13; 65:13; Jer. 31:12, 25; Ezek. 34:29; 36:29.
153. See Ps. 126; Isa. 40:1; 51:3; 57:18; 61:2; 66:13.
154. 1 Kings 22:12–13; Isa. 30:9–11; Jer. 5:31; 6:14; 23:16–17.
155. Cf. Deut. 24:10–17; Amos 2:8.
156. For other texts see Danker, *Jesus and the New Age,* 146–47; Fitzmyer, *Luke,* 1:639–40; Seneca, *De Beneficiis* 2.1.1.
157. *b. Šabb.* 31a.
158. See the sources cited by Marshall, *Gospel of Luke,* 262.
159. F. W. Danker, *Benefactor: Epigraphic Study of a Graeco-Roman and New Testament Semantic Field* (St. Louis: Clayton, 1982), 78; idem, *Jesus and the New Age,* 147.
160. Ex. 22:25; Lev. 25:35–37; Deut. 23:20; Ps. 112:5; Sir. 29:1–2.
161. Cf. Ruth 3:15; Isa. 65:6.
162. *m. Soṭah* 1:7.
163. Nolland, *Luke,* 1:301.
164. See examples in W. Schrage, "τυφλός," *TDNT,* 8:275–76, 286. The image of the blind leading the blind appears in Sextus Empiricus, *Pyrrhonic Elements* 3.259.
165. Cf. Plutarch, *De curios* 515d; Horace, *Satires* 1.3.25. The Jewish example often cited (*b. ʿArak.* 16b) is probably anti-Christian polemic dependent on Jesus' saying. It is attributed to Rabbi Tarphon (c. A.D. 100), a strong opponent of Palestinian Christians; it criticizes those (Christians?) who will not accept correction: "If one says to a man, 'Remove the spelk [*sic*] from your eye,' he will reply, 'Remove the beam from yours.'" See T. W. Manson, *The Sayings of Jesus* (London: SCM, 1949), 58.
166. U. Wilckens, "ὑποκρίνομαι, κ.τ.λ.," *TDNT,* 8:559–71.
167. A. N. Sherwin-White, *Roman Society and Roman Law in the New Testament* (Oxford: Clarendon, 1963), 123–24.
168. Cf. Luke 9:22; 20:1; 22:52; Acts 4:5, 8, 23.
169. W. Schrage, "συναγωγή," *TDNT,* 7:813.
170. W. Dittenberger, *Orientis graeci inscriptiones selectae* (Leipzig: Hirzel, 1903–5), §96; cited by Fitzmyer, *Luke* 1:652; Creed, *St. Luke,* 101.
171. For these terms and a description of Roman patronage see Bruce J. Malina and Richard L. Rohrbaugh, *SSCSG,* 326–29.
172. *m. ʾOhal.* 18:7.
173. *b. Ber.* 34b.
174. Philostratos, *Life of Apollonius of Tyana* 4.45; for other parallels see *Hellenistic Commentary to the New Testament,* 203–5; Marshall, *Gospel of Luke,* 283. A somewhat similar account of resuscitation at a funeral can be found in Apuleius of Madaura, *Florida* 9:2–6.
175. Burial customs are referred to in various rabbinic tracts, especially in the tractate *Ṣemaḥot.* See D. Zlotnick, *The Tractate "Mourning" (Ṣemaḥot): Regulations Relating to Death, Burial, and Mourning* (YJS 17. New Haven: Yale Univ. Press, 1966). Cf. *m. Ber.* 3.1–2; *m. Šabb.* 23.4–5; *m. Sanh.* 6:5; *t. Neg.* 6:2.
176. Ex. 22:22; Deut. 10:18; 27:19.
177. Jer. 6:26; Amos 8:10; Zech. 12:10.
178. Cf. Str-B 1:1047–48; *m. Ber.* 3:1–2; *b. Ketub.* 17a.

179. 4QPBless (4Q252) 1–5; cf. 1QS 9:11.
180. Isa. 26:19; 29:18–19; 35:5–6; 61:1–2.
181. See Matt. 3:3; 11:10, 14; 17:10–13; Mark 1:2–4; Luke 1:17, 76; 3:4–6.
182. Job 14:1; 15:14; 25:4.
183. *HCNT,* 207; Herodotus, *Histories* 1.141; cf. Aesop, *Fables,* 27b.
184. See Prov. 1:20–33; 8:1–9:6; Sir. 1; 24; *1 En.* 42; Wisd. Sol., *passim;* Marshall, *Gospel of Luke,* 303; G. Fohrer and U. Wilckens, "σοφία," *TDNT,* 7:465–526.
185. See Malina and Rohrbaugh, *SSCSG,* 331.
186. J. Jeremias, *The Eucharistic Words of Jesus* (trans. Norman Perrin; London: SCM, 1966), 20–21; Fitzmyer, *Luke,* 1:688.
187. BAGD, 34.
188. BAGD, 534; Bock, *Luke,* 1:696.
189. Jeremias, *Parables,* 126. Jeremias cites *t. Soṭah* 5.9; *y. Giṭ.* 9.50d.
190. See Marshall, *Gospel of Luke,* 309.
191. Malina and Rohrbaugh, *SSCSG,* 332–33.
192. Josephus, *J.W.* 2.17.6 §§426–27 (LCL, 491).
193. Marshall, *Gospel of Luke,* 311.
194. See L. Goppelt, "ὕδωρ," *TDNT,* 8:324 n.63; Str-B 4.615.
195. See 2 Sam. 15:5; Job 31:27; Luke 22:47; Rom. 16:16; 1 Peter 5:14; Cant 8:1.
196. Mark 15:40, 47; Luke 24:10; John 19:25; 20:1, 18.
197. BAGD, 303.
198. See especially Jeremias, *Parables,* 11–12, 149–51; Fitzmyer, *Luke,* 1:703.
199. Cf. *m. Šabb.* 7.2, where sowing is listed before plowing in a list of agricultural work that appears to be in chronological order; *Jub.* 11:11.
200. Nolland, *Luke,* 1:371, citing G. Dalman for typical crop yields.
201. Dan. 2:18, 19, 27–30, 47.
202. Cf. 1QpHab 7:4–5, 8; 1QS 3:23; 1 QM 3:9; 1QH 4:23–24.
203. 1QpHab 7:4–5.
204. Luke 8:10; cf. John 12:40; Acts 28:26–27; Rom. 11:8.
205. 2 Esd. 8:41; cf. 9:31.
206. Cf. *Jub.* 11:11 (see comments on 11:5); *1 En.* 90:2–4, 8–13; *Apoc. Ab.* 13:3–7.
207. *Apoc. Ab.* 13:3–7.
208. Marshall, *Gospel of Luke,* 327; citing W. Grundmann, "ἀγαθός," *TDNT,* 1:11–12; 3:538–44. See Tobit 5:14; 2 Macc. 15:12 for its use in Hellenistic Judaism.
209. J. Rousseau and R. Arav, *Jesus and His World* (Minneapolis: Fortress, 1995), 246; Fitzmyer, *Luke,* 1:729.
210. See 2 Sam. 22:16; Ps. 18:15; 104:7; 106:9; Isa. 50:2; Nah. 1:4.
211. Nolland, *Luke,* 1:398. Nolland notes that such attribution was given to, among others, Caesar, Caligula, Xerxes, Apollonius of Tyana, and Empedocles. The closest parallel is that of Apollonius, where people press to travel in the same boat because he is reportedly more powerful than storm, fire, or other dangers (Philostratus, *Life of Apollonius* 4:13).
212. Cf. *y. Ber.* 9.1; cf. the account of R. Gamaliel in *b. B. Meṣiʿa* 59b. These and other parallels are conveniently surveyed in *HCNT,* 66–68.
213. Ps. 65:7; 89:9; 104:6–7; 107:23–32.
214. Philostratus, *Life of Apollonius* 4:20 (LCL); cf. *HCNT,* 71–72.
215. Fitzmyer, *Luke,* 1:736, wryly notes that if this were the location, it would have been the most energetic herd of pigs in history.
216. *Jub.* 22:16–17.
217. *y. Ter. 1.1* [40b]; cited in *HCNT,* 72. Cf. Str-B 1:491.
218. Nolland, *Luke,* 1:409.
219. 2 Peter 2:4; Rev. 9:1–2, 11; 11:7; 17:8; 20:1, 3.
220. Lev. 11:7; Deut. 14:8.
221. See *HCNT,* 72–73, where examples are provided of the banishment of disease (epilepsy?) into wild goats and of a demon into the head of a bull.
222. See Schrage, "συναγωγή," *TDNT,* 7:847; see 8:49; 13:14; Acts 13:15; 18:8, 17.
223. See Gen. 22:16; 1 Kings 17:17–24; Jer. 6:26; Amos 8:10; Zech. 12:10.
224. Lev. 15:19–31; Ezek. 36:17.
225. Num. 15:38–39; Deut. 22:12.
226. See John 11:11; Acts 7:60; 13:36; 1 Cor. 11:30; 15:6, 18, 20, 51; 1 Thess. 4:14–15; 5:10.
227. Cf. Luke 23:46; Acts 7:59.
228. Cf. *1 En.* 22; 39:4–8.
229. Luke 24:46–48; Acts 1:1–2, 8; 2:33.
230. Manson, *Sayings,* 181, 182; *m. Ber.* 9.5.
231. See Nolland, *Luke,* 1:427.
232. Cf. Str-B 1:571.
233. Luke 12:35–40; 13:24–30; 14:15–24; cf. 22:30; see comments on 13:29; 14:15.
234. Keener, *BBC,* 213.
235. BAGD, 436.
236. *m. Ber.* 6:1.
237. Job 22:26–27 LXX; Ps. 121:1; 123:1.
238. Priests: Lev. 4:3, 5, 16; 8:12. Prophets: 1 Kings 19:16; CD 2:12; 6:1; 1QM 11:7. Kings: 1 Sam. 10:1; 16:13; 1 Kings 19:16.
239. See Sydney H. T. Page, "The Suffering Servant Between the Testaments," *NTS* 31 (1985): 481–97.
240. See Luke 20:1; 22:52; Acts 23:14; 25:15. See Nolland, *Luke* 2:466; G. Schenk, "ἀρχιερεύς," *TDNT,* 3:268–72; J. Jeremias, *Jerusalem,* 160–81; Schürer 2:213, 233–36.
241. See Jeremias, *Jerusalem,* 222–32.

242. On crucifixion see especially M. Hengel, *Crucifixion in the Ancient World and the Folly of the Message of the Cross* (tr. J. Bowden; Philadelphia: Fortress, 1977); Fitzmyer, *Luke*, 1:787.
243. *1 En.* 37–71.
244. There is a growing consensus that the *Similitudes* of Enoch (*1 En.* 37–71) are Jewish Palestinian and that they are pre-A.D. 70. See J. H. Charlesworth, *The Old Testament Pseudepigrapha and the New Testament* (SNTSMS 54; Cambridge: Cambridge Univ. Press, 1985), 89.
245. See the descriptions of angels and heavenly beings at Dan. 10:5–6; Matt. 28:3; Mark 16:5; Luke 24:4; John 20:12; Acts 1:10; Rev. 4:4; 19:14; *1 En.* 71:1, and of glorified saints at Dan. 12:3; Rev. 3:4–5, 18; 6:11; 7:9, 13; *1 En.* 62:15–16; 38:4; 104:2; *4 Ezra* 7:97.
246. See Wisd. Sol. 3:2; 7:6; Josephus, *Ant.* 4.189; cf. 2 Peter 1:15; BAGD, 276.
247. See Ex. 19:1; Num. 33:38; 1 Kings 6:1; 10:29 (cf. Judg. 5:4; Ps. 104:38; 113:1).
248. Isa. 11:11–16; 40–55; Jer. 23:7–8.
249. See Lev. 23:42; Neh. 8:14–17.
250. See Ex. 16:10; 19:9; 33:9; 40:34–35; Lev. 16:2; Num. 11:25; 1 Kings 8:10–11; 2 Chron. 5:13–14; Ps. 18:11–12; 97:2; Isa. 4:5; Ezek. 1:4, 28; 10:3–4; Zech. 2:17 (LXX); 2 Macc. 2:8. See Oepke, "νεφέλη," *TDNT*, 4:905.
251. Ex. 19:16; 20:18; 34:30; Deut. 5:5, 23–27.
252. See Wanke, "φοβέω," *TDNT*, 9:200–203; Balz, "φοβέω," *TDNT*, 9:209–12; see Luke 1:12; 2:9; 5:26; 7:16; 8:25, 35–37; Acts 5:5, 11.
253. See 2 Sam. 7:14; comments on Luke 3:22.
254. Many Old Testament persons are described as being "chosen" by God, including Abraham (Neh. 9:7; cf. *4 Ezra* 3:13; *Apoc. Ab.* 14), Moses (Ps. 105:26; Sir. 45:4), Levi and Aaron (Num. 17:5; Ps. 105:26; Sir. 45:16), Saul (1 Sam. 10:24; 12:13), David (Ps. 89:20; cf. Sir. 45:4), Solomon (1 Chron. 28:5, 6), Zerubbabel (Hag. 2:23), and others. The Teacher of Righteousness, the leader of the Dead Sea sect, is called "his elect" in 1QpHab 9:12. Throughout the intertestamental book of *1 En.*, the Messiah is called the "Elect One."
255. Gen. 22:16; 1 Kings 17:17–24; Jer. 6:26; Amos 8:10; Zech. 12:10; see comments on Luke 7:12; 8:42.
256. For the status of children in the ancient world see A. Oepke, "παῖς," *TDNT*, 5:639–52.
257. Cicero, *Pro Ligario* 33.
258. Cited by Danker, *Jesus and the New Age*, 206. For other references see Fitzmyer, *Luke*, 1:821.
259. See Nolland, *Luke* 2:534–35 for references.
260. Plutarch, *Lives* 828c; cited by Danker, *Jesus and the New Age*, 210.
261. Ex. 20:12; Deut. 5:16.
262. Cited by Nolland, *Luke*, 2:542. See also M. Hengel, *The Charismatic Leader and His Followers* (trans. J. C. G. Greig; New York: Crossroad, 1981), 8–10; Str-B 1:487–89; 4:1, 578–92; *b. Ber. 31a*.
263. Cf. Gen. 50:5; Tobit 4:3; 6:15.
264. This latter is suggested by Keener, *BBC*, 215.
265. See Marshall, *Gospel of Luke*, 412, for this and other parallels.
266. Jer. 5:6; Ezek. 22:27; Zeph. 3:3; cf. the Babylonians in Hab. 1:8.
267. Tanchuma, *Toledoth*, 32b; cited by J. Jeremias, "ἀρνός," *TDNT*, 1:340.
268. Cf. 1 Cor. 9:14; *Did.* 13:1–2.
269. Isa. 29:18–19; 35:5; see comments on Luke 7:22; 4:43.
270. See Deut. 29:23; 32:32; Isa. 1:9–10; 3:9; 13:19; Jer. 23:14; 49:18; 50:40; Lam. 4:6; Ezek. 16:46–56; Amos 4:11; Zeph. 2:9.
271. See also Str-B 1:574; 4:2; 4:1188; *m. Sanh.* 10:3.
272. Turner, *Hist. Geog.* 96.
273. Nolland, *Luke* 2:555–56.
274. E.g., Gen. 37:34; 2 Sam. 3:31; 1 Kings 21:27; Est. 4:1, 3; Isa. 58:5; Dan. 9:3.
275. See *Life of Adam and Eve* 12–16; Wisd. Sol. 2:24.
276. See Num. 21:6–9; Deut. 8:15; 1 Kings 12:14; Isa. 11:8; Ezek. 2:6; Sir. 21:2; 39:30.
277. Gen. 3:15; Rom. 16:20; Rev. 12:9; 20:2.
278. Old Testament: Ex. 32:32–33; Ps. 69:28; Isa. 4:3; Dan. 12:1; Mal. 3:16–17; Jewish Literature: *Jub.* 19:19; 30:19–23; *1 En.* 47:3; 104:1, 7; 108:3, 7; 1 QM 12:2; New Testament: Phil. 4:3; Heb. 12:23; Rev. 3:5; 13:8; 17:8; 20:12, 15; 21:27.
279. See Tobit 7:17; Judith 9:12; 1QapGen. 22:16, 21; cf. Gen. 14:19, 22.
280. 1 Cor. 1:18–31; cf. 2:6–13; 3:18–20.
281. Bar. 3:32, 36; cf. Wisd. Sol. 8:4.
282. *Pss. Sol.* 17:21, 44; 18:6.
283. Marshall, *Gospel of Luke*, 442, citing *b. Ber.* 28b; Str-B 1:808.
284. See 2 Macc. 7:9; *4 Macc.* 15:31; 17:18; *1 En.* 37:4; 40:9; 58:3; *Pss. Sol.* 3:12; 13:11; 14:10; 1QS 4:7; 4Q181 1:4; cf. R. Bultmann, "ζάω," *TDNT*, 2:855–61.
285. The command to love one's neighbor appears in *Jub.* 7:20; 36:7–8; CD 6:20–21; Sir. 7:21; 34:15; *T. Benj.* 3:3–4; *T. Dan* 5:3. The two are linked in *T. Iss.* 5:2; 7:6; *T. Dan* 5:3; cf. Philo, *Spec. Laws* 2.63.
286. 2 Sam. 12:7; cf. 2 Esd. 4:20; 1 Kings 20:40–42.
287. 1QS 1:9–10.

288. Sir. 12:1–7.
289. Josephus, *J.W.* 4.8.3 §474.
290. Luke 10:32; John 1:19; Acts 4:36.
291. See John 11:1–44; 12:1–11.
292. *m.* ʾ*Abot* 1:4.
293. Jeremias, *Jerusalem*, 363. For the role of women in Jewish society see Jeremias, *Jerusalem*, ch. 18; Malina and Rohrbaugh, *SSCSG*, 348–49.
294. *m. Soṭah* 3:4.
295. Malina and Rohrbaugh, *SSCSG*, 348.
296. See especially Kenneth E. Bailey, *Poet and Peasant* and *Through Peasant Eyes: A Literary-Cultural Approach to the Parables of Luke* (combined ed.; Grand Rapids: Eerdmans, 1983), 119–41.
297. Cf. Rom. 8:15–16; Gal. 4:6.
298. See J. Jeremias, *The Prayers of Jesus* (Philadelphia: Fortress, 1978); idem, *New Testament Theology* (London: SCM, 1971), 63–68.
299. Cited in Jeremias, *New Testament Theology*, 198.
300. Ex. 16:4; 20:20; Deut. 8:2, 16; Judg. 2:22.
301. Cf. *b. Ber.* 60b; cited by Bock, *Luke*, 2:1056.
302. Bailey, *Poet and Peasant*, 121.
303. Ibid., 122; Jeremias, *Parables*, 157, claims bread was baked daily.
304. Jeremias, *Parables*, 158, citing A. Fridrichsen.
305. Bailey, *Poet and Peasant*, 130–33.
306. Nolland, *Luke*, 2:631.
307. 2 Kings 20:8–11; Isa. 38:7–8.
308. E.g., Isa. 13:10; 34:4; Joel 2:30–31.
309. See Ps. 23; Isa. 53:6; Jer. 13:17; Ezek. 34; Zech. 10:3; 13:7; cf. comments on 10:3; 12:32; 15:4.
310. Tobit 12:15.
311. *Satyricon* 4:1; cited by Danker, *Jesus and the New Age*, 234; cf. Ovid, *Metamorphoses* 4.320–24.
312. *m.* ʾ*Abot* 2:8.
313. Jonah 1:2; cf. Nah. 1:11; 2:12–13; 3:1, 19.
314. Nolland, *Luke*, 2:657.
315. See D. C. Allison Jr., "The Eye Is the Lamp of the Body (Matthew 6.22–23 = Luke 11.34–36)," *NTS* 33 (1987): 61–83.
316. For the literature see H. Conzelmann, "σκότος, κ.τ.λ.," *TDNT*, 7:423–45; cf. 9:310–58.
317. See 7:36; 11:37; 14:1, 10; 22:14.
318. Marshall, *Gospel of Luke*, 493–94.
319. *m. Yad.* 1:1–5.
320. See *m. Kelim* 25; Str-B 1:934–35.
321. Tobit 12:8–9; cf. 4:8–11; 14:10–11; Sir. 3:30; 7:10; 29:12.
322. Lev. 27:30–33; Num. 18:21–32; Deut. 14:22–29; 2 Chron. 31:5–12; see the tractates *m. Maʿaś.* ("Tithes"); *m. Maʿaś. Š.* ("Second Tithe"), and *m. Demai* ("Produce not certainly tithed").
323. E.g., Isa. 1:17, 21; 5:7; Mic. 6:8.
324. Cf. *y. Ber.* 4b [2.1]; Str.-B 1:382; H. Windisch, "ἀσπάζομαι," *TDNT*, 1:498.
325. 1 Kings 19:10, 14; Neh. 9:26; Jer. 2:30; 26:20–24; cf. Matt. 5:12; 23:34–36; Luke 4:24; 6:23, 26; 13:34; Acts 7:52.
326. See Prov. 1:20–33; 8:1–9:6; Sir. 1; 24; *1 En.* 42; Wisd. Sol., *passim*; Bar. 3–4.
327. Ex. 20:5; Isa. 65:7; Jer. 32:18.
328. See Gen. 9:5–6; 2 Sam. 4:11.
329. Deut. 32:43; 2 Kings 9:7; Ps. 79:10; cf. *1 En.* 47; Rev. 6:10.
330. Cf. Str-B 1:940–943; Keener, *BBC*, 222.
331. Fitzmyer, *Luke*, 2:951.
332. Cf. Str-B 1:128–29; H. Windisch, "ζύμη," *TDNT*, 2:905–6.
333. Job 10:4–7; 11:11; Ps. 11:4; 33:15; 139:2.
334. *4 Macc.* 13:14–17, NRSV.
335. 2 Kings 16:3; 21:6; 23:10; Jer. 7:32; 19:4–6; 32:34–35.
336. Judith 16:17; *4 Ezra* 7:36; *1 En.* 10:13; 18:11–16; 27:1–3; *Jub.* 9:15; Mark 9:45–48; Rev. 20:10–15.
337. Manson, *Sayings*, 108.
338. 1 Sam. 14:45; 2 Sam. 14:11; 1 Kings 1:52; Dan. 3:27; cf. Luke 21:18; Acts 27:34.
339. Cf. Str-B 3:545–49; *m. B. Bat.* 8–9.
340. See Ex. 20:17; Deut. 5:21; Job 31:24–25; Ps. 49; Eccl. 2:1–11.
341. *T. Jud.* 18–19; Sir. 11:18–19; *1 En.* 97:8–10.
342. Mark 7:22; Col. 3:5; 1 Tim. 6:10; 2 Peter 2:3.
343. Old Testament and Jewish: Eccl. 2:24; 3:13; 5:18; 8:15; Isa. 22:13; Tobit 7:10; Sir. 11:19; cf. 1 Cor. 15:32 (citing Isa. 22:13). Greek parallels include Euripides, *Alcestis* 788–89; Menander, *Fragment* 301 (Fitzmyer, *Luke*, 2:973).
344. Ps. 39:6; 49:10; Eccl. 2:18.
345. See references in Fitzmyer, *Luke*, 2:978.
346. See ibid., 2:979.
347. Manson, *Sayings*, 112.
348. See Job 8:12; Ps. 37:2; 90:5–6; 102:11; 103:15–16; Isa. 37:27; 40:6–8.
349. See Jer. 13:17; Ezek. 34; Zech. 10:3; 13:7.
350. Sir. 29:8–17; Tobit 4:7–11; *Pss. Sol.* 9:5.
351. See 1 Kings 18:46; 2 Kings 4:29; 9:1; Job 38:3; Jer. 1:17; 1 Peter 1:13.
352. Fitzmyer, *Luke*, 2:988.
353. BAGD, 199.
354. Prov. 23:2; Zech. 7:6; Rom. 14:17; Ex. 32:6; Isa. 22:2; 1 Cor. 10:7; Prov. 20:1; Isa. 28:7; 56:12; Luke 21:34; Rom. 13:13; 1 Cor. 11:21; Gal. 5:21; 1 Peter 4:3.
355. Sir. 23:6; 31:29–30; 37:30–31; Tobit 4:15; *4 Macc.* 1:3.
356. Ibid., 200.
357. Homer, *Odyssey* 18.339; Herodotus 2.139; Judith 5:22; Sus. 55; 2 Macc. 1:13; Heb. 11:37.

358. See Gen. 19:24; Isa. 29:6; Ezek. 38:22; Amos 7:4; Zeph. 1:18; 3:8; Mal. 4:1; *4 Ezra* 13:10–11, 27; *1 En.* 67:13; 90:24–27; 102:1; *Pss. Sol.* 15:4–5; *Jub.* 9:15; 36:10; 1QS 2:8; 4:13; *T. Isaac* 5:21–25; *T. Ab.* 12–13.
359. Isa. 4:4; Mal. 3:2; 1 Cor. 3:10–15.
360. Ps. 18:4; 42:7; 69:1–2; Isa. 8:7–8; 30:27–28; Jonah 2:5; see also Mark 10:38.
361. *m. Soṭah* 9:15.
362. *Jub.* 23:16, 19; *4 Ezra* 6:24.
363. Job 15:2; 37:17; Jer. 4:11; Ezek. 17:10; Sir. 43:16.
364. Josephus, *Ant.* 18.3.1 §§55–59.
365. Ibid., 18.3.2 §§60–62; *J.W.* 2.9.4 §§175–77. For other incidents see Marshall, *Gospel of Luke*, 553; Fitzmyer, *Luke* 2:1006–7.
366. See also Job 8:4, 20; 22:5; Ps. 34:21; 75:10; Prov. 3:33; 10:3, 6–7, 16, 24–25; John 9:2–3.
367. Josephus, *J.W.* 5.4.2 §145; John 9:7, 11.
368. Marshall, *Gospel of Luke*, 554.
369. Jer. 8:13; 24:1–10; Hos. 9:10; Mic. 7:1; Isa. 5:1–7.
370. See Matt. 21:19–21; Mark 11:12–14, 20–21.
371. 1 Kings 4:25; 2 Kings 18:31; Isa. 36:16; Joel 2:22; Isa. 5:5; 9:10; Jer. 5:17; Hos. 2:12; Joel 1:7.
372. See also Isa. 10:34; 11:1; Jer. 46:22; Dan. 4:23; Matt. 3:10; 7:19; Luke 3:9.
373. Syriac *Ahikar* 8:35; cited in *HCNT*, 218. Cf. other parallels in Str-B 4:1, 474; Armenian Philo, *De Jona* §52.
374. Luke 4:31–41; 6:6–11; cf. 14:1–6.
375. Jeremias, *Jerusalem*, 373; Bock, *Luke*, 2:1215; *m. Ber.* 3:3; Acts 16:13; 17:4.
376. Marshall, *Gospel of Luke*, 557; Bock, *Luke*, 2:1215; Fitzmyer, *Luke*, 2:1012.
377. Luke 4:40, 41; 7:21; 13:32.
378. See Luke 8:41, 49; Acts 13:15; 18:8, 17.
379. *m. Yoma* 8:6; *m. Šabb.* 18:3; 19:2.
380. *m. Šabb.* 5:1–4.
381. Ibid., 15:1–2; 7:2.
382. CD 11:5–6 forbids taking an animal beyond 1000 cubits (1500 feet) for pasturing. The Qumran sectarians appeared to be stricter than the Pharisees, forbidding help for an animal giving birth or pulling it out of a well on the Sabbath (CD 11:13–14).
383. *m. ʿErub.* 2:1–4.
384. Keener, *BBC*, 227.
385. *m. Nid.* 5:2.
386. Marshall, *Gospel of Luke*, 561; cf. Str-B 1:669; O. Michel, "κόκκος, κόκκινος," *TDNT*, 3:810 n.1.
387. Bock, *Luke*, 2:1227.
388. *Hist. Plant.* 7.1, 2–3; noted by Fitzmyer, *Luke*, 2:1016–17.
389. Ps. 104:12; Ezek. 17:22–24; Dan. 4:10–15.
390. BAGD, 745 ("a peck and a half"); Bock, *Luke*, 2:1228.
391. Cf. 2 Esd. (*4 Ezra*) 7:47; 9:15; *2 Bar.* 44:15; 48:45–50; Str-B 1:883.
392. Danby, *The Mishnah*, 397 n.4.
393. Isa. 22:22; Rev. 3:7–8, 20; cf. Matt. 7:7; 25:10; Luke 11:9.
394. Nolland, *Luke*, 2:734; Str-B 1:469; 4:293.
395. Cf. John 7:27–28; 9:29–30.
396. Matt. 8:12; 13:42, 50; 22:13; 24:51; 25:30.
397. See also Job 16:9; Ps. 112:10; Lam. 2:16; cf. Sir. 51:3; Acts 7:54.
398. Ex. 2:24; cf. Gen. 50:24; Ex. 3:6, 15.
399. See Tobit 4:12; Judith 8:26; Sir. 51:12; Bar. 2:34; 2 Macc. 1:2; *4 Macc.* 13:17.
400. See also Isa. 6:7; Mic. 4:1–2; Mal. 1:11; cf. Isa. 51:4; 52:10; 59:19; Zech. 2:13. For the eschatological regathering of Israelites see Ps. 107:3; Isa. 43:5–6; 49:12; 66:19–20.
401. Cf. *2 En.* 42:5; *m. ʾAbot* 3:17; also the "wedding supper of the Lamb," Rev. 19:9.
402. See also Isa. 55:1–2; 65:13–14; *1 En.* 62:14; *2 Bar.* 29:1–8.
403. 1QSa (1Q28a) 2:1ff.
404. Cf. Luke 4:24; 7:16; 11:47–51; 24:19.
405. For Greek literature Fitzmyer (*Luke*, 2:1031) cites Pindar, *Pyth. Od.* 2.77.78; Plato, *Resp.* 2.8 §365c; Plutarch, *Life of Solon* 30.2; Epictetus, *Diatr.* 1.3.7–8. For the rabbinic writings see Str-B 2.200–1.
406. Ezek. 13:4; cf. Lam. 5:18; *1 En.* 89:42–50.
407. Keener, *BBC*, 228.
408. Ibid., 228.
409. See also Ruth 2:12; Ps. 17:8; 36:7; 57:1; 61:4; 63:7; 91:4.
410. The close parallel in 2 Esd. 1:33 is probably dependent on the Gospel text (see previous note); Jer. 26:9; 12:7; 22:5; cf. Isa. 24:10.
411. Cf. Str-B 1:849–50, 876.
412. *American Heritage Electronic Dictionary* (New York: Houghton and Mifflin, 1992).
413. Cf. Str-B 1:629. See Marshall, *Gospel of Luke*, 580.
414. *Lev. Rab.* 11.5 on 1:1 (commenting on Prov. 25:7); cited by Manson, *Sayings*, 278; Str-B 1:916.
415. Theophrastus, *Characteres* 21.2; noted by Manson, *Sayings*, 278.
416. See B. J. Malina and J. H. Neyrey, "Honor and Shame in Luke-Acts: Pivotal Values of the Mediterranean World," pp. 25–65 in *The Social World of Luke-Acts: Models for Interpretations* (ed. J. H. Neyrey; Peabody, Mass.: Hendrickson, 1991); Malina and Rohrbaugh, *SSCSG*, 76–77, 213–14, 309–11.
417. Malina and Rohrbaugh, *SSCSG*, 365.
418. E.g., 2 Macc. 7:9, 14; *1 En.* 103:4.
419. Josephus, *Ant.* 18.1.3 §14.
420. cf. Luke 1:52–53; 6:21, 25; 10:15; 18:14.

421. Cf. *y. Sanh.* 6:23c, 30–43. The text is reproduced in *HCNT,* 228–9 §338.
422. Cited by G. B. Gray, *The Book of Isaiah* (ICC; New York: Scribner's Sons, 1912), 1:429–30.
423. *Pss. Sol.* 17:22–25; cf. 17:30–31; *1 En.* 62:9–13.
424. The Hellenistic Jewish philosopher Philo notes that "givers of a banquet. . .do not send out the summonses to supper till they have put everything in readiness for the feast" (*Creation* 25 §78). For additional Greek and Jewish references see Marshall, *Gospel of Luke,* 587–88; Nolland *Luke,* 2:755.
425. Bailey, *Through Peasant Eyes,* 94–95.
426. Ibid., 95–96.
427. Marshall, *Gospel of Luke,* 589.
428. Bailey, *Through Peasant Eyes,* 97–98.
429. Ibid., 98–99.
430. Ibid., 99.
431. Isa. 29:18–19; 35:5–6; 61:1–2.
432. 1QSa (1Q28a) 2:2–7.
433. Gen. 29:31, 33; Deut. 21:15; Rom. 9:13.
434. See Josephus, *J.W.* 5.4.3 §§156–71 for towers in Jerusalem. For a vineyard watchtower see Isaiah 5:2; Mark 12:1.
435. Epictetus, *Dissertationes* 3.15.8; cited by Fitzmyer, *Luke,* 2:1065.
436. Philo, *Abraham* 21 §105.
437. Nolland, *Luke,* 2:765.
438. Cf. *m. Bek.* 8b; cited by Marshall, *Gospel of Luke,* 596, and Fitzmyer, *Luke,* 2:1069.
439. Marshall, *Gospel of Luke,* 596. A less likely solution noted by Marshall involves the use of salt in ovens, where it gradually loses its catalytic power.
440. Ibid., 597.
441. *Mekilta de Rabbi Ishmael,* tractate *Amalek* 3.55–57 on Ex. 18:1; cited by Bock, *Luke,* 2:1299.
442. Jeremias, *Parables,* 133.
443. Bailey, *Poet and Peasant,* 149–50 n.34.
444. Jeremias, *Jerusalem,* 100; idem, *Parables,* 134–35; Bailey, *Poet and Peasant,* 157, points out the headdress would be a Bedouin custom, while the necklace would be characteristic of a village woman.
445. Keener, *BBC,* 232.
446. Bailey, *Poet and Peasant,* 161–65.
447. *m. B. Bat.* 8:7.
448. Bailey, *Poet and Peasant,* 162–66; Manson, *Sayings,* 286–87.
449. BAGD, 782; Marshall, *Gospel of Luke,* 607.
450. Bock, *Luke,* 2:1310.
451. Marshall, *Gospel of Luke,* 608.
452. Bailey, *Poet and Peasant,* 167–68.
453. Cf. *b. B. Qam.* 82b. Cf. Str-B 1:492–93.
454. Bailey, however, claims that this is not Syrian carob (*ceratonia siliqua*), which is sweet, but a bitter variety of wild carob (*Poet and Peasant,* 171–73).
455. Rabbi Acha (c. A.D. 320) in *Lev. Rab.* 35.6 on 26.3; cited by Marshall, *Gospel of Luke,* 609.
456. *Lam. Rab.* 1.34 on 1:7; Str-B 2:215–16.
457. See references in Bailey, *Poet and Peasant,* 181–82.
458. Ibid., 185.
459. Ibid., 186–87.
460. Ibid., 168, 195–96.
461. J. D. M. Derrett, *Law in the New Testament* (London: Darman, Longman and Todd, 1970), 48–77; Ex. 22:25; Lev. 25:35–37; Deut. 15:7–8; 23:20–21.
462. Fitzmyer, *Luke,* 2:1098.
463. Cf. Sir. 38:24–34; Aristophanes, *The Birds* 1430–33.
464. Sir. 40:28.
465. Jeremias, *Parables,* 181; Marshall, *Gospel of Luke,* 618–19.
466. See Bailey, *Poet and Peasant,* 86–110.
467. See 1QM 1:3, 11, 13; 1QS 1:9; 3:13, 24–26; cf. *1 En.* 108:11. For additional references see Fitzmyer, *Luke,* 2:1108.
468. See Marshall, *Gospel of Luke,* 621 for details.
469. Cited in James B. Pritchard, ed., *Ancient Near Eastern Texts Relating to the Old Testament* (3rd ed., Princeton, N.J.: Princeton University Press, 1969), 413; cf. *HCNT,* 226–7 §335.
470. *Ex. Rab.* on Ex. 3:1; cited by Manson, *Sayings,* 293–94. For other parallels see Bock, *Luke,* 2:1335 n.27.
471. See Marshall, *Gospel of Luke,* 624 for other examples.
472. Josephus, *Ant.* 13.10.6 §298. The *Pss. Sol.* (a Pharisaic document from the first century B.C.) repeatedly condemns the unrighteous aristocracy of Jerusalem.
473. Cf. Str-B 1:937; Jeremias, *Jerusalem,* 114; Marshall, *Gospel of Luke,* 625.
474. See also Isa. 51:6; 65:17; 66:22; 2 Peter 3:7, 10; Rev. 21:1.
475. See also Isa. 40:8; 55:10–11; Bar. 4:1; 2 Esd. (*4 Ezra*) 9:36–37.
476. BAGD, 428.
477. Cf. Matt. 5:32; 19:9; Mark 10:11–12.
478. *Demotic Narrative about Setme Chamois,* in *HCNT,* 227–28 §338.
479. Marshall, *Gospel of Luke,* 635.
480. Cf. *b. Beṣah* 32b; cited by Manson, *Sayings,* 299.
481. See also Ps. 22:16, 20; 59:6, 14; Jer. 15:3.
482. See Sir. 21:9–10; *1 En.* 10:13; 2 Esd. (*4 Ezra*) 8:59; Matt. 25:41; Rev. 20:10, 14–15.
483. See Luke 16:31; 24:27, 44; Acts 26:22; 28:23.
484. 1QS 1:3.
485. See also Isa. 10:1–3; Jer. 5:26–28; Ezek. 18:12–18; Amos 5:11–12; Mal. 3:5; Deut. 15:7; 24:14, 19–21; Isa. 58:10; Isa. 3:14–15; 5:7–8.

486. See Sir. 28:2; 1QS 5:24–6:1; CD 9:3–4; *T. Gad* 6:1–7; Str-B 1:795–99. The *Testament of Gad* text is closest, but it may have undergone Christian redaction.
487. *m. Nid.* 5:2.
488. Bock, *Luke*, 2:1391.
489. *m. ᵓAbot* 2:8.
490. *m. ᵓAbot* 1:3.
491. *Pss. Sol.* 17:21–46; 18:5–9.
492. See 2 Esd. (*4 Ezra*) 5:4–10; *1 En.* 91, 93; *2 Bar.* 25–27, 53. These passages have their background in the apocalyptic passages of the Old Testament (see Isa. 24–27; Ezek.; Dan. 7–12; Joel 2; etc.).
493. Cf. *m. Ber.* 1:5; 2 Esd. (*4 Ezra*) 13:52; Str-B 2:237; 4:826–27.
494. See Josephus, *Ant.* 17.10.5 §§271–72 (Judas the Galilean); *Ant.* 17.10.6 §§273–77 (Simon); *Ant.* 17.10.7 §§278–81 (Anthronges); *Ant.* 20.5.1 §§97–99 (Theudas); *Ant.* 20.8.6 §§169–72; *J.W.* 2.13.5 §§261–63 (the Egyptian); *Ant.* 18.4.1 §§85–87 (a Samaritan).
495. Josephus, *J.W.* 2.13.4–6 §§258–65; cf. 6.5.4 §§312–13.
496. See also Ezek. 30:3; Joel 1:15; 2:1, 11, 31; Amos 5:18; Obad. 15; Zeph. 1:14; Mal. 4:5.
497. See Wisd. Sol. 10:4–6; 14:6; *3 Macc.* 2:4–5; *T. Naph.* 3:4–5; Philo, *Moses* 2:10–12 §§52–65; *Gen. Rab.* 27 on 6:5–6; Str-B 1:564. Cf. 2 Peter 2:5–7.
498. *m. Sanh.* 10:3.
499. See 2 Esd. (*4 Ezra*) 14:9, 52; *1 En.* 48:6; 62:7; Str-B 2:334.
500. A. Edersheim, *The Life and Times of Jesus the Messiah* (Grand Rapids: Eerdmans, 1971), 2:287.
501. See also Deut. 24:17; 27:19; Ps. 68:5; Isa. 1:23; 10:2; Jer. 22:3; Ezek. 22:7; Amos 5:10–13; Zech. 7:10; Mal. 3:5; Ex. 22:22; Deut. 10:18.
502. 2 Esd. 2:20; Sir. 35:17–21; Wis. 2:10.
503. Bailey, *Through Peasant Eyes*, 134–35, recounts a similar story witnessed by a Western traveler in Iraq.
504. See *m. Soṭah* 9:15; 2 Esd. 6:24; 9:1–12; 13:29–31; Matt. 24:10–12; 2 Thess. 2:3; 1 Tim. 4:1.
505. *m. B. Qam.* 10:1.
506. *m. Ṭehar.* 7:6.
507. Cf. *y. Ber.* 2.7d; cited by Manson, *Sayings*, 311. Cf. *b. Ber.* 28b; *b. Sukkah* 45b; Jeremias, *Parables*, 142; Bock, *Luke*, 2:1463 n.7.
508. This is attested in later Judaism (*b. Ta'an.* 12a) and is implied in the *Did.* 8:1, where Christians are instructed not to fast on these two days "with the hypocrites" (Fitzmyer, *Luke*, 2:1187).
509. Isa. 32:12; Jer. 31:19; Ezek. 21:12; Nah. 2:7; Luke 23:48.
510. Psalm 51:1, 3; cf. Ps. 6; 32; 38; 102; 130; 143.
511. For such blessings in Judaism see Marshall, *Gospel of Luke*, 682; Str-B 2:138.
512. Deut. 32:4; 2 Sam. 22:31; Job 36:4; cf. Matt. 5:48.
513. Ex. 20:12–16; Deut. 5:16–20.
514. Cf. Str-B 1:814; *b. Sanh.* 101a; Marshall, *Gospel of Luke*, 684.
515. 2 Chron. 1:11–12; Ps. 112:3; 128:2; Prov. 8:18; Isa. 61:6; Wisd. Sol. 8:18.
516. Ps. 62:10; Prov. 11:28; Jer. 9:23–24; 49:4–5; Sir. 5:1, 8; 40:13.
517. Isa. 29:18–19; 35:5–6; 61:1–2; Luke 4:18; 7:22.
518. *Pss. Sol.* 17:21.
519. Cf. Isa. 9:6–7; 11:1–5; Jer. 23:5–6; 33:15–16; Ezek. 37:24–25.
520. O. Michel, "τελώνης," *TDNT*, 8:97–99; Marshall, *Gospel of Luke*, 696.
521. *m. Ned.* 3:4.
522. Marshall, *Gospel of Luke*, 696; C.-H. Hunzinger, "συκάμινο, συκομορέα, συκοφαντέω," *TDNT*, 7:758–59.
523. Cf. Str-B. 4:546–47; *b. Ketub.* 50a; S. T. Lachs, *A Rabbinic Commentary on the New Testament: The Gospels of Matthew, Mark and Luke* (New York: Ktav, 1987), 331 n.6; Bock, *Luke*, 2:1482.
524. Lev. 5:16; Num. 5:7.
525. For references see Michel, "τελώνης," *TDNT*, 8:105 n.154; Marshall, *Gospel of Luke*, 698; Bock, *Luke*, 2:1520.
526. *m. Ketub.* 3:9.
527. See, e.g., Isa. 2:2–4; 35:1–10; 65:17–25; Jer. 30–31; Ezek. 37, 40–48; Mic. 4:1–5; *Pss. Sol.* 17–18; *1 En.* 45, 51; *2 Bar.* 71–74.
528. Josephus, *Ant.* 14.14.1–4 §§370–85 (Herod the Great); idem, *J.W.* 2 §§20–22; idem, *Ant.* 17.9.4 §§224–27 (Antipas); *Ant.* 17.11.1 §303 (Philip); *Ant.* 18.6.1–11 §§143–239 (Agrippa I).
529. Josephus, *Ant.* 17.8.1 §188; 17.9.3 §§213–18; 17.11.1–4 §§299–320; idem, *J.W.* 2.6.1–3 §§80–100; 2.1.3 §§8–13.
530. *m. ᵓAbot* 4:2.
531. See also *1 En.* 62:15; 96:1; Dan. 7:18, 22; Luke 12:32; 22:30; 1 Cor. 6:2–3.
532. Cf. *m. B. Meṣiᶜa* 3:10–11; Str-B 1:970–71; 2:252.
533. *m. B. Meṣiᶜa* 3:11.
534. There are many examples of this in the ancient world. See Josephus, *Ant.* 13.14.2 §380 (Alexander Jannaeus); idem, *Ant.* 14.9.4 §175; 14.16.4 §489 (Herod the Great).
535. John 11:1, 18; 12:1; cf. Luke 10:38.
536. See J. D. M. Derrett, "Law in the New Testament: The Palm Sunday Colt," *NovT* 13 (1971): 241–58; esp. 243–49.
537. Cf. Josephus, *Ant.* 9.6.2 §111.

538. *1 Macc.* 13:51.
539. Later rabbis interpreted the psalm messianically, but it is uncertain whether this interpretation goes back to Jesus' day. See Str-B 1:849–50, 876.
540. See also Jer. 13:17; 14:17; Lam. 1:1–4, 16; 3:48; Mic. 1:8; Isa. 22:4; Jer. 9:1–2, 10.
541. Josephus, *J.W.* 5.11.4–6 §§466–490; 5.12.1–4 §§491–526.
542. Ibid., 5–6.
543. Ibid., 6.3.3 §§193–195; 6.8.5 §§403–406.
544. Ibid., 6.9.3 §§420–21.
545. Ibid., 6.9.4 §434; 7.1.1 §§1–3; 7.8.7 §§375–77.
546. Cf. Str-B 1:850–52.
547. Ex. 30:11–16; *m. Šeqal.* 1:3; 2:1, 4; 4:7–8.
548. See Luke 20:1; 22:52; Acts 23:14; 25:15. See Nolland, Luke, 2:466; G. Schenk, "ἀρχιερεύς," *TDNT*, 3:268–72; J. Jeremias, *Jerusalem*, 160–81.
549. See also 2 Chron. 24:21; 36:16; Neh. 9:26; Jer. 2:30; 26:20–24; 37:15; 2 Chron. 24:19; 36:15–16; Jer. 7:25–26; 1 Kings 19:10, 14.
550. Ps. 2:7; 89:26–29; Isa. 7:14.
551. Cf. 4QFlor 1:11 (= 4Q174).
552. Fitzmyer, *Luke*, 2:1282.
553. Esp. Ps. 118:22–23; Isa. 8:14; 28:16; Rom. 9:32–33; Eph. 2:20; 1 Peter 2:6–8; 2:34.
554. BAGD, 215.
555. See also Ps. 78:36; Prov. 26:28; 28:23; 29:5; Ezek. 12:24.
556. See also Job 23:11; Ps. 27:11; 119:15; 1QS 3:8–11; CD 20:18–19.
557. Josephus, *J.W.* 2.8.1 §118. For tribute to Rome in general see *J.W.* 1.7.6 §154; idem, *Ant.* 14.10.6 §§202–3.
558. Rom. 13:1–7; Titus 3:1; 1 Peter 2:13–17.
559. Isa. 40:23; Dan. 2:21; 4:17.
560. Cf. Matt. 22:23–33; Mark 12:18–27.
561. Job 19:26; Ps. 16:9–11; Isa. 25:7–8; 26:19; Hos. 13:14.
562. Tobit 3:7–17; 6:10–8:18.
563. The same concept prevailed in Judaism, where saints receive glory and immortality *like* that of the angels; see Wisd. Sol. 5:5; *2 Bar.* 51:10; *1 En.* 104:5–6; 1QSb (1Q28b) 4:28.
564. *1 En.* 15:7; 6–10.
565. *Midrash Sifre* on Numbers 112; cited in *HCNT*, 127. Cf. *m. Meg.* 3:3; *Sifre* on Deut. 32:2.
566. See Mark 14:62; Acts 2:34; 7:56; Rom. 8:34; 1 Cor. 15:25; Eph. 1:20; Col. 3:1; Heb. 1:3, 13; 5:6; 7:17, 21; 8:1; 10:12–13; 1 Peter 3:22; Rev. 3:21.
567. Cf. *b. Giṭ.* 52a-b.
568. Cf. *Pss. Sol.* 4:1–13.
569. Josephus, *J.W.* 6.5.2 §282; 5.5.2 §200; idem, *Ant.* 19.6.1 §294; 1 Macc. 14:49; 2 Macc. 3:4–40.
570. Cf. *m. Šeqal.* 6:1, 5; cf. Neh. 12:44.
571. Aristotle, *Nikomachean Ethics* 4.1.19; cited by Danker, *Jesus and the New Age*, 328. Cf. Euripides, *Danaë* frg. 319. For a later Jewish parallel involving a widow see *Lev. Rab.* 3.5 on 1:7 (see comments on Mark 12:42).
572. Cf. Matthew 24:1–35; Mark 13:1–37.
573. Cf. *b. B. Bat.* 4a; *b. Sukkah* 41b.
574. Josephus, *J.W.* 5.5.6 §§ 222–24; idem, *Ant.* 15.11.3–7 §§ 391–425; cf. *m. Mid.*
575. Josephus, *J.W.* 6.5.3 §300–309.
576. Ibid., 6.5.4 §§312–13; cf. Tacitus, *Hist.* 5.13.
577. See 2 Chron. 15:6; Isa. 19:2; Jer. 4:20; Dan. 11:44; Joel 3:9–14; cf. Rev. 6:4, 8.
578. Earthquakes: 1 Sam. 14:15; Ps. 18:7–8; Isa. 5:25; 13:13; 29:6; Amos 1:1; Hag. 2:6, 21; Zech. 14:4; famines and plagues: Jer. 14:12; 21:6–7; Ezek. 14:21.
579. See Isa. 2:19, 21; 13:13; 24:18; 29:5–6; Ezek. 38:19; Joel 2:10.
580. See also 2 Esd. 13:31; *2 Bar.* 27:7; 70:2–8; Josephus, *J.W.* 6.5.3 § 299; cf. Rev. 6:12; 8:5; 11:13, 19; 16:18; 2 Esd. 9:1–5.
581. See Schürer, 2:427–33.
582. See also Num. 23:5; Deut. 18:18; Isa. 50:4; 51:16; Ezek. 29:21; Acts 6:10.
583. On excommunication in Judaism see Schürer, 2:431–33.
584. *m. Soṭah* 9:15; *4 Ezra* 6:24; *Jub.* 23:16, 19.
585. 1 Sam. 14:45; 2 Sam. 14:11; 1 Kings 1:52; Dan. 3:27.
586. Cf. 9:24; 17:33; John 12:25.
587. Eusebius, *Eccl. Hist.* 3.5.3.
588. 1 Kings 9:6–9; Jer. 6:1–30; 32:24–25; Ezek. 14:12–23; Dan. 9:26; Mic. 3:12.
589. Josephus, *J.W.* 6.3.4 §§201–13 (my translation).
590. 1 Macc. 3:45, 51; 4:60; 2 Macc. 8:2; *Pss. Sol.* 2:19–21; 8:14–22; 17:7–18, 22–24, 30.
591. See also Jer. 4:23, 28; Ezek. 32:7–8; Joel 2:10, 30–31; 2 Esd. 5:4–5; 7:39; *T. Mos.* 10:5.
592. Josephus, *J.W.* 6.5.3 §289; cf. *Sib. Or.* 3.797.
593. Josephus, *J.W.* 6.5.3 §§297–98; Tacitus, *History* 5:13; cf. 2 Macc. 5:2–3; *Sib. Or.* 3:795–807; 1QM 12:9; 19:1–2.
594. See 2 Esd. (*4 Ezra*) 6:24; 9:1–12; 13:29–31; *2 Bar.* 27:1–15; 70:2–8; *m. Soṭah* 9:15; 1QM *passim*; cf. 1 Cor. 7:26.
595. 1QM 1:11–12.
596. BAGD, 154.
597. Nissan 15–21; see Ex. 12:1–20; 23:15; 34:18; Deut. 16:1–8.
598. Josephus, *Ant.* 14.2.1 §21; 17.9.3 §213; idem, *J.W.* 2.1.3 §10.
599. Ex. 12:1–11; Num. 9:11–12; Deut. 16:1–8.
600. Deut. 16:3; *m. Pesaḥ.* 10:5.
601. Marshall, *Gospel of Luke*, 791.
602. *m. Pesaḥ.* 10:1.

603. J. Jeremias, *The Eucharistic Words of Jesus* (trans. Norman Perrin; London: SCM, 1966), 84–88; Fitzmyer, *Luke*, 2:1390. The use of the fourth cup in first-century Palestine is disputed; Ps. 115–118; see *m. Pesaḥ*. 10:2, 4, 7.
604. See 2 Macc. 4:2; *3 Macc.* 3:19; prologue to Sirach; Josephus, *J.W.* 3.9.8 §459 (Vespasian). See Fitzmyer, *Luke*, 2:1417 for inscriptions of Caesar Augustus and Nero using the title.
605. Danker, *Jesus and the New Age*, 348.
606. Cf. *1 En.* 62:14.
607. *Acts Pet.*, 37–38.
608. Fitzmyer, *Luke*, 2:1426.
609. *m. B. Qam.* 7:7.
610. Josephus, *J.W.* 2.8.4 §125.
611. See Ps. 11:6; 60:3; 75:8; Isa. 51:17, 21–23; Jer. 25:15–29; 49:12; 51:57; Lam. 4:21; Ezek. 23:31–34; Hab. 2:16; Zech. 12:2.
612. See also Prayer of Azariah 26; Tobit 5:17, 22; Bar. [Letter of Jeremiah] 6:7; 2 Esd. (*4 Ezra*) 5:15, 31; 7:1; 1 Kings 19:5–8; Ps. 91:11–12; Dan. 3:28; 10:16–19; cf. Heb. 1:14.
613. *Jos. and Asen.* 4:11; see Marshall, *Gospel of Luke*, 832, for additional sources.
614. See Bock, *Luke*, 2:1761.
615. See also 2 Sam. 15:5; Song 8:1; 1 Esd. (3 Ezra) 4:47; Rom. 16:16; 1 Cor. 16:20; 2 Cor. 13:12; 1 Peter 5:14.
616. Josephus, *J.W.* 2.13.2–3 §253–54.
617. Ps. 2:7; 89:26; Isa. 7:14.
618. Cf. *y. Sanh.* 1.1, 18a; Josephus, *Ant.* 20.9.1 §§ 200–203.
619. See Sherwin-White, *Roman Society and Roman Law*, 12–23.
620. Ibid., 24–27.
621. Josephus, *J.W.* 2.8.1 §118.
622. Schürer 1:343. See sidebar on *Herod the Great* at 1:5.
623. For individuals staying silent at their trials see Josephus, *Ant.* 15.7.5 §235 (Mariamne, the wife of Herod the Great); Diogenes Laertius 3:19 (Plato); 9.115 (the sophist philosopher Timon). Cf. Danker, *Jesus and the New Age*, 365.
624. Philo, *Embassy* 38. It is not certain whether this episode was before or after Jesus' crucifixion.
625. Sherwin-White, *Roman Society and Roman Law*, 27.
626. Luke 23:17 does not occur in the best Greek manuscripts and is probably a later scribal harmonization; Matt. 27:15; Mark 15:6; John 18:39.
627. R. L. Merritt, "Jesus Barabbas and the Paschal Pardon," *JBL* 104 (1988): 57–68.
628. Josephus, *Ant.* 17.10.5 §§271–72; idem, *J.W.* 2.8.1 §118 (Judas the Galilean); idem, *Ant.* 17.10.6 §§273–77 (Simon); *Ant.* 17.10.7 §§278–81 (Anthronges); *Ant.* 20.5.1 §§97–99 (Theudas); *Ant.* 20.8.6 §§169–72; idem, *J.W.* 2.13.5 §§261–63 (the Egyptian); idem, *Ant.* 18.4.1 §§85–87 (a Samaritan).
629. See Josephus, *Ant.* 20.8.10 §186–88; idem, *J.W.* 2.13.3 §254; 2.17.6 §425; 4.7.2 §400.
630. Josephus, *J.W.* 7.8.1 §253–54.
631. See Josephus, *Ant.* 18.3.1 §55–59; Philo, *Embassy* 38.
632. Tacitus, *Ann.* 15.44.
633. Josephus, *Ant.* 18.3.3 §§63–64.
634. Shlomo Pines, *An Arabic Version of the Testimonium Flavianum and Its Implications* (Jerusalem: Israel Academy of Sciences and Humanities, 1971), 16.
635. Josephus, *J.W.* 5.11.1 §451.
636. *Digesta iuris Romani* 48.19.28.15, cited in Hengel, *Crucifixion*, 50. Cf. Quintilian, *Training in Oratory* 274.
637. Brown, *Death*, 853–958; Sherwin-White, *Roman Society and Roman Law*, 46.
638. BAGD, 574.
639. Eusebius, *Eccl. Hist.* 5.1; Suetonius, *Caligula* 32; *Domitian* 10; Dio Cassius, *Roman History* 54.3; BAGD, 291; Marshall, *Gospel of Luke*, 870.
640. Gen. 2:8–10, 15; Josephus, *Ant.* 1.1.3 §37; *1 En.* 20:7; 60:8.
641. See also *4 Ezra* 4:7; 6:2; 7:36, 123; *1 En.* 32:3; *T. Dan* 5:12; *T. Levi* 18:11.
642. Isa. 13:9–13; Joel 2:10; 3:14–15; Amos 5:18, 20; 8:9; cf. Ex. 10:21–23.
643. Darkness is reported with reference to the deaths of Alexander the Great (Ps-Callisthenes 3.3.26); Caesar (Virgil, *Georgics* 1.463ff.), Aeschylus (Aristophanes, *Ael. Aristid.* 32.32), and others (see BAGD, 757; H. Conzelmann, "σκότος," *TDNT*, 7:439; for rabbinic parallels see Str-B 1:1040–41).
644. Ex. 26:33–37; 27:16.
645. Josephus, *J.W.* 5.5.4 §212.
646. Josephus, *J.W.* 6.5.3 §293–96.
647. Isa. 32:12; Jer. 31:19; Ezek. 21:12; Nah. 2:7.
648. See Josephus, *J.W.* 4.5.2 § 317; *Ag. Ap.* 2.29 §211; Philo, *Flaccus* 83–84; Tobit 1:17–18.
649. Marshall, *Gospel of Luke*, 879; Rathamin (1 Macc. 11:34) and Ramathain (Josephus, *Ant.* 13.4.9 §127) may designate the same location.
650. Finegan, *Archaeology*, 166–68; 181–219; Rachel Hachlili, "Burials, Ancient Jewish," *ABD* 1:789–91; Rousseau and Arav, *Jesus and His World*, 164–69.
651. *m. Šabb.* 23:5.
652. Josephus, *Ant.* 4.8.15 §219.
653. Philo, QG 4:15.
654. See J. Finegan, *Archaeology*, 198, 202.

655. Gen. 18:2; 19:1, 10; Josh. 5:13; Judg. 13:6–11; Tobit 5:4–5; cf. Heb. 13:2.
656. See also *1 En.* 71:1; 2 Macc. 11:8; Acts 1:10; Rev. 4:4; 19:14.
657. Judg. 6:22–23; 13:22; Dan. 8:16–17; 10:10–11.
658. Fitzmyer, *Luke*, 2:1561–2; Marshall, *Gospel of Luke*, 892.
659. See Sydney H. T. Page, "The Suffering Servant Between the Testaments," *NTS* 31 (1985): 481–97.
660. Cf. Luke 18:32; 20:17; 23:47; Acts 2:25ff.; 4:25–26.
661. See 2 Macc. 3:34; Euripides, *Orestes* 1496; idem, *Helen* 605–6; Virgil, *Aeneid* 9.656–58.
662. 1 Sam. 28:3–19; Isa. 8:19; 19:3.
663. Dan. 12:2; 2 Macc. 7:9, 14; *1 En.* 103:4; see also Luke 8:55; 14:14; 20:27.
664. Acts 2:25–28, 34; 13:33–35; 2:17–21; 13:47; 15:16–18.
665. Isa. 32:15; Ezek. 36:26–27; Joel 2:28–32; cf. Jer. 31:33; see Acts 2:14–21.
666. Enoch: Gen. 5:24; Heb. 11:5; Sir. 44:16; 49:14; *1 En.* 17–36; 39:3; Elijah: Sir. 48:9, 12; *1 En.* 89:52; 93:8; Jos. *Ant.* 9 §28; Bar.: *3 Apoc. Bar.* 10–17; Moses: *As. Moses.* In Greco-Roman traditions too, heroes and gods sometimes ascend. Dio Cassius, *Roman History* 56.46 describes the ascent of Caesar Augustus, supposedly witnessed by the senator Numerius Atticus. For this and other examples see *HCNT*, 309 §485.
667. Acts 2:32–36; 5:31; Eph. 1:19–23; Phil. 2:9–11; Heb.

## *Sidebar and Chart Notes*

A-1. Cf. A. W. Mosley, "Historical Reporting in the Ancient World," *NTS* 12 (1965–66): 10–26; and C. J. Hemer, *The Book of Acts in the Setting of Hellenistic History*, ed. C. H. Gempf (WUNT 2.49; Tübingen: Mohr, 1989), 43–44, 75–79.
A-2. On Luke's value as a historian see the above-mentioned works; also M. Hengel, *Acts and the History of Earliest Christianity* (Philadelphia: Fortress, 1979).
A-3. Josephus, *Ag. Ap.* 1.1 §§1–4.
A-4. Josephus, *Ag. Ap.* 2.1 §§1–2.
A-5. The fascinating story of Herod the Great is given in great detail by the Jewish historian Josephus in his *Antiquities of the Jews*. See *Ant.* 14.15.2 §403 (Edomite or "1/2 Jewish" heritage); 15.7.3 §§215–17 (allegiance switched to Caesar); 15.7.4–6 §§230–39 (execution of Miriamme); 15.10.4 §365 (Jewish taxes relieved); 15.11 §§380–425 (building the temple); 17.7.1. §§182–87 (execution of sons); 17.6.5 §§174–78 (death of key Jews ordered); 17.8.1 §§188–92 (death of Herod).
A-6. See especially J. Neusner, W. C. Green, and E. S. Frerichs, eds., *Judaisms and Their Messiahs at the Turn of the Christian Era* (Cambridge: Cambridge Univ. Press, 1987).
A-7. See 2 Esd. (*4 Ezra*) 12:32; 13:3–11, 26–38; *1 En.* 48:10; 49:3; 62:2.
A-8. See 4QFlor (4Q174); 4QPBless (4Q252); 4QpIsa[a] (4Q161); 4Q504; 4Q285.
A-9. Cf. 1QS 9:11; 1Qsa 2:11–21; 1QSb; 4QTestim. For a survey of this material see M. L. Strauss, *The Davidic Messiah in Luke-Acts* (JSNTSup 110; Sheffield: Sheffield Academic Press, 1995), ch. 2.
A-10. Josephus, *J.W.* 2.8.2 §§120–121.
A-11. Ex. 12:17–20; 34:18; Lev. 23:6.
A-12. Ex. 23:14–17; Deut. 16:16; cf. *m. Ḥag.* 1:1, which provides exceptions.
A-13. Josephus, *Ant.* 18.5.2 §§116–119.
A-14. See Jeremias, *Jerusalem*, 233–45; idem, "γραμματεύς," *TDNT*, 1:740–42.
A-15. Recent research has challenged traditional views of the Pharisees. See the bibliography and history of interpretation in A. J. Saldarini, "Pharisees," *ABD*, 5:303.
A-16. Important references to the Pharisees in Josephus include *J.W.* 1.5.2 §110; 2.8.14 §§162–65; idem, *Ant.* 13.5.9 §§171–72; 13.10.6 §§297–98; 17.2.4 §§41–45; 18.1.4 §16.
A-17. Prov. 3:13; 8:34; 14:21; 16:20; 28:20; Sir. 31:8.
A-18. Isa. 3:11; 5:8; Jer. 48:1; 50:27; Zech. 11:17.
A-19. Nolland, *Luke*, 1:280; Isa. 30:18; Dan. 12:12; *Pss. Sol.* 17:44; 18:6–7.
A-20. Lysias, *Pro Milite* 20.
A-21. 1QS 10:18–19.
A-22. *Counsels of Wisdom*, lines 41–45; from the translation by W. G. Lambert, *Babylonian Wisdom Literature* (Oxford: Clarendon, 1960), 101.
A-23. For other texts see Fitzmyer, *Luke*, 1:637–38; Nolland, *Luke*, 1:294–96; Seneca, *De Beneficiis*, 4.26.1.
A-24. 1QS 1:9–10.
A-25. Cf. 1QS 10:19.
A-26. Matt. 13:55–56; Mark 6:3; cf. Matt. 12:46; Mark 3:31.
A-27. Acts 12:17; 15:13; 21:18.
A-28. Cf. Fitzmyer, *Luke*, 1:723–24 who rejects the "cousin" view, but suggests that "brothers" could refer to a more distant relationship than a physical brother.
A-29. See R. J. Bauckham, *Jude and the Relatives of Jesus in the Early Church* (Edinburgh: T. & T. Clark, 1990).
A-30. Josephus, *Ant.* 20.9.1 §§ 200–203; ca. A.D. 61.

A-31. Eusebius, *Eccl. Hist.* 1.7.14.
A-32. Ibid., 3.19.1–3.20.8.
A-33. For other Jewish parallels see Str-B 4:1, 527–35.
A-34. Josephus, *Ant.*8.2.5 §§42–45.
A-35. For examples of such incantations see H. D. Betz, ed., *The Greek Magical Papyri in Translation* (Chicago: Univ. of Chicago Press, 1986).
A-36. On the Samaritans, see Jeremias, *Jerusalem*, 352–58; idem, "ὁδός," TDNT, 7:88–94; R. J. Coggins, *Samaritans and Jews: The Origins of the Samaritans Reconsidered* (Oxford: Blackwell, 1975); R. Pummer, *The Samaritans* (Leiden: Brill, 1987).
A-37. Josephus, *Life* 269.
A-38. *HCNT,* 262–63.
A-39. Josephus, *Ant.* 20.6.1 §118.
A-40. See Luke 10:25–37; 17:16; John 4:4–42.
A-41. Fitzmyer, *Luke*, 2:920.
A-42. There are many other suggestions related to the meaning. See Marshall, *Gospel of Luke*, 472–73; Fitzmyer, *Luke*, 2:920.
A-43. *T. Sol.* 3:2–5; 4:2; 6:1–3.
A-44. *Jub.* 10:8; 11:5; 19:28; cf. Hos. 9:7.
A-45. 1QS 1:18, 24; 2:5, 19; *Jub.* 1:20; *T. Dan* 5:10; see 2 Cor. 6:15.
A-46. Malina and Rohrbaugh, SSCSG, 136, 191.
A-47. Martial, *Epigrams* 1.20 (LCL, 43); Juvenal, *Satires* 5 (LCL, 69–83); Pliny, *Letters* 2.6 (LCL, 109–13).
A-48. Martial, *Epigram* 3.60 (LCL, 201).
A-49. See Josephus, *J.W.* 4.8.3 §§459–75.
A-50. Turner, *Hist. Geog.* 234, citing Kathleen M. Kenyon, *Archaeology of the Holy Land* (New York: Praeger, 1960), 42ff.
A-51. Josephus, *Ant.* 13.5.9 §171–73; 13.10.6 §297–98; 18.1.4 §16; idem, *J.W.* 2.8.14 §§164–65. For rabbinic views of the Sadducees see Str-B 1:885–86.
A-52. See Josephus, *Ant.* 12.3.3. §138. But cf. also *Ant.* 11.4.7 §105.
A-53. Josephus, *Ant.* 14.9.4 §175.
A-54. On crucifixion see especially Hengel, *Crucifixion*.
A-55. Seneca, *Dialogue* 6 (*To Marcia On Consolation*) 20.3.
A-56. See Hengel, *Crucifixion*, 29–32.
A-57. On the original excavation findings see N. Haas, "Anthropological Observations on the Skeletal Remains from Giv'at ha-Mivtar," *IEJ* 20 (1970): 38–59. On a reassessment of the evidence see J. Zias and E. Sekeles, "The Crucified Man from Giv'at ha-Mivtar—A Reappraisal," *IEJ* 35 (1985): 22–27; and J. Zias and J. H. Charlesworth, "Crucifixion: Archaeology, Jesus, and the Dead Sea Scrolls," in *Jesus and the Dead Sea Scrolls*, ed. J. H. Charlesworth (New York: Doubleday, 1992), 273–89.

# CREDITS FOR PHOTOS AND MAPS

Claycombe, Hugh . . . . . . . . . . . . . . . . . . . . . . . . . . . . . . . . pp. 13, 150–51, 180
Franz, Gordon . . . . . . . . . . . . . . . . . . . . . . . . . . . . . . . . . . . . . . pp. 61, 140
Isachar, Hanan . . . . . . . . . . . . . . . . . . . . . . . . . . . . . . . . pp. 33, 52, 69, 92, 69
King, Jay . . . . . . . . . . . . . . . . . . . . . . . . . . . . . . . . . . . . . . . . . pp. 24, 67, 127
Kohlenberger, John R. III . . . pp. 9, 15, 18, 33, 35, 60, 67, 80, 91, 95, 100, 149, 183
Radovan, Zev . . . . . . . . . . . . pp. 26, 35, 40, 46, 49, 55, 58, 71, 73, 74, 83, 94, 106, 117, 120, 121, 123, 136(2), 146, 154, 157, 160, 163, 164, 166, 169, 170, 174
Ritmeyer, Leen. . . . . . . . . . . . . . . . . . . . . . . . . . . . . . . . . . . . . . pp. 4, 11, 30, 178
Zondervan Image Archive (Neal Bierling) . . pp. 2–3, 18, 22(3), 24, 26, 29, 32, 37, 43, 44(2), 49, 62, 69, 73, 75, 80, 87(2), 92, 99, 107, 108, 110, 112, 113, 137, 146(2), 147, 152, 154, 155, 156, 162, 163, 172, 173, 176, 177, 181, 182

# ALSO AVAILABLE

Printed in the USA
CPSIA information can be obtained
at www.ICGtesting.com
LVHW081125281223
767069LV00001B/4